SCREENING TORTURE

Edited by
MICHAEL FLYNN and FABIOLA F. SALEK

SCREENING TORTURE

MEDIA REPRESENTATIONS OF
STATE TERROR AND POLITICAL DOMINATION

 COLUMBIA UNIVERSITY PRESS   NEW YORK

Columbia University Press
Publishers Since 1893
New York   Chichester, West Sussex
cup.columbia.edu
Copyright © 2012 Columbia University Press
All rights reserved

Library of Congress Cataloging-in-Publication Data
Screening torture : media representations of state terror and political domination / edited by Michael Flynn and Fabiola F. Salek.
    p. cm.
Includes bibliographical references and index.
ISBN 978-0-231-15358-4 (cloth) — ISBN 978-0-231-15359-1 (pbk.) — ISBN 978-0-231-52697-5 (e-book)
 1. Torture in motion pictures. 2. Torture on television. I. Flynn, Michael, 1962– II. Salek, Fabiola F.

PN1995.9.T67S37 2012
791.43'6352—dc23
                                                              2011049965

Cover design: Catherine Casalino

For my Mathiso and family with love

Fabiola F. Salek

Contents

Screening Torture: An Introduction   1
Michael Flynn and Fabiola F. Salek

Part I   Torture and the Implications of Masculinity   19

1. Countering the Jack Bauer Effect: An Examination of How to Limit the Influence of TV's Most Popular, and Most Brutal, Hero   21
   David Danzig

2. Mel Gibson's Tortured Heroes: From the Symbolic Function of Blood to Spectacles of Pain   35
   Lee Quinby

3. It's a Perfect World: Torture, Confession, and Sacrifice   53
   Michael Flynn and Fabiola F. Salek

Part II   Torture and the Sadomasochistic Impulse   69

4. *Lust, Caution*: Torture, Sex, and Passion in Chinese Cinema   71
   Chris Berry

5. The Art of Photogenic Torture   93
   Phil Carney

6. Beyond Susan Sontag: The Seduction of Psychological Torture   109
   Alfred W. McCoy

7. Stanley Kubrick's *A Clockwork Orange* as Art Against Torture   143
   Carolyn Strange

Part III Confronting the Legacies of Torture and State Terror   165

8. "Accorded a Place in the Design": Torture in Postapartheid Cinema   167
   Elizabeth Swanson Goldberg

9. Confessing Without Regret: An Israeli Film Genre   191
   Livia Alexander

Part IV Torture and the Shortcomings of Film   217

10. Movies of Modern Torture as Convenient Truths   219
    Darius Rejali

11. Torture at the Limit of Politics   239
    Faisal Devji

12. Doing Torture in Film: Confronting Ambiguity and Ambivalence   257
    Marnia Lazreg

13. Documenting the Documentaries on Abu Ghraib: Facts Versus Distortion   273
    Stjepan G. Mestrovic

List of Contributors   293

Index   295

SCREENING TORTURE

Screening Torture
AN INTRODUCTION

Michael Flynn and Fabiola F. Salek

Marathon Man was released in 1976. Its protagonist, Thomas "Babe" Ryan (Dustin Hoffman), is a Columbia graduate student majoring in history and a committed runner. His father was an esteemed professor at Columbia who got caught up in the McCarthy hearings and committed suicide when Babe and his brother, Henry (aka "Doc") (Roy Scheider), were young. Babe believes that his brother is an oil executive, but he is actually an agent who works for a secret government agency. Doc visits Babe in New York knowing that Dr. Christian Szell (Laurence Olivier), an ex-Nazi dentist who worked in the concentration camps and has been hiding in Uruguay, is coming to New York to pick up a valuable cache of diamonds. The agency Doc works for is headed by Peter Janeway (William Devane) who, unbeknownst to Doc, is a double agent working with Szell to get him to inform on other Nazi war criminals. Babe strikes up a relationship with a German woman, Elsa Oppel (Marthe Keller), who has worked as a courier for Szell, but Babe has no idea of this. Doc meets Szell in a night meeting and Szell critically wounds him with a spring blade concealed in his coat sleeve. Doc makes it back to Babe's apartment where he dies in Babe's arms.

Thinking that Doc confided something to Babe as he died (though he didn't), Szell's henchmen kidnap Babe and set him up to be tortured by Szell, who wants him to confess. Janeway believes that Doc didn't reveal anything to Babe. The henchmen tie Babe—who knows that Szell will try and hurt him—to a chair. Szell repeatedly asks, "Is it safe?" Babe is confused by the question and first answers, "Yes, it's safe," and then says, "No, it's not safe, it's dangerous." Szell then inserts a dental device into an existing cavity in Babe's mouth, causing him great pain. Szell brings him back into the room and says that he is "disappointed with your silence," and then tortures him again by drilling into a healthy tooth. There is no doubt that Szell is an old sadist who is revisiting techniques he used on Jews in the concentration camps. The audience feels a great deal of empathy for Babe and none for Szell, who expresses contempt for human decency. Torturing Babe is a senseless act (unless Szell wants to revisit his past project of domination); the confession Szell wants is from someone who knows next to nothing about the matter at hand, and is a pawn in a game that is well beyond him. Using his running skills, Babe escapes from Szell's warehouse, ends up killing Janeway, and apprehends Szell after he has obtained the diamonds from a safety-deposit vault at a bank. He then takes his prisoner to the Central Park reservoir, where Szell falls down the stairs and accidentally stabs himself with his spring blade.

Man on Fire was released in 2004. Its protagonist, John Creasy (Denzel Washington), is a former CIA assassin and torturer who worked to put down leftist insurgencies in the name of patriotism. With time he becomes horrified by his murderous and destructive acts and becomes an alcoholic, suicidal drifter, moving from place to place in search of redemption and death. He decides to visit an old CIA partner, Rayburn (Christopher Walken), in Mexico, and Rayburn, sensing his despair, urges him to become a bodyguard for a seemingly wealthy half-Mexican, half-American family. The young girl of the family, Pita (Dakota Fanning), shows Creasy "that it was all right to live again," and they develop a loving relationship that is far deeper than she has with her feckless parents. Pita is kidnapped by rogue cops working for a professional kidnapper called "the Voice," and after a botched ransom exchange everyone assumes that Pita has been killed. Creasy is seriously wounded during the kidnapping and refuses to return to the United States to obtain the medical care that could help him. Instead he vows to kill anyone associated with the kidnapping and engages in a vigilante campaign in which he tortures and kills his enemies. He becomes an "artist of death," at last able to "paint his masterpiece."

He first tortures a crooked cop who was involved in the kidnapping. This torture scene lasts over six-and-a-half minutes, and in it the victim literally swims in his own blood, yet few in the audience feel any sympathy or empathy for the cop; he is an immoral man whose only delight lies in his prowess for destructiveness and death—and when Creasy kills him after torturing him the audience experiences a sense of expiation. The audience feels much more empathy for the torturer, and his plan to go after all of those involved with Pita's death makes him a hero, someone who will restore social order to a society stricken with criminality. Although torture is the "clumsiest"[1] way to extract information—paid or unpaid informants impart far more reliable information—in the post–September 11 era torture has been given magical qualities. Torture victims are thought to rarely confabulate, and instead name names and give locations and dates with an empirical accuracy that is hardly seen in actuality. The torture ends in a confession that ends up breaking open the case and reinforces the notion that torture and sacrifice will yield the desired results. In the course of his crusade Creasy discovers that Pita has not been killed and arranges to exchange himself for her—and he dies a martyr in the kidnapper's car.

Screening Torture addresses the representation of torture in film and television. Torture scenes have proliferated in most genres of film over the past decade, and the period has given birth to a new mutation, the "torture-porn" flick. These films—*Hostel*, *Saw*, and *Wolf Creek* are examples—differ from older horror films by virtue of their "high production value" and the fact that they feature "explicit scenes of torture and mutilation"[2] that are highly sexualized. David Edelstein, coiner of the term, states, "I am baffled by how far this stuff goes and why Americans seem so nuts these days about torture."[3] These films aren't the sole culprits; scenes of torture have been placed in comedies, dramas, and especially action films for little discernable reason other than audiences' excitement and delight. Some of the mainstream American films that feature torture scenes include *Man on Fire* (2004), *The Passion of the Christ* (2004), *Mr. and Mrs. Smith* (2005), *Syriana* (2005), *Casino Royale* (2006), *The Good Shepherd* (2006), *V for Vendetta* (2006), *The Bourne Ultimatum* (2007), *In the Valley of Elah* (2007), *Rendition* (2007), *Shoot 'Em Up* (2007), *Body of Lies* (2008), *The Dark Knight* (2008), *Taken* (2008), *Inglourious Basterds* (2009), *Public Enemies* (2009), *The Expendables* (2010), *Salt* (2010), and *Unthinkable* (2010). As A. H. Hamrah states, "The ingeniously imagined punishment devices in these movies, along with their chummy torture chamber repartee and quick recovery from pain and abuse, aren't so much about the fear of torture as they are about the joy of it—and its necessity."[4] Other than *In the Valley of Elah*, *Rendition*, and two documentaries, *Taxi to the Dark Side* (2007) and *The Ghosts of Abu Ghraib* (2008), the exceptions to this trend have been foreign films: *The Last King of Scotland* (2006), *The Lives of Others* (2006), *Pan's Labyrinth* (2006), *Hunger* (2008), *Mesrine: Killer Instinct* (2008), and *La Soga* (2009). Torture in these films is devoid of redeeming qualities, and no defense of it is mounted; torture is represented as an exercise in "brutal senselessness"[5] by authoritarian regimes or institutions.

While recognizing the increasing number of films featuring torture scenes, it is also important to note that many well-known pre–September 11 films address the issue of torture. Some of the more recognized films, outside the horror/slasher genre, include: *Rome, Open City* (1945), *The Battle of Algiers* (1966), *The Good, the Bad and the Ugly* (1966), *A Clockwork Orange* (1971), *Dirty Harry* (1971), *Midnight Express* (1978), *First Blood* (1982) (and all the subsequent *Rambo* films), *Missing* (1982), *1984* (1984), *Mississippi Burning* (1988), *The Siege* (1988) (notable for its antitorture message), *Reservoir Dogs* (1992), *Death and the Maiden* (1994), *Garaje Olimpo* (1999), and *3 Kings* (1999). The depiction of torture in these films is quite variable; in some of the films the torture scenes are graphic (some would argue that they verge on the pornographic), in other films the depiction is quite ephemeral and incomplete, and in still others torture is represented only through the characters' verbal recounting of past experiences. In most of these films torture is not presented as a spectacle, and the torturer is depicted as a desperate, depraved, and brutal individual; the viewer is more likely to identify with the victim than with the torturer (the exceptions here are *Dirty Harry* and *Mississippi Burning*).

It is difficult to overestimate the draw of film. Film has consistently gained in viewership and "has been one of the most important kingdoms of our century."[6] Its appeal has widened with capitalism's growing influence,[7] and the schooled and unschooled, elite and impoverished, "care about movies, await them, respond to them, talk about them . . . are grateful for some of them."[8] Films also have an instructional power that should not be underestimated: "people learn to kiss, to talk, to live, according to the shadows they make."[9] People watch films to feel pleasure, to be entertained, and to think, but also because films "elicit" certain emotions.[10] Many male film theorists have devalued this aspect of film because feeling has been consigned to femininity and bathos, and have favored instead the more abstract realms of ideology and aesthetics—as if these qualities could be estranged from emotion. They have also made the mistake of believing that emotion is divorced from an intellectual appreciation of film.[11]

Films are profoundly influenced by and implicated in the cultural, political, and historical conditions of their time. In order to be relevant they must simultaneously reflect, contest, or undermine the dominant ideological currents of the era of their making.[12] Films are a way "articulating the world."[13] The filmmaker is continually involved in making decisions regarding the means of representation, sequencing, proportion, and duration of events as well as subject matter, intensity, and vividness. Despite the efforts of many academic film theorists to reduce film to the play of images, film is a pluralistic medium, one that contains music, dialogue, sound, and narrative. It is a medium "that can take and assimilate more."[14] As with other forms of art and entertainment, films have to have one foot in the real; a successful film has to actuate conscious and unconscious meanings. Filmmakers (even documentarians) are not simply interested in recording reality; they enter a project with the desire to "artistically refigure reality,"[15] to expand the filmgoer's understanding of existence and its predicaments. As V. F. Perkins argues, it would be absurd to claim that films are "like life," but the special magic of the moving image, dialogue, story, sound, and music can "impress us as being more lifelike than any other form of narrative."[16] The dilemmas faced by protagonists have a far greater intensity than is usually faced in everyday life, and the world represented by the filmmaker is "more shaped."[17]

We attend films because they expose us to characters that we don't encounter in our daily lives, places we will never visit, and situations that are foreign to us; films expose us to that which is "beyond our real life experience."[18] When viewing films we never forget that we are watching a work created for our pleasure or entertainment—we also experience it as "a world."[19] When viewing a film in a theater the viewer has much less control that when contemplating a photograph or reading a novel—this is not true for film that demands our "continuous attention."[20]

Until recently, the basis of film was photographic, although film was never a simple assembling of photographic images; it always has involved editing and sound and other qualities.[21] The scene in a photograph invokes a contemplative turn of mind, but the scene in a film possesses an "existential momentum" that demands to be experienced and "inhabited."[22] Photographs, unlike films, don't tell stories, and the story in a film has an immediacy that is unmatched. Cinema projects an intentional world in which the motives and subjectivity of the characters are identifiable. Film is experienced in an intuitive, erotic, subjective, embodied manner, and perhaps more than any other medium "beautifully and gracefully mingles with our minds."[23] It also has the capacity to make "us feel like eye-witnesses of the events which it portrays."[24] This presents a problem in films and television shows where torture is represented, because the accepted "iconography"[25] of torture is misleading.

Shortly after the attacks on the World Trade Center and the Pentagon, members of the Bush administration set to work crafting a policy that would make torture their "secret weapon in the War on Terror."[26] They took this action knowing full well that the prohibition against torture was the cornerstone of the international rule of law and in complete disregard of the fact the United States was a signatory of all the treaties banning torture. They also did so knowing that confessions obtained through torture were usually false. They delegated the task of redefining torture to a group of young attorneys, ideologically committed to a form of extreme neoconservatism. These attorneys believed that victory in this war would necessitate fighting on the "dark side"[27] and sought to make illegal detentions, rendition, torture, and political murder legal. They were a paranoid[28] group who believed that the existing principles governing the rules of war and the treatment of prisoners were "quaint"; they favored "war without limits."[29]

The U.S. use of torture began long before this redefinition project was completed, before the "death-worlds"[30] of Guantánamo and Abu Ghraib were established. U.S. servicemen in Afghanistan tortured their prisoners long before memos on torture were vetted by the secretary of defense and the attorney general, and many times they were guided by television shows and movies they watched before being deployed.[31] With the establishment of the offshore prisons at Bagram Air Force Base, Guantánamo, and Abu Ghraib, torture became routinized, and the number of victims grew exponentially. The torturers at Guantánamo regularly watched the television series 24, a show in which torture produces confessions that otherwise would not be made. Diane Beaver felt that this show "encouraged" the interrogators "to see themselves as being on the frontline—and to go further than they otherwise might."[32] The torture and defilement at these locations was highly sexualized—witness the Abu Ghraib photographs. Photographs of suffering are usually "documents of protest: they show us what happens when we unmake the world."[33] The Abu Ghraib photographs were not, quite obviously, exercises in protest. The photographs raised almost no "moral outrage"[34] at the site, and the claim made by the photographers/war criminals that they were simply documenting the torture and defilement were quite specious—many of the acts were performed for the camera. These torture and harsh interrogation methods were countenanced at Guantánamo and Abu Ghraib by Major General Geoffrey Miller and additionally at Abu Ghraib by General Ricardo Sanchez, but this didn't mean that the women and men were "neutral"[35] regarding torture. They derived much pleasure from the torture and abuse they inflicted. Many of the torture scenes depicted in the Abu Ghraib photographs could have been directly lifted from Pasolini's film *Salò*.

Torture is usually a man's pursuit. For most men Western masculinity is based on the principle of domination: men must be able to "dominate some men and all women."[36] Intelligence officers and military personnel are socialized to think of themselves as warriors, individuals dedicated to protecting national security, and their integrity is tied to their ability to dispense violence particularly against those perceived as enemies. At Guantánamo 20 percent of the interrogators were women, and they regularly sexually tormented the detainees in hopes of "severing their relationship with God."[37] Female interrogators wiped fake menstrual blood on a detainee (which made him feel dirty and prevented him from praying), rubbed their breasts against the prisoners' backs and mocked their erections, roughly grabbed the prisoners' genitals, threatened them with rape, and often interrogated Muslims who were forced to wear bikinis, lingerie, and thong underwear. But the methods they employed weren't solely confined to these sexual hijinks; they also defiled the Qur'an, banged the detainee's heads on tables, and bent back the thumbs of several detainees.[38] Much criticism has been aimed at the enlisted female "bad apples," but women high in the chain of command also condoned torture and abuse, including Lieutenant Colonel Diane Beaver, Captain Carolyn Wood, Brigadier General Janis Karpinski, and Major General Barbara Fast.

The United States is hardly singular in its acceptance of torture. More than one-half of the signatories to the treaties banning torture countenance the practice. Old-fashioned brutal torture, including methods that maim and leave scars, is still practiced in some countries, but it has been replaced, particularly in democracies, with "clean torture."[39] These methods, intended to escape detection by human rights groups, are no less painful, but leave no signs of the torturer's brutality. Punishment is one way the state becomes "evident."[40] Torture is one form of punishment that regimes, both authoritarian and liberal, employ. The state must be careful in its decisions regarding whom and what to punish; its power should not be used arbitrarily, and any punishment must be dispensed in the "name of a value and ideal."[41] The ideal proposed by the Bush administration was that torturing al-Qaeda and Taliban operatives would "protect American lives." Despite the claims of Dick Cheney, the intelligence produced by the torture of prisoners at Abu Ghraib, Guantánamo (where the worst of the worst[42] were detained), and the CIA's black sites was negligible.

Torture is rarely a public event anymore, and when it was it didn't lack for spectators. In the contemporary world torture takes place in prison camps that are surrounded by razor wire and armed guards. The crimes committed by intelligence officers and their adjuncts are usually invisible to the public, at least until a released prisoner testifies to his or her maltreatment. Representations of torture both "revile" and "titillate" the "imagination";[43] the scene of an individual held captive and being tortured both seduces and disgusts the viewer. This is why many have turned to novelists, poets, painters, sculptors, and filmmakers to make sense of the practice; for these figures torture has exerted a "dark fascination."[44] Beginning with the Greek comic playwrights, the public has always relied on artists to represent the suffering of the victim, the reasoning of the judges and leaders who order the torture, and the torturer's emotional and patriotic motives. In early Greek, Roman, and Renaissance sculpture and painting, the pain of the torture victim was aestheticized, eroticized, and rationalized (this equation was later reversed by Goya, Picasso, Shahn, and Golub).[45] Torture was frequent in medieval mystery plays and was the source of "pleasure" for the audience—"we cannot insist upon this emphatically enough: if people hadn't liked torture, they could not have tolerated the sight of it."[46] We now rely on film and television shows to represent the interpersonal dynamics of the torture chamber. Most of these films and shows present torture as melodrama, though in reality it has none of the attributes of melodrama.

Not all classes of people are equally torturable; a certain selection takes place. In ancient Greece the slaves and foreigners were the torturable classes, and in Rome the *humiliores*.[47] Then it was the Christians, the criminals, apostates, witches, and freethinkers. In the first half of the twentieth century the Jews and Stalin's scapegoats were the "designated victims";[48] during the Cold War, according to Graham Greene, the torturable classes expanded to include the "poor of Latin America, Central Europe and the Orient"—Catholics have always been "more torturable than Protestants."[49] Greene's book *Our Man in Havana* was published in 1958, long before the rise of a new "torturable class," the Muslims. Public intellectuals have written about the effectiveness of torture on this population, often invoking the "ticking time-bomb" scenario. In many films Muslims are depicted as religious or political fanatics immune to standard interrogation practices. The procedures that get Christians, Jews, and Hindus to spill their secrets, their violent plans, are simply a fool's errand with Muslims. They maintain their defiant silence even when subjected to moderate violence; it is only extended and brutal torture than makes them confess.

The tortured individual, powerless and dependent, often worries that the torturer will kill him or her (*Garaje Olimpo, Reservoir Dogs, The Good Shepherd, Taken*). The torturer intends the infliction of pain in the name of deriving a confession, and knows that bodily pain always has a psychological consequence, that it is traumatic, and that the victims will be haunted by it for the rest of their lives. As Maurice Merleau-Ponty argues, body and mind possess an intimacy that is undeniable—"I am aware of the world through the medium of my body."[50] The mind's higher functions, including perception, cognition, memory, and wanting, are "anchored in the body,"[51] and when one undergoes torture (or any other traumatic event) these capacities are significantly altered. The torturer knows that destruction of the body will result in the "annihilating negation"[52] of consciousness and the abrogation of the soul. The survivor of trauma is one who has, physically or psychologically, been in proximity to death; "a survivor is one who has encountered, been exposed to, or witnessed death and has himself or herself remained alive."[53] Traumatized individuals are not able to completely take in the traumatic experience; they undergo a process of "psychic numbing"[54] as a way to protect themselves against the death anxiety and helplessness occasioned by the traumatic experience. Those who suffer psychic numbing lose the capacity to feel with the intensity and passion they were capable of before the traumatic event. Psychic numbing is a "necessary psychological defense" and is adaptive in that it allows the individual to "avoid psychological death,"[55] but if uninterrupted it can lead to despair and depression. Trauma brings up the "issue of death and the crises of life,"[56] and many traumatized people feel immobilized by the predicaments and conflicts life puts before them, so withdrawal and isolation often become the preferred mode of being. The traumatized person can no longer see the world as a place where decency reigns, where there are natural barriers against humiliation and degradation, where one can trust that people will abstain from deriving satisfaction, even fulfillment, from the infliction of pain. Jean Améry argues that "at the first blow," the tortured person "loses something we will perhaps temporarily call 'trust in the world,'"[57] and that this loss is irreparable. In the aftermath of the traumatic experience the individual feels "invaded" by the event, and it becomes a "dominating feature "of the person's "interior landscape";[58] consequently, the traumatized person feels entrapped by what has happened and is often demoralized.

Améry, an essayist and Holocaust survivor, cautions against "exaggeration" when "speaking about torture," and also writes that "torture is the most horrible event a human being can retain in himself."[59] Améry also emphasized the permanence of torture's destructiveness: "Whoever was tortured stays tortured. Torture is ineradicably burned into him, even when no clinically objective traces can be found."[60] The psychological state of most torture survivors is very precarious; they struggle with despair and depression, social withdrawal, psychic numbing and death anxiety, sleep disturbances, and a pervading sense of mortification. Their sense of self is usually very fragmented; torture survivors often actively consider suicide, and they consider themselves to be broken. In many of the films made before and after September 11, these consequences are not shown; torture has no lasting psychological effects and can even strengthen an individual's character and resolve. In the *Rambo* and *Lethal Weapon* films the protagonists' intensity and retaliatory power increases after being tortured, in *Body of Lies* torture cures Leonardo DiCaprio's character of his romantic and professional ambivalences, and in *V for Vendetta* the Natalie Portman character recovers her parents' revolutionary fervor after being tortured.

Many contemporary films and television shows support the myth that torture leads to truthful confessions (*24*, *Man on Fire*, *Taken*); that the individual suffering the torturer's ministrations will, after a period of resistance, always confess; and that this confession will disclose details and actualities unobtainable in any other fashion. This forced confession always takes place within the context of "a power relationship" in which the torturer "requires the confessing" and offers salvation or death that will end the suffering.[61] The films perpetuate a fantasy that physical punishment will result in the victim confessing to diabolical conspiracies aimed at the state. It is not surprising that these films were so popular during a time of neoconservative ascendancy, given that political movement's autocratic contempt for "rights and the individual."[62] The obsession with confession also manifests a deep insecurity regarding the competence of national security agents, particularly those in the intelligence services. Coerced confessions are usually false, something that Frederick the Great of Prussia realized long before the writings of Voltaire and Beccaria.[63] Moreover, as Peter Brooks contends, "There is something unstable and unreliable about the speech-act of confession, about its meaning and motives."[64] Films that disclose the lie about the torture-truth hermeneutic include *The Dark Knight*, *Marathon Man*, and *Unthinkable*.

"Almost anyone looking at the *physical* act of torture would be immediately appalled and repulsed by the torturers."[65] Yet in many contemporary American films and television shows the torturer is represented as a messianic figure, or at least a serious man, whose administration of "world-destroying"⁶⁶ pain is righteous and even necessary (*Inglourious Basterds, Man On Fire, Taken, Unthinkable, V for Vendetta*). The torture victim's bodily pain is represented as an essential and beneficial quality, intrinsic to the restoration of social and political order, the saving of "innocent" lives. In many of these films torture is a spectacle in which the filmgoer empathizes with the torturer, not the victim. The torturer is transformed from a war criminal into a benevolent "outlaw," one willing to transcend the law to save civilization.

The torturers in these films are often troubled men, suicidal or drug-addicted, but they rarely seem disquieted by the torture they inflict. In many cases they seem to be amplified by it, such that the pain felt by the victim boosts the torturer's "growing sense of self."⁶⁷ This contradicts most social science and anecdotal accounts. Merle Pribbenow, a former CIA agent, states, "One of my main objections to torture is what it does to the guys who actually inflict the torture. It does bad things."⁶⁸ Some of these "bad things" include constant anxiety, sleep disturbances, paranoia, and alcoholism or drug addiction. In the presence of women these characters are frequently withdrawn and juvenile, and often sexually inert. They are vital only in the presence of men, with whom they laugh, tease, and cavort. Perhaps this shouldn't be a surprise; torture is a practice that intends the negation of the other, and the torturer's contempt for any decent "contract,"⁶⁹ including the rule of law, is well established. The torturer derives great pleasure from engaging in actions that eradicate the feminine and elevate "the father who is beyond all laws."⁷⁰

In many of the action films the protagonists operate without physical or ethical limits. In *Unthinkable* the "private contractor" torturer (who is working for the CIA), H., says to the FBI agent, "He has to believe I have no limits." Given this disregard for limits, it isn't surprising that scenes of torture are becoming more popular, and a new technique is needed to show the protagonists' dominating power. Practices of punishment are closely associated with cultural values:⁷¹ in America the consensus is that rehabilitation is a failed approach and that criminals and terrorists, actual or perceived, must be dealt with harshly, and film audiences often enjoy watching "bad guys" being maimed and sacrificed. Many American filmmakers believe that displays of graphic violence and torture make their films more tantalizing, so they feature scenes in which victims disgorge pints of blood or undergo dismemberment—the audience winces and cringes and often applauds, not realizing the banality of the scene they have just internalized.

In films made prior to 2001 the torturer was usually a fascist, a depraved outlaw, a rogue cop or serviceman, or a madman. Over the last decade the torturers have been counterterrorism agents, CIA or former CIA agents, and even Batman is one—when superheroes and agents sworn to uphold the Constitution are torturers, the ethical and professional rot is profound. Many American films and television shows promote the fiction of "efficient, selective, professional torture,"[72] even when the torture results in false confessions. Some of these films and television shows clearly legitimize torture, endowing it with an effectiveness it does not possess.[73] In other films the message is opaque, but few American films made over the last decade openly condemn the practice. These films transmit the concept that torture can be absorbed by a civil society, that the consequences for the victims, the perpetrators, and the system are insignificant. As Lawrence Weschler argues, this is a dangerous precedent: "'There are all kinds of things wrong with torture,' Gaspari told me, 'but one of the main ones is that it poisons the system. For one thing, a sort of gangrene sets in. . . . The agencies working extralegally inevitably start behaving illegally as well. . . . This leads to a terrible indiscipline and institutional instability.'"[74]

Writing about film is a complex and difficult endeavor. Film, as a medium, is elusive and often escapes the author because of its motion and its unfolding and revelatory nature—"its materiality cannot be grasped."[75] We asked film scholars (Chris Berry, Elizabeth Goldberg, Livia Alexander) and academics whose primary area of research is not film—sociologists, political scientists, historians, American studies scholars, and psychologists—to join us for what should be an interesting conversation on the representation of torture in cinema and television.

In these inconsistent times writing about torture invites disputation, and interpreting cinematic torture scenes can be an effort in soliciting resistance. We didn't invite people who favor torture, because we didn't want to collaborate with the project of state terror. When writing about torture it is obvious that some articles will invite controversy, but it is our position that to invite neutrality is to court indifference. The opinions of our authors reflect their own personal judgments and are not indicative of the editors' points of view.

In part I, "Torture and the Implications of Masculinity," David Danzig argues in "Countering the Jack Bauer Effect: An Examination of How to Limit the Influence of TV's Most Popular, and Most Brutal, Hero" that the torture techniques and effectiveness of the hero of 24 are admired and sometimes emulated by American soldiers. He also discusses a documentary he coproduced, *Primetime Torture*, that debunks the effectiveness of the practice. Torture is present in many of Mel Gibson's films, and many critics have argued that his films promote torture. In her chapter addressing *The Passion of the Christ*, *Braveheart*, and *Apocalypto*, Lee Quinby argues that Gibson's films don't condone torture, that torture is an act that cruel and despotic leaders perpetrate on their citizens, and that these films "condemn the use of torture." The male characters in these films are victims of torture, a torture that often ends in sacrifice, and the suffering that they endure grants them a purified and patriarchal masculinity that invites honor. Michael Flynn and Fabiola Salek address three action films: *Taken*, *Man on Fire*, and *Unthinkable*. All three contain a variant of the ticking time-bomb scenario, and in each the protagonist employs torture to get the terrorist, or organized crime member, to confess.

In part II, "Torture and the Sadomasochistic Impulse," Chris Berry's treatment of *Lust, Caution* highlights the connection between torture and sexuality in Chinese filmmaking, and he also discusses the differences in the American and Chinese receptions of the film. The film was a sensation in China and not in America, in part because of the sadomasochistic sex scenes between the torturer, Mr. Yee, and the woman who is planning his assassination, Wong Chia-Chih. Berry locates *Lust, Caution* in the context of other earlier Chinese films that depict the "direct representation of torture and bodily torment on screen." In light of the revival of torture during the global war on terror, Carolyn Strange argues for a reexamination of *A Clockwork Orange* and makes a case for its continued relevance. She argues that the film operates as "art against torture" and that it indicts state terror. In her article she addresses the Ludovico Technique—which was used to domesticate Alex—and uses it as an example of techniques employed by the state (including drug therapy) to "control the deviant, the criminal, and the mentally ill." In "Beyond Susan Sontag: The Seduction of Psychological Torture" Alfred W. McCoy provides a history of the CIA's use of psychological and physical torture. He also reflects on the unreleased photographs from Abu Ghraib and the sexual nature of the abuse and humiliation inflicted on detainees there. His analysis discloses the erotic, even sadomasochistic, dimensions of torture and the manner in which they are "advertised" in contemporary film and video games. In "The Art of Photogenic Torture" Phil Carney addresses the films *Psycho* and *Peeping Tom*. Carney interrogates the dynamics of sexual power and desire and how these can lead to murder and torture. In his analysis of both films he proposes that the killers are people who are capable of living "ordinary" lives and that monstrosity has migrated from "the body to the mind."

In part III, "Confronting the Legacies of Torture and State Terror," Elizabeth Goldberg analyzes two South African films, *Forgiveness* and *Zulu Love Letter*, and argues that both of them find fault with South Africa's Truth and Reconciliation Commission, particularly its emphasis on the forgiveness of torture. Goldberg is critical of *Forgiveness* but lauds *Zulu Love Letter* for its engagement with the history of apartheid and the consequences of the antiapartheid struggle on familial and communal relationships, as well as its depiction of traumatized individuals. In "Confessing Without Regret: Israeli Soldiers Talk to the Camera" Livia Alexander examines how in the films *One of Us*, *Waltz with Bashir*, and *Z32*, "confession and forgiveness in Israeli cinema take place outside the official space of state practice and institutional structures. Confession unfolds between individuals and the recording lens of the camera, between the former soldier and filmmaker." These films privilege the predicaments of the Israeli soldier and minimize the suffering of the Palestinian and Lebanese people. The confessions in these films lack any engagement with the direct victim.

In part IV, "Torture and the Shortcomings of Film," Darius Rejali argues that torture is frequently misrepresented in classic and contemporary film. Directors and actors often choose the accepted iconography of torture that won't challenge filmgoers' preconceived notions. In his analysis of *The Battle of Algiers*, Rejali argues that torture didn't have the effectiveness in the "short run" that the director, Gillo Pontecorvo, gave it. Rejali also argues that torture is the least efficient way of obtaining necessary information (though in many films it "makes the man"), and that relying on informants (as the French did in Algeria) is far more reliable. Faisal Devji, in his incisive and erudite chapter, critiques work by Hannah Arendt, Michel Foucault, and Darius Rejali on torture. Devji analyzes the Indian film *Black Friday* and martyrdom videotapes made by Muslim extremists. He argues that when torture becomes visible in media such as film it cannot be represented without throwing into question the integrity of modern institutions. Marnia Lazreg maintains that *The Battle of Algiers* didn't capture the centrality of torture in the French counterinsurgency effort in Algeria. Decisions about the use of torture were made by the French political and military elites. The film *Standard Operating Procedure* minimizes the effects of torture on the Abu Ghraib detainees and doesn't represent the victims' suffering or experience. *Taxi to the Dark Side*, however, discloses the extent of the United States torture program, elucidates the decisions that made torture a key element in the United States counterinsurgency program in Iraq and Afghanistan, and gives the torture victims a voice. In his chapter Stjepan Mestrovic argues that the documentaries *Standard Operating Procedure* and *The Ghosts of Abu Ghraib* fail to adequately capture the humanity and the dilemmas of victims and perpetrators at Abu Ghraib. These films also avoid framing the abuse and torture as official government policy and focus on the enlisted "bad apples," minimizing the role played by the commanding officers.

NOTES

1. Darius Rejali, *Torture and Democracy* (Princeton: Princeton University Press, 2007), 478.
2. David Edelstein, "Now Playing at Your Local Multiplex: Torture Porn," *New York Magazine*, February 6, 2006.
3. Ibid.
4. A. S. Hamrah, "We Love to Torture," *Los Angeles Times*, December 18, 2006.
5. Elaine Scarry, *The Body in Pain: The Making and Unmaking of the World* (New York: Oxford University Press, 1985), 29.
6. Dana Polan, "'Above All Else to Make You See': Cinema and the Ideology of Spectacle," *boundary* 2, 11 (Fall 1982): 131.
7. Jonathan Beller, *The Cinematic Mode of Production: Attention Economy and the Society of the Spectacle* (Hanover, NH: Dartmouth College Press, 2006).
8. Stanley Cavell, *The World Viewed*, enlarged edition (Cambridge, Mass.: Harvard University Press, 1979), 5.
9. Polan, "'Above All Else to Make You See,'" 131–132.
10. Carl Plantinga, *Moving Viewers: American Film and the Spectator's Experience* (Berkeley: University of California Press, 2009), 2.
11. Ibid.
12. Robert Kolker, *A Cinema of Loneliness*, 3rd ed. (New York: Oxford University Press, 2000), 13–14.
13. Ibid., xiii.
14. Leo Braudy, *The World in Frame* (Chicago: University of Chicago Press, 2002), 10.
15. Daniel Frampton, *Filmosophy* (London: Wallflower, 2006), 4.
16. V. F. Perkins, *Film as Film: Understanding and Judging Movies* (New York: Da Capo, 1972)
17. Ibid.
18. Frampton, *Filmosophy*, 151.
19. Cavell, *The World Viewed*, 168. See also Frampton, *Filmosophy*.
20. Braudy, *The World in a Frame*, 34.

21. Noël Carroll, *The Philosophy of Motion Pictures* (Malden, Mass.: Blackwell, 2008).
22. Vivian Sobchack, *Carnal Thoughts: Embodiment and Moving Image Culture* (Berkeley: University of California Press, 2004).
23. Frampton, *Filmosophy*, 9.
24. Perkins, *Film as Film*.
25. See chapter 10 in this book.
26. Alfred W. McCoy, *The Question of Torture: CIA Interrogation, from the Cold War to the War on Terror* (New York: Henry Holt, 2006), 108.
27. Jane Mayer, *The Dark Side: The Inside Story of How the War on Terror Turned Into a War on American Ideals* (New York: Doubleday, 2008).
28. Ibid.
29. Anne Norton, *Leo Strauss and the Politics of the American Empire* (New Haven: Yale University Press, 2005).
30. Edith Wyschogrod, *Spirit in Ashes: Hegel, Heidegger, and Man-Made Mass Death* (New Haven: Yale University Press, 1985).
31. Joshua E. S. Phillips, *None of Us Were Like This Before: American Soldiers and Torture* (New York: Verso, 2010).
32. Phillipe Sands, *Torture Team: Rumsfeld's Memo and the Betrayal of American Values* (New York: Palgrave, 2008), 62.
33. Susie Linfield, *The Cruel Radiance: Photography and Political Violence* (Chicago: University of Chicago Press, 2010), 33.
34. Judith Butler, *Frames of War: When Is Life Grievable?* (New York: Verso, 2009).
35. Leigh Payne, *Unsettling Accounts: Neither Truth nor Reconciliation in Confessions of State Violence* (Durham: Duke University Press, 2007), 16.
36. Martha Huggins, Maria Haroitos-Fatouros, and Philip Zimbardo, *Violence Workers: Police Torturers and Murderers Reconstruct Brazilian Atrocities* (Berkeley: University of California Press, 2002), 85.
37. Erik Saar, *Inside the Wire: A Military Intelligence Soldier's Eyewitness Account of Life at Guantánamo* (New York: Penguin, 2005), 228.
38. Center for Constitutional Rights, *Report on Torture and Cruel, Inhuman, and Degrading Treatment of Prisoners at Guantanamo Bay, Cuba* (July, 2006), 10.
39. Rejali, *Torture and Democracy*.
40. Keally McBride, *Punishment and Political Order* (Ann Arbor: University of Michigan Press, 2007), 9
41. Ibid., 11.
42. Karen Greenberg, *The Least Worst Place: Guantanamo's First 100 Days* (New York: Oxford University Press, 2010).
43. Jody Enders, *The Medieval Theater of Cruelty: Rhetoric, Memory, Violence* (Cornell: Cornell University Press, 1999), 6.
44. J. M. Coetzee, *Doubling the Point: Essays and Interviews* (Cambridge, Mass.: Harvard University Press, 1992).
45. Stephen Eisenman, *The Abu Ghraib Effect* (London: Reaktion, 2007).

46. Enders, *The Medieval Theater of Cruelty*, 12.
47. Edward Peters, *Torture* (Philadelphia: University of Pennsylvania Press, 1996).
48. Robert Jay Lifton, *The Broken Connection: On Death and the Continuity of Life* (New York: Simon and Schuster, 1980), 323.
49. Graham Greene, *Our Man in Havana* (New York: Penguin, 1958).
50. Maurice Merleau-Ponty, *The Phenomenology of Perception*, 2nd ed. (Routledge, 2002).
51. Taylor Carman, *Merleau-Ponty* (New York: Routledge, 2008).
52. Scarry, *The Body in Pain*, 36.
53. Robert Jay Lifton, *The Future of Immortality and other Essays for a Nuclear Age* (New York: Basic Books, 1987), 235.
54. Ibid., 239.
55. Ibid., 239.
56. Cathy Caruth, *Unclaimed Experience: Trauma, Narrative, and History* (Baltimore: Johns Hopkins University Press, 1996).
57. Jean Améry, *At the Mind's Limit: Contemplation by a Survivor of Auschwitz and Its Realities* (New York: Schocken, 1986), 28.
58. Kai Erikson, *A New Species of Trouble: The Human Experience of Modern Disasters* (New York: Norton, 1994), 228.
59. Améry, *At the Mind's Limit*, 22.
60. Ibid., 34.
61. Michael Foucault, *The History of Sexuality*, Vol. 1, *An Introduction* (New York: Vintage, 1990)
62. Norton, *Leo Strauss and the Politics of the American Empire*,
63. John Langbein, *Torture and the Law of Proof: Europe and England in the Ancien Regime* (Chicago: University of Chicago Press, 2006).
64. Peter Brooks, *Troubling Confessions: Speaking Guilt in Law and Literature* (Chicago: University of Chicago Press, 2000).
65. Scarry, *The Body in Pain*, 35.
66. Ibid., 88
67. Ibid., 36
68. Regali, *Torture and Democracy*, 502.
69. Gilles Deleuze, *Masochism: Coldness and Cruelty* (Cambridge, Mass.: Zone, 1991).
70. Ibid.
71. Philip Smith, *Punishment and Culture* (Chicago: University of Chicago Press, 2008).
72. Rejali, *Torture and Democracy*, 478.
73. Ibid.
74. Lawrence Weschler, *A Miracle, A Universe: Settling Accounts with Torturers* (New York: Pantheon, 1990).
75. D. N. Rodowick, *The Virtual Life of Film* (Cambridge, Mass.: Harvard University Press, 2007), 22.

PART I

Torture and the Implications of Masculinity

24 – FOX television series (2010–2011)

1

Countering the Jack Bauer Effect

AN EXAMINATION OF HOW TO LIMIT THE INFLUENCE OF TV'S MOST POPULAR, AND MOST BRUTAL, HERO

David Danzig

> "You say that nuclear devices have gone off in the United States, more are planned, and we're wondering about whether waterboarding would be a bad thing to do? I'm looking for Jack Bauer at that time!" [Sustained applause.]
>
> —Tom Tancredo, Republican presidential debate,
> May 15, 2007, University of South Carolina

To some, Jack Bauer, the hero of the FOX television program 24, is just the sort of guy the U.S. needs to counter the threat from extremist groups like al-Qaeda. Bauer never flinches when confronting a terrorist. In its first six seasons 24 broadcast eighty-nine scenes that feature torture.[1] Bauer has used nearly every torture technique imaginable over the lifetime of the series. He has stabbed, shot, kicked, choked, electrocuted, drugged, blackmailed, threatened family members of terrorists with death, and used other exotic forms of torture in his abusive quest for information. Terrorists who are willing to die for their cause routinely reveal critical secrets seconds after Bauer turns on the pain. 24 is at the leading edge of a new trend in television. Since September 11 there has been a lot more torture on TV—an average of more than 120 scenes a year on prime time.[2]

The torturers have changed too. The heroes on programs like *LOST*, *The Shield*, and even *Star Trek: Enterprise* turn to torture regularly to gain information. When "the good guys" use torture, it almost always works. All this torture has had an impact. Junior U.S. soldiers—and even interrogators at the detention facility in Guantánamo Bay—have copied abusive interrogation techniques they have seen portrayed on TV.[3] And military educators say that *24* is one of the biggest problems they have in their classrooms, because young people preparing for a career in the armed services routinely point to the program as evidence that it is necessary to use torture at times to save lives.

A number of public figures have also turned to *24* in explaining their own views on torture. In doing so they have perpetuated the myth that Bauer, or at least men like him, exist. At a jurists' conference in Canada, for example, Justice Antonin Scalia reportedly said, "Jack Bauer saved Los Angeles. . . . He saved hundreds of thousands of lives."[4] He went on to explain that no jury would convict Bauer of a crime for his use of abusive interrogation techniques. President Bill Clinton, in explaining his position on torture during the run-up to the 2008 Presidential elections, told NBC's *Meet the Press*, that any law that approved torture would soon become abused. But, he said, there are security agents like Bauer who might decide to use torture even though it is illegal. "If you're the Jack Bauer person, you'll do whatever you do and you should be prepared to take the consequences," Clinton explained.[5] "When Bauer goes out there on his own and is prepared to live with the consequences, it always seems to work better," the former president added. In December 2006 the Intelligence Science Board, which serves as an expert advisory panel to the U.S. intelligence community, released a report stating, "Most observers, even those within professional circles, have unfortunately been influenced by the media's colorful (and artificial) view of interrogation as almost always involving hostility and the employment of force—be it physical or psychological—by the interrogator."[6]

Copying Bauer

The story of how the Bush administration pulled back from the United States' long-standing commitment to the Geneva Conventions is well known. As Tony Lagouranis, an interrogator who served at Abu Ghraib, explains in his book *Fear Up Harsh: An Army Interrogator's Dark Journey Through Iraq*, interrogators who served in Iraq in 2002 and 2003 were told "to take the gloves off" and encouraged to develop their own interrogation techniques.

"We were told explicitly that the interrogator needed the freedom to get creative," Lagouranis writes. "So basically there were no limits."[7] In more than one case interrogators turned to television and the movies for inspiration. Lagouranis said that his unit, based in Iraq in 2003, would watch TV programs together and then discuss using the torture techniques they had just viewed on the Iraqis in their custody.

Lagouranis's unit was not the only one that was inspired by on-screen fictional accounts of interrogation. Lieutenant General Paul Mikolashek, who served as inspector general of the army, was sent into the field in 2004 with a team of investigators to conduct a systemic review of interrogation methods in an effort to determine how widespread the use of torture had become.

Mikolashek's final report identified "no evidence of a pattern of abuse." [8] But the field, or "scoping," notes recorded by one investigator are troubling. A platoon leader said that "at the point of capture, non-commissioned officers were using interrogation techniques they literally remembered from the movies." [9]

Diane Beaver, the highest-ranking uniformed military lawyer at Guantánamo, told Philippe Sands, a lawyer and journalist, that the second season of 24 directly influenced the way that interrogations were conducted at the facility. Sands recounts the conversation in his book, *Torture Team: Rumsfeld's Memo and the Betrayal of American Values*. "We saw it on cable," Beaver told Sands.[10] "People had already seen the first series. It was hugely popular." "He gave people lots of ideas," Beaver continued, saying that interrogators directly copied Bauer. "You could almost see their dicks getting hard as they got new ideas."

Torture on *24*

24 is set up to knock down whatever hesitations you might have about Bauer's methods. It is, in a perverse way, an advertisement for torture that ran for eight seasons, every Monday night, from when it first aired on November 6, 2001, to its last episode on May 24, 2010. Bauer is a hero who not only fights terrorists but also all of us who believe that his methods won't work.

Just about the only assistance that Bauer needs comes from technology (and a squeaky-voiced tech who runs the computers named Chloe). Virtually everyone else—especially those easy-to-hate government bureaucrats—tries to keep Bauer from "taking the gloves off."

Bauer was often restrained—and sometimes even arrested or otherwise detained—by superiors at the White House and the Counter-Terrorism Unit (CTU, the fictional agency where Bauer is employed), who fear he will use abusive interrogation tactics inappropriately. However, he repeatedly manages to escape, torture the bad guys, gain necessary information, and convince his superiors to continue letting him do his job. In season 4, for example, when Bauer apprehends a suspected terrorist, his superiors prevent him from participating in the interrogation, preferring instead to use more humane questioning tactics. They get nowhere, and the clock is ticking. The terrorist is known to be a part of a cell planning a high-level political assassination. The program heightens the tension by placing a small clock at the bottom of the screen. It counts down as Bauer paces outside the interrogation room.

One of the innovations of the program is the introduction of this clock, which purports to be tracking real time in Bauer's life. A season, made up of twenty-four episodes, recounts one day of Bauer's life. After less than ten seconds Bauer decides to take action. He boldly strides toward the interrogation room, knocks out the armed guard on duty, breaks into the room, and shoots the detainee in the knee. "What is your target?" Bauer screams, as he points the gun at the detainee's other leg. "Secretary of defense," shouts back the prisoner. While all of this takes place, the CTU director and a colleague are watching (and listening) from behind a one-way mirror connected to the interrogation room. When Bauer first enters they scream at him to stop. When the information is blurted out, they immediately call the White House to warn of the attack. Seconds later Bauer's boss sends him out to protect the secretary.

Every character who questions the use of torture on the program is ultimately proved to be wrong. Even Bauer's commitment to abusive interrogations wavers at one point, before he quickly realizes that he has to keep doing "whatever it takes." In season 6 Bauer actually opposes the torture of a suspect for the first time, only to watch slack jawed as an associate jams a knife into the suspect's knee, causing him to immediately reveal secrets. Indeed, torture is presented as such a perfect tool when it comes to countering terrorism that just about the only person that it does not compel to talk is Bauer himself. Bauer actually (briefly) dies during a torture scene in season 2 rather than talk. But he quickly comes back to life, and can be seen effectively torturing terrorists later that episode.

Bauer's Appeal

Interrogators and soldiers in the field were not the only ones who were influenced by Bauer's tactics. In the summer of 2004, one year after Diane Beaver and her colleagues watched the second season of 24, I began renting DVDs of the program and quickly became hooked on the adrenaline rush that 24 provided. I was an unlikely fan. Days after the revelations of abuse at

Abu Ghraib, I was tapped to serve as the manager of Human Rights First's campaign to end torture. I would spend my days talking to government officials, reporters, and activists about the damage the use of torture had done to the United States.

But at night, as I watched more and more 24, I found that Bauer was chipping away at my ironclad resolve that torture should not ever be employed. I found myself wondering what a U.S. agent should do if he faced the ticking time-bomb situations Bauer faced every Monday night on 24. The experience was unsettling. After all, if this program could have this impact on me—a person who spends his days working to stop torture—I wondered what impact the program might have on the broader viewing public. And I wondered what, if anything, Human Rights First might do about it.

In the fall of 2005 I called Lieutenant Colonel Gary Solis, a retired Marine Corps officer and an attorney who had developed a course on torture and the laws of war that he was teaching at the U.S. Military Academy at West Point. Solis told me, "24 is one of the biggest problems I have in my classroom."[11] He explained that some professors at West Point felt compelled to watch the program in order to argue with their students about why what Bauer had done on the program the night before would never work in the field. During its first four seasons the program boasted more than 15 million regular viewers, and was especially popular among seventeen- to thirty-five-year-old men, according to Nielsen ratings. (After that peak, the program's ratings ebbed, but ratings show that it continues to be one of the top ten most-viewed programs on TV, with a steady viewership of more than 12 million people.)

On the phone Solis, a combat-decorated veteran of the Vietnam War, asked me, "Have you ever been in a position where you shot someone in combat? Because I can tell you that in real life, it doesn't sound the same or even smell the same as it does on TV." Solis said his students were particularly swayed by the scene during the fourth season where Bauer breaks into the interrogation room, shoots the suspect, and finds out about plans to target the secretary of defense. Solis told Jane Mayer of the *New Yorker*, "I tried to impress on them that this technique would open the wrong doors, but it was like trying to stomp out an anthill."[12]

Nudging Hollywood

For the next year I corresponded with Colonel Stuart Herrington, a legendary intelligence officer who had operated behind enemy lines in Vietnam, interrogated Noriega's henchmen in Panama, and directed the interrogation of high-value detainees in the first Gulf War. When we began our on-again, off-again e-mail conversation, Herrington wrote, "I bet every prisoner I interrogated would buy me a drink if I saw him on the street again today."[13] His approach was decidedly un–Jack Bauer. "Torture," Herrington told me, "is pure amateur hour. Experienced, professional interrogators don't need it." And over time, he told me stories of how he "broke" detainees without laying a hand on them.

In Herrington's view humane treatment was not just morally right; it was also more effective. The stories that Herrington, and other interrogators, told me were riveting. But they were not the sort of interrogation stories one saw on TV. In the fall of 2006 I asked Herrington if he would join Human Rights First for a trip to Hollywood to talk to writers, producers, studio executives, and actors about the way interrogation and torture are portrayed on television.

Our hope was that we might be able to gently nudge the industry to portray interrogators more like Herrington and less like Bauer. Brigadier General Pat Finnegan, the dean of the U.S. Military Academy at West Point, and Joe Navarro, a former FBI special agent and supervisor who wrote a key textbook the FBI uses to train agents on interrogation, joined us for the trip. We met with the executive producers of 24 and *Lost*, a popular ABC drama that features a number of scenes of torture each season, and we learned that the producers and the writers of these two programs, which often depicted torture and interrogation, had never met a professional interrogator prior to our visit.

What Hollywood Wants

We met with the writing team and the executive producers of 24 in a conference room on the first floor of the low-slung brick building that serves as the program's set just north of Los Angeles. The setting and the atmosphere were casual. Many of the writers wore t-shirts and jeans. Seconds after we sat down at a large square table Bob Cochran, an attorney and cocreator of the show, asked Herrington and Navarro what they would do if they faced a ticking time-bomb scenario.

The conversation lurched backward and forward as the interrogators explained that the situation that Bauer faced on the program was—as Navarro said—"preposterous." You would never know, Navarro argued, with certainty that you had "the one guy" who had exactly the information you sought. And it was absurd to suggest that they would "break" if they were tortured. "These are determined people," Navarro explained. "They are not going to give you information just because you pull out a few fingernails."[14]

Herrington provided the writers with typed notes on seventeen humane interrogation techniques he had used successfully. Looking at the list, executive producer Howard Gordon slammed the table with his hand and said, jokingly, "You are hired!"

The next day, Jeff Pinkner, an executive producer of *LOST*, told us, "Quite honestly, when looking at an interrogation or torture scene and trying to decide whether or not we will include it, it comes down to the entertainment value. What do we think will capture the audience's attention?"[15] We met with Pinkner and another *LOST* executive producer, Carlton Cuse, in an effort to convince them that torture should not be presented on their program as a facile tool that always generates reliable information. "Before speaking with you guys," Pinkner said, "we never thought that what we came up with in our fevered minds might have any impact on the way these things were done in the real world."

But during the visit to Hollywood we saw repeatedly how the line between the TV world and the real world was sometimes hard to see. One morning I waited with General Finnegan to meet with Kiefer Sutherland, the actor who plays Bauer, to talk to him about the way that interrogation is portrayed on the program. Finnegan, who was dressed in a classic army uniform complete with medals and ribbons, was approached by an actor who gave him a friendly, light punch in the arm. "Hey man," said the actor, who was dressed as an LAPD officer, "when is our first call?" It seems that the actor mistook General Finnegan for an extra on the set.

Part of the problem with 24 is that many aspects of the show are produced with such an attention to detail the fantasy seems real. When you bring a real general to the set, he is indistinguishable from the fake ones. Sutherland told us later that he is often confused for the character he plays. "Recently," he said, "a woman on the street ran away from me screaming, 'Don't hurt me Jack Bauer!'"[16] But Sutherland, who reportedly is paid $10 million a season, told us that "in almost every interview" he stresses the fact that what they produce is "just entertainment." It is not meant to be copied or to influence the political debate.

A Film of Our Own

Soon after our first trip to Hollywood, we called Howard Gordon, 24's executive producer, and asked him to participate in a short "training" film that would be distributed for free to military educators. The purpose of the film, we explained, was to show young people training for a career in the armed services the difference between the way Jack Bauer operates and the way experienced interrogators obtain information. Gordon agreed to be interviewed on camera. Several months later, while our cameras rolled, he told us, "It would be great if we knew that torture worked. It would."[17] "But Jack Bauer is not a handbook," he said. "The premise of our program—that this hero can get all of this done in twenty-four hours—is absurd."

Our hope, in producing the film, was to show that Bauer is not a superhero. He is simply a Hollywood creation developed by writers who know nothing about interrogation. We juxtaposed the interview with Gordon (as well as Pinkner and Cuse, the two producers from *LOST*) with interviews with Herrington, Navarro, and a former U.S. Army Special Forces interrogator named Ken Robinson.

The most dramatic moment in our film, entitled *Primetime Torture*, comes from Denzel Washington, who tells Bruce Willis, in a key moment in *The Siege*, that once the United States starts using torture it will spread like wildfire. We show the scene in its entirety in our film. "You can't do this!" says Washington. "Who is next? If you torture this man today then who will it be tomorrow? Another and another." "If you do this, then they've won," Washington adds. The film has been sent to more than 1,200 military educators and is now in use in ROTC classes and a handful of elite institutions, including the U.S. Military Academy at West Point.

Humane, Effective Interrogations on Screen

I have asked dozens of interrogators and intelligence officials to point me to films and TV shows that show the way successful, humane interrogations are actually performed in the field.

There have been a number of compelling portrayals on the large screen of what can go wrong when torture is employed including memorable scenes in *Other People's Lives* and *The Marathon Man*, among others. But it is difficult for most interrogators to point to many TV programs or movies that capture the art of questioning a hostile subject effectively and humanely.

Some point to a scene in *L.A. Confidential* where a young detective, played by Guy Pearce, manipulates a pair of prisoners such that each believes the other is cooperating with the police. Fearing that his former partner in crime is ratting him out in exchange for a deal, one of the criminals begins to cooperate.

The Wire, an HBO award-winning cop show set in Baltimore, features a slapstick version of virtually the same scene in the opening sequence of the fifth season.

An interesting, recent program called *Lie to Me*, featuring Tim Roth as Doctor Cal Lightman, shows how a skilled interrogator might use "nonverbal clues" to unlock secrets. "But being an interrogator is not like what you see in the movies," Lagouranis, who was stationed at Abu Ghraib said. "You don't get the information and rush out and save lives. The truth is, it's a lot of paperwork and recording boring information."[18]

Jacob Epstein, a longtime TV writer who used to work on the police drama *Hill Street Blues* explained, "A lot of writers simply don't have the time to go through complex scenes where an interrogator and a prisoner build rapport. Torture scenes only take a few seconds. And one-hour programs are really only forty-two minutes when you cut out the commercials." Pinkner, the executive producer from *LOST*, said, "Torture is just a convenient dramatic device. It moves the plot along quickly."

The lack of TV and films that depict humane, true-to-life interrogation scenes leaves general viewers with few cultural reference points for understanding how professional interrogators actually operate. As Robert Destro writes in the introduction to the Intelligence Science Board's three-hundred-page report on interrogation,

> Prime-time television increasingly offers up plot lines involving the incineration of metropolitan Los Angeles by an atomic weapon or its depopulation by an aerosol nerve toxin. The characters do not have the time to reflect upon, much less to utilize, what real professionals know to be the "science and art" of "educing information." They want results. Now. The public thinks the same way. They want, and rightly expect, precisely the kind of "protection" that only a skilled intelligence professional can provide. Unfortunately, they have no idea how such a person is supposed to act "in real life."[19]

Chasing Saddam—Made for TV?

Consider the story of Eric Maddox, the U.S. Army interrogator who was responsible for developing the intelligence that led to the capture of Saddam Hussein. Maddox's story—as recounted in his book *The Hunt for Saddam*—is gripping. But he is no Jack Bauer. Indeed, Maddox says that when he teaches interrogation to older students, they often compare his approach to the TV police detective Columbo. Columbo, played by Peter

Falk, was an unlikely hero in a popular 1970s crime series that ran on ABC. He combined a practiced absentmindedness with what seemed like a careless approach to gathering clues. The seemingly bumbling detective put perpetrators of crimes completely at ease. They felt it was unlikely that this incompetent cop would catch them, so they told him information they probably should not have.

In much the same way, Maddox explains to the interrogators he trains that one of the most difficult challenges an interrogator questioning a hostile subject faces is getting him to talk. "I just act dumb," Maddox told me. "An interrogation is probably the most important moment in that detainee's life, and he is thinking about a lot of things, especially about whether he is ever going to get out and see his family. . . . My job is to give him hope. To let him taste freedom."

In the hunt for Saddam Hussein Maddox would hunker down opposite a suspected Iraqi insurgent in Tikrit, Iraq, and make up an absurd charge. "Look," he would say. "I have to fill out some paperwork." Then he would consult his papers. "It says here that you were Osama Bin Laden's driver." "What happens then for the detainee," Maddox explained, "is that he has a glimmer of hope. . . . He probably went into the interview thinking, 'I am not going to say anything'. . . but then he thinks, 'They have me for the wrong thing. Maybe they don't know who I am after all.' And he starts talking."

The way Maddox operates is more cerebral than Bauer. Maddox is an information junkie. He found Saddam by interviewing hundreds of individuals who he believed were close to the former Iraqi president and piecing together their stories. He gobbled up facts in an effort to draw as complete a portrait of Saddam as possible. Ultimately, Maddox learned a key piece of information that led almost directly to Saddam's capture from the former dictator's cook. Saddam insisted on eating Mafooz, an Iraqi fish, every day. When Maddox learned during an interrogation that one of Saddam's former bodyguards owned a fish farm where one could get excellent Mafooz, a lightbulb went off in the interrogator's head. The former Iraqi president was found on the farm soon afterward hiding in a hole a few hundred feet from the river. Stories like Maddox's may not lend themselves to being told on TV. They take a commitment that an eight-second torture scene does not require.

An Ongoing Struggle

Since our initial trip I have visited Hollywood another half-dozen times to speak with producers, actors, writers, and others about torture. And I have introduced members of the creative community to Maddox and other interrogators with a track record of success.

Some members of the creative community have embraced our call to show torture in a more nuanced fashion. Adam Fierro, executive producer of *The Shield*—a popular cable program about a rogue cop—wrote for *24* before moving into the lead writing position at *The Shield*. He built the plot of his current program's second season around a story line involving an innocent man who is tortured to death by the police. The story arc shows what can go wrong when torture is employed.

Fierro, who participated in our initial conversation with *24*, told NPR that he realized there was "a dramatic opportunity" to tell stories on TV about torture that more accurately reflect what really happens in the field when these techniques are used. Fierro and his team were nominated for an ALMA award for "outstanding writing" that season.

24 has also struggled to move beyond the over-simplified depictions of torture that characterized the program's first six seasons. The seventh season, which began in January of 2009, starts with Bauer under investigation for his use of torture. In the run-up to the program's initial air date, Evan Katz—a writer on the program—told the *Chicago Tribune* that the writers were "a little sick of" writing so many torture scenes, and he said that the seventh season would not contain much more of the same. Yet the season continued to peddle the story line that torture works. For example, an adamantly antitorture FBI agent decides that she must use torture only two hours after meeting Bauer, and of course, the man she tortures immediately gives her useful information.

Bauer, in turn, delivers stirring speeches to easy-to-hate politicians about how he has "no regrets" for using the techniques he did. But the seventh season also presents, for the first time, heroic characters who oppose torture, including a strong president. And the seventh season contains the lowest number of torture scenes (seven) of any season since the first. Unfortunately, the eighth and final season does not continue this trend. Bauer engages in an orgy of violence and torture in the program's final episodes.

The Challenge

Too often the public debate around interrogation policy focuses on the use of torture. Fuelled by TV programs like *24*, the assumption at the root of this debate is that torture and abuse are effective ways to obtain information. This is not a valid assumption. The United States' extensive experience questioning prisoners shows that the most effective interrogation techniques, rarely seen on TV or in the movies, have been legal and humane.

Yet many of the stories of success are not well known. Most Americans do not realize that the most wanted men in Iraq—Saddam Hussein and Abu Musab al Zarqawi[20]—were successfully tracked down by interrogators who played by the rules.

Indeed, the United States has a long and proud tradition of success in the interrogation booth led by interrogators who never laid a hand on their subjects.

- Recently, the work of PO Box 1142 has been declassified. PO Box 1142 was a top-secret U.S. intelligence operation located at Fort Hunt, Virginia, during World War II. Many of Germany's top scientists were sent to Fort Hood for interrogation. U.S. interrogators, who often spoke fluent German and had deep operational and analytic support, questioned them using techniques that did not rely on abuse.
- A recent DIA study, *Interrogation: WWII, Vietnam and Iraq*, shows that the respectful treatment of Japanese soldiers by their American captors led directly to cooperation. Japanese soldiers said later that they expected to be tortured, and when they were treated humanely it changed their minds about their one-time enemy.
- The same study documents how three interrogators during the Vietnam War parlayed decent treatment, cultural and linguistic knowledge, and an understanding of human psychology to obtain cooperation from some of the enemy's most dedicated soldiers.

It is up to our political leaders to explain to interrogators, intelligence officials, military police officers, translators, and others who interact with detainees in the field that these are the men and women whose work ought to be emulated, not the superheroes who torture people on TV. But this will take aggressive action on the part of leaders in the White House, the Pentagon, and the intelligence community. A recent survey of U.S. combat troops deployed to Iraq found that one in ten said they mistreated civilians and more than a third condoned torture to save the life of a comrade.

For human rights advocates like me there is still much work to be done.

NOTES

1. *Study of Torture Scenes on Television*; July 15, 2007. The Primetime Torture Project, Human Rights First.
2. Ibid.
3. Philippe Sands, *Torture Team: Rumsfeld's Memo and the Betrayal of American Values* (New York: Palgrave, 2008), 63.
4. Colin Freeze, "Judge Scalia Cites Jack Bauer as Example in Discussion Over Torture," *The Globe and Mail*, June 20, 2007.
5. Bill Clinton, interview by Tim Russert, *Meet the Press*, NBC, Sept 30, 2007.
6. Intelligence Science Board, *Educing Information* (Washington, D.C.: December 2006), 95.
7. Tony Lagouranis, *Fear Up Harsh: An Army Interrogator's Dark Journey Through Iraq* (New York: NAL 2007), 131.
8. Paul Mikolashek, *Detainee Operations Inspection* (Department of the Army, the Inspector General, Washington, D.C., July 21, 2004), http://www.washingtonpost.com/wp-srv/world/iraq/abughraib/detaineereport.pdf.
9. ACLU.org, "Army Documents Show Systematic Failures in Treatment of Detainees," http://action.aclu.org/torturefoia/released/091505/.
10. Sands, *Torture Team*, 63.
11. Gary Solis (retired Marine Corps officer), phone conversation with the author, October 8, 2005.
12. Jane Mayer, "Whatever It Takes," Letter from Hollywood, *New Yorker*, February 19, 2007.
13. Stuart Herrington (former intelligence officer), e-mail correspondence with the author, November 12, 2005.
14. Author notes from meeting with producers of *24* and *LOST*.
15. Jeff Pinkner (executive producer of *LOST*), interview with the author.
16. Kiefer Sutherland (the actor), discussion with the author.
17. *Primetime Torture*, produced by David Danzig (Human Rights First, 2007), http://www.humanrightsfirst.org/our-work/law-and-security/torture-on-tv/.
18. Ibid.
19. Intelligence Science Board, *Educing Information*, ix.
20. The former "emir" of al-Qaeda in Iraq, Al Zarqawi was responsible for a series of bombings, beheadings, and other attacks during the Iraq War intended to destabilize the country. He was tracked down by a group of interrogators who used humane techniques. The hunt for Zarqawi was chronicled in Matthew Alexander's book, *How to Break a Terrorist* (New York: Free Press, 2008).

The Passion of the Christ, 2004

2

Mel Gibson's Tortured Heroes
FROM THE SYMBOLIC FUNCTION OF BLOOD TO SPECTACLES OF PAIN

Lee Quinby

In their list of the "ten best torture scenes in American cinema," Fat Guys at the Movies not only places scenes from Mel Gibson films in four of the ten slots, they give *The Passion of the Christ* top honors, admitting with discernible glee that Gibson's "torture extravaganza" exceeds a single scene.[1] Their list goes directly to a knotty point about depictions of torture in film: cinematic torture entertains—or at least captivates—even as it provides possibilities for critique of the gruesome brutalities human beings can and have wrought upon one another. Of course, there are numerous films that showcase a plentitude of blood and gore extracted from bodies writhing in pain that exhibit little or no interest in condemning torture. But Mel Gibson films are not of that genre. While Gibson heroes—with the exception of Jesus in *The Passion*—are ferocious toward their enemies, they do not condone torture per se.[2] Indeed, they are cast as valiant victims of it. In the Gibson schema revenge is what good guys justifiably inflict on their enemies. Torture is what the bad guys do.

Whether Gibson is starring or directing, the primary empathic focus in all of his films is on the body of the hero who has been seized and assaulted by torturers—the perpetrators of evil who are often holders of official power. In each case the hero's stoic endurance is the means by which he manifests exemplary manhood, even when half divine, to become a moral champion of suffering. In each instance the main character's heroic stature depends on his being tortured, sometimes to death. Gibson's depiction of the symbolic function of masculine suffering and blood sacrifice by way of cinematic spectacles of pain is the key reason that, despite his overt denunciation of torture, his films are sometimes construed as protorture.

The contradictions that arise from condemning torturers on the one hand, condoning the tortured hero's revenge on the other, and representing both through media spectacle make Gibson's films provocative, controversial, and—given his own stated goals—misguided.

The Tortured Hero of Filmmaking

I focus on three Gibson films—*Braveheart* (1995), *The Passion of the Christ* (2004), and *Apocalypto* (2006)—in which this complex and, more importantly, confusing depiction of torture is paramount. Despite their quite different historical settings and eras, all three tell stories of heroes who have opposed, in word or deed, the corrupt oppression of cruel rulers. *Braveheart*, which won five Academy Awards, including best picture, centers on the violent medieval revolt led by Scotsman William Wallace against Edward I, the King of England. *The Passion of the Christ* focuses on the final hours of Jesus of Nazareth as he is made to stand trial and condemned to death for blasphemy by crucifixion under the authority of Pontius Pilate, the Roman governor of Judea. *Apocalypto*, which is set in the more recent past, just prior to the Spanish conquest of the Mayan civilization, tells the story of a tribal member, Jaguar Paw, whose tribe has been largely slaughtered, with surviving members taken captive to be sacrificed to the gods by Mayan priests.

My choice of these three films over futuristic ones like *Mad Max* (1979) or crime thrillers like *Lethal Weapon* (1987) and *Payback* (1999), all of which are notably violent, is to accentuate the disjunction between Gibson's elevation of suffering from torture as that which makes a man heroic and his condemnation of torture by an abusive governing power in the historical past. Significantly, Gibson was the director of all three (and also the starring actor in *Braveheart*), so these films reflect his personal vision most clearly. My interest in exploring Gibson's commemoration of suffering and sacrifice is to point out its inherent contradictions, not only as an antiquated and questionable model of masculine morality, but also as a scathing though inept critique of torture conducted by a governing body. In the case of these three films in particular, the internal incongruities emerge from the three main values that Gibson overtly espouses, both in interviews and through his films: a religiously conservative moral vision, the denunciation of abusive governing power, and the usefulness of entertainment to spark reflection.

Anyone familiar with the hilarious and unusually offensive portrayal of Mel Gibson in the 2004 *South Park* episode called "The Passion of the Jew" may be surprised by and/or resistant to my claim that his films provide any sort of critique worthy of serious attention. There he is dismissed as demented as well as anti-Semitic. There is no question that his (post-*Passion*) statements upon arrest for a July 2006 DUI charge in California were anti-Semitic, as he ultimately, and perhaps begrudgingly, acknowledged. Furthermore, as I will discuss later, his portrayal of Jews in *The Passion of the Christ* is primarily (though not exclusively) crude, reductive, and incendiary. Nevertheless, simply to reiterate the overripe scorn expressed in the *South Park* episode is to miss an opportunity to understand why Gibson films in general and these three in particular are so compelling to so many viewers. Given the fact that his films have such widespread reach, it seems crucial to grasp more fully the nature of Gibson's vision. I stress his efforts to critique torture because, in my view, that theme is too often ignored by those who would dismiss him as one who merely wallows in gore. Granted, his films not only wallow, they also stumble, heave, and lurch in gore, but not merely.

Findings of and responses to the 2009 Pew Foundation study "The Religious Dimensions of the Torture Debate" provide some clues about the convoluted logic surrounding torture in Gibson's films. One finding was that 62 percent of white evangelical Protestants "say that the use of torture against suspected terrorists in order to gain important information can be often or sometimes justified." This contrasts with 46 percent of nonevangelical Protestants and 40 percent of nonreligiously affiliated Americans. The analysis of this finding goes on to point out that several intertwining factors beyond religious affiliation are strong predictors of this view, naming conservative ideology, education, and geographic region explicitly, but pointing out that religion also has a shaping force with these factors. More specifically, Republicans defend its use over Democrats, 64 to 36 percent, whites slightly edge out blacks, and southerners justify it more than residents of other regions of the country.[3]

In a *Washington Post* opinion piece Susan Brooks Thistlethwaite, a professor at and former president of the Chicago Theological Seminary, makes a direct connection between these findings and *The Passion of the Christ*. She attributes the wider acceptance of torture by evangelicals to what is called "the penal theory of atonement," the theological view that holds that "the way Jesus paid for our sins is by this extreme torture inflicted on him." Pointing to *The Passion of the Christ* as providing evidence for the connection, Thistlethwaite explains that "evangelical Christians flocked to this movie, promoted it and still show it in their churches, despite the fact that it is R-rated for the extraordinary amount of violence in the film. It is, in fact, the highest grossing R-rated movie in the history of film. The flogging of Jesus by the Romans goes on for fully 40 minutes. It is truly the most violent film I have ever seen."[4] Thistlethwaite further argues that the "message of the movie, and a message of a lot of conservative Christian theology, is that severe pain and suffering are not foreign to Christian faith, but central."

There are two points that are askew in this logic. First, while it is accurate to say that both the movie and a majority of conservative Christians see Christ's severe pain and suffering as integral to salvation for believers, what is not clear is that *The Passion of the Christ* in any way or at any point endorses torture. Second, findings indicating that a majority of evangelical Christians condone torture in order to extract information from a terrorist do not really explain why they would flock to a film that shows their avowed savior being brutally flogged, humiliated, and nailed to a wooden cross. And yet Thistlethwaite is not alone when she makes this leap of logic. This same slippage may be found among those who describe films as advocating torture, being forgiving of it, or just plain loving it.

So why are Gibson's depictions of torture, which are actually cast in all three films as inhumane and barbaric, so often seen as condoning torture? And why don't these three films in particular manage to convert audiences, especially the Republican evangelical Christians of the Pew poll, to an antitorture perspective? In response to the second question I would say that the more likely correlation for the 62 percent of white evangelical Protestants who consider torture permissible under conditions of extracting information is their acceptance of apocalyptic belief as depicted in the Book of Revelation, where Jesus is cast as a messianic warrior who brings torturous suffering and death to all but the chosen. But the Jesus of *The Passion* is not that Jesus. Hardly wrathful, he suffers, endures, and forgives. As I will indicate in the final section of this chapter, Gibson's use of spectacle to present the theme of masculine endurance of torture as an unsurpassed virtue is what enables many viewers to conflate these two depictions of Jesus. This also holds true for *Braveheart* and *Apocalypto*. But this is not the only factor at work in the confusion over Gibson's antitorture stance. There is actually a confluence of factors that, together, undermine the films' overt denunciation of torture.

One of the confluent factors contributing to the confusion surrounding the depiction of torture in these films is the reputation Gibson acquired when they were being released. His public homophobic remarks, the DUI arrest, an affair leading to an out-of-wedlock pregnancy and a divorce from his wife of twenty-eight years, and nightclub altercations have unsurprisingly led to sharp criticism of his emotional maturity and intelligence. He is often simply characterized as mentally unstable.[5] Such assessments of his personal life often blur into critical descriptions of his films, aligning him with their most barbaric characters—the torturers.

This coupling of Gibson and torture is further provoked by his outspoken religious views, which emerge from the Traditionalist Catholicism in which he was raised. Many of Gibson's remarks on this score are erratic and contradictory, but they circulate widely, and rather wildly, on the Internet and in comedic monologues. For example, his well-known remark that his (then) wife might likely go to hell, since, although she is a good woman and a practicing Episcopalian, she isn't in the church, was later contradicted by his conceding that non-Catholics could also go to heaven. The public stances he has taken on homosexuality and Jewish blame are theologically within the framework of his conservative Catholicism—but he has expressed them in virulent and coarse ways. When criticized for his statements, he tends to step back and grant as much. His insistence on essential differences between men and women and insulting remarks about feminists are countered, in his view, by his claims of devotion to women.

Not only have such concessions and counterclaims done little to create an impression of tolerance or respect for those whose views are different from his, his frequent tone of moral righteousness (regardless of which way the wind is blowing on any given topic) prompts exasperated reactions to him both personally and as a filmmaker. And those reactions tend to feed into his feeling of being unfairly judged, which he also expresses from time to time. Again, the line between Mel Gibson as a person and as the heroes of his films tends to get blurred, both in public perception and in his own, it would seem. This is particularly pronounced in *Braveheart*, not only because he plays the role of the film's hero, William Wallace, but also because Wallace's temperament, as portrayed in the film, does bear a resemblance to Gibson's own brashness, although when Gibson claims to suffer unfair attacks on his work, he also seems to identify with the leading characters in the other two films, Jesus and Jaguar Paw. He becomes the tortured hero of filmmaking.

This kind of back and forth was especially pronounced in relation to *The Passion of the Christ*, around which all of these factors came together most intensely. Even before release of the film, a number of Jewish organizations and the Anti-Defamation League undertook educational campaigns in an effort to stave off anti-Semitic reactions spurred on by it. Controversy escalated to the point of making it difficult for Gibson to get distribution in the United States. Twentieth Century Fox turned him down, and he ultimately used his own company, Icon Entertainment—a decision that paid off with huge profits from the film.[6] He also engaged in innovative marketing by widely circulating the film to evangelical groups, a move that critics saw as further evidence of his fomenting anti-Semitism among conservative Christians. Thus even though his business acumen rendered the film a huge financial success, his sense of this turmoil and rejection fed into his view that he was victimized, that he was the one who was being sacrificed to enemies who wished to squelch the truth he was struggling to tell about Christ's sacrifice.

Amid this furor Gibson's interviews tended to oscillate between assertive self-defense, penitent self-accusation, and rather charming self-deprecation. In regard to the pervasive violence of *The Passion*, for instance, he said, "I wanted it to be shocking. And I also wanted it to be extreme. I wanted it to push the viewers over the edge . . . so that they see the enormity—the enormity of that sacrifice—to see that someone could endure that and still come back with love and forgiveness, even through extreme pain and suffering and ridicule." In contrast to this directorial assuredness, he explains that it was his own state of bankrupt spirituality that led him to the point of despair, and then on a path back to Christianity. As he put it, "I think I just hit my knees. I just said, 'Help.' You know? And then, I began to meditate on it, and that's in the Gospel. I read all those again. I remember reading bits of them when I was younger." *The Passion* was his attempt to share his profound belief that "pain is the precursor to change, which is great. That's the good news."[7] That his own comments get him into trouble is something that he also acknowledges. He has said, for example, that he should refrain from doing much publicity "because I'm an idiot when I open my mouth. I might as well shut up and go away," adding that "once you go out there, you end up engaging in the nasty kind of editorial name-calling, which I didn't want to do, because that's what this isn't about."[8]

In short Mel Gibson films are often perceived within the context of his celebrity persona, one that is quite inconsistent, thus attracting myriad points of view. How one views a Gibson film is likely colored by whether one sympathizes with, distances oneself from, or is simply intrigued by that persona. With regard to *The Passion* the impasse so often expressed seems to depend on whether one sees the film as about Christ's suffering or as an exposé of how much responsibility Jews had in his crucifixion. In the case of the former view, held especially by evangelical viewers, it is likely that they have accepted Gibson's spiritual self-narrative as a sinner who has fallen and struggled to redeem himself, and are predisposed to focus on Christ's suffering as redemptive for him and his followers. In the case of the latter view, however, which includes those who railed against the film's depiction of Jews, it is likely that they are predisposed to see him as anti-Semitic in the first place and to focus on the most egregiously negative depictions of the Jews who called for Christ's death, sometimes disregarding the film's depictions of the Roman persecutors or the Jews who aligned with Christ. In other words, people don't see the exact same film, depending on how they regard Gibson himself.

In this light it is worth observing how Gibson has described his own objectives for his films. In an interview with Todd Gilcrest following the release of *Apocalypto*, he responded to a question about what he wants his "audiences to take away from this movie" in a way that straightforwardly indicates his approach to popular film:

> Okay, I think there are some good lessons. I think the whole fear aspect of life, you know. There are a lot of things happening in our civilization now where the environment is being destroyed, there's conspicuous consumption, using just for its own sake. There's the use of fear, I think in the media as a manipulation tool, and fear itself; fear drives people to do things that they wouldn't do if they thought about it a bit longer. Those are valuable lessons, I think, and we're all susceptible to these things as human beings. And there's no such thing as a hopeless situation, and I don't know—I just think the film is uplifting and spiritual on that level, and also visceral and kinetic on an action, kind-of thriller level, and also educational in that it does look at a culture that hasn't really been addressed on film before. It takes place at a certain time in that culture when things are starting to get a little rough, but what are you gonna do—talk for two hours about the guy who invented the calendar? But above all, I want people to be entertained and moved by it, you know?[9]

I quote this response at length because it encapsulates how Gibson's directorial vision so effectively reflects prevalent attitudes and responds to them in ways that show his emotional recognition of such concerns. Poll after poll indicates that Americans are indeed fearful about the issues he mentions—the environment, reckless spending, media manipulation—and fear itself. So, too, expressed desire for a more meaningful life and a better understanding of other cultures past and present are well-worn popular sentiments. What makes Gibson especially insightful as a director is his awareness that two hours packed with "visceral and kinetic" action in a historical setting can leave audiences feeling that their fears and concerns have been heard and that they have been educated about certain historical and cultural details in the process.[10] Moreover he is particularly skilled in fostering the heightened excitement and calmer resolution of the action-thriller genre. Even more crucial (although admittedly speculative on my part) is the way that emotional reactions to and enjoyment of his films may spark identification with Gibson, even when he is not starring in the film. When detractors show disdain for his vision—whether for its historical or scriptural acuity or its violent extravagance—their criticisms have been construed as disparaging of these fears and concerns and, by extension, of the audiences who have them. To some extent the process of fusing Gibson with his heroes seems to be replicated by audiences identifying with him, precisely because he has tapped into fears that are vital to them. Thus they too become tortured heroes vilified by elitist critics.

"Purified by Pain"

Despite dramatic divisions in perception of the overall meaning of the three Gibson films, one theme does seem to be understood by virtually all viewers as integral to their plots: in the course of each film the hero undergoes inordinate physical abuse and, because of it, is shown to be—in the phrase used in *Braveheart* when William Wallace is sentenced to be brutally broken, disemboweled, and beheaded—"purified by pain." It is precisely this theme that so confuses Gibson's stance against torture within the logic of each film. The confusion swirls around the way Gibson portrays morality and masculinity through the archaic blood logic central to a system of power relations based on kinship and the law.

There are two likely and related reasons for why Gibson is attached to this theme. One is personal: his ideological affinity with the most conservative form of Catholic theology upholds this ancient schema of hierarchical power relations that Michel Foucault has called the "deployment of alliance." The second is historical: all three films take place in societies where such power relations did actually predominate. The issue at hand in each film is what the most admirable form of masculine morality might be in the face of this hierarchical power. The question at stake here, however, is the extent to which this archaic morality is also being put forward as a contemporary ideal, especially for men. All three films strongly suggest that this mode of masculine morality would be better for our own era as well.

Foucault's descriptions of the system of alliance are most readily found in the final section of *History of Sexuality*, volume 1, in which he contrasts the power of a sovereign's right of death over his subjects to contemporary society's administrative powers over life itself, what he calls "biopower." Even though Foucault's division between these two forms of power relations is too stark and too sharply separated historically, the basic outline of each system is valuable for understanding Gibson's contradictory vision. Gibson espouses an ancient system of masculine morality but uses contemporary modes of normalizing biopower relations to circulate his views to as wide an audience as possible, with the dual intention of educating and entertaining them.

Foucault describes the system of alliance as a "society of blood" in which "power spoke *through* blood: the honor of war, the fear of famine, the triumph of death, the sovereign with his sword, executioners, and torturers; blood was *a reality with a symbolic function*."[11] Rather than contemporary formations of power that discipline bodies and normalize populations, the system of alliance operated by seizure and execution. It was quite literally a bloody undertaking, but as Foucault asserts, blood also carried symbolic meaning. Within the framework of Catholic theology to which Gibson adheres, the crucifixion of Jesus was a bloody torture inflicted by the corrupt ruling delegates of sovereign power. The symbolic function of Jesus' blood, according to the gospels, is as the "blood of the new testament," as Jesus declares at the Last Supper, which is reenacted ritually in the Catholic Mass.

That these figures are male heroes also stems from the historical moment of each film. These are patriarchal cultures in which male-to-male conflict is the power dynamic that is both most potent and most vulnerable to change. Patriarchal values associated with overcoming earthly evil also come to the forefront. In the case of *Braveheart* and *Apocalypto* the heroes initially use violence as an effort to overthrow the evil sovereigns. Those vicious conflicts also make up the greater portion of each film, underscoring Gibson's point quoted earlier about the cinematic value of depicting scenes that are "visceral and kinetic on an action, kind-of thriller level." *The Passion*, however, upholds endurance over revenge, and by the end of *Braveheart* and *Apocalypto*, that theme is also ultimately embraced as the higher calling. In each case the overriding message is that undergoing torture rather than exacting revenge makes the man a hero if he withstands it with nobility, bravery, and honor. For these heroes suffering bloody torture—not inflicting it—is what makes them worthy in Gibson's eyes.

The patriarchal concept of purity that is integral to the system of alliance is meant to secure kinship lines, so that bloodlines are kept, literally, unadulterated. In both *Braveheart* and *Apocalypto* rape by the enemy is a pronounced threat against which their respective heroes struggle to protect their wives. But the theme of purity of line is also disrupted in a telling way in *Braveheart*, when the film indicates that Wallace has consensually impregnated the king's French daughter-in-law, Isabelle, thus assuring his blood lineage as a means to "right" the wrong done to his wife (and therefore to him, according to alliance), since she was killed by the enemy soldiers. This starkly fictional element of the film makes sense only within the retrograde logic of the blood function of alliance, whereby Wallace defeats his enemy in the future by insuring that his own blood line is continued in the English royal family. Moreover any implication that their sexual union was an impure act is rectified through the surplus of blood that purifies his body prior to his death. He gains full honor and nobility because he has refused Isabelle's offer of the means to subdue the pain of his torture, and even when the crowd beseeches the torturer to stop, he refuses their mercy by crying "freedom" with his dying breath.

The idea that the body of the tortured hero gains purity through enduring pain is underscored in the concluding scene of *The Passion*. In direct opposition to the scene of Judas's suicide, in which a maggot-infested carcass symbolizes his impurity, the scene of Jesus' resurrected body visualizes purity in the flesh: radiant and washed clean of blood. For the film's final image the camera zooms in on Jesus' torso in profile, his hand resting against his thigh. A gaping hole in the middle of his hand, where the deadly nails had held him to the wooden cross, directs viewers to peer through to his naked body just as a final movement reveals his buttocks and upper thighs as he steps forward. The film cuts to a black screen. For viewers steeped in Freudian suggestion, this scene shocks for its sexual innuendo. And yet, as presented, it seems intended to desexualize his body by showing how his death has released his human side from all fleshly desire and rendered him pure innocence. Again much of Gibson's vision seems at odds with itself.

With regard to the power formation of alliance, Gibson's moral vision is equally at odds: it is simultaneously conservative and revolutionary. It is conservative to the extent that he accepts the hierarchy of Traditionalist Catholicism, which is premised on rejection of the Catholic reforms in the second half of the twentieth century. In keeping with the system of alliance the church is seen as a proper hierarchy based on the authority of divine law. Yet Gibson's moral vision is revolutionary to the extent that it justifies overturning a ruling power that is not sanctioned by divine authority if it is abusive to its subjects. In this light his allegiance to William Wallace in his battle against the British king is understandable, despite Wallace's own predilection for brutality. Even so, Wallace's vicious resistance is not the final or the highest form of masculine morality portrayed in that film.

Although overcoming the oppressive sovereign, his appointees, and their persecutory rule of law is cast as a goal, in all three films it is one that is deferred over time and possibly beyond time in an afterlife. In place of immediate triumph the highest ideal is physical suffering, and even death, at the hands of the despot. For Gibson's theology the first instance is Jesus, but this mode of morality through suffering subsequently applies to all adherents of the higher law of God. This is plainly visible in *The Passion*, but it also plays out in *Braveheart* and *Apocalypto*. All three heroes are captured by tyrannical rulers. Two of them, Jesus and William Wallace, are menacingly tortured in bloody, body-piercing ways to the point of an agonizing death. The third, Jaguar Paw, although captured and in line to have his heart ripped from his soon-to-be-carved-open chest, manages to escape. He too, however, endures myriad physical abuses at the hands of the enemy rulers, manifesting immense courage in the face of cruelty. In each case the tortured hero is seen as purified by the pain he undergoes.

But in order to be a hero, each of these figures requires an enemy. In each film that role is portrayed by the historical ruler of the time, a figure whose devious and cruel rule infuses his empire with corruption and viciousness. All three films stand strong against these murderous and ruthless ruling powers, and the condemnation of their use of torture is consistent and clear. Yet this is also where the portrayal of blood becomes the problematic feature of Gibson's moral vision. Although it makes sense, given the historical focus of these three films, to depict a "society of blood" as well as to accentuate the symbolic function it played at the time, what happens in the process of doing so cinematically through an excess of explicit detail and lingering close-ups of torn flesh is that blood moves from symbol to spectacle.[12] This shift from the controlled meaning of blood as a symbol within the logic of alliance to the proliferating meanings of torturous bloodletting as a large-screen spectacle is something about which Gibson seems either unaware or naïve. Or else he thinks he can have it both ways, using blood and torture as spectacle while retaining control of its meaning to project the moral message he wants to uphold.

"Dude, That Was Graphic"

Again it is worth considering what Gibson has said about his use of media spectacle in order to grasp his way of thinking rather than automatically dismissing it as merely gratuitous or erroneous. What is to be gained by witnessing portrayals of flesh ripped open by axes, whips, and knives? In an interview about *The Passion* he provides an anecdote that gets to this point:

> The most interesting reaction was from the guy who lives over the fence. He's known my boys since he was a little kid. He wanders in, goes through the refrigerator, helps himself to food, comes in, plops in front of the TV. We're watching it, so he catches it only from about halfway through, from the flagellation. He forgot to eat. He had his food, but he forgot to eat it. When it's over, he just has this stunned silence and doesn't really know quite how to react. He sits there for a couple of minutes, and I'm was [sic] watching him. And he finally turned to me and he said, "Dude, that was graphic."
>
> Now that's an understatement, but it indicated to me that he was really thinking. He was searching. And I think people don't usually say much after the film. They can't really talk, which is a good reaction, I think, because they are introspective—which is what I hoped to achieve: introspection.[13]

When I first read this, I laughed out loud at the neighbor's response. I think Gibson meant for us to laugh at this point. But when I read the second paragraph about what Gibson makes of it, I laughed again, in initial disbelief. I don't think that reaction is what he intended. I think he meant it in earnest—and this is what most engages me about the story.

Introspection is surely in keeping with what Gibson has said about his own journey of falling into temptation and finding his way back. His remark that "pain is the precursor to change" points to his identification with his heroes and the pain they endure. Within the framework of his religious beliefs, recognizing that one has been lost in sin can only cause dire pain for the sinner, but that recognition is also what allows the change in moral direction to be made. This way of thinking also makes sense in light of Gibson's stated criticism of the Bush administration's war against Iraq at the time *Apocalypto* was released. In interviews he commented on the way the film is meant to designate the common tendencies of civilizations in decline. In his words, "The precursors to a civilization that's going under are the same, time and time again," further indicating that his specific example of a nation in decline was the United States, explicitly citing the war in Iraq as he pointedly went on to ask, "What's human sacrifice if not sending guys off to Iraq for no reason?"[14] On second thought, then, I accept Gibson's *belief* that his films prompt introspection of the sort he intends. Furthermore I imagine that for many viewers of *The Passion*, especially the evangelical Christians who often attend the film together and meet for discussions about it afterwards, his kind of moral introspection associated with the symbolic function of blood is likely.

Introspection of the type Gibson is after has obviously not been the response of the film's critics, however. And what is even less clear is the extent to which the kind of moral introspection that he seeks is likely to be the outcome for the majority of viewers of *Braveheart* and *Apocalypto*, both of which lack the religious theme of *The Passion* and are given over more overtly to the action/thriller mode. As Richard Walsh has explained in an insightful essay about Gibson's use of violence as spectacle, *Braveheart* draws most explicitly from recognizable features of action films in which a hero with a death wish gets his way, undergoing a violent rite of passage that insures him a heroic stature of epic proportion. Walsh further points out that *The Passion* not only follows this same scenario but also extends the level of gore by thematically borrowing from horror films, increasingly a mainstay of media spectacle. He cites three main connections between *The Passion* and the popular horror genre. One is the theme of demonic possession, exemplified by Judas. Another is the figure of "Gibson's tempting, androgynous Satan," a figure reminiscent of slasher films in which evil is depicted as supernaturally "monstrous." The third—and most important, Walsh says—is the film's violence, which he claims "is not gratuitous. It signals the world of horror" and is meant to produce horror emotions of "shock, fear and disgust."[15]

Walsh goes on to indicate that by "maximizing the violence, *The Passion* threatens not only to obscure its own providence story but also to expose the gospel's providential story as yet another horror story."[16] This is a point that Gibson seems to miss: his desire for a moral message that is in keeping with the symbolic function of blood is actually jeopardized by his creation of spectacles of pain. Perhaps that is not surprising, given the logic of a society (the one "going under," as he puts it) that has become so thoroughly immersed in the spectacular. But his portrayal is thus more aligned with the horror genre's lack of (or ironic take on) moral judgment than his personal moral vision warrants.

Another unintended consequence of this use of torture as spectacle revolves around the unsettling of traditionally sexualized gender categories.

This seems particularly inadvertent, given Gibson's repeated acceptance of a strict gender dualism: masculinity and femininity. It may seem initially that Gibson's films follow a standard binary division, depicting men as active and aggressive, even to the point of sadism, and women as passive and willing to suffer, even to the point of masochism. It is true that in many of his films, especially the early ones in which he starred, his role was that of the "manly man" taking revenge on the brutal killers of his beloved wife. *Braveheart* has this plotline. Yet even with this gender divide at work, a traditional masculine role does not hold steady. The male body of the hero—disrobed, flogged, and stretched out and bound before his tormentors—is posed in a manner these days most often associated with the female body in pornography. Jeffrey A. Brown argues that films in which Gibson plays the hero portray this gender reversal while also managing to restore the hero's body to the pose of traditional manliness because of Gibson's "accumulative star image," which has three key qualities: a tough-guy demeanor, a wisecracking stoicism in the face of torture, and his own status as sex symbol. According to Brown, the sex-symbol and tough-guy qualities work together to create a hero that "incorporates the momentary disempowerment within a symbol of greater manliness." As he explains it, it is the character's wisecracking stoicism that mediates between the two extremes.[17]

Interestingly, although Brown does not include *The Passion* or *Apocalypto* in his analysis—neither of which have Gibson as the star—his argument about this dynamic of temporary disempowerment within greater manliness also holds to a significant extent for Jesus and Jaguar Paw in the two films, respectively. It is therefore not just Gibson's sex-symbol image that partially aligns him with the disempowered feminine role that is at work in this blurring. Provisional disempowerment is in keeping with his morality based on kinship and blood, to the extent that it can be seen as honor in the face of overwhelming odds and sacrifice in the face of persecution. Within the symbolic function of a blood society as envisioned by Gibson, these would not be seen as feminine traits. Rather they are cast as the highest ideals of manliness.

Yet in a society given over to spectacle, and in scenes that employ techniques of spectacle, as Gibson's torture scenes do, these same traits may be seen by many viewers, either favorably or unfavorably depending on taste, as a kind of pornography in which gender roles are reversed and torture is sexualized as acts of sadism and masochism. Media spectacle, in other words, operates within contemporary biopower relations that function, as Foucault has argued, through the proliferating meanings of the deployment of sexuality rather than the older system of alliance. *New York Times* columnist Frank Rich minces no words in making just such a connection: "With its laborious build-up to its orgasmic spurtings of blood and other bodily fluids, Mr. Gibson's film is constructed like nothing so much as a porn movie, replete with slo-mo climaxes and pounding music for the money shots."[18] Rich's critique reportedly infuriated Gibson, who was quoted as saying, "I want to kill him. I want his intestines on a stick. . . . I want to kill his dog."[19] This hyperbolic response, of course, is in keeping with the symbolic function of blood, and although I don't think Gibson was literally threatening doing any such thing to Rich—and there may be some intended humor with the exaggerated dog remark—it is understandable why Rich's comments about the film's depictions of Jesus' torture as pornographic would incense Gibson.

This kind of impasse between Gibson and his critics may well be irreconcilable. As I have indicated, after all of the furor raised by *The Passion of the Christ*, his next film, *Apocalypto*, also employed the spectacles of pain and torture that have become his mark and trade.[20] Again critics assailed the scenes of torture as well as the film's historical inaccuracies, and Gibson strongly defended the film in terms of his dual goals of education and entertainment. And yet there were some significant differences in *Apocalypto*'s depiction of the tortured hero. For one thing Jaguar Paw defeats his immediate enemies and lives on to begin a new life. And for another the hero's wife not only does not get killed off, but instead saves her children (one of whom she gives birth to while in hiding) and survives by her own wits and courage to rejoin her husband. Together they symbolize a new Adam and Eve, but they do not enter a new Eden, given the allusions to two sons as a possible Cain and Abel recurrence, and with Spanish ships on the horizon, future strife is clearly suggested. This shift indicates some rethinking on Gibson's part of what the symbolic function of blood amounts to in societies that grow large and imperious.

Given the likelihood of Gibson continuing to make blockbuster films in which violence plays an essential role, it seems to me that the most fruitful approach for critics of Gibson's work is to avoid wholesale attacks on his films, which ironically help to demonize him every bit as much as he does the enemies of his films, and to try instead to enlist him in representing heroism that is less susceptible to such contradictory ends. Perhaps he would be willing to engage in a little more introspection himself about why sheer spectacles of pain circumvent his espousal of manly morality and honor.

NOTES

1. The other Gibson films on the list are *Payback* (1999), *Lethal Weapon* (1987), and *Braveheart* (1995). Fat Guys at the Movies, "The Ten Best Torture Scenes in American Cinema," Film School Rejects, June 10, 2007, http://www.filmschoolrejects.com/opinions/the-10-best-torture-scenes-in-american-cinema.php.
2. For evangelical Christians who adhere to the Book of Revelation's figure of Jesus as a godly avenger, he too is ferocious toward his enemies, but Revelation's messianic warrior is not the Jesus depicted in *The Passion*.
3. The Pew Forum, "The Religious Dimensions of the Torture Debate," April 29, 2009, and "The Torture Debate: A Closer Look," May 7, 2009, http://pewforum.org/docs/?DocID=417.
4. Susan Brooks Thistlethwaite, "Why the Faithful Approve of Torture," *Washington Post*, May 1, 2009.
5. For example, Gibson's next reported project was described in an offhand manner that mirrors the *South Park* depiction: "Noted crazy Mel Gibson will star in the film *The Beaver* for noted lesbian Jodie Foster, who will direct and co-star. The film, once thought to be a project for Steve Carell, is about a man who finds comfort in a beaver hand puppet. So it'll be a cheapish quirky indie type affair, although it will star one of the most vociferously strange movie stars of the past twenty years. Could be great! Could be awful." Richard Lawson, "Mel Gibson Hoping You'll Pay $12 to Watch Him Have Conversations with a Puppet," Gawker.com, July 10, 2009, http://gawker.com/5311791/mel-gibson-hoping-youll-pay-12-to-watch-him-have-conversations-with-a-puppet.
6. John Horn, "Gibson to Market 'Christ' on His Own, Sources Say," *Los Angeles Times*, October 22, 2003, http://articles.latimes.com/2003/oct/22/business/fi-mel22.
7. ABCNews, "How Despairing Gibson Found 'The Passion,'" February 17, 2004, http://abcnews.go.com/Primetime/Oscars2005/Story?id=132399&page=3.
8. Mel Gibson, interview by Paul Fischer, "Gibson Defends His Passion," IOFilm, http://www.iofilm.co.uk/feats/interviews/m/mel_gibson_passion_of_christ.php.
9. IGN, "Interview: Mel Gibson," December 15, 2006, http://movies.ign.com/articles/751/751225p2.html.
10. Numerous errors in historical treatment have been pointed out in all three films. Thus my point here is not to suggest that viewers are being educated accurately, but that they are made to feel as though they are because of the way these films use realism in setting and details of everyday life.
11. Michel Foucault, *The History of Sexuality*, Vol. 1, *An Introduction*, trans. Robert Hurley (New York: Vintage Books, 1990), 147.
12. The concept of spectacle is most closely associated with Guy Debord's 1967 study, *The Society of the Spectacle*, but much has been written subsequently about its power dynamics and evolution under advanced capitalism. For a useful discussion of both aspects, see Douglas Kellner, "Media Culture and the Triumph of the

Spectacle," (unpublished paper, GSEIS, UCLA), http://www.gseis.ucla.edu/faculty/kellner/papers/medculturespectacle.html.
13. David Neff and Jane Johnson Struck, "'Dude, That Was Graphic': Mel Gibson Talks About *The Passion of The Christ*," *Christianity Today*, February 23, 2004, http://www.christianitytoday.com/movies/interviews/2004/melgibson.html.
14. Associated Press, "Mel Gibson Criticizes Iraq War at Film Fest," MSNBC.com, September 25, 2006, http://www.msnbc.msn.com/id/15001985/.
15. Richard Walsh, "The Passion as Horror Film: St. Mel of the Cross," *Journal of Religion and Popular Culture* 20 (Fall 2008): 9–10, http://usak.ca/relst/jrpc/art20-passionashorror-print.html.
16. Ibid., 11.
17. Jeffrey A. Brown, "The Tortures of Mel Gibson: Masochism and the Sexy Male Body," *Men and Masculinities* 5 (2005): 124–25.
18. Frank Rich, "Mel Gibson Forgives Us for His Sins," *New York Times*, March 7, 2004.
19. Peter J. Boyer, "The Jesus War: Mel Gibson and *The Passion*," *New Yorker*, September 15, 2003, quoted in Rhonda Hammer and Douglas Kellner, "Critical Reflections on Mel Gibson's *The Passion of the Christ*" (unpublished paper, GSEIS, UCLA), http://www.gseis.ucla.edu/faculty/kellner/essays/gibsonspassion.pdf.
20. For an extended analysis of some of the contradictions in *Apocalypto*, see my discussion in Lee Quinby, "The Days are Numbered: The Dance of Death, Doom, and Deferral in Contemporary Apocalypse Films," in *The End All Around Us*, ed. John Walliss and Kenneth Newport (Sheffield, UK: Equinox, 2008).

Man on Fire, 2004

3

It's a Perfect World

TORTURE, CONFESSION, AND SACRIFICE

Michael Flynn and Fabiola F. Salek

There was nothing cold about the Cold War. It was marked by the insanity of the nuclear arms race and the principle of mutually assured destruction, and this legacy still haunts and endangers the civilian population. The sponsored proxy wars, insurgencies, death squads, and torture centers resulted in a casualty count in the millions. Both sides built up their militaries to obscene levels and supplied warring factions with armaments that are still used and make for a very unstable global climate.[1] The costs of interventions into the political, economic, and societal affairs of the third world were atrocious. From the perspective of the United States the war was conducted to ensure the viability of capitalism, individualism, and democracy; it seems laughable now, but many believed that the war was being waged to counter "Soviet world supremacy."[2] The Soviets' expansionist capacities were far more impaired than those of the United States; they were deeply worried about the "precariousness and insecurity of Central and Eastern Europe."[3] Both sides were possessed with an "apocalyptic fear"[4] that the other was stronger and each adopted a "policy of confrontation."[5] Yet the "cold war ethos—for those who accepted it—was at least as alluring and evocative as the imperialistic ethos that it replaced."[6]

America has been an interventionist and imperialistic power since its infancy. It sought to impose its standards of action, and will, on people perceived to be politically, spiritually, and economically immature. Throughout the Cold War the Soviet Union promoted "an alternative form of modernity,"[7] one that U.S. business and governmental elites perceived as quite dangerous. They approved of forms of economic and military intervention dedicated to prohibiting the establishment of leftist governments that would embrace "collectivist" economic and social models and restrict the influence of American models. The United States employed both overt and covert methods to accomplish this goal. During the Cold War presidential administrations used the CIA as their "personal, secret, unaccountable army,"[8] and charged it with creating political unrest, carrying out assassinations (sometimes unsuccessfully), and sponsoring guerilla wars and insurgencies (not to mention lying to Congress and engaging in domestic spying). The CIA reports to the president and takes great pains to obscure its covert actions; when they are revealed the CIA "protects the president by taking the blame, this is what is meant by 'plausible deniability.'"[9] This is a well-rehearsed game; once the agency assumes responsibility for its actions, and the media and impotent congressional committees have closed their review, the "president's men treat the alleged excess with great gentleness."[10] The intelligence failures of the CIA are legendary, and just a few need to be listed; it failed to predict the North Korean invasion of South Korea, the strong Cuban response that foiled the Bay of Pigs fiasco, the 1973 Arab attack on Israel, the disintegration of the Soviet Union, the terror attacks on September 11, 2001, and the recent uprisings in the Middle East.

CIA agents have tortured or advised torturers in South Vietnam, Uruguay, Honduras, Paraguay, Iran, Chile, El Salvador, Bolivia, and the Philippines, and this is only a partial list. It is also responsible for publishing two interrogation manuals, The *Kubark* and the *Human Resources Training Manual* (HRET); the *Kubark* was published in 1963 and the HRET In 1983. In 1985 the English version of HRET was revised to "remove objectionable discussion of torture, but the Spanish version was not."[11] These manuals are not "how-to" guides for aspiring torturers, but they "do itemize" torture techniques (ibid., 428), and the manuals argue that pain should be used to encourage the captive's "psychological regression."[12] This is accomplished by inducing "existential chaos"[13] and subjecting detainees to sleep deprivation, extreme heat or cold, and stress positions, as well as threatening the use of drugs or isolation.

During the war on terror the CIA chose fourteen operatives and instructed them in "six authorized torture techniques"; the victims were all highly placed al-Qaeda operatives. The authorized techniques included forceful shaking, slapping, "forced standing," "the cold cell," and water torture (Rejali, *Torture and Democracy*, 500). With time many more CIA operatives began to torture, and the methods they used were not limited to these six techniques. CIA operatives murdered at least five detainees. Additionally, soldiers who witnessed CIA agents torturing prisoners in Afghanistan used these techniques themselves on prisoners in Afghanistan and Iraq. The extraordinary rendition program started before the Bush Administration came into power, but "since 2001, the CIA and allied intelligence agencies" have apprehended over three thousand suspects and transported them to countries where torture is commonplace; how many of these people were not members of terrorist organizations is unknown, but the numbers are "likely to be high" (ibid., 504).

Spies, at least American spies, are agents of imperialism. Although spies are patriotic they usually have a deeply ambivalent relationship with authority and power. In most American films the spy is male, usually manifests a "straight, orthodox masculinity,"[14] is a skilled fighter, a crack shot, and a wizard with technological gadgets. The spy must also be a master of secrecy—his success and his survival depend on his ability to be a confidence man, "a manipulator or contriver, who creates an inner effect, an impression, an experience of confidence that surpasses the ground for it."[15] Spies are usually represented as loners, often contemptuous of interpersonal bonds and "social order." This alienation is central to their appeal, and the ordinary film viewer fantasizes about what it would be like to be so detached, so "invulnerable to sentiment," and to "belong nowhere."[16]

Film's most famous spy is James Bond, and it is estimated that over half of the world's population has watched at least one Bond film.[17] A key element of spy films is the "thrill" that often unites "dissimilar components of hazard, fear, pain, eros, aggression, boldness, athleticism."[18] The thrill is often manifested through chase scenes; often the spy is the one chasing an antagonist, but it is not unusual to have the protagonist being chased and needing to elude an enemy who is trying to kill or capture him. These scenes are occasions where the spy can display his athleticism and masculine courage because they involve "transgressing boundaries"[19]—dogging cars, scaling buildings, swimming great distances.

This chapter will address the films *Man on Fire* (2004), *Taken* (2008), and *Unthinkable* (2010). The protagonists in *Man on Fire* and *Taken* are ex-CIA agents; in *Unthinkable* the protagonist is protected by the CIA. None of these films were critically well received, and we concur with the critics' appraisal, but *Taken* grossed over $200 million, and *Man on Fire* grossed over $100 million. The films are pertinent because their protagonists have been trained in the craft of torture and other methods of state terror by the United States, in the films they violently intervene in the political and cultural affairs of other nations, and they suffer morally and emotionally from their training and interventions. All three are action films, which have become a Hollywood specialty. They are extremely popular among adolescents and young men, and the foreign sales of these films often outpace domestic revenues. The genre is an amalgam: borrowing from the western, film noir, the police procedural, and disaster films.[20] Action movies don't make many emotional or intellectual demands of the filmgoers, and this accounts for their wide appeal; they "favor parody over interrogation, self direction over self-reflection."[21] As Leo Braudy argues, "Serious films exist in themselves, genre films are so conscious of their audience and their manipulation of that audience that the feelings of the viewers can often be the most important subjects."[22] This genre must showcase "scenes of physical action, be they fistfights, gunfights, swordfights . . . or other derring do."[23] Action films depend on violence and destructiveness, and this is carried out in an "excessive" fashion[24]—exploding cars, bombed buildings, lots of blood and gore, and huge numbers of casualties and deaths. The protagonists are usually male, "hard–bodied,"[25] and rather unreflective; when faced with a conflict it is apparent that they would prefer to resolve it with violence, even when they make the decision to do otherwise.

Taken is by far the most pedestrian of the three films. It was released in 2008 and earned worldwide receipts of more than $226 million. The protagonist, Bryan Mills (Liam Neeson), is an ex-CIA agent whose dedication to his job means that he spends most of his time away from his family and daughter. Long divorced from his wife, he has quit the agency and moved to Los Angeles to repair his relationship with his daughter, Kim (Maggie Grace). When Kim decides to go to Europe to follow the band U2 on tour, Mills fears for her safety but allows her to go. On her first day in Paris she is kidnapped by an Albanian crime organization that specializes in getting young girls addicted to drugs and then selling them into sexual slavery. Mills is told that he has a ninety-six-hour window to get Kim back or she will be lost forever. He leaves immediately for Paris, and once he arrives he immediately starts looking for her. He uses his "spy skills" to unravel the case and very soon starts killing members of the Albanian mob. When he finds the man, Marko, who kidnapped his daughter, he tortures and wins a "true" confession from him and then kills him. The confession leads him to a sex-slave dealer named Patrice St. Claire who is auctioning off Kim to wealthy Arab men; St. Claire's henchmen knock Mills out and St. Claire orders them to murder Mills. Using skills he acquired while working for the

CIA, Mills manages to escape, and kills most of St. Claire's henchmen and executes St. Claire. He then shoots the Arab man who has bought Kim and is planning her sexual humiliation.

Unthinkable is the only film of the three that didn't merit a theatrical release; it was released directly to video in 2010. The plot is quite trite; an ex-army explosives expert, Stephen Arthur Younger (Michael Sheen), states that he has planted three nuclear devices in three separate cities and they will explode in three days if his demands are not met. Younger is an American convert to Islam and has changed his name to Yusuf Atta Mohammed. *Unthinkable* contains the most prolonged and graphic torture scenes of any nonhorror American film. Mohammed is subjected to electrical torture and water torture, his fingernails are pulled off, his fingers are dismembered by a hatchet, he is nearly asphyxiated, his teeth are drilled, he is hung like a side of beef, his wife's neck is slit in front of him, and his children are threatened with torture (hence the film's title). The torturer is Henry Harold Humphries (Samuel L. Jackson)—aka "H." The film implies that American converts to Islam are far more dangerous than Muslims raised in the Magreb or the Levant, being more fanatical and willing to endure suffering than most other Muslims. Mohammed arranges his apprehension by the police, knowing full well that he will be a prime candidate for torture under the ticking time-bomb scenario, and he is quite prepared to assume the martyr mantle—"I let myself be caught.... I choose to meet my oppressors."

The film reveals little regarding H.'s past, as is fitting for a man in a witness-protection program. He has two adorable children and is married to a Bosnian woman who was raped by three men who also murdered her son—after the war she killed the three men and their wives and children. H. obviously has tortured scores of individuals. He is arrogant, violent (he viciously attacks an enlisted soldier), and contemptuous of decency and authority. H. is represented as an African American Mephistopheles, a combination of a nineteenth-century romantic devil, capable of "good as well as evil, urbane as well as brutal, a proponent of love as well as strife," and a twentieth-century devil, oriented toward negation and "intolerable coldness."[26] He takes great delight in the fact that the military torturers believe him to be evil, an "animal"; his contempt for their clean methods of torture is quite obvious—they don't have the courage to go beyond the established procedures. He also takes delight in the fact that he is called into service by top military and governmental officials, and that "no agency will claim" him. He is an "independent contractor," a man without a home and beholden to no one. The torture he perpetrates is moral violence—"What I'm doing is good for my people"—directed against a Muslim fanatic who has designs to kill "six to ten million" citizens.

The film revolves around the relationship between H. and Helen Brody (Carrie-Anne Moss). Brody is an F.B.I. agent in the bureau's counterterrorism unit and a Harvard Law School graduate. She is a career-oriented, by-the-book agent who doesn't believe in torture. She first meets H. after inadvertently seizing him and taking him into the bureau's Los Angeles office; he is upset at having his anonymity breached and is quite brusque with her. Her next meeting with him takes place at the Centralized Command Facility where he has been requisitioned by the government to torture Yusef. H. says that he wants her to assist him because she is the only one with "integrity." It is quite clear that H. wants to break down the torture firewall between the FBI and the CIA; he wants to corrupt Brody and the FBI. She is a strong believer in regular interrogation methods and is appalled by H's brutal tactics; she strongly opposes them by stating that they are "unconstitutional" and against American "values," and that torture "doesn't work"— to which H. retorts, "That's why they've been doing it since the beginning of human history." Mohammed is able to see her idealism and the ex-army explosives expert is able to run rings around her; after he sets her up and kills fifty-three civilians her opposition to torture wanes, and she even considers torturing him. Toward the end of the film H. starts to believe that he cannot make Mohammed "crack" and, realizing that Mohammed wants to be sacrificed, and he says to Brody and the government agent, "If you tell me to stop I will." Neither instructs him to stop, and Brody later tells him to "do what you have to do."

Even when his children are threatened with torture it is difficult to feel any empathy for Mohammed. He is represented as a fanatic throughout the film, a man with no attributes outside his religiosity and a capacity to endure torture. The Muslims' predilection for fanaticism has been remarked on by Voltaire, Hegel, Canetti, and many other writers from the "liberal" states. According to Hegel, Muslims have always been inclined toward fanaticism in part because of their enthusiasm for the "abstract" and "abstract worship" and their rejection of "the singular or concrete form of subjectivity, understood as freedom."[27] When Mohammed makes his demands they are quite clichéd: the nonsupport for puppet regimes in the Middle East and the withdrawal of U.S. forces from Islamic countries. He seems to have no theological depth, choosing to mouth the platitudes "Allah believes in a just war" and "I love my religion." Representing Mohammed as a fanatic is a very cheap move: not only does it aggrandize stereotypes that have bounced around film even before September 11, it also reinforces the notion that Muslims prefer death to life, the "cult of death" to ordinary existence. Mohammed is represented as a cold man, lacking empathy—a man who rejects rational, calculative modes of being, doesn't understand the "limits of faith,"[28] disavows the state's regulatory function, and rejects the dynamics of representation and fetishizes the "real."[29]

Man on Fire was released in 2004. It received a mixed critical reception but made over $130 million at the box office. It features Denzel Washington in the title role and also stars Christopher Walken, Marc Anthony, and Dakota Fanning. Washington plays John Creasy, an ex-CIA assassin who has traveled to Mexico to visit his former partner, Rayburn (Christopher Walken). Both joined the CIA out of patriotic and imperialistic zeal, thirsty with a desire to "remake the world." Both men are haunted by their murderous pasts. When Creasy asks Rayburn, who moved to Mexico to open a security firm and married a Mexican woman, "Do you think that God will forgive us for the deeds we have performed?" Rayburn answers with a quick and unequivocal "no." Creasy is a Jack Daniels–swilling, bible-reading, sexually inert, suicidal man (from his facility with biblical passages we assume he is Protestant, since few Catholics memorize scripture). We learn that he was a very effective agent, though he regrets his past actions. As he tells a nun, "I am the sheep that got lost, Madre."

Rayburn convinces Creasy to apply for a job as a bodyguard for the daughter of a seemingly wealthy half-Mexican, half-American family. His job is to protect her from the wave of kidnappings that has targeted Mexico's upper class, since 90 percent of those kidnapped end up murdered. Creasy's charge is Pita (Dakota Fanning), a precocious and angelic little blond girl who could melt the heart of Lucifer. She manages to overcome Creasy's cynicism and hostility in short order, and they develop a deep and loving bond that is much more sustaining and involved than the relationship Pita has with her parents. This is all standard Hollywood fare: the young child as an agent of regeneration bringing the haunted, sinner man back into worldly affairs; the "lost" child drawn both to the physical strength and spiritual despair of the itinerant wanderer—but it is done rather well here, particularly for an action film.

Before she is kidnapped Pita gives Creasy a St. Jude medal. Jude, an apostle and martyr, is the patron saint of lost causes and "cases despaired of." He is called on to perform miraculous cures when the petitioner is considering giving up, often in cases of life and death. In a common prayer to Jude the petitioner recites, "I am helpless and alone. . . . Please bring me visible and speedy assistance." Jude, like Creasy, traveled widely, but whereas Jude preached the gospel and urged both political and spiritual revolution, Creasy delivered death to third-world leftists and radicals. Jude is commonly represented iconically with a small Pentecostal flame over his head; he is the original nonviolent Christian "man on fire." Both Pita and Creasy are cases despaired of for very different reasons.

Creasy is unable to protect Pita. She gets kidnapped after a shootout in which Creasy performs heroically, killing four would-be kidnappers. He is shot several times during the fighting. The kidnappers are crooked Mexican policemen and members of La Hermandad, an organization that operates with impunity in the region. The cops are in cahoots with a kidnapper named La Voz. The kidnapping has been arranged by Pita's father (Marc Anthony) and the family's attorney (Mickey Rourke) in order to pay the family's debts. After a botched ransom exchange everyone believes that Pita has been killed by the kidnappers. After partially recovering from his wounds, Creasy refuses Rayburn's offer to take him to the border so he can get the medical care he needs; instead he enlists Rayburn to find him an arms dealer who in turn supplies him with enough explosives, rocket launchers, and guns to outfit a small army. Creasy then embarks on a campaign of vengeance, torturering and killing anyone directly involved in Pita's kidnapping and assumed murder. He counters the "bad violence" of the kidnappers with his form of "good," retributive violence and becomes a kind of "man on fire," a continually bleeding, vengeance-obsessed, Christlike martyr on his own private march to Golgotha. He knows that his campaign will end in his death, and he desires a martyr's death, but he will paint his "masterpiece of death" before he is killed. He tortures his first victim by cutting off his fingers and cauterizing the wounds with a car's cigarette lighter, and then kills him; he tortures and shoots his subsequent victims. His principal tool for breaking the crime ring is torture; it is through torture that he gains his information, which is always accurate and allows him to eventually save Pita—who, in fact, is still alive. In *Man on Fire* Creasy is represented as a professional torturer, a man who takes his time and perceives torture as a ritual. There is nothing slapdash about his efforts—in some ways he belongs to the Middle Ages. Creasy (like Mills in *Taken*) carries out the torture with a quiet assurance that the criminal's confession will be true and will allow him to punish those responsible for Pita's kidnapping.

The film is disturbing in many ways. One of the main problems is the way it unites the practices of torture, murder, and love. Many psychologists and theologians have discussed the connection of sacrifice and cosmic order, and martyrdom performed in the pursuit of justice. Martyrdom is often represented as an act of love, perhaps the ultimate loving act: love for the principle of justice, but also for one's oppressed or persecuted people. Creasy is a haunted nomad beholden to no tribe or nation; his allegiance is singular, to one girl—Pita—who he believes has been murdered in cold blood. His final campaign of torture and murder is not simply a "masterpiece of death" but an act performed to settle accounts in the name of love. The film elevates martyrdom performed by an American.

Since the attacks of September 11 much has been written regarding the CIA's use of "clean torture" (Rejali, *Torture and Democracy*). Clean torture is physically painful and leaves little evidence of the torturer's practices; these clean methods are used to hinder the detection of torture by human rights organizations. Alfred McCoy has written about the CIA's use of sensory deprivation and other forms of psychological torture that result in the victim's feeling that the pain experienced has been self-inflicted. The torture depicted in *Man on Fire* (as well as *Taken* and *Unthinkable*) shares nothing with these "new" developments—the torture is brutal and extremely dirty. The victims are beaten, brutalized, scarred, and sacrificed. Creasy 's decision to use brutal forms of torture is grounded in the perception that his victims are redundant, that they have no inherent dignity, and that after the torture they must be murdered (this is also the case in *Taken* and *Unthinkable*). We wonder if these films are advocating a return to the old practices of torture, to the days of naked and unapologetic brutality, and forget this "effete" concern with nuance.

Anyone familiar with the United States' involvement in the political and social affairs of Latin American countries is well aware of the centrality of the CIA in campaigns of torture, assassination, and the arming and training of death squads in Guatemala, Chile, El Salvador, Uruguay, Honduras, and Bolivia to name just a few countries. The targets of the campaigns in the sixties, seventies, eighties, and nineties were usually leftists or socialists. The chaos depicted in *Man of Fire* is not orchestrated by leftists or atheistic revolutionaries but by working-class Catholic members of organized crime syndicates. These are the post–Cold War Latin American demons. The film does a very good job of representing Mexican criminals as physically ugly and like little Eichmanns (throughout the film they repeat that that they are "professionals," they are just doing their duty). Watching *Man on Fire* the audience feels no sympathy for those tortured or killed during Creasy's rampage, a rampage that is represented as both sacred and noble and restrained (he doesn't kill women or children or seniors, just criminals).

Creasy's victory in the film is only partially successful because it does not restore social order, though it is melodramatic, saves one little angelic girl from a rotten death, and rids the world of some of its sleaziest characters. Creasy is also represented as a far more effective agent of "justice" than Mexico's mostly corrupt and incompetent police force and politicians. Over the past couple of years we have seen an increase in media coverage of the violence in Mexico and a worry about "spillover" into the United States (never mind the fact that well over 70 percent of the weapons used are manufactured in America). We are left with the question of whether the film is arguing for the necessity of agents like Creasy. Are agents of the Protestant "redeemer" nation the only ones capable of bringing some form of justice and moral order to an anarchic, Catholic Latin American country before it's too late?

The representation of masculinity in these films is quite disturbing. These men are capable of loving children for short periods of time and are oddly disconnected from women. They lack spontaneity and rarely seem emotionally or spiritually present to those around them. Once they have embarked on their vengeance quest they show no remorse, no mercy, and derive great pleasure and delight in killing and torturing their enemies. They emotionally harden themselves and perceive their enemies as subhuman; they become servants of death and ruin, and violence is seen as the absolute solution to their dilemmas; they become individuals with a "passion to transform that which is alive into something unalive."[30] It isn't surprising that these films were produced during a neoconservative era. Each of the protagonists believes he is engaged in a war, and war to them is a man's game. Many neoconservatives believe that war "restores virtue" and "rescues men" from civilization, which renders them soft and equivocal; war also separates men from women . . . war makes men manly."[31]

In *Man on Fire* and *Taken*, Creasy and Mills become avenging vigilantes once their loved ones are kidnapped. H. is a different kind of vigilante, hired to do the dirty and illegal work that law enforcement and intelligence personnel can't legally get away with; he is a vigilante protected by top military and governmental officials. The vigilante occupies an esteemed position in American cultural memory and in action films; he is seen as a courageous man who will confront and engage dangerous criminals—an agent of the state minus the state's protection—with the purpose of restoring "social order and stability."[32] In American history the vigilante movement was strongest in frontier towns where the established law enforcement was lacking. Both Creasy and Mills became vigilantes because of the indifference and corruption of the Mexican and the French police, respectively. For all three men the move into vigilantism is not difficult; all have lived transient lives in which they manifested a contempt for social norms and the "values of community."[33] The protagonists are all "marginalized" men, and this "provides them with the strongest of all motives" for their vigilante action—"the desire to remount the pedestal... to recover their lost halos."[34] The "heroes" in these films have transformed themselves into bloodthirsty predators and have little patience for weak punishments; they want their enemies to suffer and die. The American vigilante ideology was grounded in the principle of responding to "a threat to individual or collective identity"[35]—Creasy defends his honor, Mills rescues his only child from a life of sexual slavery, and H. attempts to prevent the nuclear slaughter of millions. The principle of popular sovereignty was also a central feature of vigilante ideology. This principle held that "the people are the real sovereigns"[36] and they have the duty and right to pursue justice when agents of the law are absent or ineffectual. This principle resonated with Americans no matter their political affiliation. In the early years of American vigilantism the punishment was whipping and social exclusion, but as time passed "killing became the... customary sentence."[37]

When the wound—or the anticipated wound—is profound, vigilantism and vengeance complement each other. In each of these films the protagonists feel a sense of "moral anger," provoked by the evil actions of an individual or group they perceive to be morally inferior to them.[38] This moral anger is intensified because the threatened individuals are innocent; they have done nothing to deserve the danger they now encounter. Each of the protagonists has been trained to fight in a "savage" war,[39] a war in which one's enemies are considered uncultivated, black-hearted, and bestial. Engaging in conventional combat against foes such as these is suicidal; to prevail one must employ tactics (i.e., torture) and weapons that can't be countered—a certain "regression to a more primitive state"[40] is required to survive. Because the actions of the enemy are perceived as disgraceful, any hostile response is suitable. None of the protagonists worries about the degree of injury he inflicts on his opponents.[41] In both *Taken* and *Man on Fire* it is the vengeance of the outsider, the exspook from America with little cultural knowledge, that bestows justice and cleanses the criminal element. The corrupt Mexican and French law-enforcement and intelligence agencies are willing to accommodate organized crime networks because they receive kickbacks, so it is only the Americans who have the moral gumption to rescue the children that the authorities would rather see sacrificed. These films promote the idea that the criminal justice system aids and abets criminals, or inadvertently sentences people to death because of its slowness in responding to threats. Justice is served by stepping outside the law and pursuing a speedy course, free from the chains of command and the bureaucracy, punishing the criminals with methods long declared barbaric.

In *Man on Fire* and *Unthinkable* there is a disturbing racialization of violence. In both films it is the black man who tortures and kills, and the white man or woman who is the promoter of nonviolence and limits. Rayburn, after serving in the CIA, has sworn off violence, and Brody continues to insist on nonviolent interrogation through the first half of their respective films. This representation reinforces certain stereotypes about black men and violence. H. tortures Mohammed with a clinical detachment and coldness that is akin to the sadism of the Nazis. He is represented as having a captured tiger's obsessions and preoccupations, always anticipating the zookeeper's mistakes, and waiting for the opportunity to create mayhem. Creasy, after Pita's kidnapping, is represented as a cold-blooded killer who shows no mercy, and after he tortures and sacrifices his first victim he says, "The revenge is best served up cold." When Rayburn speaks with the attorney general he says that Creasy is an "artist of death" who is about to "paint his masterpiece."

The three films illustrate that fear is often a prime motivator of torture. Usually presented as a practice performed by tough men—spooks, soldiers, cops—the torturer, in film, is often depicted as a man in total control, a man unacquainted with fear or at least practiced at its disavowal. Yet in *Unthinkable* and *Taken* H. and Mills carry out their respective interrogation programs with the knowledge that if torture doesn't secure a true confession, Mill's daughter will be lost into sexual slavery and millions will die in a nuclear holocaust. Creasy's torture and murder campaign is an attempt to replace the fear caused by the loss of Pita—a girl who "showed him it was alright to live again"—with moral anger and rage. In *Taken* and *Man On Fire* the torture is effective, and Creasy and Mills get instant confessions that allow them to "crack the case." This a fictional conceit, one that has little bearing in reality; as Darius Rejali argues, the problem is that "physical interrogation methods ... take time, time that interrogators do not have in emergencies. Real torture—not the stuff on television—takes days, if not weeks" (Rejali, *Torture and Democracy*, 474). Torturing someone in an "emergency situation" often results in increased resistance; the victim either won't produce a confession or will manufacture a false one. In such emergencies torturers must eschew slow techniques for brutal tactics that run the risk of causing trauma and "insensitivity, unconsciousness and inadvertent death" (ibid.). H.'s torture of Mohammed demonstrates the futility of torture, but also argues for its viability; the film offers no other option for getting the information needed to find the bombs. H.'s threat to torture Mohammed's children gets him to reveal the location of three nuclear devices, but not the fourth. Torture is often performed in these situations because "this kind of stuff just makes people feel better, even if it doesn't work" (ibid., 535). Torture gives the impression that those charged with national security are engaged in real work and not rendered passive by terrorists or organized crime figures.

In the wake of the terrorist attacks on the World Trade Center and the Pentagon, the preferred victims of torture on television and film were terrorists or individuals believed to be terrorists. In *Unthinkable* the torture victim is a terrorist, but in *Taken* and *Man on Fire* the tortured are members of organized crime rings. In some ways this shift was a response to a desire to distance film productions from the 24 phenomenon. Terrorists are easy to demonize; they attack undefended civilians, and in the current era they are no longer interested in simply making a symbolic statement about the weakness of the nation-state—they try and kill as many people as possible, and their victims often include children. Terrorism is indefensible, yet terrorists' motives are grounded in something other than personal gain; their attacks are frequently a response to imperialistic and oppressive practices of more militarily advanced nations. Often terrorists are defending what they believe are "sacred values," such as a commitment to "honor religion and justice." The values are "inviolable and absolute," and are defended without any consideration for materialistic or financial gain.[42] In many ways members of organized crime make more satisfying torture victims than terrorists. These men aren't motivated by political or religious intentions and they aren't responding to another country's desire to inflict pain on their nation and its citizens; their pursuit is only in increasing their own profit. Kidnappers, more than any other criminals, are worthy of opprobrium; they prey on children with the hope of increasing their organization's riches, often killing them in the process, and sentence their parents, whose only "crime" is wealth, to a lifetime of grief and guilt.

For Michel Foucault, the "gloomy festival of punishment" came to an end by the early nineteenth century.[43] Torture was no longer a staged event, a spectacle designed to "make everyone aware, through the body of the criminal, of the unrestrained power of the sovereign."[44] As described in the opening pages of *Discipline and Punish*, the ritual of torture was staged to elicit excesses of "blood and pain"[45] and always ended with the execution of the victim, a death that was agonizing and prolonged. After the decline of torture, according to Foucault, the object of punishment shifted from body to soul, and punishment was aimed at the deprivation of rights and wealth, not physical suffering. In these films (like many in the post–September 11 period) we witness the recrudescence of the spectacle of torture; the scenes are long, and the fear, desperation, and physical suffering of the tortured are developed with loving detail. The audience experiences little empathy or sympathy for the tortured because the torturer is inflicting moral, good violence as opposed to the criminal's depraved violence. The sacrifice must take place, and for a moment the audience believes that the sacred has returned. And the sovereign—does he, late at night, watch these films?

NOTES

1. Eric Hobsbawm, *The Age of Extremes: A History of the World, 1914–1991* (New York: Vintage, 1996), 230.
2. Ibid., 240.
3. Ibid., 238.
4. Odd Arne Westad, *The Global Cold War: Third World Intervention and the Making of Our Times* (Cambridge: Cambridge University Press, 2007), 397.
5. Hobsbawm, *The Age of Extremes*, 225.
6. Westad, *The Global Cold War*, 5.
7. Ibid., 39.
8. Chalmers Johnson, *Nemesis: The Last Days of the American Republic* (New York: Metropolitan, 2008), 93.
9. Thomas Powers, *Intelligence Wars: American Secret History from Hitler to Al-Qaeda* (New York: New York Review of Books, 2004), 55.
10. Ibid., xi–xii.
11. Darius Rejali, *Torture and Democracy* (Princeton: Princeton University Press, 2007), 428. Hereafter cited in text.
12. Alfred W. McCoy, *A Question of Torture: CIA Interrogation, from the Cold War to the War on Terror* (New York: Metropolitan, 2006).
13. Ibid., 51.
14. Toby Miller, *SpyScreen: Espionage on Film and TV from the 1930s to the 1960s* (New York: Oxford University Press, 2003), 8.
15. Gary Lindberg, *The Confidence Man in American Literature* (New York: Oxford University Press, 1982), 7.
16. Allan Hepburn, *Intrigue: Espionage and Culture* (New Haven: Yale University Press, 2005), 13.

17. Miller, *SpyScreen*, 129.
18. Hepburn, *Intrigue*, 24.
19. Ibid., 25.
20. Eric Lichtenfeld, *Action Speaks Louder: Violence, Spectacle, and the American Action Film* (Wesleyan: Wesleyan University Press, 2007), 4.
21. Ibid., 342.
22. Leo Braudy, *The World in a Frame: What We See in Films, 25th Anniversary Edition* (Chicago: University of Chicago Press, 2002), 117.
23. Lichtenfeld, *Action Speaks Louder*, 5.
24. Ibid., 342.
25. Susan Jeffords, *Hard Bodies: Hollywood Masculinity in the Reagan Era* (New Brunswick, N.J.: Rutgers University Press, 1993).
26. Jeffery Burton Russell, *Mephistopheles: The Devil in the Modern World* (Cornell: Cornell University Press, 1990), 169.
27. Albert Toscanno, *Fanaticism: On the Uses of an Idea* (London: Verso, 2010), 154.
28. Ibid., 157.
29. Ibid., 27.
30. Erich Fromm, *The Anatomy of Human Destructiveness* (New York: Holt, 1992), 408.
31. Anne Norton, *Leo Strauss and the Politics of the American Empire* (New Haven: Yale University Press, 2005), 153.
32. Richard Maxwell Brown, *Strain of Violence: Historical Studies of American Violence and Vigilantism* (New York: Oxford University Press, 1975), 96.
33. Ibid., 97.
34. Rikke Schubart, "Passion and Acceleration: Generic Change in the Action Film," in *Violence and American Cinema*, ed. J. David Slocum, 194–95 (New York: Routledge, 2000).
35. Robert Jay Lifton, *The Broken Connection: On Death and the Continuity of Life* (New York: Simon and Schuster, 1980), 149.
36. Brown, *Strain of Violence*, 117.
37. Ibid., 109.
38. Peter A. French, *The Virtues of Vengeance* (Lawrence, Ka.: University Press of Kansas, 2001), 95.
39. Richard Slotkin, *Gunfighter Nation: The Myth of the Frontier in Twentieth Century America* (New York: Harper Perennial, 1993), 12.
40. Ibid., 431.
41. French, *The Virtues of Vengeance*, 141.
42. Scott Atran, *Talking to the Enemy: Faith, Brotherhood, and the (Un)Making of Terrorists* (New York: Harper Collins, 2010), 353.
43. Michel Foucault, *Discipline and Punish: The Birth of the Prison* (New York: Vintage, 1977), 8.
44. Ibid., 48.
45. Ibid., 16.

PART II

Torture and the Sadomasochistic Impulse

Lust, Caution, 2007

4

Lust, Caution

TORTURE, SEX, AND PASSION IN CHINESE CINEMA

Chris Berry

Emilie Yueh-yu Yeh notes two brief appearances made by a German shepherd guard dog in Ang Lee's 2007 film, *Lust, Caution* (*Se Jie*). It first appears in the credit sequence, then again in the middle of the second sex scene in the film, in a cutaway shot punctuating the shift from foreplay to penetration. What is it doing here? Its appearance is somewhat mysterious, because there is no evident narrative motivation. The absence of narrative motivation makes it impossible to give a definitive answer about the meaning of the dog. For Yeh the shots of the dog function as a "crisp visualizing of 'caution,'" reminding us on the animal's second appearance of the nervous tension that punctuates the lust between a collaborator with the Japanese invaders and his would-be patriotic assassin. On the basis of this insight she details how the relationship between lust and caution is communicated cinematically in the film through montage techniques.[1] However, as I hope to demonstrate, the dog can also be understood as a crisp visualization of torture, and it is therefore key to my reading of the film.

Lust, Caution is often thought of as a sort of *Last Tango in Shanghai*—another sexually explicit film about a torrid, dangerous, and even sadomasochistic affair between an older man and a younger woman, but set during the Japanese occupation of Shanghai in the 1937–1945 War of Resistance against Japan. Indeed some critics have made direct comparisons to Bertolucci's 1972 film, *Last Tango in Paris*.[2] However, I argue here that Lee's film is both an ideal jumping-off point for the examination of existing cinematic discourses on torture in China and a significant intervention into those same discourses. The film's usefulness as an avenue for examining existing discourse stems partly from Ang Lee's status as a leading director of transnational cinema. Because he aims his films at very different audiences in different countries, *Lust, Caution* invokes at least two existing cinematic discourses on torture. One is a Western discourse about China as the "land of a thousand cuts." The other is the revolutionary idealism of the People's Republic of China (PRC), which depicts prerevolutionary China as a society populated by revolutionary heroes and reactionary villains, many of whom are also torturers.

However, before we set out on this exploration of *Lust, Caution* and torture, we need to establish that there is a connection to torture. This is not obvious. The film follows a lethal game of lust—or is it love?—and death. On one side is Mr. Yee, who works for the puppet regime collaborating with the Japanese invaders. On the other side is Wong Chia-Chih, who works for the Chinese KMT Nationalists. A naïve and patriotic young woman, Wong has been recruited and sent on a mission to seduce Mr Yee and then set up his assassination. The connection to torture is present in the plot through Mr. Yee's character. He is not just any old traitor, but a torturer who extracts confessions from patriotic Chinese resistance fighters and then sends them to be executed. However, we do not see any torture on screen, nor do we see the bruised and battered victims of Mr. Yee's professional attention. This is where the dog comes in.

The German shepherd works for Mr. Yee. The dog may signify caution for Emilie Yueh-yu Yeh, but for me it also signifies Mr. Yee's appalling

The German shepherd dog punctuates the sex scene in *Lust, Caution*.

profession. The dog is the closest we get to seeing images of torture or its results. It functions as a detachable part of the off-screen torture scenario that stands in for the whole and reminds us of what is going on behind the scenes. What does it mean that a little bit of torture is suddenly inserted without any apparent reason in the middle of this long sex scene? What is the significance of so much visible sex and so little visible torture? I will argue that the decision to crystallize the visible evidence of torture down to this one rather indirect visual image has important consequences. First, as I will demonstrate below, the dog as stand-in for both of the discourses on torture mentioned above simultaneously frustrates the expectations associated with those discourses. Furthermore minimizing the visible evidence of torture lays a necessary foundation for *Lust, Caution*'s huge success with younger audiences. This is not only because it enables those viewers to ignore the torture and enjoy the available pleasures of the moment. As I will argue, it goes beyond merely not delivering on the expectations of the older revolutionary idealist discourse of the People's Republic and radically undermines the fundamental viability of that discourse.

International Failure and the Frustration of Stereotypes

First, the appearance of the dog helps to explain the failure of the film with foreign audiences. Ang Lee and his colleagues certainly tried to make *Lust, Caution* appealing to non-Chinese viewers. In addition to invoking orientalist stereotypes of supposed Chinese erotic cruelties, there is plenty of beautiful period detail taking us back to old Shanghai. The city's pursuit of European and American modernity in the 1930s can be read as flattering the West's sense of its own superiority, and therefore this element can also be described as aimed at the Western box office. In addition the casting of Tony Leung Chiu-wai, against type as Mr. Yee, is designed to enhance the film's global appeal. Leung is a Hong Kong star whose soulful eyes usually make him a sympathetic romantic lead. He is well known to international audiences from his roles in films like Wong Kar-wai's *In the Mood for Love* (*Hua Yang Nian Hua*) (2000). Ang Lee is also internationally renowned for box-office smashes like *Crouching Tiger, Hidden Dragon* (*Wo Hu Cang Long*) (2000). Nevertheless the box office revenue for *Lust, Caution* in the United States was a disappointing $4,604,982.[3] This compares unfavorably with the much smaller territory of Hong Kong, where it ranked third at the annual box office for 2007 and took in $6,249,342.[4] In the People's Republic it was also a big hit, taking $5.4 million in the first four days of its release alone.[5]

No doubt there are many reasons for the film's lack of appeal to international audiences. But I would argue that the dog—or rather what the dog promises and the film does not deliver—is a contributing factor. For those audiences the dog not only recalls Mr. Yee's profession but also invokes the long history of Western ideas about China. Western popular culture overflows with orientalist fantasies about China as a land of fiendish and cruel torture. Examples include the Fu Manchu novels by Sax Rohmer and figures like Dr. No in the James Bond movie of the same name.[6]

One of the earliest images of "Chinese cruelty" to circulate in the West was the practice of "death by a thousand cuts." Lurid illustrations circulated widely in the late nineteenth century, followed by photographs.[7] Such photographs caught Georges Bataille's eye when shown them by his analyst in the late 1920s. He wrote about them often and reproduced five of them in *The Tears of Eros*.[8] In her discussion of his fascination with these photographs, Susan Sontag insists that "Bataille is not saying that he takes pleasure at the sight of this excruciation," and goes on to argue that he is instead examining the link between extreme suffering and exaltation.[9] Despite Sontag's efforts the association of Bataille's treasured photographs with the possibility of erotic arousal has been persistent and disturbing, helping to reinforce some of the most repugnant orientalist prejudices about premodern Chinese culture and its supposed cruelties.

In their recent book, *Death by a Thousand Cuts*, Timothy Brook, Jérôme Bourgon, and Gregory Blue have made an important corrective intervention into the Western discourse about torture, torment, and cruelty in Chinese culture. They point out that because it is not intended to elicit a confession or other information, the penalty is more correctly termed a torment rather than a form of torture.[10] Discussing the execution of Wang Weiqin in 1904, they write:

> This form of the death penalty is known in Chinese as *lingchi chusi*, "to put to death by lingchi." Western observers have variously translated this as "death by a thousand cuts," "death by slicing," and "the lingering death"—all graphic phrases, and none of them an accurate description of the procedure. The executioner did not leave Wang to linger at death's door while cutting away at his body slice by slice. Nor did it take him a thousand cuts to get from his first slicing to his last. And as painful as the punishment of lingchi must have looked to those who watched, Wang was in all likelihood under heavy opium sedation before it started (ibid., 2).

Furthermore the photographs that fascinated Bataille and those of Wang Weiqin's execution discussed by Brook, Bourgon, and Blue captured some of the last instances of *lingchi* to take place, as the Qing government moved to abolish the penalty, starting in 1905. Therefore "European photographers preserved the gap between Chinese and European penal practices that the Qing state was about to close, making these shocking deaths a permanent memorial of cultural difference" (ibid., 6).

As well as correcting the facts about *lingchi* and reminding us that culture is not fixed but contested and ever changing, Brook, Bourgon, and Blue also place *lingchi* in both Western and Chinese lineages of cultural conceptions about torment and torture. On the one hand, they point out the special horror attached to the idea of the loss of "somatic integrity" involved in this form of execution for Chinese culture (ibid., 11–17). On the other hand, they add that the photographs show that although the executions took place in public, they did not take place on a stage. This contrasts with the European Catholic tradition, through whose terms and practices *lingchi* was first understood as a *supplice*, or torture, in which the body was not just killed but first put on display on a platform in a ceremonial sacrifice (ibid., 21ff.). Whereas such events were not only part of premodern European social life but also frequently circulated as drawings and other forms of representation, that was not the case in Chinese culture. Although the punishments of hell were imagined in China, representations of earthly torture and torment have been few and far between.

With this history in mind Ang Lee's *Lust, Caution* stands in an ambiguous position for international audiences. This is not unusual for Lee, as he often constructs his films in a manner that enables different judgements to be made about characters and events by different audiences.[11] In this case the off-screen quality of the torture is a source of ambiguity.

On the one hand, keeping the torture off-screen means that *Lust, Caution* invokes the idea of Chinese torture and all the baggage of the Western lineage of representations and associations, including the sensational and the disturbingly erotic. In this sense Lee could be said to be exploiting those associations. Indeed the shot of the German shepherd in the second sex scene can be understood as cutting *away* from the sex scene to the torturer's dog, or as cutting the torturer's dog *into* the sex scene. Either way the sex substitutes for the vision of torture that the dog invokes and that the narrative of the film reminds us of so often. In the process the torture that is otherwise so carefully kept invisible is held in the audience's mind. Furthermore the sex itself resembles a form of torture in the film. This is not only because of its aggressive, slightly sadomasochistic quality but also because the sex leads Wong to develop feelings for Mr. Yee, who she is convinced also has feelings for her. When he arranges fittings at a jeweller's shop for a very expensive and impressive diamond ring, she sets up the assassination. But, moved by him, she also utters the words that prompt him to flee and escape assassination. If torture is a manipulation of the body intended to force words out, then Wong's sex with Mr. Yee ends up having an analogous effect by making her speak a truth she is supposed to conceal from him.

On the other hand, although Lee delivers plenty of on-screen sex, any disturbing appetite for scenes of torture whetted by the site of the slavering German shepherd dog remains unsatisfied. In this sense Lee's practice subverts expectations by arousing and then refusing them.

Polarized Reactions in China

Lust, Caution was a box office hit with Chinese audiences. Presumably, they did not expect or want to see spectacles of oriental cruelty. Even before its release two factors created a buzz around the film. As will be explained, both were less interesting to international audiences. But both factors also suggested a polarization of responses based on age, which further research has confirmed. Understanding these polarized responses provides a foundation for understanding the film's status as an intervention in cinematic discourses of torture in Chinese culture.

The first factor to create a buzz was the sex scenes, which were scandalously intriguing for Chinese audiences. English-language audiences have become used to such scenes since at least *Last Tango in Paris*. But when sex scenes "even now run the gamut from tame to nonexistent in most Chinese cinema," the extensive nudity and torrid sex in *Lust, Caution* grabbed the attention of Chinese audiences.[12] Ironically, in the PRC the majority of the sex scenes were cut. There is no film classification system in China, and films are either passed for general release or not passed at all. This means the censors can only pass material suitable for audiences of any age. According to Robert Chi, there is a sixteen-minute difference between the version of the film released in Hong Kong, Taiwan, and the United States and the mainland Chinese version, which is even longer than the cuts mentioned by various critics.[13] For the most part the excised material consists of sex scenes.[14] The mainland Chinese interest in these scandalous excised scenes was so strong that one man even sued the State Administration of Radio, Film, and Television (SARFT) for infringing on his consumer rights.[15] At the same time the possibility of seeing the unexpurgated version on the big screen boosted mainland Chinese tourism to Hong Kong.[16] For those who could not make it to Hong Kong, the sex scenes could be downloaded, and bootleg DVDs of the unexpurgated version were available within weeks (if not days) of its release in China.[17]

The scandalous quality of the sex scenes in *Lust, Caution* was further underlined by a bizarre incident that took place a few months after the initial release of the film in the PRC. In March 2008 SARFT issued a notice banning the broadcast of a commercial featuring Tang Wei, who played Wong Chia-Chih, the female lead in the film. Effectively, she lost the right to work in China. No explanation of the ban was offered, but it was widely assumed that *Lust, Caution* was the reason, and it was reported that all *Lust, Caution* video clips had been pulled from Youku and Tudou, the Chinese equivalents of Youtube.[18] Since no punishment was meted out to the male actors who had worked on the film or the men on the crew, this belated punishment also implied gender bias. A storm of Internet protest, and even a petition against the ban, followed.[19]

A second factor polarizing responses to the film in China concerned the fame—and infamy—of the author of the short story it was based on. Eileen Chang (Zhang Ailing) may not be a draw card for foreign audiences, but she is one of China's best-known writers. Growing up in difficult times and living through the Japanese occupation of Shanghai, Chang became famous for her intricately observed stories about emotional complexities and ambiguities. Hers was a time when public discourse maintained an "either you are with us or you are against us" line on political allegiance and ideology, yet betrayal, collaboration, and confusion were everywhere. Chang captured this strange atmosphere in her work.[20]

Furthermore her own life and the stories she wrote were closely intertwined. Indeed, after the war she was widely condemned for her short and disastrous marriage to a collaborator. Many readers believe this is the basis for the short story "Lust, Caution," and the reason for her decision to hold it back and rework it continuously from 1953 until she finally published it in 1977.[21] Others point to similar events that occurred at the time, such as Zheng Pingru's failed attempt to assassinate the secret police chief Ding Mocun in Shanghai in 1939.[22] Chang's complex political background meant that her work was effectively banned in the PRC until the late 1980s, but since then many younger readers there have rediscovered her.[23]

Implicit in the buzz generated by these factors is an age divide. It might be supposed that older audiences, brought up in a more sexually and politically conservative era when even kissing on the mouth did not appear on-screen and Eileen Chang's work was denounced, would be outraged by the film. This hypothesis prompted a research project conducted by Shen Liyun in the months following the film's PRC release. Shen examined published responses to the film. She notes that while many of the negative critiques of both the film and Eileen Chang came from an older generation of critics in the PRC, those she could identify as coming from the post-1980 generation tended to be more favorable.[24] Shen followed this up with online-questionnaire work and some focus-group work with Chinese students based in the United Kingdom. Limited resources meant the size of the sample was too small to be considered reliable, and it was not chosen in any manner to ensure representativeness across the population of the PRC. Nevertheless there is a very strong correlation of responses to age in her results.

Shen divided her online respondents into four age groups: 19 to 28, 29 to 38, 39 to 48, and 49 to 58 years old, and worked with the first fifty responses received in each age group (ibid., 19–20). The older the respondents, the more likely it was that they had read the original short story, but the less likely it was that they had seen the full version of the film released in Hong Kong and only available in pirated versions on the mainland. The younger the respondents, the less likely they were to have seen the censored mainland version of the film. Every member of the oldest age group felt the sex scenes in the film were harmful to society, although almost none of them had seen the version of the film with these scenes in it. On the other hand, almost all the youngest respondents felt the scenes were necessary and harmless (ibid., 23–25).

When it comes to the plot of the film Shen's questionnaire continues to show starkly different responses according to age. The vast majority of the older generation disliked the ending in which Wong Chia-chih betrays her comrades out of love for Mr. Yee, whereas the younger generation overwhelmingly felt the ending was essential. Fully 80 percent of the youngest cohort agreed with the statement that in Wong's position, they too would have fallen in love with Mr. Yee. In contrast the vast majority of the oldest cohort said they would have completed the mission and killed Mr. Yee without hesitation, regardless of whether they had fallen in love with him (ibid., 25–27).

On-Screen Torture

The results of Shen's research are very striking. They suggest a clear divide between those who were born during the Maoist era and those born afterward. It is remarkable that members of the youngest generation agree that they could fall in love with a man who is not only a traitor but also a professional torturer and a sadist. Why? Here we can only speculate. Although anecdote has limited value for extrapolation, when I discussed the film with young mainland Chinese students in my seminar in the months following its release, I noticed that all them were aware of Tony Leung and felt he was a very charismatic star. However, many of them were confused about history and were unsure whom exactly Mr. Yee was working for. Others assumed that the patriotic would-be assassins must be Communist guerrillas, when in fact they are affiliated with the Communists' rivals, the KMT Nationalist Party. Perhaps this is because until very recently the KMT Nationalists have always appeared as villains in mainland cinema. It seems the students were not interested in the historical backdrop and ignored it, possibly because it was very far from their own experience, and they were so overexposed to more conventional materials about those times that they had stopped paying attention altogether. The fact that we do not see any of the torture may also make it easier for them to overlook it or push it into the margins of their experience of the film.

The idea that the pre- and post-1980s generations have very different values and ideas about romance and desire is certainly a very plausible part of the overall explanation and comes up frequently in the various published commentaries on the different reactions to the film. However, what has not received any particular attention so far is the cinematic intertext. Closer consideration will show that this also forms an important part of the "horizon of expectations"[25] that the older generation held and that was disappointed and even violated by *Lust, Caution*.

As noted, Brook, Bourgon, and Blue argue in *Death by a Thousand Cuts* that images of earthly torture and torment were relatively rare in premodern China, unlike premodern Europe. However, in modern Chinese culture, including Chinese cinema, this is no longer the case. Between the times that they write about and the release of *Lust, Caution* a very different cinematic intertext was established, and *Lust, Caution* violates its conventions in various ways. Put simply, before *Lust, Caution* the invocation and sometimes direct representation of torture and bodily torment on screen was not only acceptable but a common convention of Chinese cinema, whereas sex was taboo. In this sense the on-screen sex in *Lust, Caution* not only substitutes for the torture within the text, as is suggested by the cutaway to the German shepherd and then back to the sex, and by the torturous nature of the sex act, which makes Wong Chia-chih spit out the words that send her and her comrades to a certain death. It also substitutes for torture in terms of the horizon of expectations for older Chinese audiences that remember the way movies were before marketization and opening up to the world started in earnest in the 1980s.

What are some of the more iconic examples of this pre–Deng Xiaoping legacy of screen torture and torment? Working backward, Cultural Revolution model opera and ballet films often feature such moments. For example, the heroine of *Azalea Mountain* (*Dujuan Shan*) (1974), the underground Communist Party worker Ke Xiang, has been arrested when the film opens. Liberated from captivity by peasant guerrilla forces, she makes her first appearance by bursting through the gates of the compound where she has been held. Both of her wrists are manacled and linked by a heavy chain. As she sings and gestures, her revolutionary fervor apparently enables her to defy the weight of the chains even as she thrusts them before us, conjuring up images of dungeonlike prison conditions and mistreatment.[26]

Chains like these feature as metonyms for torture equipment and torture in general in many films. Xie Jin's well-known *Two Stage Sisters* (*Wutai*

Chunhua almost passes out while tied to a pillar in *Two Stage Sisters*.

Jiemei) (1964) is about two young traditional opera singers and their travails. When they refuse the advances of landlord Ni, who expects them to entertain him with more than just singing, he seizes one sister while the other one is arrested and then sentenced to be tied to a pillar in a public place for a period of days. The film graphically displays her pain, how she sweats through the heat, becomes dehydrated, and almost passes out. Scenes designed to have similar effects can be found as far back as the pre-revolutionary left-wing cinema of the 1930s. Sun Yu's famous 1934 film, *Big Road* (aka *The Highway*) (*Da Lu*) foreshadows *Two Stage Sisters* in a subplot about two two young women in a sisterly relationship who find that being guests of the local landlord in the big house leads to expectations of sexual favors. Together with their male companions they are imprisoned in his dungeon. Again chains and whips feature heavenly in the mise-en-scène.

Robert Chi has written about the importance of displays of somatic suffering in his analysis of an earlier Xie Jin film, *The Red Detachment of Women* (*Hongse Nianzijun*) (1961), set on tropical Hainan Island in the South China Sea. The main character is Wu Qionghua; maid to local warlord Nan Batian,

Qionghua displays her wounds in *The Red Detachment of Women*.

she is cruelly abused, and in one scene she is chained up in a water prison. She runs away, but is recaptured and then flogged. Eventually, the Communist cadre Hong Changqing rescues her. He frees her after Nan gives him to her as a servant, and he sends her to try and join the eponymous Red Detachment of Women. One of the most dramatic moments in the film comes when the commander of the Red Detachment asks her why she wants to join. To the accompaniment of dramatic music she pulls back her clothing to reveal her scars. This display of bodily sites of memory is intended not only to license her own passionate denunciations of Nan Batian but also to arouse a somatic response and sympathy in the audience. As Robert Chi points out, the director, Xie Jin, understood this as a form of "memoropolitics," in which the audience responds collectively with a resonance that "resides at the intersection among affect, cognition, soma and memory.... In other words, the revolutionary call to action consists not only of ideological education but of moving the spectatorial body—moving both as somatic gesture and as emotional stimulation."[27]

A clear pattern emerges from these examples. First, all these scenes of torture take place in what has been called "the old society" since the 1949 revolution, as in "the bad old society." Any kind of negative depiction is permitted in the cinema of the PRC, just so long as it appears as a feature of the corrupt feudal and semicolonial world the revolution claims to have liberated Chinese citizens from. In most of these examples class politics are at work, with landlords operating as evil torturers and tormentors, and ordinary citizens—and in particular the peasants and workers—as victims. A patriotic or revolutionary dimension in these films is also common, with the heroes and heroines fighting for revolution and/or against the Japanese, who invaded China progressively from the early 1930s on. Few if any such scenes appear in films set after 1949 until the late 1970s, when the myth of socialist infallibility was dropped and negative depictions of the Cultural Revolution era (1966–1976) started to appear in films such as Chen Kaige's *Farewell My Concubine (Bawang Bieji)* (1993).

Second, the display of bodily suffering is frequently a feature of these scenarios. As noted earlier, Brook, Bourgon, and Blue have argued that although executions might have sometimes taken place in public, they did not take place on platforms as part of mass spectacles, nor did illustrations of them circulate widely. While that might have been true of premodern China, the lineage indicated by both the example of real-life displays of torment and screen examples indicates all that changed in China's long twentieth century. However, it must be noted that there is an important difference between off- and on-screen torment and torture in the modern era. The tortured and tormented are established as objects of pity and often of empathy in the cinema. Off screen, after the revolution, they were used to mobilize class hatred by encouraging accusations and provoking the memories of onlookers through "speaking bitterness."

However, despite these differences, display itself remains a common feature of both off- and on-screen torment and torture during the modern era. Although nothing quite as ghastly as the *lingchi* "death by a thousand cuts" occurs in any of the examples described here, there are striking formal similarities with that practice, *except for display*. In the photograph that Bataille found so compelling the condemned man is bound, immobilized by ropes, and arranged frontally for the camera. He also appears delirious. The chains draped around the victims in films are also marks of their immobilization. In *Two Stage Sisters* Chunhua is tied to a pillar, her sweat-soaked (albeit fully clothed) body arranged frontally for the camera. As time passes she also descends into a semiconscious state, which we are made aware of when little Chunhua takes pity on her and gives her some water to drink. However, whereas the executed man in the *lingchi* photograph is at ground level in a crowd that has cleared a space for the photograph to be taken, the punishment represented in *Two Stage Sisters* not only entails public display, as the victim is tied to a pillar in a square, but is also shot from below, placing her above us, just as the victims of the Cultural Revolution were put up on stages and tortured before the crowd.

A third common feature of the conventions shaping the cinematic lineage of displays of physical punishment and torture in Chinese culture is that the moral and political dimensions of this established scenario are absolutely clear. The torturers are pure villains without any redeeming features whatsoever. Their victims are heroic fighters for justice who never waver in their commitment to the cause and also hate their torturers with a burning anger that never dims. With the visual allusion to torture limited to a shot of a dog, younger audiences less aware of or invested in this long lineage may be able to watch the scenes between Mr. Yee and Wong Chia-Chih in *Lust, Caution* without being reminded of these conventions and unaware of the fact that *Lust, Caution* violates their fundamental principles. Perhaps, for them, the fact that the torture remains off screen means it will not trouble their enjoyment of the intense sexuality on screen. However, older viewers will recognize the settings, period, and characters as invoking a lineage they are steeped in. They are therefore less likely to overlook the fact that Mr. Yee is a villain who gets away with it rather than getting his just deserts. They are also unlikely to miss the fact that Wong Chia-Chih is not the unwavering heroine portrayed in the earlier films. Instead of resisting she is seduced by her torturer and ends up betraying herself and her comrades, rather than sacrificing herself for the cause.

Caution, Lust

From the above discussion, it can be seen that the dominant conventions concerning the depiction of torture and torment in Chinese cinema are strict. With the exception of a smattering of films about "errors" made after the 1949 establishment of the PRC, such depictions are largely confined to the "old society." Furthermore they are only acceptable as part of the process of mobilizing political commitment by inciting passionate sympathy for the victim—who is always patriotic and revolutionary—and passionate anger toward the villain—who is always either an invader or a class enemy. Even here learning to control one's passions and to obey discipline is a key convention. Wu Qionghua in *Red Detachment of Women* joins the group to seek revenge against Nan Batian. But she must learn to control her personal anger and submit to the discipline of the Revolution. *Lust, Caution* clearly violates these conventions. But what does sex have to do with it? I have argued that sex appears in *Lust, Caution* where there might be torture in other films, and that sex functions like torture in the film. The insertion of the shot of the dog, unnecessary to the narrative, makes this substitution visible. But what are the consequences of making this connection? This substitution takes *Lust, Caution*'s intervention beyond mere nonfulfillment of expectations to an active undercutting of the foundations of revolutionary idealism. This might fuel the anger of older viewers even as it pleases younger audiences.

In the earlier discussion of the examples of torture and torment in the Chinese cinema, it will not have escaped the reader's attention that all the victims are women. While there is no statistical research on this question, female victims and male tormentors and torturers appear to constitute the dominant pattern in PRC cinema. However, it must be acknowledged that the pattern is not an exclusive one. Men are sometimes consigned to dungeons, too. For example, *Song of Youth* (*Qingchun zhi ge*) (1959) is a bildungsroman movie set in the prerevolutionary era and directed by Cui Wei and Chen Huaikai. (Ironically, Chen Huaikai is the father of Chen Kaige, whose *Farewell My Concubine* depicted the torture of his father, whom he felt he had betrayed.) It follows the development of Lin Daojing's political consciousness through her relationships with three different men. The second one is a Communist underground leader, Lu Jiachuan, who helps her to see the correct way forward and take action as an underground worker. Arrested, Lu is thrown into a dungeon in chains, his clothes torn, with bruises and wounds visible. He refuses to talk and is executed.

How are sexual desire and torture involved in the process of Lin Daojing's political maturation? First, Lin herself is never shown sexually desiring, but men are shown as desiring her. The first man, Yu Yongze, rescues her from a suicide attempt and then marries her. On the other hand, neither Lu Jiachuan nor his successor, Jiang Hua, shows any kind of physical interest in her. It seems that sexual desire would be considered an unsuitable trait not only for a good woman, but also for a good Communist man. The only romance here—and it is an intense one—is the political romance inspired by patriotism and revolution. Indeed, as discussed elsewhere, there is a strange parallel between the narratives of revolution and romance in this film. Instead of it ending with marriage vows at the altar, the film ends with Lin Daojing swearing her oath of allegiance as she joins the Communist Party, with the camera cutting back and forth between her and the red Chinese Communist flag as it might between bride and groom in a conventional romance.[28]

This parallel extends to the moment Lin gets seriously involved in revolutionary activity for the first time. Before Lu Jiachuan's arrest he leaves a packet with her, telling her to burn it if he does not come to collect it within three days. When he does not, she opens it. However, upon seeing that it contains flyers with the slogan "Long Live the Communist Party!" she remembers his words but does not burn the flyers. Fired up by her memories of Lu, she instead goes out and pastes them up under cover of dark. The film cuts back and forth from this scene to the scenes leading up to Lu's execution, as he too shouts, "Long live the Communist Party!" Although Lin does not know what is happening to Lu, she is excited by her memories of him, and both become almost ecstatic. Presumably, for the viewer, who does see what happens to Lu, the sight of injustice is supposed to mobilize a passionate commitment to the cause as is the case with Lin. However, there is nothing like the cutaway shot to the German shepherd dog in this, nothing that might make the homologous relationship to sexual passion that I am suggesting exists explicitly in *Lust, Caution*. Furthermore, after Lu's death Lin's relationship with her third male mentor, Jiang Hua, is far less personal, as her commitment has already gone beyond any individual and to the Party.

In contrast the more dominant pattern where women are the victims of torture is often more clearly related to sexual desire. In the cases of *Two Stage Sisters* and *Big Road* it is thwarted lust that drives (or licenses) the male villains to torture their female victims. Again this is not always the case. After Lu's death *Song of Youth* reverts to a more usual pattern, with Lin Daojing and two other women thrown into jail. Although the iconography of chains, wounds, and bruises is all there, along with the threat of torture, no sexual element is added.

However, the idea of sexuality and torture as two dangerously exciting physical activities that need to be suppressed or denied is crystallized most powerfully and succinctly in a scene from an iconic 1930s film, *New Women* (*Xin Nüxing*) (1934), directed by Cai Chusheng. The heroine is a music teacher. Asked by her principal to entertain a wealthy patron of the school where she works, she is taken out to a ballroom. Among the cabaret acts is a performance involving a Caucasian woman in a prisoner's outfit, adorned in chains, and her partner, who wields a whip. A shot and reverse-shot exchange between the patron and the scene on the dance floor indicates that he is very excited by this scenario. Another shot and reverse-shot sequence involving the heroine and the scene on the dance floor shows her imagining herself in the position of tormented prisoner. This scene is crucial in the development of her growing political and moral consciousness in the film, and that of the audience. Again, as is the case with the more directly revolutionary films, this heroine is an apprentice character whose political maturation the audience is encouraged to identify with and be mobilized by, as surely as she is mobilized by both her identification with the dancer and her disgust at the patron's response to what he sees.

A variety of patterns occur in these films. In some cases torture appears by itself as a negative inspiration for revolutionary fervor. In other cases the connection between refusal of sex and physical punishment also acts as a negative model inspiring eschewal of sexual passion in favor of political commitment. *New Women* is a rare instance where the sight of torture itself is arousing for the villain and therefore helps to drive the heroine and the audience away from sexuality and toward political commitment.

If these films suggest sexuality and individual passion are dangerous forces that must be disciplined and redirected toward "higher" goals, then *Lust, Caution* scrambles all these elements and in the process both undermines the presumptions they depend on and opens up other possibilities. In the conventional model sexual desire and torture—and the rarer excitement at the prospect of torture—are all exclusive attributes of the male villains that the female victims learn to resist with the guidance of male heroes. In this narrative Wong Chia-Chih is a young virgin cynically used by the KMT Nationalists for their own ends and with no regard for her feelings. To get her prepared for her mission to seduce Mr. Yee, she is expected to have sex with the only other member of the young student group who is sexually experienced. When she tells her political masters that she cannot cope with the impact of her torrid relationship with Mr. Yee, they simply expect her to knuckle down. Yet the impact of her submission to political discipline is made clear in the later scene where she warns Mr. Yee.

It could be argued that Wong is expected to submit herself to discipline, to know right from wrong, and that she gets confused and egoistically fails to sacrifice herself for the cause. But it could also be argued that the film displays a fundamental skepticism about the possibility of idealism. For the very people who normal conventions dictate will lead Wong away from the dangers of the flesh here lead her straight into them. Her supposed comrades betray and abandon her as surely as her father did when he left

The teacher imagines herself as a prisoner in *New Women*.

her in war-torn China and fled to England. There are no pure heroes to rescue Wong from the depredations of villainous sexual desire and torture, because the would-be heroes are the ones that abandon her to these forces.

This fundamental skepticism toward the very possibility of idealism takes *Lust, Caution* beyond a simple failure to deliver according to the normal conventions and turns it into an attack on the foundations of those conventions. For older audiences whose very identities and life histories are built on those foundations, such an attack could be experienced at a deeper level than a mere failure to deliver on their expectations and therefore may contribute to their vehement rejection of the film. But for younger audiences whose identities and lives—after the failure of idealist movements from the Revolution itself to the democracy movement of 1989—have been built around denying idealism and instead pursuing personal wealth and pleasure, *Lust, Caution* may offer both the affirmation of their values and beliefs and a new model of transcendence through individual romance.

In a recent book Rey Chow has called for more attention to the importance of affect and feelings (*qing*) and not just signification and meaning in Chinese cinema. In a postscript on Ang Lee's *Brokeback Mountain* she quotes Ang as saying, "Whatever I bring into my own films, I am forever trying to update and recapture that feeling. I call it juice—the juice of the film—the thing that moves people, the thing that is untranslatable by words."[29] Instead of discovering this juice in revolution, Wong Chia-Chih discovers it in her personal battle with Mr. Yee and her effort to overcome his sexual torture and touch his heart. On the surface she may seem to fail, for he captures and executes her and her comrades after she betrays them. Yet in a final coda to film he is seen alone in her bedroom, accompanied by her absence. The implication is that although she has died, she has breached his defences and touched his feelings after all. It is not his commitment to his political principles and his job or even his cynical pursuit of self-interest and survival that have triumphed, but romance.

Postscript

If Rey Chow and Ang Lee both end with a coda or postscript, so will I. Ang Lee's *Crouching Tiger Hidden Dragon* tells the story of a young girl who refuses all the conventions and codes of the world of chivalry to pursue her own passions. It was answered, so to speak, by Zhang Yimou's *Hero* (*Ying Xiong*) (2002), which restored the normative principle of self-sacrifice in the service of the establishment and maintenance of a virtuous order in the world. So perhaps it is not surprising that *Lust, Caution* also seems to have inspired its own response.

In 2009 another Taiwan-born director, Chen Guofu, codirected the PRC film *The Message* with Gao Qunshu. Like *Lust, Caution*, this was a big budget drama set during the Japanese occupation and inside the puppet government. The film emphatically restores the order disturbed by *Lust, Caution*. Sex never rears its ugly head. Because the Japanese try to use torture to find out who is leaking messages from their headquarters, torture scenes are plentiful and at least as salacious as the sex scenes in *Lust, Caution*. The first of these scenes is particularly graphic, featuring a female victim and a German shepherd dog, perhaps to emphasize the film's status as a correction to *Lust, Caution*. Certainly, it confirms the idea that the dog signifies torture. Both the pre-1949 period setting and the display of torture in *The Message* appear according to convention. There is never any question about who the good guys and the bad guys are, although the process of revealing the good message sender's identity is what drives the narrative of the film. Here, again perhaps not surprisingly, the virtuous individual is a young woman. Self-sacrifice in order to defend the correct political ideal is restored to the transcendent status that *Lust, Caution* so radically undercuts, but whether it can really overcome the impact of *Lust, Caution*'s intervention remains to be seen.

NOTES

1. Emilie Yueh-yu Yeh, "Montage of Attractions: Juxtaposing Lust, Caution," in *Lust/Caution from Eileen Chang to Ang Lee*, ed. Peng Xiao-yen and Whitney Dilley (New York: Routledge, forthcoming).
2. See, for example, Richard Alleva, "Hope Abandoned," *Commonweal* 134, no. 20 (2007): 20–21.
3. BoxOfficeMojo.com, domestic sales information for *Lust, Caution*, directed by Ang Lee, http://www.boxofficemojo.com/movies/?page=weekend&id=lustcaution.htm (accessed March 9, 2010).
4. "Hong Kong Yearly Box Office," BoxOfficeMojo.com, http://www.boxofficemojo.com/intl/hongkong/yearly/?yr=2007&p=.htm (accessed March 9, 2010).
5. Associated Press, "Ang Lee's 'Lust, Caution' a Hit in China, Despite Major Cuts by Chinese Censors," BLNZ.com, November 6, 2007, http://www.blnz.com/news/2007/11/06Lees_Lust_China_1427.html (accessed August 24, 2009).
6. Jachinson Chan, "Sax Rohmer's Dr. Fu Manchu: Scrutinizing the Inscrutable," in *Chinese American Masculinities: From Fu Manchu to Bruce Lee* (New York, Routledge: 2001), 27–50.

7. Timothy Brook, Jérôme Bourgon, and Gregory Blue, "Chinese Torture in the Western Mind," in *Death by a Thousand Cuts* (Cambridge: Harvard University Press, 2008), 152–202. Special thanks to Chou Yu-Ling, whose work on *lingchi* in a different context drew the practice to my attention while I was working on this project.
8. Georges Bataille, *The Tears of Eros*, trans. Peter Connor (1961; San Francisco: City Lights, 1989), 204–206. See Jonathan David York, "Flesh and Consciousness: Georges Bataille and the Dionysian," *Journal for Cultural and Religious Theory* 4, no. 3 (2003): 42.
9. Susan Sontag, *Regarding the Pain of Others* (New York: Picador, 2003), 98–99.
10. Brook, Bourgon, and Blue, "Chinese Torture in the Western Mind," 9; hereafter cited in text.
11. For example, in a previous essay I examine how this works in his film *The Wedding Banquet (Xiyan)* (1990); see Chris Berry, "*Wedding Banquet*: A Family (Melodrama) Affair," in *Chinese Films in Focus II* (London: British Film Institute, 2008), 235–42.
12. Howard W. French, "Censored on the Mainland, Ang Lee's 'Lust, Caution' Is a Hit in Hong Kong," A Glimpse of the World Web site, January 7, 2008, http://www.howardwfrench.com/archives/2008/01/07/censored_on_the_mainland_ang_lees_lust_caution_is_a_hit_in_hong_kong/ (accessed August 24, 2009).
13. Robert Chi, "Exhibitionism: *Lust, Caution*," *Journal of Chinese Cinemas* 3, no. 2 (2009): 184.
14. However, according to the Wikipedia entry on the film, sex was not the only thing cut. A scene of Chia-Chih, the female lead, walking past the corpses of refugees on the street went, too. The stabbing scene was greatly shortened. The most obvious political intervention was a small change in the dialogue in the diamond shop scene, the effect of which is to make it unclear whether Chia-Chih does in fact betray her colleagues in order to save Mr. Yee from assassination. Presumably, such blatant treachery was too much for the censors to accept. "*Lust, Caution*," *Wikipedia*, last modified September 22, 2011, http://en.wikipedia.org/wiki/Lust,_Caution_(film) (accessed April 15, 2009).
15. Joel Martinsen, "Unsatisfied with the *Lust, Caution* Edits? Sue!" DanWei.org, November 14, 2007, http://www.danwei.org/film/unsatisfied_with_the_lust_caut.php (accessed September 2, 2009).
16. French, "Censored on the Mainland, Ang Lee's 'Lust, Caution' Is a Hit in Hong Kong."
17. *Economist*, "Censorship in China: Caution: Lust," January 10, 2008, 37.
18. Joel Martinson, "Tang Wei Too Hot for TV," March 7, 2008, DanWei.org, http://www.danwei.org/media_regulation/tang_wei_too_hot_for_tv.php (accessed September 2, 2009).
19. Eric Mu, "A Petition to Stop the Ban on Tang Wei," DanWei.org, March 26, 2008, http://www.danwei.org/film/an_online_petition_about_tangw.php (accessed September 2, 2009). More recently, it has been reported that Tang Wei will play

Mao's first wife in an upcoming movie. This means the ban has been lifted, at least, although what it means for her political standing depends on what we are supposed to think about Mao's widow, I suppose. Jeremy Goldkorn, "Formerly Blacklisted Actress Tang Wei to Play Mao Zedong's First Girlfriend in Party Film," September 2, 2010, http://www.danwei.org/film/formerly_blacklisted_actress_t.php (accessed September 9, 2010).

20. The writing on Chang is too extensive to list here. However, as an indication of the detailed attention she receives, Leo Ou-fan Lee (Li Ou-fan) has written a whole book on *Lust, Caution* and its adaptation for the screen, *Di Se Jie: Wenxue, Dianying, Lishi* [Looking at *Lust, Caution*: Literature, Film, History] (Hong Kong: Oxford University Press, 2008). Some of the careful and painstaking comparison between the original short story and the film is glossed in Leo Ou-fan Lee, "Ang Lee's *Lust, Caution* and Its Reception," *boundary 2* 35, no. 3 (2008): 223–38.
21. William Leung, "Sex, China and Propaganda: Ang Lee's *Lust, Caution*," *Metro*, no. 156 (2008): 52.
22. Robert Chi, "Exhibitionism," 179.
23. Leung, "Sex, China and Propaganda," 52.
24. Shen Liyun, "How Does the Generational Gap Affect the Reading of Ang Lee's *Lust, Caution*? Representation of Individual Value in Mainland China," graduation thesis (London: Goldsmiths, University of London, 2008), 7–8. Cited with permission of the author. Hereafter cited in text.
25. Hans Robert Jauss, *Toward an Aesthetic of Reception*, trans. Timothy Bahti (Minneapolis: University of Minnesota Press, 1982).
26. For a close analysis of the aesthetic structure of this scene, see Chris Berry and Mary Farquhar, *China on Screen: Cinema and Nation* (New York: Columbia University Press, 2006), 62–65.
27. Robert Chi, "*The Red Detachment of Women*: Resenting, Regendering, Remembering," in Berry, *Chinese Films in Focus II* (London: British Film Institute, 2008), 194–95.
28. Berry and Farquhar, *China on Screen*, 117–18.
29. Rey Chow, *Sentimental Fabulations, Contemporary Chinese Films* (New York: Columbia University Press, 2007), 197.

Peeping Tom, 1960

5

The Art of Photogenic Torture

Phil Carney

Sometime during the late 1950s and early 1960s the photographic spectacle changed. Mass media and commerce had expanded in a striking way since the Second World War, delivering a mass consumer culture to the West. Rock and pop, perfume and clothes, catwalks and models, TV entertainment and televised sports—all accompanied by a new kind of celebrity—percolated through consumerist spaces to a much broader spread of age groups and social classes. Suddenly, we found ourselves immersed in an ostensibly classless and ageless mass marketplace of the image.

Photographic spectacle had progressively expanded since its first stirrings in the mid-nineteenth century.[1] One important turning point was the decade of the 1920s, when a truly mass cinematic culture coincided with both the appearances of news and fashion magazines and the increasing popularity of portable snapshot cameras.[2] Another turning point was the moment of interest here, a moment in which proliferated the image world of television, youth consumerism, fashion, and pop music, and which was accompanied by further developments in camera technology enabling even faster, more portable cameras. Out of this world emerged a new class of professional photographers and a photography that no longer deferred to the world in its lens. Class barriers seemed for a moment to dissolve. In London, for example, young, brash, working-class photographers such as David Bailey, Terence Donovan, and Justin de Villeneuve exploited their social mobility and commanded the arena of the celebrity image.

In the middle of this cultural moment a strange, disturbing film briefly hit the screens of the British cinema. Bearing the suggestive name *Peeping Tom*, its release was separated only by a matter of months from Hitchcock's

Psycho, Fellini's *La Dolce Vita*, and two pulp British B movies: *Circus of Horrors* and *Horrors of the Black Museum*.[3] It was 1960, an important year for the image, particularly a type of image that was later recognised as "predatory" and "punitive." All four films act as a discourse reflecting on a particular dynamic of the wider spectacle at this moment in the postwar period, in the expanding society of consumerism and mass media. One might go as far as to argue that they are—in the midst of their excited entertainment—better than any more sober theoretical discourse of that time or even since.

The ultimate aim of this chapter is to explore how we might understand torture in the image. Haunting this discussion is the well-known set of war-on-terror images from Camp X-Ray (2002) and Abu Ghraib (2004), but its purpose is to open out the argument to a more general consideration of the play of power and desire across the surface of the predatory photograph. We could use the term "photogenic torture" in a deliberate distortion of the common meaning of the word "photogenic," but in the service of a return to its more literal meaning. This is not a torture that looks better (or worse) in the image; rather it is a torture created both in and through the image. It is photogenic in the sense that it is a product of the photograph. The photograph is both scene and means of torture. But we should also take into account that photogenic torture is, like other forms of torture (when reduced to their basic forces), an intersection between power and desire, between a power over another body and the desire to wield that power.

The Dangerous Image

Fellini's celebrated film *La Dolce Vita* baptised the paparazzo, relaying the atmosphere of a culture of consumption and celebrity already decaying from its inception. It was a culture in which spectating and the image play central roles, as the popping flash bulbs around the bodies of the famous attest. This was the dawn of our late-modern phase of consumerism, yet the awakening from a night of economic depression and wartime austerity to a bright new morning of economic expansion was already infected with a certain boredom and disappointment at the changes in society. Kennedy's assassination and Marilyn Monroe's death struck blows to the invulnerability of the celebrity image. At the same time consumerist hedonism seemed to age as soon as it was born. The sense of an essential emptiness inside the bright, novel, fashionable consumerist social forms, inside the mass image itself, was portrayed in *La Dolce Vita* and also depicted in Antonioni's photographic meditation *Blowup*.

When they don't ignore it, social theorists of the 50s and early 60s are disturbed by the commercial spectacle. For Horkheimer and Adorno it is a culture industry, a factory churning out low-grade entertainment for the distracted masses, while for Barthes it is a modern mythology coding the ideology of late capitalism. Meanwhile Debord accuses the spectacle of worse: rendering its audience passive and inert worshippers of the commodity as image, and the image as commodity. Later Baudrillard describes the essentially meaningless nature of a culture of simulated images, echoing Daniel Boorstin's description in 1963 of the evaporation of the American dream into empty imagery.[4]

Something deathly seems to move through the fabric of this new world, and though Fellini's character Paparazzo looks innocent enough, he, too, was born in the mid-1950s, emerging from the cynical chrysalis of the mass culture industry. All these cultural forms are at one with the intentions and effects of *Peeping Tom*, *La Dolce Vita*, and, later, *Blowup*. It is not so much that there is an absence, an emptiness at the core of the new culture, as it is that something new emerges: a violent force that operates on the surface of the photographic spectacle.

As always the B-movie industry was prepared to comment on these times, though not without ensuring that we were cheaply and efficiently entertained. *Circus of Horrors*, a strange film in which much else happens, features a circus entertainment that becomes more successful as its performers fall victim to a series of fatal accidents staged, in fact, by its new owner. In effect it is a film that reflects on the hunger of the spectator for horror: the more real, the better. In other places in the spectacle "factual" image making at this time is more candid, frank, especially in the new wave of documentary and war photography. It is also part of a new entertainment ethic. But this desire for real horrors has its dangers.

Horrors of the Black Museum, another British B movie, was shot in Hypno-Vista with the tag line, "It actually puts YOU in the picture: can you stand it?" A crime writer—a popular criminologist no less—is suffering a creative block, so he arranges for real crimes to be committed as a stimulus for his jaded writing. The infamous opening story of the film features a pair of murderous binoculars that, when put to the eyes of the viewer, trigger two deadly spring-loaded spikes. This instrument is a fatal punishment for one who dares to look through an optical apparatus. Perhaps the sinner here is the voyeur, but the punishment is also intended to cause the movie audience a certain delighted discomfort from the outset of the film. It plays the game, which the movie audience embraces with delight, that film spectatorship is essentially voyeuristic, and therefore transgressive and liable to punishment. If it puts the audience in the picture, it is to remind them of the dangers, horrors, and delights of spectating. The publicity for the film informed the audience that these binoculars, according to legend on display at the real-life Black Museum of Scotland Yard, were associated with a true crime.

The producer of this film had his finger on the cultural pulse: coming from the United States, he had been prominent for his work on the late 1950s classics *I Was a Teenage Werewolf* and *I Was a Teenage Frankenstein*, films that, with no little irony, tapped into anxieties about changing youth culture of the time. With a characteristic appetite for social commentary disguised as horror, he had turned his gaze to the gaze itself, one of the most important sources of fascination and fear in the developing culture of spectacle.

Also preoccupied by the gaze, Hitchcock's *Psycho* depicts a voyeur killer, Norman Bates, and implicates the audience in his murderous desires. The argument of the film, or rather the way in which the audience is folded into the camera's action, is set up in the opening frames, as we pan across a cityscape, close in on a hotel block, and then on a half-open window. In a technique derived from innovations by Orson Welles in *Citizen Kane*, the camera then climbs through the open gap into the dark space inside, revealing an illicit hotel room scene with the characters of Marion Crane and her lover. The audience is a true cinematic voyeur peeping at the half-undressed couple. Much later Norman Bates peers through a peep hole in a picture on his motel office wall. On the other side is Marion Crane. In the celebrated shower murder scene we learn that the killer has entered the room through an open window, just the kind of aperture through which the audience entered the film. *Psycho* also asks, Who is Norman Bates? At the end of the film the answer of the mock-psychoanalyst is intended to reassure the audience and lighten the mood, at least until the death grin of his mother is briefly superimposed on the distracted face of Norman Bates. Throughout this film Hitchcock's clever camera work performs another kind of action, fusing in the same point of view, and in the same movements, the audience and the voyeur-killer. If we believe the psychiatrist, Norman Bates is a pathological, transvestite killer, irredeemably fused with the identity of his mother. Reassuring. But if we watch Hitchcock's camera, the subliminal action renders the audience complicit in the power and desire of the camera, in its voyeurism, in its violence, and in its capacity to kill. These films are part of a turning point, a decisive moment in postwar culture. They deal with the desires and dangers of spectating and the spectacle.

Peeping Tom

The most important film of all, *Peeping Tom*, was given the tell-tale X certificate, marketed badly as sleazy smut, and was so reviled by the critics that it was withdrawn after a week. In effect it destroyed what was left of Michael Powell's career. Farmed out for a short time in a cut-down version to the flea pits of the suburbs, it soon disappeared from sight altogether until the late 70s. Martin Scorsese was important in its revival, and no doubt it was also given a boost by Susan Sontag's mention of it in her 1979 treatise on photography.[5]

The central character of *Peeping Tom* is Mark Lewis, who works as a focus puller in the film industry. He occupies his spare time in two ways, first earning pennies on the side as a glamour photographer, taking sleazy pictures of the undressed for under-the-counter sale at a corner shop. His second, unpaid hobby is his work as a serial killer, which is of a particularly perverse variety. His victims are women involved in one way or another with the allure of the spectacle: a street prostitute, a glamour model, and an actress.[6] Somewhere between amateur and professional, he draws them into a conversation with his own 16 mm movie camera, and then kills them with a knife unsheathed from one leg of the camera tripod. A parodic phallus, no doubt. His camera is both an erotic apparatus and an instrument of death, and he keeps it running as he murders its targets, thus capturing the faces of victims in the throes of their last agonised breath. We later learn that he is making a documentary, one that will culminate in his own death, for which he is well-prepared in the movie's final sequence and which he has clearly engineered from the start. This final coup de grâce does not, however, provide us with any comfortable moral closure: his death continues rather than solves the cruel perversity of his gaze. This is just as disturbing and important as Kafka's story "In the Penal Colony," where the operator of a cruel punishment machine, when questioned by a traveller to the colony, submits himself to its fatal operation.

In what now appears to be a motif of the time, the audience is directly involved in the opening shots of the film, a point of view through the lens of Lewis's own camera when he kills his first victim. Rather like Hitchcock's subliminal opening sequence of *Psycho,* this puts the audience in the position of the protagonist, looking through his camera's viewfinder with its sniperlike crosshairs, and actively participating in the active gaze of his murderous camera.

Following this opening scene we see Mark Lewis rubbing shoulders with the photographers and writers of the press as they gather with the police around the scene of his crime. He not only commits the murders with his camera but also records the news spectacle they trigger. Perhaps here he is a Weegee figure, arriving at the scene of the crime first. In this way he also films the police arriving at the scene of what is his own carefully choreographed and recorded death at the end of the film.

Played by Carl Boehm, Mark Lewis is a good-looking, diffident, sensitive, soft-spoken, uncomfortably appealing character. Despite all that we know, we are, from the outset, encouraged to sympathize with him, and thus understand the attraction that Helen, the woman he does not kill, has for him. He elicits this sympathy in spite of the fact that he knows exactly what he is doing, whereas *Psycho*'s Norman Bates is a genuinely split person, a transvestite murderer completely unknown to the shy motel receptionist.

As in Hitchcock's *Psycho*, we are provided at the close of *Peeping Tom* with a reassuring psychological explanation in which we learn that Mark's father had been a behavioral scientist who made a study of his own son, filming a series of cruel experiments investigating the nature of fear. The psychologist locates the source of murderous aggression in a poor, pathological individual, the tragic victim of a cruel upbringing. So, again, we have fearful disturbance followed by a reassurance that it is, after all, the pathology of a warped individual.

Some have attributed the troubled gaze of *Peeping Tom* to difficult times in postwar Britain,[7] when people were prone to panic about rebellious and delinquent youth—teenage werewolves and Frankensteins—but also about potential obscenity, such as was at stake in the prosecution of D. H. Lawrence's *Lady Chatterley's Lover*, the British echo, perhaps of the U.S. legal proceedings against Allen Ginsburg's *Howl*. Yes, we can detect anxieties about sex and horror films, about permissiveness on TV, about rebellious youth, about salacious scandal in the newspapers, about rising crime. But more than anything else, here we are in the midst of a changing culture of spectatorship and of the spectacle, of the sound and light of the consumer world, of new configurations of desire and power in the photographic spectacle.

More specifically, *Peeping Tom* also resonates with the new phenomenon of the paparazzi, whose emblematic shot is of the suffering star whose privacy has been invaded by an aggressive camera. At some point in the mid- to late 1950s a small group of street photographers in Italy changed the way they photographed the celebrities who strutted the fashionable streets of the big cities.[8] Instead of the usual deferential practice of politely requesting permission, they deliberately invaded the spaces celebrities regarded as their own, snapping them in their cars, at restaurant tables, in nightclubs, in intimate trysts. The ideal shot was of the upset star; better still if the target tried to stop the photograph being taken or gave chase to the photographer. With teamwork a double viewpoint was possible: through the lens of the stalker and from the viewpoint of an observing third party. A photography of action and reaction, it brought together the action of a stalking, predatory, invasive camera, and the reaction of a distressed prey.

In this image culture of celebrity the resulting shots sold for as much as five times the price of a polite photograph. The viewing public wanted the usual diet of studio portraits and carefully engineered red-carpet images to be spiced up with a violence that would punish the newly exalted class of imaged bodies.[9]

Psycho sets up the predatory camera and the pleasures and compulsions of both the filmmaker and the audience. *Peeping Tom* helps us develop this story further as the camera moves from an implicit to an explicit instrument of predation. The camera is seen. But *Peeping Tom* adds a final perverse twist, which we discover toward the end of the film. In addition to its knife our focus puller's camera is equipped with a mirror. Not only does the killer capture and replay the face of the victim at the moment of death, but she can also see her own face in its death throes. *Peeping Tom*'s filmmaker kills the victim and captures the victim's face as she *sees her own death*. These victims are terrorized by their own terror. If these films resonate with the paparazzo as aggressive intruder, *Peeping Tom* adds an important refinement, that the celebrity victim of such intrusion is destined, through mass circulation, to see his or her own face at the time of the aggression, as in a mirror.

Perhaps it is tempting to see the film as comparable to the game of reflections and the gaze in Velázquez's *Las Meninas*.[10] But there is another painting much closer to our world of the spectacle, Manet's *Bar at the Folies-Bergères* in the Courtauld, London. In this image we see a woman serving behind the bar, and in the mirror we are are aware that, first, it is a space of entertainment and, second, we occupy the position of a customer who is not just buying a drink but also attempting to buy the woman. Her face is not welcoming but sadly resigned to her position as a commodity among others in a hall of mirrors.

Peeping Tom also deals with the hall of mirrors of a commercial spectacle that combines erotic desire and violent power. In his grubby glamour photography studio above a newsagent, Mark Lewis caters to the demand for semi-illicit photographic erotica. In his day job he works in the commercial movie industry as a photographic cog in the mass-culture machine. And his murders will attract the popular press, always hungry for a sensational crime. *Peeping Tom*'s murder victims are figures in a visual world that mixes erotic glamour, mainstream movies, and crime scene spectacle as elements in the film's representation of photography, which are also the key features provoking concern and anxiety in the expanding photographic spectacle of the time. *Peeping Tom* is quite uncanny insofar as it manages within 109 minutes to comment on so much of what was happening in the spectacle as the 1950s turned to the 1960s.

Some elements of the film, for example, anticipated McLuhan's 1964 depiction of the photograph as the "brothel-without-walls" in *Understanding Media*.[11] Here McLuhan parodies Malraux's optimistic vision of mass photography as a "museum without walls."[12] What Walter Benjamin[13] had ambivalently considered a loss of aura through mass culture, André Malraux sees as an educational advance, opening up the treasures of the museum to a mass gaze. While Malraux is interested in the high-cultural possibilities of the photograph, McLuhan examines a low-cultural, even gutter-bound, popular photographic practice. For McLuhan the gaze of the camera is frankly erotic, directed at an array of celebrity bodies from Hollywood films, fashion magazines, and the images of pop music. These bodies circulate in a commercial spectacle. In these new meretricious places they are commodities for sale. It is, in effect, a new form of prostitution, asserts McLuhan. Just as the riches of the museum are delivered to a mass audience, so, too, are erotic bodies sold to spectators, and both processes occur through the agency of the photograph. For McLuhan the photograph is a brothel without walls.

But the 1961 films of Michael Powell and Alfred Hitchcock go further. In them the photograph does not merely bring down the screens of modesty separating the voyeuristic gaze from its erotic object, it is now an active predatory force, breaching the screen, seeking to do violence to the erotic object. Mark Lewis introduces the violent camera to McLuhan's brothel. He combines his roles as glamour photographer and serial killer. The targets of his destructive image apparatus are precisely those bodies McLuhan envisaged in the brothel without walls. Eros and Thanatos combine forces.

Critics acknowledge *Peeping Tom* as a key participant in a turning point of the so-called horror genre. As in *Psycho*, the killer here is no longer a physical monster or alien but, at least on the surface, an ostensibly normal person living a normal life. Monstrosity has moved from the physical to the psychological, from the outside to the inside, from the body to the mind.[14] In contrast, however, what we have seen in the social developments of this period obliges us to move beyond this individualizing approach in order to examine these films not so much as symptoms of an interior psychology but as *indicators* of their culture. Mark Lewis is, like the paparazzo, not so much a pathological person holding a camera but a person driven by the camera and its desires. The drives do not erupt from a dark interior but circulate in the exterior where desires flow in a flux between bodies and technologies at the level of the social and cultural.

Desire: From Psychology to Culture

A particular kind of psychoanalytic fantasy is tempted to understand the mirror on Mark Lewis's camera as somehow emblematic of the perversion of a mirror phase in infant development, perhaps of narcissistic rage. This fantasy is at one with psychologizing theory. From Cooley to Lacan to Winnicott the mirror finds a central place in the theory of the formation of the self.[15] We have looking-glass selves: we are formed in the gaze of others.

In this fantasy life of psychoanalysis another kind of imaginary will work in the Oedipal register, where there is a desire for the other combined with the fear of an amputating punitive response to a forbidden desire. If this is not properly negotiated it will be expressed either through aggression against a representative of the other or through fetishistic attachment to a part object, a "little other," a trace that acts partially to discharge sexual desire. This Oedipal theatre is Freud's "primal scene" in which the infantile gaze is associated with the fantastic desire to unite with the mother, and hence with a fear of castration by the jealous father or an amputating punishment by the law that forbids incest.[16] Thus an amputating, punitive modality of power is summoned up, and submission to its threats is a socially adaptive course of action. Of course submission is never total, and another fantasy lurks around the margins of the social: that of transgressing the power of law, overturning that which wields an amputating force.

Here, according to psychoanalytic discourse, is where the voyeur is supposed to come into play in a secret, fantastic domination of the other that evades a castrating law. We are supposed to play this out in our relationship with cinema.[17] In this way the cinematic spectator may also be regarded as a fetishist, taking a little symbol or token of the other, with the image as a little other, or a fetishistic object: a substitute for possession.

Hence, in this perspective, the figures of both Mark Lewis and Norman Bates offer to the cinematic spectator a symptomatic and attenuated expression of a universal kind of frightened and murderous voyeurism born in Freud's primal scene.

But instead of reducing these violent dynamics to a psychology, we would do better to look at all of these mirrors and movements of desire as indicators of something happening in the wider culture. We might still use the term "narcissism" but in a more more socially and historically situated way, so that the self we speak of is not a universal identity but the particular self of a narcissistic culture.[18] More simply and directly, the mirror in question has a much more material presence as a technology of the image. It indicates another "mirror with a memory," as Oliver Wendell Holmes called it, that of photograph.[19] For us this mirror is indicative of photography, photographic spectacle, and photographic festival.

In the cultural realm these violent fantasies of psychoanalysis are not the repressed feature of a universalized infantile development, but a life at the level of social processes rather than the psychological interior. The psychoanalytic analysis of desire represses the material and bodily forces that operate at the level of the social and the cultural. First, it misses the rather more *tangible* processes we have elucidated in these films: the forces of the photograph that fold in the corporeal spectator. We need less of a symptomatic and semiotic analysis of desire and more of an *indicative* analysis. As Steven Shaviro has argued in *The Cinematic Body*, we should attend less to what appears to be symbolized or coded or symptomatic in these films, and more to the active entrainment of the spectatorial body.[20] We are dealing with a set of visual-material forces rather than a set of semiotically coded signs or symptoms. Desire is transmitted rather than "read." Second, the psychoanalytic viewpoint *universalizes* when it should be much more specific and situated. Freud's theories of voyeurism and fetishism are intended to apply to all times and all places, taking no account of sociohistorical specificities in the production of the image. To ignore the time and place in which *Peeping Tom* was produced is to repress its most important forces.

This has implications for a critical approach to the kind of images presented in these films. Power, if it could be given the status of a person, would be quite happy with psychoanalytic representations of itself and its relation to desire, because it does not, for the most part, operate in this way. Power would also be quite content with this representation of torturing desire as Oedipal, interior, repressed, secret, and universal. Power is not challenged at the level of its operation in the social. Instead the engagement with power is turned into a psychological struggle with the maladapted self.

It is no surprise that both *Psycho* and *Peeping Tom* use reassuring psychoanalytic interpretations of photogenic torture, but it would be a mistake to ignore the ironic way in which both filmmakers deploy them. If what is disturbing in the images and narrative of these films has its sting pulled out by the psychoanalytic interpretation, then we are reminded to think of it in another way.

The sociohistorical imperatives that should inform a critical approach to photogenic torture and its desires do not attempt to uncover secret, universal, psychological motivations but instead observe the surface of the film as a play of forces relayed by the film medium itself, the nature of the camera, and the apparatus and images of photography in a particular time and place. The point is to take an anti-Oedipal view of what happens, deliberately rejecting the psychoanalytic interpretation, which soothes, reassures, and places the killer in a maladapted pathological category formed in a cruel childhood.[21] Yes, indeed, this is a desire to look in order to violate, and to violate in order to look, but the proper level of analysis is in the register of a camera culture rather than the dark interior of perversion. Mark Lewis is an expression of that culture. And the reason why this film is so disturbing is, first, the protagonist is not a monster; if anything he might attract a certain degree of sympathy. Second, he is one of us because his desire is the desire of a whole culture, a paparazzi culture, a culture that has learned to punish through the photographic gaze.

Though our society still holds on to the fiction that torture might be useful in certain circumstances, we should have learned that torture can serve no instrumental purpose other than to terrorize into submission the community from which the tormented individual comes.[22] This practice has been elaborated into a science and technology of terror, a *savoir* of counterinsurgency, whose cancer has metastasized through the post–World War II world in the form of manuals and training programs.[23] Leaving aside the use of torture as information gathering (the convenient fantasy of which still inhabits our debates today), the use of torture as terror is also in doubt as a means to an end other than more violence. We are faced with the prospect that torture serves no other purpose than itself. It is this fundamental and inescapable expressive nature of torture that is suffused with the dynamic of desire.

Orwell's *Nineteen Eighty-Four* took a journey with Winston Smith in search of this desire.[24] It began with the telescreen, the device of both surveillance and spectacle, and took us into the cellars of the Ministry of Love, and thus into the bosom of the power playing across the surface of the telescreen. Beginning with flickering images and sounds, the narrative journey moved through ideologies and systems of thought, and finally arrived at the meeting point of power and desire in a scene of torture. The end point, the final sentence of the novel, is this: "He loved Big Brother." Orwell's theoretical journey is important, for its understanding of how desire and power operate is found in both the culture of the image we have encountered and at the heart of torture itself. But it is important to understand that this is a circular journey taking us back to the surface of the image.

The basements of the windowless Ministry of Love, Minilove for short, are places of torture and death, repression and espionage. Perhaps it is named in a deliberate reversal of meaning (like the Ministry of Peace, the Ministry of Truth, and the Ministry of Plenty). But, as in all of these names, inversion of significance is not the only game Orwell is playing. The designation "Ministry of Love" is not merely a manifestation of doublethink. Love really is at the heart of this ministry: it is a love of power. At what seems like the culmination of his torture, Winston Smith is told by his persecutor, O'Brien,

> The Party seeks power entirely for its own sake. We are not interested in the good of others; we are interested solely in power. Not wealth or luxury or long life or happiness: only power, pure power. . . . We know that no one ever seizes power with the intention of relinquishing it. Power is not a means, it is an end. One does not establish a dictatorship in order to safeguard a revolution; one makes the revolution in order to establish the dictatorship. The object of persecution is persecution. The object of torture is torture. The object of power is power.

O'Brien continues: "But always—do not forget this, Winston—always there will be the intoxication of power, constantly increasing and constantly growing subtler. Always, at every moment, there will be the thrill of victory, the sensation of trampling on an enemy who is helpless. If you want a picture of the future, imagine a boot stamping on a human face—for ever" (chapter 3).

Winston has learned how power works: power is desired for the sake of power, torture is desired for the sake of torture. Using Orwell as our theoretical resource, we can now understand the great surplus to the ostensibly practical use of torture in the hands of our military and security technologists of terror and counterterror. A tormenting desire operates in the rituals of torture, which no table of military or security interests can account for. It is continuous with photogenic torture, such as the kind we've seen in Camp X-Ray and Abu Ghraib, and which emerged in our spectacle in the early years of mass consumerism. Following Orwell we can only understand this punitive gaze as a meeting of power and desire.

But psychology has no place here. This desire is not confined to the criminal and pathological individuals who make up the infamous characters of our popular literature and documentaries of atrocity. It is not merely found in a Sadean fantasy or a figure lurking in the shadows of Edgar Allen Poe's work. Nor is it buried deep in the badly bolted dungeons of our unconscious. Rather, in the form of photogenic torture, it flows through the bright lights of our social world, across the visible surfaces of our culture, and parades itself in our photographic spectacle.

NOTES

1. Phil Carney, "Crime, Punishment and the Force of Photographic Spectacle," in *Framing Crime: Cultural Criminology and the Image*, ed. Keith Hayward and Mike Presdee (London: Routledge, 2010).
2. Siegfried Kracauer, *The Mass Ornament: Weimar Essays*, trans. Thomas Y. Levin (Cambridge, Mass.: Harvard University Press, 1995).
3. For an account of the social context in which the British films appeared, see Sarah Street, *British National Cinema* (Oxford: Routledge, 1997); and David Pirie, *A Heritage of Horror: The English Gothic Cinema, 1946–1972* (London: Avon, 1973). Pirie calls the three British films a "Sadean trilogy."
4. Theodor Adorno, *The Culture Industry: Selected Essays on Mass Culture*, ed. J. M. Bernstein, (London: Routledge, 1991); Roland Barthes, *Mythologies*, trans. Annette Lavers (London: Jonathan Cape, 1972); Guy Debord, *The Society of the Spectacle*, trans. Donald Nicholson-Smith (New York: Zone, 1994); Jean Baudrillard, *Simulations*, trans. Paul Foss, Paul Patton, and Philip Beitchman (New York: Semiotext(e), 1983); Daniel Boorstin, *The Image, or What Happened to the American Dream* (Harmondsworth, UK: Pelican, 1963).

5. Susan Sontag, *On Photography* (London: Penguin, 1979).
6. Note that Carol Clover in *Men, Women and Chainsaws: Gender in the Modern Horror Film* (London: British Film Institute, 1992), sees more than the now conventional film-theory perspective on the sadism of the masculine spectator (of the horror-slasher film). She argues that there is a more complex, interacting, less gender-determined set of identifications.
7. See Marcia Landy, *British Genres: Cinema and Society, 1930–1960* (Princeton: Princeton University Press, 1991); and Pirie, *A Heritage of Horror*.
8. See, for example, Karen Pinkus, *The Montesi Scandal: The Death of Wilma Montesi and the Birth of the Paparazzi in Fellini's Rome* (Chicago: University of Chicago Press, 2003).
9. For the punitive analogy, see Anthony Burgess's prefatory essay in Daniel Angeli and Jean-Paul Dousset, *Private Pictures* (London: Jonathan Cape, 1980).
10. Michel Foucault, *The Order of Things: An Archaeology of the Human Sciences*, trans. Alan Sheridan (London: Tavistock, 1971).
11. Marshall McLuhan, *Understanding Media: The Extensions of Man* (London: Routledge and Kegan Paul, 1964).
12. André Malraux, *The Voices of Silence*, trans. Stuart Gilbert (Princeton: Princeton University Press, 1978).
13. Walter Benjamin, "The Work of Art in the Age of Mechanical Reproduction" in *Illuminations*, ed. Hannah Arendt, trans. Harry Zohn (London: Jonathan Cape, 1970).
14. Robert Yanal, "Two Monsters in Search of a Concept," *Comtemporary Aesthetics* 1 (2003).
15. Charles H. Cooley, *Human Nature and the Social Order* (New York: Scribner, 1902); Jacques Lacan, "The Mirror Stage as Formative of the Function of the I as Revealed in Psychoanalytic Experience," in *Ecrits: A Selection*, trans. Alan Sheridan (New York: Norton, 1977); D. W. Winnicott, "Mirror-Role of Mother and Family," in *Playing and Reality* (Harmondsworth, UK: Penguin, 1974).
16. Sigmund Freud, "Three Essays on the Theory of Sexuality," in *The Standard Edition of the Complete Psychological Works of Sigmund Freud*, ed. John Strachey, 7:133–243 (London: Hogarth Press, 1953).
17. See, for example, Andrea Sabbadini, "Watching Voyeurs: Michael Powell's *Peeping Tom*," *International Journal of Psychoanalysis* 81 (1960): 809–813; and Elisabeth Bronfen, "Killing Gazes, Killing in the Gaze: On Michael Powell's *Peeping Tom*," in *Gaze and Voice as Love Objects*, ed. Renata Salecl and Slavoj Žižek (Durham: Duke University Press, 1996).
18. Christopher L. Lasch, *The Culture of Narcissism* (New York: Norton, 1979).
19. Oliver Wendell Holmes, "The Stereoscope and the Stereograph," *Atlantic Monthly*, June 1859, 738–48.
20. Steven Shaviro, *The Cinematic Body* (Minneapolis: University of Minnesota Press, 1993).

21. Gilles Deleuze and Félix Guattari, *Anti-Oedipus: Capitalism and Schizophrenia*, trans. Robert Hurley, Mark Seem, and Helen R. Lane (London: Athlone, 1984).
22. Ruth Blakeley, "Why Torture?" *Review of International Studies* 33 (2007): 373–94.
23. See chapter 6 of this book and Alfred W. McCoy, *A Question of Torture: CIA Interrogation, from the Cold War to the War on Terror* (New York: Metropolitan, 2006). See also Neil McMaster, "Torture: from Algiers to Abu Ghraib," *Race and Class* 46, no. 2 (2004): 1–21.
24. George Orwell, *Nineteen Eighty-Four* (London: Secker and Warburg, 1949).

Casino Royale, 2004

6

Beyond Susan Sontag

THE SEDUCTION OF PSYCHOLOGICAL TORTURE

Alfred W. McCoy

Just four weeks after CBS Television broadcast those sixteen photographs of abuse at Abu Ghraib prison in April 2004,[1] Susan Sontag published a subtle yet sensational cover story in the *New York Times Magazine*. She simply asked us to look again at that iconic image we all thought we knew so well, the one showing a hooded Iraqi standing on a box, electrical wires hanging from his outstretched arms. By expanding the photo's frame a fraction of inch, Sontag captured a casually dressed American soldier in the right foreground, nonchalantly adjusting the setting on his digital camera.

"The photographs," Sontag concluded, "are us." To explain that controversial remark, she continued: "An erotic life is, for more and more people, that which can be captured in digital photographs and on video." Then, commenting on other photographs in her article showing naked Iraqis simulating sex, she stated, "Most of the torture photographs have a sexual theme." In fact, she argued, referencing the notorious Private Lynndie England, "most of the pictures seem part of a larger confluence of torture and pornography: a young woman leading a naked man around on a leash is classic dominatrix imagery. And you wonder how much of the sexual tortures inflicted on the inmates of Abu Ghraib was inspired by the vast repertory of pornographic imagery available on the Internet—and which ordinary people, by sending out Webcasts of themselves, try to emulate." In the midst of this sharp condemnation of Americans and their culture, Sontag then inserted a key clause asserting, without any evidence or elaboration, that many of these "torture photographs are interleaved with pornographic images of American soldiers having sex with one another."[2]

Where? Where were those sensational "pornographic images of American soldiers having sex with one another"? Not in the pages of that *New York Times* article. Not anywhere on the Internet that a Google search could find. Something was missing. Sontag had shown us what we thought were the worst of the photographs—Iraqis naked, forced fellatio, piles of naked male bodies. But as bold as that essay might have been, Sontag was holding back. There was something important, something she had apparently seen but was not going to share—not the photographs, not any description beyond those few words. Despite her sedulously cultivated self-image as a cultural iconoclast who could stare with sangfroid into the most horrific image of Nazi death camps or Southern lynchings, she had finally found, in this her last major essay, some recess of the human mind too dark, too disturbing for even Susan Sontag.

After nearly two years with little publication of any more leaked images, an Australian television network grabbed headlines around the globe in February 2006 by releasing more, and much grittier, Abu Ghraib photographs.[3] A few days later a Compact Disc (CD) appeared in my mailbox via airmail from Sydney, Australia. The disc's first document was a report, with attached spreadsheets, from the U.S. Army's Criminal Investigation Command indicating that "a computer forensic examination" had recovered some 1,600 photographs from two perpetrators of abuse at Abu Ghraib, Private Lynndie England and Corporal Charles Graner.[4]

To view these photographs I selected my computer's "slide show" function and clicked on the first file marked "CG CD Marks 1." The first image, "0001.jpg," was of a woman sucking hard on an erect penis. The next one, "0002.jpg," showed the same woman with eyes closed, smiling and holding the pink head of an erect circumcised penis. In "0005.jpg" she appeared again, midcoitus, her face blurred. Then in "0009.jpg" she was staring directly into the camera, lifting her shirt to expose her breasts. Private Lynndie England. In "00027.jpg" a male soldier was kissing her left breast and holding her right breast. Corporal Charles Graner. Finally, after dozens of photographs of Lynndie England in nude poses, "0055.jpg" showed an Iraqi woman in a prison cell lifting her shirt to expose her breasts.

Next, in the file called "CG CD Marks 3," I found eight photographs of U.S. soldiers in a prison corridor with two leashed German shepherds. The first one, "0001.jpg," showed soldiers leading a dog, its fangs visible, toward an Iraqi prisoner with his hands behind his head and his penis exposed.

The file "CG CD Marks 4" revealed a half-dozen photographs of Iraqi prisoners shackled in contorted positions. The image "0008.jpg" captured an Iraqi male prisoner chained to a bed frame with women's underwear on his face and his penis exposed. In "0020.jpg" Private Lynndie England lead an Iraqi male crawling completely naked on the floor, leashed like a dog. In "0024.jpg" U.S. soldiers were forcing three Iraqi male prisoners to lie down in the corridor, their naked bodies touching and hands intertwined. In another image, "0032.jpg"—the one Sontag had published in the *Times*—a hooded Iraqi stood on a box with an unknown U.S. soldier adjusting the digital camera. Then there was "0034.jpg," in which Corporal Charles Graner lay in a pile of four hooded, semiclothed Iraqis, punching one in the back of the head with his gloved fist. One last image, "0038.jpg," showed an Iraqi hooded and naked, sitting on another naked prisoner while Private Lynndie England pointed to his penis smiling, thumbs up.

Though repulsive, these photographs are nonetheless revealing—not about the private lives of ordinary Americans, *pace* Susan Sontag, but about torture as U.S. public policy. And in particular they reveal the erotic dimensions in a distinctively American form of psychological torture that has been recently refined, under the exigencies of the war on terror, to exploit cultural and, above all, sexual sensitivities. With the exception of a few egregious incidents of physical abuse, almost all these photographs show techniques within the ambit of psychological and psychosexual abuse. Moreover the sequencing and time dates on the thousand-plus photographs on that army computer log indicate that Corporal Graner and Private England interleaved their off-duty, autoerotic photography with on-duty, on-camera sexual humiliation of Iraqi prisoners. This degradation was, moreover, exceptional in its sexualized brutality. From Highland New Guinea penis gourds to National Hockey League (NHL) cup protectors, human civilizations across time and space have proven circumspect about exposing the male organ in combat, real or simulated. These photographs with their graphic display of sexual torture are thus a gateway into that dark, deeply disturbing recess of the human mind where pain and pleasure commingle in ways that make torture, particularly the psychological torture displayed so relentlessly in these images, both deeply erotic and powerfully seductive—attributes that may help explain the surprising persistence of this practice.

In seeking some explanation for torture's adoption as a formal prerogative of American power in the decade since September 11, 2001, we are confronted with a mystifying contradiction. On the one hand, the United States has long joined the international community in enacting conventions, declarations, and laws that make torture and inhumane treatment illegal. There is, moreover, an overwhelming body of evidence, codified in the interrogation doctrines of the U.S. Army and the FBI, that torture is counterproductive, yielding useless information and precluding the possibility of coaxing accurate, actionable intelligence. Throughout this recent debate the only justification for torture that its proponents have offered is the so-called ticking time-bomb scenario, a hypothetical elaboration of an academic exercise in philosophy that has almost no factual basis.[5] And just as the French learned in Algeria and the Americans should have learned in Vietnam, every informed U.S. national security official discovered, in the aftermath of Abu Ghraib, the high political cost of violating this international norm. Yet in defiance of law, reason, and morality, Washington has embraced torture as state policy and refused to repudiate the practice. Why? To understand this contradiction we need to move beyond the realm of rationality and explore the symbolic, subliminal forces that can help explain elite and popular support for torture as a weapon in the arsenal of American power.

Unbeknownst to both the U.S. Congress and the American public, the CIA spent the first decade of the Cold War developing an array of sophisticated, scientific psychological techniques that have remained, for the past half century, the foundation of a distinctive U.S. interrogation doctrine. Since the research was highly classified and carefully compartmentalized, for decades we knew surprisingly little about the psychopathology of the mental torture that Washington has applied so globally, first against communism, now against terrorism. Some future fusion of cognitive science and communication studies may someday map the neural pathways of mental stimulus between pornography, sadism, masochism, and torture, but for now we shall have to rely on an array of external evidence, documents and images, to glimpse something of torture's eroticism in both performance and perception.

To explore this uncomfortable dimension of torture, we must look beyond Susan Sontag to an unconventional source—Pier Paolo Pasolini's *Salò, or the 120 Days of Sodom*, arguably the most abhorrent feature film ever made. Despite the literary bow to the Marquis de Sade's long-banned book *The 120 Days of Sodom*, Pasolini's film transposes Sade's timeless France to Mussolini's short-lived Republic of Salò (1943–1945), transforms his generic aristocrats into four fascist archetypes (president, bishop, duke, magistrate), and translates Sade's pure sadomasochism into sexualized power. After Nazi soldiers deliver eighteen young captives to a crumbling villa in the film's first scenes, the four fascists, in an allusion to

Dante, lead their victims in a descent through the Circle of Mania, Circle of Shit, and Circle of Blood—ever downward from coerced copulation and coprophagia to voyeuristic evisceration. In the final scene two soldiers who have seen it all, surrogates for moviegoers who sit through this horrific spectacle, dance a diffident waltz, seemingly showing how torture both enraptures and brutalizes everyone, perpetrator and spectator alike. On the set Pasolini said he was "making a film about the modern world," and described his four perpetrators as "Nietzschean supermen"—a point he drives home when these debauchers debate whether a quote ("Without bloodshed, there is no forgiveness") is from Baudelaire or Nietzsche's *Genealogy of Morals*. With uncommon insight about torture's pathological escalation into a paroxysm of violence, Pasolini also observed that "the torturer, because he can undertake his [sodomitic] gesture only once upon any single victim . . . must kill thousands in order to be able to repeat his gesture."[6]

By his juxtaposition of perverse tortures and political power, Pasolini takes us deep into that dark realm where eroticism and cruelty cohabit— empowering the perpetrator, destroying the victim, and enticing the rest of us. Torture, he tells us, is power. Not the abstraction of law or constitution, but the visceral, sexually charged power over life and death, procreation and extinction, that expands the perpetrators' egos and enthralls the rest of us. Countless reviewers have commented, since the film's first showing in 1975, that its images of blood, shit, bared genitalia, brutalized bodies, and eroticized cruelty are burned indelibly and disturbingly into the brain. Not surprisingly, therefore, the CBS broadcast of just sixteen snapshots of the same subjects from Abu Ghraib, even though sanitized with blackouts over bared genitalia, shocked the sensibilities of humankind, provoking emotional protests around the globe. Although the elegant cinematography and careful scripting give Pasolini's film the power of great artistry, it remains nonetheless a faint simulacrum of the same subjects revealed in the full, uncensored archive of Abu Ghraib's 1,600 digital snapshots. Their painful reality leads us more directly into that dark, disturbing recess of the human mind where torture has such perverse power.[7]

Physical torture is a relatively straightforward matter of sadism that leaves behind broken bodies and useless information. Psychological torture, by contrast, is a mind maze that can destroy its victims, even while entrapping its perpetrators in a compensatory, almost erotic, sense of empowerment. With egos inflated beyond all imagining as masters of life and death, pain and pleasure, perpetrators and the powerful who command them can become forceful proponents of abuse when in office, striding across the political landscape like those "Nietzschean supermen." Just as these perpetrators are seduced and empowered by the eroticism of torture, so they sometimes derive support from politicians and the public who share in the vicarious stimulation through private or public simulations, through secret reports or feature films.

For both perpetrators and the powerful, torture seems to have a seductive psychological appeal, whether assuaging insecurity in times of crisis or arousing a darkly erotic sense of empowerment. "When feelings of insecurity develop within those holding power," wrote two CIA cognitive scientists about Soviet leaders in 1956, "they become increasingly suspicious and put great pressures upon the secret police to obtain arrests and confessions. At such times police officials are inclined to condone anything which produces a speedy 'confession,' and brutality may become widespread."[8] Even when the abuse is initially intended for a few spies or subversives, it soon expands almost uncontrollably in two directions—rapid proliferation to the torture of many and an inexorable escalation in the scale of brutality. So strong is torture's appeal, the powerful, whether in the Kremlin or the White House, will often concoct rationales to preserve their prerogative of torture, ignoring strong evidence of its ineffectiveness in interrogation and clear signs of its high political cost.

Historical Antecedents

In both its medieval and modern iterations the closeted, often secretive practice of torture has been mimed by public displays of eroticized inhumanity in artistic works that serve to legitimate the practice. Indeed there is certain continuity from medieval and early modern representations of the aestheticized abuse of Christ and his martyrs to present-day projections of eroticized torture in film and television.

In medieval Europe the growing use of torture in civil and canonical courts paralleled a proliferation of religious art with almost anatomical displays of physical scourging. After a church council abolished trial by ordeal in 1215, European civil courts revived Roman law and its reliance on torture to obtain confessions—an approach that persisted for the next five centuries.[9] With the parallel rise of the Inquisition, church interrogators used torture for both confession and punishment, a procedure that was formalized under Pope Innocent IV in 1252. By the fourteenth century the Italian Inquisition had routinized the physical scourging of heretics through use of the strappado to suspend the victim with ropes and weights in five degrees of escalating duration and severity.[10]

The impact of judicial torture on medieval culture went far beyond the courts, coinciding with a subtle shift in theological emphasis from the life of Jesus to the death of the Christ—a change reflected in artistic representations of his body being scourged and crucified. From the slender details of Christ's agonies in the gospels, medieval artists, in the words of art historian Mitchell B. Merback, "approximated these grisly violations with the unerring eye of a forensic pathologist," creating an artistic convention of the pain inflicted on his battered body that mimed, and may have legitimated, the increasingly gruesome legal spectacles of torture and public execution.[11]

Later in the sixteenth and seventeenth centuries Europe's early-modern states elaborated on this judicial embrace of torture and artistic display of suffering. "Military torture was prodigious," wrote Alec Mellor of these absolutist regimes, "religious torture was regularized; and judicial torture was enriched daily by new varieties."[12] In the religious realm the Counter-Reformation fought challenges to church authority by establishing the Roman Inquisition in 1542 while pursuing military campaigns against Muslims and Protestants. In this age of royal and religious patronage of the arts, there were, as art historian Stephen Eisenman argues, close parallels between state practice and artistic representation. One of Michelangelo's frescos in the Sistine Chapel, *The Execution of Haman* (1511), captures its subject with the "finely articulated musculature of the body" that "signals ecstasy as much as torment," while next door in the Sala Regia *The Massacre of the Huguenots* (1572) by the artist Giorgio Vasari depicts the bloody slaughter of these thirty thousand "leering blasphemers" as "the triumph of Catholicism over heresy." In this same spirit Vasari covered the great Sala di Cosimo I at the Palazzo Vecchio in Florence with a fresco (1560) showing Saturn using a ponderous metal scythe to castrate his father, Uranus, who lies prone and passive while a naked goddess nearby fondles her breasts in orgasmic pleasure. When the Counter-Reformation begat the Baroque aesthetic, this "cult of sacred and eroticized violence" spread further as "the combined erotic and sanguinary desires of noble and religious patrons" took form, for example, in Jusepe di Ribera's *Martyrdom of St. Bartholomew* (1644), showing the saint's torturer as "a divine instrument in the miracle of salvation."[13]

But in the eighteenth century the Enlightenment slowly eclipsed the twinned practice of judicial scourging and artistic celebration of torture as "eroticized chastisement."[14] Amid growing disquiet among jurists about the accuracy of evidence from torture, evaluation of evidence on its merits replaced forced confessions in civil courts. Following his coronation in 1740 Frederick II of Prussia banned torture after writing a dissertation that criticized it for being "as cruel as it is useless," while his friend Voltaire famously condemned the practice, sparking a movement that led to its abolition across Enlightenment Europe by the early 1800s.[15] The arts followed the state's retreat from torture, a trend exemplified by Édouard Manet's painting of *The Mocking of Christ* (1865), showing a "pasty skinned, knobby-kneed Frenchman" surrounded by motley inquisitors—projecting a modern sensibility that torture degrades both perpetrator and victim.[16]

Psychological Torture

The recent revival of torture as U.S. state policy has its origins in the hidden history of the CIA's mind-control research. In the early years of the Cold War the agency became concerned that the Soviets had somehow cracked the code of human consciousness and launched a "special interrogation program" whose working hypothesis was, according to a 1952 CIA memo, that "medical science, particularly psychiatry and psychotherapy, has developed various techniques by means of which some external control can be imposed on the mind or will of an individual, such as drugs, hypnosis, electric shock and neurosurgery."[17]

Although the CIA tested all these exotic techniques aggressively during the 1950s and 1960s, none proved successful in breaking potential enemies or obtaining reliable information.[18] Starting in 1951, however, the CIA also collaborated with British and Canadian defense scientists to promote classified behavioral research into "methods concerned in psychological coercion." Within months the agency defined the aims of its now top-secret program, code-named Project Artichoke, as the "development of any method by which we can get information from a person against his will and without his knowledge."[19] In launching the successor program, MKUltra, in April 1954, Richard Helms wrote his CIA director that this effort would test chemicals that "could potentially aid in discrediting individuals, eliciting information, and implanting suggestions and other forms of mental control."[20]

This secret research produced two discoveries central to the CIA's emerging protocol for psychological torture. In classified experiments conducted from 1951 to 1954, famed Canadian psychologist Donald Hebb found that he could induce a state akin to drug-induced hallucinations and psychosis in just forty-eight hours without drugs, hypnosis, or electrical shock. For two days student volunteers at McGill University simply sat in a comfortable cubicle deprived of sensory stimulation by goggles, gloves, and earmuffs.[21] "It scared the hell out of us," Hebb said later, "to see how completely dependent the mind is on a close connection with the ordinary sensory environment, and how disorganizing to be cut off from that support." This discovery, soon confirmed and elaborated by hundreds of scientific papers, led to the development of a torture technique called "sensory deprivation."[22]

During the 1950s as well, a neurologist and cardiologist at Cornell University Medical Center, working under CIA contract, found that the most devastating torture technique of the Soviet secret police, the KGB, was to force a victim to stand for days while the legs swelled, the skin erupted in suppurating lesions, and hallucinations began. This procedure is now euphemistically called "stress positions."[23]

Four years into this project American prisoners in North Korea suffered what was then called "brainwashing," sparking a sudden surge of interest in the defensive uses of these mind-control techniques. In August 1955 President Eisenhower ordered that any soldier at risk of capture must be given "specific training and instruction designed to . . . withstand all enemy efforts against him." Consequently, the air force developed a program it dubbed SERE (Survival, Evasion, Resistance, Escape) for training pilots to resist psychological torture.[24] Thus two intertwined strands of mind-control research developed: aggressive techniques for breaking enemy agents and defensive methods for training Americans to resist enemy inquisitors.

In 1963 the CIA distilled its decade of research into the *Kubark Counterintelligence Interrogation* manual, which stated that sensory deprivation was effective because it made "the regressed subject view the interrogator as a father-figure . . . strengthening . . . the subject's tendencies toward compliance."[25] Refined through years of practice on human beings, the CIA's psychological paradigm came to rely on a mix of sensory overload and sensory deprivation via seemingly banal procedures—extremes of heat and cold, light and dark, noise and silence, feast and famine—all meant to attack the sensory pathways into the human mind. Embedded within this formal doctrine was an inclination to explore yet another cognitive pathway through psychosexual abuse. Apart from these particular methods the U.S. psychological torture doctrine was distinguished, throughout its fifty-year history, by a scientific methodology that produced a succession of detailed manuals by both contract psychologists and security practitioners—from CIA's

Kubark manual (1963) to the U.S. Army's Guantánamo interrogation handbook (2003).

After codifying these methods, the CIA spent the next thirty years propagating these torture techniques within the U.S. intelligence community and among anticommunist allies worldwide. Along the global arc of anticommunist containment the CIA trained allied agencies in these coercive counterintelligence techniques in Iran, South Vietnam, the Philippines, and Latin America. In almost every application these psychological techniques broke out of their controlled, clinical bounds, crossing a troubled cognitive terrain between pain and pleasure, sensuality and sexual perversion, into the realm of psychosexual torture.

During the Vietnam War, when the CIA's Phoenix program used torture to eliminate top-level Vietcong cadres, the interrogation effort soon degenerated into a lurid physical brutality and proliferated into a counterproductive slaughter. Appearing before Congress in 1971, a senior CIA official, William Colby, testified that Phoenix had killed 20,587 Vietcong suspects since 1968. The Saigon government provided figures attributing 40,994 Vietcong kills to the same program.[26] In these hearings K. Barton Osborn, a Military Intelligence veteran who had worked with the CIA's Phoenix program in 1967–68, described "the use of electronic gear such as sealed telephones attached to the . . . women's vagina[s] and the men's testicles . . . [to] shock them into submission." During his eighteen months with the Phoenix program, not a single Vietcong suspect had survived agency interrogation.[27]

Despite this extreme violence CIA officers reported that the program captured almost no Vietcong leaders. As he left Saigon in 1970, the Phoenix program's founder, CIA official Robert Komer, described it as "a small, poorly managed, and largely ineffective effort." Indeed one Pentagon study of Phoenix's operations found that, in 1970–71, only 3 percent of the Vietcong "killed, captured, or rallied were full or probationary Party members above the district level." Over half the supposed Vietcong captured or killed "were not even Party members."[28] The CIA chief for Gia Dinh Province in 1968, Ralph W. McGehee, was even blunter, stating: "The truth is that never in the history of our work in Vietnam did we get one clear-cut, high-ranking Viet Cong agent."[29] In retrospect the Phoenix program shows the psychodynamic power of torture to erupt from bureaucratic controls into an uncontrollable paroxysm of sexualized cruelty and lethal blood lust increasingly detached from any rational military objective.

Although the Phoenix program was the CIA's largest interrogation effort, its Latin American operations produced documented instances of institutionalized psychosexual perversion. As civil war intensified in Central America during the late 1970s, the CIA sent Honduran soldiers to the United States for instruction by its own experts. "I was taken to Texas with 24 others for six months between 1979 and 1980," Sergeant Florencio Caballero told the *New York Times*. "There was an American Army captain there and men from the CIA," said the sergeant, who "taught me interrogation in order to end physical torture in Honduras. They taught us psychological methods—to study the fears and weaknesses of a prisoner. Make him stand up, don't let him sleep, keep him naked and isolated, put rats and cockroaches in his cell, give him bad food, serve him dead animals, throw cold water on him, change the temperature."[30] According to its *Human Resources Exploitation Manual—1983* the CIA taught Honduran interrogators to "manipulate the subject's environment . . . to disrupt patterns of time, space, and sensory perception"—in short, to assault the basic sensory pathways into human consciousness.[31]

After their training these soldiers joined Battalion 316, a special Honduran army intelligence unit supported by the CIA. One of those interrogated by Sergeant Caballero's unit, a young Marxist named Ines Murillo, was subjected to eighty days of torture with psychosexual techniques. Following her capture in 1983 she was taken to a secret army safe house in the town of San Pedro Sula where she was stripped naked and subjected to electrical shocks for thirty-five days. Then she was moved to a second secret prison near Tegucigalpa where her questioners "gave her raw dead birds and rats for dinner, threw freezing water on her naked body every half hour for extended periods and made her stand for hours without sleep and without being allowed to urinate."[32]

Philippine Parallels

The Philippines provides perhaps the most poignant testimony to the sexualized abuse embedded in the CIA psychological paradigm. From 1972 to 1986 torture was a key instrument in President Ferdinand Marcos's martial-law rule, creating a cohort of young military officers who refined this dimension of the agency's methods. As the regime's human rights abuses deepened steadily after 1975, Marcos's two top torturers were reportedly sent to the United States for CIA training. By probing human consciousness in the ad hoc laboratory of thousands of torture sessions over the span of fourteen years, these officers and their subalterns discovered the capacity of sexual humiliation to damage the human psyche, simultaneously devastating the victim and empowering the perpetrator.[33]

A rural Filipino priest tortured by Marcos's interrogators offers acute insight into these psychological tactics. Arrested for subversion in October 1982, Fr. Edgardo Kangleon was subjected to two months of constant psychological abuse before breaking down, confessing to being a communist agent and naming fellow clergy as subversives. A week after his release from military custody Fr. Kangleon composed a perceptive twenty-five page memoir describing the mix of sensory deprivation, sexual humiliation, and physical pressure that culminated in his capitulation.

> Inside I was made to sit on a stool. I felt a small table being placed in front of me. Then, I heard voices—new voices! Three or four of these voices—the more commanding ones—took their places around me. And with actors in their places, the most crucial stage of my detention started to unfold.
>
> "Now, Father, you are going to answer our questions!"
>
> "What's the name of that sister you used to visit at the Sacred Heart College? She is your girlfriend, *ano*? You are fucking her? How does it feel? . . .
>
> "For me, he is not a priest. Yes, your kind is not worthy of a respect of a priest."
>
> "OK, take off his shirt. Oh, look at that body. You look sexy. Even the women here think you are macho. You are a homosexual, *ano*?"
>
> "Lets see if you are that macho after one of my punches." A short jab below my ribs.
>
> "Hey, don't lean on the table. Place your arms beside you. That's it." Another jab.
>
> "You, take that stool away from him." I stood up. A blow landed behind my ears. I started to plead that they stop what they are doing to me. I started to cower. More blows.
>
> "You better answer our questions or else you will get more of this." With that, a short blow landed in my solar plexus.
>
> I was already quaking with fear. The psychological and physical aspect . . . of my interrogation had finally taken its toll. I finally broke down. "Yes. Go call Ltc. Figueroa. I am now willing to cooperate."[34]

Among the regime's many victims, it was a twenty-three-year-old journalism student, Maria Elena Ang, who provided the most detailed description of these psychosexual methods. In her account Philippine military torture was aimed ultimately at effecting a psychological breakdown by sexual humiliation.

> I remember that while being restrained in a high-backed chair, several men, about 10 to 20, swelled the ranks of those already in the room. Immediately, they swamped me with a battery of questions and psywar tactics. They threatened to kill me, get my relatives and friends and torture them in front of me. They kept telling me nobody saw them taking me in.
>
> Failing to answer one of their questions, I immediately received a slap in the face and a blow in the thighs....
>
> Then, several agents began clamoring that I be given what they called the MERALCO treatment—MERALCO being the supplier of electricity in Manila.
>
> An agent then forcibly removed my blouse and bra and unzipped my fly. Another brought in a hand-cranked electric generator used in military telephone.... Suddenly, the current shot painfully through my body. I could do nothing but scream and plead and scream but he only turned the crank until I was screaming continuously.... The electric shock session lasted for nearly two hours and was repeated in the evening....
>
> After the electric shock session, the military authorities still were not satisfied.... This time I was stripped naked and forced to lie on a short table [for] ... the start of the water cure, which they laughingly called the NAWASA session—NAWASA being the supplier of water in Manila.... This time, besides four men restraining my hands and feet, another formed my hair into a bun and pulled my head down so that it kept hanging on the air until I felt that the water was racing through my brains. I passed out twice but they kept pouring water until I thought I would die.
>
> Besides pouring water, several agents mashed my breasts while another contented himself by inserting his fingers in my vagina after failing to make me masturbate.[35]

What is the impact of such psychological torture on the torturer? Reading statements by victims like Fr. Kangleon and Maria Ang, it seems that these military interrogators did not operate as impersonal technicians, attaching electrodes and scaling the voltage calmly upward to extract information. They generally engaged in perverse, often sexual, tortures to establish psychological dominance over their victims. As I have argued in detail elsewhere, such experience empowered these young officers for future political warfare.[36] Through their extraordinary duties in the service of dictatorship, they acquired an inflated sense of themselves as supermen who could capture the state. Instead of reflecting and rejecting their experiences in the safe houses, these rebel officers invested this violence with a romantic power, making them the main force in a protracted military revolt against the Philippine state, launching a half-dozen abortive coup attempts from 1986 to 1990.

Eroticized Decision Making

When the Bush administration revived CIA torture after the September 11 attacks, the psychosexual aspect of the agency's methods was soon evident—in Abu Ghraib, Guantánamo, and the White House. Right after his public address to a shaken nation on September 11, 2001, President Bush gave his White House staff secret orders for torture, saying: "I don't care what the international lawyers say, we are going to kick some ass."[37] Reflecting this approach, the president ordered, in February 2002, that "none of the provisions of Geneva apply to our conflict with al-Qaeda in Afghanistan or elsewhere throughout the world," thereby removing any requirements for "minimum standards for humane treatment."[38] In the seven years of torture that followed, the parameters of these techniques, including the psychosexual method, were grounded in interrogation manuals, legal memoranda, and staff meetings that communicated authorization from the administration's apex down the chain of command to field interrogators in Abu Ghraib, Guantánamo, and secret CIA prisons from Thailand to Poland.

In the ten-year hiatus between the end of the Cold War and start of the war on terror, the only U.S. agency that had preserved an institutional memory of harsh methods, either defensive or offensive, was the Pentagon's Joint Personnel Recovery Agency (JPRA). For decades its staff psychologists had trained thousands of U.S. troops to withstand enemy methods such as "sensory deprivation, sleep disruption, stress positions, waterboarding, and slapping." Starting in early 2002 the JPRA psychologists advised both the Defense Department and the CIA about ways to "reverse engineer" these defensive methods for effective enemy interrogation.[39] Inside CIA headquarters there was, however, a "high level of anxiety" about possible prosecution for methods officials knew to be internationally defined as torture.[40]

In response to White House inquiries about the legality of such techniques, Assistant Attorney General Jay Bybee, assisted by his subordinate

John Yoo, found grounds in their now notorious August 2002 memo for exculpating any CIA interrogator who tortured but later claimed the intention was to gather information instead of inflicting pain. "For purely mental pain or suffering to amount to torture," the memo stated, "it must result in significant psychological harm . . . lasting for months or even years"—an outrageously permissive standard.[41]

Further up the chain of command Condoleezza Rice, then national security advisor, later recalled that "in the spring of 2002, CIA sought policy approval from the National Security Counsel (NSC) to begin an interrogation program for high-level al-Qaida terrorists." Consequently, she "convened a series of meetings of NSC principals in 2002 and 2003 to discuss various issues . . . relating to detainees."[42]

These principals—including Vice President Dick Cheney, Attorney General John Ashcroft, Secretary of State Colin Powell, and CIA director George Tenet—met dozens of times inside the White House Situation Room. According to ABC News, "Some of the interrogation sessions were almost choreographed—down to the number of times CIA agents could use a specific tactic." After watching agency employees pantomime what Rice called "certain physical and psychological interrogation techniques," these leaders, their imaginations stimulated by graphic visions of human suffering, repeatedly authorized extreme psychological techniques stiffened by hitting, walling, and waterboarding. During one of these meetings Attorney General Ashcroft asked aloud: "Why are we talking about this in the White House? History will not judge this kindly." Nonetheless this national security team apparently authorized every CIA request for torture. Even after the Abu Ghraib photographs had sparked worldwide protests, these national security principals met again inside the White House in mid-2004 to approve the use of CIA torture techniques on still more terror suspects. Despite growing concern about the damage that Abu Ghraib was doing to America's reputation, Condoleezza Rice commanded agency officials in the cool demeanor of a "dominatrix" who fused "sex and power" into an aura of authority. "This is your baby," she reportedly said. "Go do it."[43]

Their recommendations were delivered to President Bush, who told ABC News in April 2008: "Yes, I'm aware our national security team met on this issue. And I approved."[44] As noted earlier, so strong is torture's appeal to the powerful that they often ignore all evidence of its high political costs to persist in the practice.

Operating under this broad White House interrogation protocol, on December 2, 2002, Defense Secretary Rumsfeld approved a military request for use of fifteen aggressive interrogation techniques for the military prison at Guantánamo.[45] Simultaneously, Rumsfeld appointed General Geoffrey Miller to command Guantánamo with a correspondingly wide latitude for interrogation, making this prison an ad hoc behavioral science laboratory. Under Miller interrogators stiffened the psychological assault of the CIA's paradigmatic techniques by exploring Arab "cultural sensitivity" to sexuality, gender identity, and fear of dogs.[46]

Moving beyond the formal, clinical bounds of the general's protocol, interrogation at Abu Ghraib veered into the realm of the psychosexual. Reflecting the notion among Bush administration neoconservatives that "Arabs are particularly vulnerable to sexual humiliation," Guantánamo's command had already begun to probe such sensitivities, using female interrogators to humiliate these Muslim males.[47] According to a sergeant who served under General Miller, female soldiers regularly removed their shirts, and one wiped red ink on a detainee's face saying she was menstruating, leaving him to "cry like a baby." Singled out for tough treatment, the alleged hijacker Mohamed al-Kahtani was subjected to a "special interrogation plan" that combined rigorous sensory deprivation with novel psychological tactics called "ego down," "futility," and "gender coercion via some domination." During forty-eight days of interrogation, often with only four hours of sleep, al-Kahtani was "told his mother and sister were whores," told he had "homosexual tendencies and that other detainees knew," "forced to dance with a male interrogator," "forced to wear a bra and a thong . . . on his head," "led around by a leash tied to chains," "forced to stand naked in front of a female interrogator," and held down while a female interrogator "straddled" his groin.[48]

When U.S. forces occupied Iraq in March 2003 this interrogation protocol became standard military procedure. After General Miller visited Baghdad in September 2003 to deliver a detailed manual and DVD of Guantánamo's methods, the U.S. commander for Iraq, General Ricardo Sanchez, issued orders for abusive interrogation at Abu Ghraib prison using three of the four basic techniques from this psychological doctrine—sensory disorientation, self-inflicted pain, and cultural humiliation.[49] Indeed my own review of the thousand classified photographs collected by the army at Abu Ghraib reveals an incessant repetition of these same three torture techniques: first, frequent hooding for sensory deprivation; second, short shackling, long shackling, and enforced standing for self-inflicted pain; and, third, total nudity, sexual humiliation, and dogs for that recent innovation, exploitation of Arab cultural sensitivities. It is no accident that Private Lynndie England was photographed famously leading an Iraqi detainee leashed like a dog.

In a sharp break with past policy the White House also allowed the CIA its own global network of prisons and planes to seize suspects anywhere, subject them to extraordinary rendition, and incarcerate them endlessly inside a supranational gulag of eight secret "black sites" from Thailand to Poland.[50] The Bush administration also approved the CIA's ten "enhanced" interrogation methods designed by agency psychologists, including waterboarding.[51]

During the first year of this CIA program, early 2002 to mid-2003, the absence of guidelines or supervision made the black sites a lurid Grand Guignol of what the agency itself later called "unauthorized, improvised, inhumane, and undocumented . . . interrogation techniques." Reflecting torture's inexorable escalation in brutality, the CIA inspector general later found that these "improvised actions" ranged from the cruel to possibly criminal, including strangling with both hands "to restrict the detainee's carotid artery" in July 2002; staging "mock executions" by brandishing or firing handguns in September to October; confining a detainee "in a cold room, shackled and naked," in December; racking "an unloaded semi-automatic . . . once or twice" and revving a "power drill" close to a detainee's head in December; threatening, through an Arabic interpreter, to begin "sexually abusing female relatives in front of the detainee"; telling a high-level prisoner, "We're going to kill your children"; and beating an Afghani detainee to death "with a large metal flashlight" in June 2003. When asked about some of this abuse, one CIA interrogator replied with an empowered arrogance, "How cold is cold?"[52]

After CIA headquarters issued clear guidelines in January 2003, such improvisation slowly ended and interrogation inside the agency's secret prisons began to follow a uniform roster of standard and enhanced techniques. As described in the agency's classified 2004 *Background Paper on CIA's Combined Use of Interrogation Techniques*, each detainee was reduced to "a baseline dependent state" through "nudity, sleep deprivation (with shackling . . .), and dietary manipulation." For "more physical and psychological stress" CIA inquisitors used coercive measures such as "an insult slap or abdominal slap" and then "walling," that is, slamming the detainee's head against a cell wall. If these techniques failed, interrogators escalated to waterboarding, which the Bush Justice Department called "the most intense of CIA interrogation techniques."[53]

In defiance of sound interrogation procedures, this extreme method was applied to al-Qaeda captive Abu Zubaydah "at least 83 times during

August 2002" and Khalid Sheikh Mohammad 183 times in March 2003—an excess best explained by the sadomasochistic appeal of psychological torture.[54] Significantly, agency investigators concluded that "there was no *a priori* reason to believe that applying the waterboard with the frequency and intensity with which it was used by the psychologist/interrogators was either efficacious or medically safe."[55]

Advertising Torture

Throughout these years of escalating abuse after September 11, the Bush administration's secret embrace of aggressive methods drew some political sustenance from the sexualized display of torture in film and television. While violence had long been a staple of Hollywood films, the sudden emergence of torture as a major multimedia theme was distinct post–September 11 phenomenon. Through the invisible tendrils that tie media to the modern state, U.S. television networks broadcast hundreds of hours of popular television dramas in the aftermath of September 11 portraying torture as effective, even exciting, video games with elaborate torture scenarios proliferated, and major Hollywood films featured graphic torture scenes. Surveying the most popular of these displays indicates, moreover, that there was a progressive coarsening of representation, with ever more explicit violence paralleling the administration's increasingly overt embrace of torture. By the time Bush left office in late 2008, screens large and small across America were saturated with torture simulations, conducting an ad hoc mass indoctrination of the public into a belief in the efficacy of torture—a sordid, even repulsive practice whose ugly reality was softened by its eroticized representation.

While studying the effect of media on individual behavior is difficult, and positing any precise correlation between national broadcasts and public opinion is doubly so, the temporal coincidence of the two in the case of torture is undeniable. By simultaneously showing torture as effective for interrogation and eroticizing the experience for both perpetrator and victim, mass-media representations may have played a central albeit intangible role in fostering public support for abuse.

According to the Parents Television Council, torture scenes on network broadcasts shot upward from just twenty per annum in the five years before September 11 to over 150 annually in the four years thereafter. Instead of the deviant drug dealers or the evil Nazi torturers in the older shows, most post–September 11 torture perpetrators were upright U.S. officials defending America from terrorists or other malefactors.[56]

Television's first sustained engagement with torture was relatively restrained. For 261 shows over twelve seasons from 1992 to 2005, Detective Andy Sipowicz, the everyman hero of ABC Television's top-rated series *NYPD Blue*, put his badge and pension on the line by deciding to "tune-up" this week's suspect with threatened or actual beatings. Although the suits from the district attorney's office moved in and out of the plot regularly, telling the detectives that threats and violence were morally and legally wrong, Sipowicz's approach was always vindicated, extracting timely information to solve or stop yet another horrible crime. Looking at and learning from Andy Sipowicz, Americans, or at least the twenty million who watched weekly, might well believe that the "tune-up" was regrettably necessary for effective interrogation.[57] But in a show famous for showing its attractive lead actors in partial-nudity shots, it was the balding, potbellied Sipowicz who extracted confessions through simple physical force by punching, pushing, choking, and threatening—violent yes, but sexual no.

If *NYPD Blue* exhibited a certain ambiguity about the morality of abuse, Fox Television's hit show *24* was an unrestrained advertisement for torture. First broadcast in November 2001 just weeks after the September 11 attacks, *24* soon became the informal signature program of President Bush's war on terror. By the end of his presidency in late 2008, the show had broadcast 192 episodes over the span of eight seasons, attracting an average of 10 to 13 million viewers. Significantly, *24* was also at the top in its depiction of torture, with sixty-seven such scenes during its first five seasons.[58] Each week, as a large clock ticks menacingly, Agent Jack Bauer of the Counter Intelligence Unit, played by Kiefer Sutherland, uses torture to save Los Angeles or the nation from the threat of terrorists armed with horrific weapons of mass destruction, often a nuclear bomb. Although some liberals such as the show's fictional president might waver, Jack's torture is graphically brutal and stunningly effective, always producing timely, accurate intelligence. In episode six of season five, broadcast on January 31, 2006, for example, Russian separatists acquire dozens of nerve gas canisters for terrorist attacks that could kill millions. At the last moment Jack Bauer, in the presence of the president, interrogates his chief of staff, Walt Cummings, a traitor who knows the location of these lethal weapons. As the camera closes in, Jack poises the glinting steel point of his hunting knife above the traitor's moist eyeball, an enticing orb inviting penetration—much as Salvador Dalí and Luis Buñel did so famously with a straight razor in their surrealist short film *Un Chien Andalou* (1929).

JACK: I don't know what this man has told you, but we need to find this nerve gas now, and I mean immediately—before it is too late.
PRESIDENT LOGAN: It's already too late.
JACK: What do you mean?
PRESIDENT LOGAN: Apparently it's on its way out of the country....
JACK: Where is it? [He keeps hitting Walt.]
PRESIDENT LOGAN: He told me he doesn't know!
JACK: He's lying to you, sir.
WALT: The man I had inside has gone dark. I don't know.
[Jack pulls out a knife and holds it near Walt's eyes. Logan grimaces.]
JACK: I'm done talking with you.... The first thing I'm going to do is take out your right eye, and then ... take out your left, and then I'm going to ... keep cutting you until you give me the information that I need. Do you understand me? So for the last time, where is the nerve gas?
WALT: I don't know.
[Jack moves the knife closer to his eye ...]
WALT: Stop! Stop! Stop! I'll tell you. I'll tell you. It's on a freighter leaving the port at Longbridge at 2:30.[59]

Setting aside the rule of law embodied by the chief executive, Jack tortures the White House chief of staff in the president's presence and, once again, demonstrates both the success and the sensuality of torture. Indeed the next season's opening episode, broadcast in January 2007, shows Jack, back from eighteen months of being abused inside a Chinese prison, stripping his shirt before two male colleagues to show the stigmata of torture's tracks down his eroticized body, shaven and sculpted in the conventions of homoerotic pornography. Instead of a real-life torture survivor shaking with trauma, emaciated, disfigured by scabrous lesions, and covered with human waste, Jack's bared, muscled torso and smooth alabaster skin is alluring—making his torture experience, as both perpetrator and now victim, seem doubly enticing.

In the elision of film and reality common to American culture, the show's interrogation scenario, rendered as an exciting and even erotic experience, affirmed for millions of loyal viewers, from active-duty soldiers to Supreme Court justices, that torture is a necessary weapon in the war on terror. "Jack Bauer saved Los Angeles.... He saved hundreds of thousands of lives," Justice Antonin Scalia told a 2007 legal seminar in Ottawa. "Are you going to convict Jack Bauer?" he asked. "Say that criminal law is against him?... Is any jury going to convict Jack Bauer? I don't think so."[60]

In case the televised version of 24 left any doubt, its video-game version is one of several that allow millions of players to simulate the torture experience. Released in early 2006 for Playstation 2 by Sony Computer Entertainment, *24: The Game* programs a torture scenario into the buttons that move the chief character, Jack Bauer, with a disconcerting effect. As media critic Mark Sample argues: "Torture is no longer . . . confined to an ambiguous moral and legal territory; it has instead been incorporated deep within the structure of the game, normalizing what would otherwise be an affront to human dignity."[61] But in the world of video games the brutalization had just begun. In the 2008 edition of *World of Warcraft*, which sold a record 2.8 million copies on the first day of its release, the player uses a "Neural Needler," which "inflicts incredible pain to target," and thereby extracts accurate information from a bound sorcerer.[62] In another gratuitous entertainment devoid of any exculpatory narrative, the "free and increasingly popular" *Torture Game* 2 appeared on Internet portals in 2008, featuring "ragdoll physics [that] lend a sickeningly hypnotic charm to . . . every touch of your cruel hand, every cut of the chainsaw" as the player dismembers a bleeding humanoid.[63] By 2009 interactive torture scenarios were integral to a wide range of popular video games—*Bethesda's Brink, the Punisher, Red Faction: Guerrilla, Killzone 2*, and *Grand Theft Auto: Vice City*, to name just a few.[64]

The temper of these times also made torture a significant theme in a surprising number of feature films with leading stars—George Clooney in *Syriana* (2005), Daniel Craig in *Casino Royale* (2006), and Matt Damon in *The Good Shepherd* (2006). Admittedly, liberal Hollywood later produced a few films critical of torture—notably, *Rendition* (2007), a box-office bust that grossed a lackluster $27 million worldwide despite major stars such as Jake Gyllenhaal, Reese Witherspoon, and Meryl Streep.[65]

With a script that was little more than a frame for sadistically erotic, utterly gratuitous torture scenes, *Hostel* (2005) became a surprising box-office hit, earning an impressive $81 million worldwide on a meager investment of $4.5 million.[66] At the opposite pole of moviemaking, the big-budget studio version of *Casino Royale* (2006) revitalized the fading James Bond franchise with a script whose chief innovation was an extended genital torture scene. This film depicts brutal homoerotic sadism, far removed from the original novel's portrayal of what its author, Ian Fleming, called a "sexual twilight where pain turned to pleasure and where hatred and fear of the torturers turned to masochistic fascination."[67] In past Bond films the agent's genitals were threatened with a certain decorum, notably in the famed *Goldfinger* (1964) scene showing Agent 007 lashed to a metal table, fully clothed. A laser beam moves slowly between his legs burning a smoking groove in the steel sheet—until it suddenly stops just short of his crotch when Bond cleverly deceives the evil Goldfinger. In *Casino Royale*, by contrast, secret agent Bond is lashed to a chair completely naked. His shaved, muscled torso writhes in eroticized pain while an empowered terrorist leader pounds at his genitals with a knotted rope. Instead of the clever escape from an impossible situation mandatory in past Bond films, our contemporary 007, played by the ruggedly handsome Craig, is entombed in a concrete dungeon, illuminated in the dramatic down lights of inescapable isolation, stolidly passive before the power of sexual torture. Just as the villain prepares to castrate Bond for his refusal to talk, another terrorist breaks in and, angry over the villain's failures, executes him and frees 007. In an otherwise lackluster script minimizing the stunning scenery and elaborate stunts of past Bond movies, this scene of sexual torture is the film's focal point—serving as the story's dramatic denouement and spicing the script with the visual conventions of gay S-M pornography. By portraying torture as both alluring and potent, this simulation may well have helped *Casino Royale* become a box-office smash with $594 million in total sales—the highest grossing of the twenty-one Bond films.[68]

Even in a nominally religious film, *The Passion of the Christ* (2004), director Mel Gibson reverted to the medieval focus on the physicality and sensuality of Christ's torture en route to Golgotha. From just nine words about Christ's flogging in the gospels—three words in Matthew 27:26 ("after flogging Jesus") and eight more in John 19:1 ("Then Pilate took Jesus and had him flogged")—Gibson creates an elaborate torture sequence. In a scene running for a full eight of the film's 125 minutes, uniformed Roman soldiers lead Christ into a stone courtyard where he drops his robe and is chained to a pedestal, revealing a lean, shaved, blemish-free torso. Before a crowd of a hundred spectators, three burly soldiers scourge Christ, first selecting rods and cat-o'-nine-tails from a rack of standard torture implements, and then beating his back into a mass of oozing lesions, laughing with satisfied, sadistic pleasure while wiping his spattered blood from their faces. Periodically, the camera, reprising a technique from Leni Riefenstahl's *Triumph of the Will* (1935), frames the faces of both torturers and spectators, allowing viewers to insert themselves into the cinema's reality as imagined participants in this ancient spectacle.[69] Again, the hero/victim seems a compliant participant in his own torture, reacting with a suffused masochistic silence that transforms a vulgar inhumanity into the aestheticized mutuality of S-M bondage.

Just as grisly medieval canvasses depicting Christ's suffering normalized that era's gory rituals of punishment and public execution, so this film's blood-soaked scourging of the messiah may have prepared the American public for quiet acceptance of the Abu Ghraib photographs. On February 25, 2004, Gibson's gruesome film was released on 4,643 movie screens across America, and by the end of March was the country's highest-grossing R-rated film, eventually earning $611 million. Four weeks later, on April 28, Americans reacted blandly to CBS Television's broadcast of those iconic images of prisoner abuse at Abu Ghraib.[70] Two months after the release of these photographs, an ABC News/*Washington Post* poll found that 35 percent of Americans still felt torture was acceptable in some circumstances—providing some indication of the media's possible influence on public perception of abuse.[71]

Impunity

As criticism rose at home and abroad this tacit consensus for torture weakened in the wake of the Abu Ghraib scandal. Within weeks of the original CBS broadcast the Pentagon held a closed-door slide show for Congress of hundreds of classified Abu Ghraib photographs. Legislators emerged grim and shaken. "I saw cruel, sadistic torture," said Senate Majority Leader Bill Frist (Republican, Tennessee). Senator Richard J. Durbin (Democrat, Illinois) said, "It felt like you were descending into one of the rings of hell, and sadly it was our own creation." On May 10, after the Senate unanimously condemned this abuse, President Bush obliquely acknowledged the problem, stating that there would be "a full accounting for the cruel and disgraceful abuse of Iraqi detainees."[72]

Apart from such criticism in Congress and the press, the Bush administration faced its sharpest challenge in the courts. In June 2006 the U.S. Supreme Court ruled in Hamdan v. Rumsfeld that Bush's military commissions at Guantánamo were illegal because they did not meet the requirement, under Common Article Three of the Geneva Conventions, that detainees be tried with "all the judicial guarantees . . . recognized as indispensable by civilized peoples."[73]

On September 6, in a dramatic bid to legalize his policies in the aftermath of this adverse decision, President Bush announced, before an applauding audience of September 11 families in the East Room, that he was transferring fourteen top al-Qaeda captives from the secret CIA prisons to Guantánamo Bay. Speaking with clipped diction and secret-agent argot reminiscent of Jack Bauer in the show 24, Bush told his national television audience a thrilling tale of covert action derring-do. After "they risked their lives to capture some of the most brutal terrorists on Earth," courageous American agents, he said, "worked day and night . . . to find out what the terrorists know so we can stop new attacks" until they scored a major breakthrough by capturing "a trusted associate of Osama bin Laden" named Abu Zubaydah. But once in custody, the president said, Zubaydah was "defiant and evasive." Knowing that "captured terrorists have . . . intelligence that cannot be found any other place," the CIA, with White House approval, applied an "alternative set of procedures" and extracted timely information that "helped in the planning and . . . execution of the operation that captured Khalid Shaikh Mohammed." Once in custody "KSM was questioned by the CIA using these procedures," producing intelligence that stopped a succession of ticking time bombs. To allow continuation of this critical "CIA program" with its "alternative set of procedures," both phrases transparent euphemisms for torture, Bush said that he was sending legislation to Congress that would protect CIA interrogators from prosecution and legalize these same executive actions now challenged by the Supreme Court.[74]

Miming the dialogue of televised spy thrillers such as 24, President Bush thus made a convincing public appeal for the preservation of the president's prerogative to torture. Just four weeks later Congress passed, without any amendment or real opposition, an omnibus antiterrorist bill called the Military Commissions Act of 2006 that, as he had directed, prevents prosecution of CIA interrogators and permits the president to order torture.

In the transition from Bush to Obama after the 2008 presidential elections, the dynamics of partisan wrangling over CIA interrogation produced a surprising bipartisan move toward impunity for past human rights abuse. Showing the extraordinary power of images in shaping this public debate, President Obama announced his refusal to release more torture photographs in May 2009, arguing that the abuse shown in these images "was carried out in the past by a small number of individuals."[75]

In this slide toward impunity, public pressure from the Republican right seemed to push the Obama White House toward compromise on its commitment to human rights. Only days after a suicide-bombing attempt on a Northwest Airlines flight near Detroit in December 2009, Liz Cheney, the former vice president's daughter, launched a new patriotic group, Keep America Safe. Using the distinctive visual format of the television show 24, the group's Web site mocked Obama's response to this incident, juxtaposing video clips of federal officers surrounding the aircraft at Detroit with the president playing golf in Hawaii. The group's manifesto blasted Obama, saying: "He should inform Attorney General Holder that he will no longer allow the Justice Department . . . to investigate or prosecute CIA officials who kept us safe after 9/11, or disbar or otherwise punish the lawyers who provided the legal framework for programs that saved American lives."[76]

Within weeks this pressure proved effective. In February 2010 Obama's Justice Department reversed an earlier finding that Bush lawyers Jay Bybee and John Yoo had been "guilty of professional misconduct" in writing those 2002 memos that gave the CIA authority for abuse. Instead Justice now found that they merely acted from an "extreme, albeit sincerely held view of executive power," thereby exempting them from any threat of disbarment.[77]

So what meaning can we extract from this sordid narrative and its interleaving of state practice and public displays of torture? Playing on the dark, still unexplored recesses of the human mind, torture seems, from recent U.S. history, so seductive that there is no such thing as a little bit of torture. No matter what euphemism we might use—"enhanced interrogation" or "alternative methods"—torture is so powerfully erotic that even the most clinical, controlled methods soon erupt uncontrollably into the Dantean abuse of Abu Ghraib, the CIA black sites, and Guantánamo. So overwhelming is the erotic stimulus of torture that the only possible restraint is the rigid enforcement of the rule of law. Unfortunately, in post–September 11 America we have come to believe that the rule of law is somehow optional.

NOTES

1. Dan Rather, "Abuse at Abu Ghraib," *60 Minutes II*, CBS, http://www.cbsnews.com/stories/2004/05/05/60II/main615781.shtml?tag=currentVideoInfo;videoMetaInfo (accessed February 21, 2010).
2. Susan Sontag, "Regarding the Torture of Others," *New York Times Magazine*, May 23, 2004, 25–29, 42.
3. Associated Press, "New Abu Ghraib Abuse Photos Broadcast in Australia," *Independent*, February 15, 2006, http://www.independent.co.uk/news/world/

middle-east/new-abu-ghraib-abuse-photos-broadcast-in-australia-466680.html (accessed February 3, 2010).
4. David A. England (computer crime coordinator, 10th MP Bn [CID], 3d MP Group [CID], Baghdad, Iraq), "Agent's Investigation Report," January 2004, personal collection. A spreadsheet on this same CD labeled "CG CD5.xls" lists 1,640 images. In mid-2004 the *Washington Post* apparently obtained a copy of a similar CD but published very few of these photographs. See Sherry Ricchiardi, "Missed Signals," *American Journalism Review*, August/September 2004, http://www.ajr.org/Article.asp?id=3716 (accessed February 21, 2010). After this CD arrived from Sydney in February 2006, Salon.com received similar material which it summarized by quoting a report by Special Agent James E. Seigmund: "A review of all the computer media submitted to this office revealed a total of 1,325 images of suspected detainee abuse, 93 video files of suspected detainee abuse, 660 images of adult pornography, 546 images of suspected dead Iraqi detainees, 29 images of soldiers in simulated sexual acts, 20 images of a soldier with a Swastika drawn between his eyes, 37 images of Military Working dogs being used in abuse of detainees and 125 images of questionable acts." Of these thousand-plus photographs, Salon.com released just eighteen on its Web site. See Mark Benjamin, "Salon Exclusive: The Abu Ghraib Files," Salon.com, February 16, 2006, http://www.salon.com/news/feature/2006/02/16/abu_ghraib/ (accessed February 22, 2010).
5. Michael Walzer, "Political Action: The Problem of Dirty Hands," *Philosophy and Public Affairs* 2, no. 2 (1973): 167; Alfred W. McCoy, "The Myth of the Ticking Time Bomb," *Progressive*, October 2006, 20–24.
6. Gideon Bachman, "Pasolini and the Marquis de Sade," *Sight and Sound* 45, no. 1 (Winter 1975–6): 69–71; and *Salò, or the 120 Days of Sodom*, directed by Pier Paolo Pasolini (1975; New York: Criterion Collection, 2008), DVD, no. 17d.
7. See Keith Breese, "Salò or the 120 Days of Sodom," filmcritic.com, http://www.filmcritic.com/reviews/1976/salo-or-the-120-days-of-sodom/; Steve Biodrowski, "Salò (1975) Borderland Review," *Cinefantastique*, http://cinefantastiqueonline.com/2008/08/borderland-salo-1975/; and Cole Smithey, "Salò (Classic Film Pick)," *The Smartest Film Critic in the World*, http://www.colesmithey.com/capsules/2009/07/salo.html (all accessed November 13, 2010).
8. Lawrence E. Hinkle Jr. and Harold G. Wolff, "Communist Interrogation and Indoctrination of 'Enemies of the States': Analysis of Methods Used by the Communist State Police (A Special Report)," *Archives of Neurology and Psychiatry* 76 (1956): 135.
9. John Langbein, *Torture and the Law of Proof: Europe and England in the Ancien Regime* (Chicago: University of Chicago Press, 1977), 7; Edward Peters, *Torture* (Philadelphia: University of Pennsylvania Press, 1996), 40–62.
10. Peters, *Torture*, 62–67; Malise Ruthven, *Torture: The Grand Conspiracy* (London: Weidenfeld and Nicolson, 1979), 57–59.

11. Mitchell B. Merback, *The Thief, the Cross, and the Wheel: Pain and the Spectacle of Punishment in Medieval and Renaissance Europe* (Chicago: University of Chicago Press, 1999), 69–70, 129–57, 199–217; James Carroll, "The Bush Crusade," *Nation*, September 20, 2004, 17.
12. Alec Mellor, *La Torture: Son Histoire, Son Abolition, Sa Réapparition au XXe Siecle* (Paris: Horizons Litteraires, 1949), 105–15; Merback, *The Thief, the Cross, and the Wheel*, 158–70.
13. Stephen F. Eisenman, *The Abu Ghraib Effect* (London: Reaktion Books, 2007), 60–69.
14. Ibid., 73.
15. Langbein, *Torture and the Law of Proof*, 10–12, 60–69; Ruthven, *Torture*, 12–15; John H. Langbein, "The Legal History of Torture," in *Torture: A Collection*, ed. Sanford Levinson, 93–100 (New York: Oxford University Press, 2004); Peter Gay, *Voltaire's Politics: The Poet as Realist* (New York: Vintage, 1965), 275; Marcello Maestro, *Voltaire and Beccaria as Reformers of Criminal Law* (New York: Columbia University Press, 1942), 86–88.
16. Eisenman, *The Abu Ghraib Effect*, 88.
17. Central Intelligence Agency, "Proposed Study on Special Interrogation Methods" (CIA Behavior Control Experiments Collection, John Marks Donation, National Security Archive, George Washington University, Washington, D.C., February 14, 1952).
18. The CIA's audit staff found that the main drug testing program, MKUltra, suffered from procedures "that produced gross administrative failures." See U.S. Senate, 94th Congress, 2nd Session, *Final Report of the Select Committee to Study Governmental Operations With Respect to Intelligence Activities, Book 1* (Washington, D.C.: Government Printing Office, 1976), 409.
19. Ibid., 387–88.
20. Ibid., 399.
21. Woodburn Heron, "The Pathology of Boredom," *Scientific American*, January 1957, 52–56.
22. Donald O. Hebb, "This Is How It Was" (address to the Canadian Psychological Association, ca. 1980, from the personal papers of Donald O. Hebb, copy provided by Mary Ellen Hebb).
23. Lawrence E. Hinkle Jr., "A Consideration of the Circumstances Under Which Men May Be Interrogated, and the Effects That These May Have Upon the Function of the Brain" (CIA Behavior Control Experiments Collection, John Marks Donation, National Security Archive, George Washinton University, Washington, D.C., ca. 1958), 1, 5, 6, 11–14, 18; Hinkle, and Wolff, "Communist Interrogation and Indoctrination of 'Enemies of the States,'" 115–74.
24. Joseph Marguilies, *Guantánamo and the Abuse of Presidential Power* (New York: Simon and Schuster, 2006), 120–25; Dwight D. Eisenhower, "Executive Order 10631—Code of Conduct for Members of the Armed Forces of the United

States" (Santa Barbara: American Presidency Project, University of California at Santa Barbara, August 17, 1955), http://www.presidency.ucsb.edu/ws/index.php?pid=59249 (accessed July 19, 2009).

25. Central Intelligence Agency, *Kubark Counterintelligence Interrogation* (CIA Training Manuals, National Security Archive, George Washington University, Washington, D.C., July 1963), 87–90. The term "Kubark" is a cryptonym that the CIA used for itself.

26. Victor Marchetti and John D. Marks, *The CIA and the Cult of Intelligence* (New York: Knopf, 1974), 246.

27. *U.S. Assistance Programs in Vietnam, Hearings Before the Subcommittee of the Committee on Government Operations*, 92nd Congress, 1st Session (Washington, D.C.: Government Printing Office, 1971), 319–21, 327, 349; *Nomination of William E. Colby to Be Head of Central Intelligence, Hearings Before the Committee on Armed Services*, 93rd Congress, 1st Session (Washington, D.C.: Government Printing Office, 1973), 101–17 (July 2, 20, and 25, 1973); Dale Andradé, "Pacification," in *Encyclopedia of the Vietnam War*, ed. Stanley Kutler (New York: Scribner's, 1996), 423.

28. Andrew F. Krepinevich Jr., *The Army and Vietnam* (Baltimore: Johns Hopkins University Press, 1986), 228–29.

29. Ralph W. McGehee, *Deadly Deceits: My 25 Years in the CIA* (New York: Sheridan Square, 1983), 156.

30. Central Intelligence Agency, "Special Review: Counterterrorism Detention and Interrogation Activities (September 2001–October 2003)" (CIA, Office of the Inspector General, May 7, 2004, Washington, D.C.), 10, http://graphics8.nytimes.com/packages/pdf/politics/20090825DEAIN/2004CIAIG.pdf (accessed, November 1, 2010); James LeMoyne, "Testifying to Torture," *New York Times Magazine*, June 5, 1988, 47, 62.

31. Central Intelligence Agency, "Special Review," 10; Central Intelligence Agency, *Human Resources Exploitation Training Manual—1983* (CIA Training Manuals, National Security Archive, George Washington University, Washington, D.C.).

32. LeMoyne, "Testifying to Torture," 45–47, 62–65.

33. For the details of this U.S. training and a description of the impact of torture on the Armed Forces of the Philippines, see Alfred W. McCoy, *Closer Than Brothers: Manhood at the Philippine Military Academy* (New Haven: Yale University Press, 1999), chapter 6.

34. Edgardo Kangleon, "A Moment of Uncertainty" (manuscript, December 8, 1982), 13–16, enclosed in a letter addressed, "Dear Papa/Mama/Rey," September 30, 1983. A copy was furnished through the kindness of Fr. Niall O'Brien, St. Columban's Mission Society, Bacolod City. An excerpt of this letter was published in Promotion of Church People's Rights, *That We May Remember* (Quezon City: PCPR, May 1989), 168–73.

35. Task Force Detainees, Association of Major Religious Superiors in the Philippines, *Political Detainees in the Philippines, Book 2* (Manila: Association of Major Orders of Religious Superiors, March 31, 1977), pp. 8–9.
36. See McCoy, *Closer Than Brothers*, chapter 6.
37. Richard A. Clarke, *Against All Enemies: Inside America's War on Terror* (New York: Free Press, 2004), 24.
38. U.S. Senate, Committee on Armed Services, *Inquiry Into the Treatment of Detainees in U.S. Custody*, 110th Congress, 2nd session (Washington, D.C.: Government Printing Office, 2008), xiii, http://www.democrats.com/senate-armed-services-committee-report-on-torture (accessed, July, 21, 2009); George W. Bush to the vice president and others, "Humane Treatment of Taliban and al Qaeda Detainees," memorandum, February 7, 2002, the White House, Washington, D.C., http://www.pegc.us/archive/White_House/bush_memo_20020207_ed.pdf (accessed July 27, 2009).
39. U.S. Senate, *Inquiry Into the Treatment of Detainees in U.S. Custody*, xiv–xvi.
40. Jane Mayer, "The Black Sites," *New Yorker*, July 21, 2009, http://www.newyorker.com/reporting/2007/08/13/070813fa_fact_mayer (accessed July 20, 2009); U.S. Senate, *Inquiry Into the Treatment of Detainees in U.S. Custody*, xiii.
41. Jay Bybee (office of the assistant attorney general) to Alberto R. Gonzales (counsel to the president), "Standards of Conduct for Interrogation under 18 U.S.C. §§ 2340–2340A," memorandum, August 1, 2002, 1, http://www.washingtonpost.com/wp-srv/nation/documents/dojinterrogationmemo20020801.pdf (accessed July 19, 2009); U.S. Senate, *Inquiry Into the Treatment of Detainees in U.S. Custody*, xv–xvi, xxi.
42. U.S. Senate, *Inquiry Into the Treatment of Detainees in U.S. Custody*, xv, xx–xxi, 16–17.
43. Jan Crawford Greenburg, Howard L. Rosenberg, and Ariane de Vogue, "Top Bush Advisors Approved 'Enhanced Interrogation,'" *ABC News*, April 9, 2008, http://abcnews.go.com/thelaw/lawpolitics/Story?id=4583256&page=4 (accessed December 24, 2008); Robin Givhan, "Condoleezza Rice's Commanding Clothes," *Washington Post*, February 25, 2005, http://www.washingtonpost.com/ac2/wp-dyn/A51640-2005Feb24?language=printer (accessed November 16, 2011).
44. Jan Crawford Greenburg, Howard L. Rosenberg and Ariane de Vogue, "Bush Aware of Advisers' Interrogation Talks," *ABC News*, April 11, 2008, http://abcnews.go.com/TheLaw/LawPolitics/story?id=4635175 (accessed December 24, 2008).
45. U.S. Senate, *Inquiry Into the Treatment of Detainees in U.S. Custody*, xix; William J. Haynes II (general counsel, Department of Defense) to secretary of defense, "Counter-Resistance Techniques," memorandum, November 27, 2002, http://www.washingtonpost.com/wp-srv/nation/documents/dodmemos.pdf (accessed June 28, 2004).

46. M. Gregg Bloche and Jonathan H. Marks, "Doctors and Interrogators at Guantanamo Bay," *New England Journal of Medicine* 353, no. 1 (July 7, 2005): 7; Jonathan H. Marks, "The Silence of the Doctors," *Nation*, December 7, 2005, http://www.thenation.com/doc/20051226/marks (accessed July 19, 2009).
47. Seymour M. Hersh, *Chain of Command: The Road from 9/11 to Abu Ghraib* (New York: HarperCollins, 2004), 38–39.
48. John Burns, "Ten Sunnis Suffocate in Iraqi Police Custody," *New York Times*, July 13, 2005; Neil Lewis, "Report Discredits F.B.I. Claims of Abuse at Guantanamo Bay," July 14, 2005; U.S. Department of Defense, "Army Regulation 15–6: Final Report: Investigation into FBI Allegation of Detainee Abuse at Guantanamo Bay, Cuba Detention Facility" (Washington, D.C., April 1, 2005; amended June 9, 2005), 12, 14–21, http://www.defenselink.mil/news/Jul2005/d20050714report.pdf (accessed July 18, 2005); *Guantanamo Bay Detainee Treatment, Hearings Before the Senate Armed Services Committee*, 109th Congress, 13–17 (July 13, 2005), http://web.lexis-nexis.com/congcom/printdoc (accessed July 18, 2005); Human Rights Watch, *The Road to Abu Ghraib* (New York: Human Rights Watch, June 2004), 13; Natasha Korecki, "Burge Gets 4 1/2 Years for Perjury," *Chicago Sun-Times*, January 28, 2005; Carol Leonnig and Dana Priest, "Detainees Accuse Female Interrogators," *Washington Post*, February 10, 2005.
49. Ricardo S. Sanchez to C2, Combined Joint Task Force Seven, Baghdad, Iraq 09335, "CJTF-7 Interrogation and Counter-Resistance Policy," memorandum, September 14, 2003; Ricardo S. Sanchez to C2, Combined Joint Task Force Seven, Baghdad, Iraq 09335, "CJTF-7 Interrogation and Counter-Resistance Policy," October 12, 2003, http://www.aclu.org/SafeandFree/SafeandFree.cfm?ID=17851&c=206 (accessed March 30, 2005).
50. Stephen Grey, *Ghost Plane: The True Story of the CIA Torture Program* (New York: St. Martin's Press, 2006), 87, 181, 227, 269–308; Scott Shane, "CIA Expanding Terror Battle Under Guise of Charter Flights," *New York Times*, May 31, 2005.
51. Douglas Jehl, "Report Warned CIA on Tactics in Interrogation," *New York Times*, November 9, 2005.
52. Central Intelligence Agency, "Special Review," 42–44, 69–79, 102–3.
53. Steven G. Bradbury (Office of Legal Counsel) to John A. Rizzo (senior deputy general counsel, CIA), "Application of 18 U.S.C. §§ 2340-2340A to the Combined Use of Certain Techniques in the Interrogation of High Value al Qaeda Detainees," memorandum, May 10, 2005, 53–56; Central Intelligence Agency, "Special Review," 29–30, 103;Mark Mazetti and Scott Shane, "CIA Abuse Cases Detailed in Report on Detainees," *New York Times*, August 26, 2009.
54. Steven G. Bradbury, Office of the Principal Deputy Assistant Attorney General, Office of Legal Counsel, "Memorandum for John A. Rizzo Senior Deputy Counsel, Central Intelligence Agency: Re: Application of United States Obligations Under Article 16 of the Convention Against Torture to Certain Techniques That

May be Used in the Interrogation of High Value al Qaeda Detainees," May 30, 2005, 38, http://media.luxmedia.com/aclu/olc_05302005_bradbury.pdf (accessed June 29, 2011).

55. Bradbury to Rizzo, "Application of 18 U.S.C. §§ 2340–2340A," May 10, 2005, 43.
56. Martin Miller, "'24' Gets a Lesson in Torture from the Experts," *Los Angeles Times*, February 13, 2007, http://articles.latimes.com/2007/feb/13/entertainment/et-torture13 (accessed February 15, 2010); Jesse Holcomb, "Tortured Logic: Do Shows Like 24 Help Make Torture Acceptable?" *Sojourners Magazine*, June 1, 2007, http://www.sojo.net/index.cfm?action=magazine.article&issue=soj0706&article=07064b (accessed February 15, 2010).
57. Associated Press, "'NYPD Blue' Signs Off After 12 Seasons," MSNBC.com, March 2, 2005, http://msnbc.msn.com/id/7052431/print/1/displaymode/1098/ (accessed June 13, 2005).
58. Miller, "'24' Gets a Lesson in Torture from the Experts."
59. David Fury, "12:00 pm–01:00 pm," 24, season 5, episode 6, directed by Jon Cassar, aired January 30, 2006, transcript provided by KAT for Twiztv.com, http://www.twiztv.com/scripts/24/season5/24-506.htm (accessed February 19, 2010).
60. "24 (TV Series)," *Wikipedia*, http://en.wikipedia.org/wiki/24_(TV_series) (accessed September 4, 2009); Colin Freeze, "What Would Jack Bauer Do?" *Globe and Mail* (Toronto), June 16, 2007, http://license.icopyright.net/user/viewFreeUse.act?fuid=NzI2NDYxOA%3D%3D (accessed February 26, 2010).
61. Mark L. Sample, "Virtual Torture: Video Games and the War on Terror," *Game Studies* 8, no. 2 (December 2008), http://74.125.95.132/search?q=cache:MsjUcyujRsEJ:gamestudies.org/0802/articles/sample+video+games+%22torture%22&hl=en&gl=us&strip=1 (accessed March 1, 2010).
62. Clive Thompson, "Why We Need More Torture in Videogames," *Wired*, December 15, 2008, http://www.wired.com/gaming/virtualworlds/commentary/games/2008/12/gamesfrontiers_1215 (accessed March 1, 2010); Daniel Terdiman, "'WoW: Wrath of Lich King' Sets Sales Record," *Cnet News*, http://news.cnet.com/8301-13772_3-10103951-52.html (accessed March 1, 2010).
63. Winda Benedetti, "Should You Take 'Torture' Seriously?" *MSNBC*, http://www.msnbc.msn.com/id/25337373/ns/technology_and_science-games/ (accessed March 1, 2010).
64. A. J. Glasser, "Torture in Video Games," *Kotaku*, September 10, 2009, http://kotaku.com/5353873/torture-in-video-games?utm_source=feedburner&utm_medium=feed&utm_campaign=Feed%3A+kotaku%2Ffull+%28Kotaku%29 (accessed, March 2, 2010).
65. "Rendition (Film)," *Wikipedia*, http://en.wikipedia.org/wiki/Rendition_(film) (accessed March 2, 2010).
66. "Hostel (Film)," *Wikipedia*, http://en.wikipedia.org/wiki/Hostel_(film) (accessed September 4, 2009).
67. Eisenman, *The Abu Ghraib Effect*, 92–93.

68. "Casino Royale (2006 Film)," *Wikipedia*, http://en.wikipedia.org/wiki/Casino_Royale_(2006_film) (accessed September 4, 2009); Chuck Kleinhans, "Imagining Torture," *Jump Cut: A Review of Contemporary Media* 51 (Spring 2009), http://www.ejumpcut.org/currentissue/ (accessed September 4, 2009); Eisenman, *The Abu Ghraib Effect*, 31–32.

69. *The Passion of the Christ*, directed by Mel Gibson (Los Angeles: Newmarket Films, 2004); "Part 6 of 12 (Full Movie)," Youtube video, from *The Passion of the Christ*, http://www.youtube.com/watch?v=gMnKpB6trUs&feature=related (accessed February 20, 2010); Oxford University Press, *The New Oxford Annotated Bible* (New York: Oxford University Press, 1994), 43, 154.

70. "The Passion of the Christ," *Wikipedia*, http://en.wikipedia.org/wiki/The_Passion_of_the_Christ (accessed February 20, 2010). For figures on the film's early earnings, see Peter A. Maresco, "Mel Gibson's *The Passion of the Christ*: Market Segmentation, Mass Marketing and Promotion, and the Internet," *Journal of Religion and Popular Culture* 8 (Fall 2004), http://www.usask.ca/relst/jrpc/art8-melgibsonmarketing.html (accessed February 20, 2010); "Passion of Christ," *Killer Movies*, http://www.killermovies.com/p/passion/ (accessed March 29, 2005).

71. Michael Ignatieff, "Mirage in the Desert," *New York Times Magazine*, June 27, 2004, 14.

72. "Iraqi Prisoner Abuse," *NewsHour with Jim Lehrer*, PBS, May 4, 2004, http://www.pbs.org/newshour/bb/military/jan-june 04/abuse1_05_04.html (accessed June 14, 2004); *New York Times*, May 11, 15, and 25, 2004; White House, "President Outlines Steps to Help Iraq Achieve Democracy and Freedom," news release, May 24, 2004, http://www.whitehouse.gov/news/release/2004/05/print/20040424-10.html (accessed June 14, 2004); Jim VandeHei, "Kerry Assails Bush on Iraq," *Washington Post*, May 13, June 22, 2004; Doulas Jehl and David Johnson, "Rule Change Lets CIA Freely Send Suspects Abroad to Jails," *New York Times*, May 8, 2004; Douglas Jehl, "The Trusted Troubleshooter," *New York Times*, May 12, 2004.

73. Salim Ahmed Hamdan v. Donald H. Rumsfeld, 548 U.S. 557 (2006), opinion of Justice Stevens, 6, 69–73; Jeffery Gettlemen, "Shiite Fighters Clash with G.I.'s and Iraqi Forces," *New York Times*, March 27, 2006; Linda Greenhouse, "Justices, 5-3, Broadly Reject Bush Plan to Try Detainees," *New York Times*, June 30, 2006.

74. Kate Zernicke and Neil Lewis, "Plans for Tribunals Would Hew to First Series," *New York Times*, September 7, 2006; Adam Liptak, "Interrogation Methods Rejected by Military Win Bush's Support," *New York Times*, September 8, 2006; White House, "President Discusses Creation of Military Commissions to Try Suspected Terrorists," news release, September 6, 2006, http://www.whitehouse.gov/news/releases/2006/09/print/20060906-3.html (accessed September 8, 2006). See also McCoy, "The Myth of the Ticking Time Bomb."

75. Chris Cillizza, "The Left Rises up against Obama," *Washington Post*, May 13, 2009.

76. Alesssandra Stanley, "Another Terrorist Plot, Another Very Long Day *New York Times,* January 14, 2010; "Statement by Liz Cheney in Response to President Obama's National Security Remarks," Keep America Safe Facebook group, January 6, 2010, http://www.facebook.com/note.php?note_id=243193612065 (accessed January 23, 2010).
77. Eric Lichtblau and Scott Shane, "Report Faults Two Authors of Bush Terror Memos," *New York Times*, February 20, 2010.

A Clockwork Orange, 1971

7

Stanley Kubrick's *A Clockwork Orange* as Art Against Torture

Carolyn Strange

Between the publication of Anthony Burgess's novel *A Clockwork Orange*[1] and its film adaptation by Stanley Kubrick in 1971 "the golden age of American film violence" emerged, as film critics have noted and as moral guardians decried at the time.[2] When the U.S. Motion Picture Association of America revised its film classification code in 1968 and effectively expanded the range of films adults could watch in public, filmmakers, led by Sam Peckinpah, seized the opportunity to depict violence more graphically than it had previously been screened in mainstream theaters.[3] At the same time sexually confronting films, such as *Midnight Cowboy* and *Medium Cool*, as well as the lighter-hearted *Bob and Carol and Ted and Alice*[4] reconstituted film-watching communities. By the end of the 1960s, while Kubrick was occupied with *2001: A Space Odyssey*,[5] shifts in the aesthetic, legal, and cultural landscape created a new niche for a film adaptation of *A Clockwork Orange (ACO)*.[6] When it appeared late in 1971 *ACO* joined *Dirty Harry, The French Connection,* and *Straw Dogs* as the year's most notable violent films.[7] None would generate the controversy that *ACO* provoked and continues to stir, however.

Reactions were polarized from the moment of *ACO*'s release. More than one critic described the experience of watching its brutal beatings, rape, and a frenzied murder, all narrated with pleasure and panache by the chief perpetrator, as torture.[8] The film "clamps open" the viewer's eyes "to witness the horrors that Kubrick parades across the screen," one reviewer complained.[9] Her description played ironically on "the Ludovico Treatment," the mind-controlling aversion-therapy program to which the film's main character, Alex DeLarge, is subjected by government scientists to eradicate his criminal inclinations. Drugged and forced to watch violent film scenes, the once-cocky criminal is robbed of his will and driven mad. In spite of *ACO*'s capacity to disturb, however, many critics found merit in Kubrick's work, which won the New York Film Critics Awards for best director and picture in 1971 and earned four Academy Award nominations.[10]

Most studies of ACO trace its emergence as a cult object to its initial X-rated release. Reception studies of the film, led by Janet Staiger's benchmark analysis, were augmented by works that have analyzed the film's politicization in the United States and Great Britain.[11] Attempts to censor the film, as well as accusations that the fictional Alex's sadistic acts and sartorial style, had inspired real-life assaults, rapes, and murders convinced Kubrick that he had to edit out the film's most violent scenes to comply with R-rating film classification standards in the United States. In Britain, however, he responded to public outrage by pulling "the illicit citrus" from circulation.[12]

While film studies scholars have connected the film to these divisive 1970s debates concerning the effects of violence, its representation, and its regulation, *ACO*'s status as an antiauthoritarian text has been overlooked, despite Kubrick's explicit invitation to read it as such. The film presents the Ludovico Treatment unequivocally as torture, and it portrays Alex's reprogramming "therapy" as a greater crime than the depredations any criminal could commit, as the director and his lead actor claimed: "The violence done to Alex in the brain-washing sequence is in fact more horrifying than anything he does himself. . . . It was absolutely necessary to give weight to Alex's brutality, otherwise I think there would be moral confusion with respect to what the government does to him."[13]

But the film's casting choices, musical inventiveness, and cinematic experimentation made it a complex, multilayered text without crudely drawn lines between good and evil.[14] Some questioned the clarity of its message. Critics such as Pauline Kael accused *ACO* of moral ambiguity in presenting Alex as a charismatic force of nature—helped, in great measure, by the choice of Malcolm McDowell to play the lead. Yet some welcomed Kubrick's critique of the liberal state's capacity to justify rights violations, while observers beyond the film community saw a strong resemblance between the fictional Ludovico Treatment and real experiments then underway in penal and medical institutions.

The recrudescence of torture, authorized in the course of the global war on terror as a necessary "extraordinary measure" invites a reconsideration of *ACO* in a light sympathetic to Kubrick's declared message and preferred reading. To consider the film as art against torture is not nearly as perverse as it might seem, even if its depiction of state violence has generated little scholarly or fan-based attention. Nevertheless this line of inquiry faces two challenges. First, is it credible to interpret Alex's treatment in prison as torture? And second, what difference does it make to frame the film from this perspective at this historical juncture, almost forty years after its release? The first question can be answered legalistically, by measuring Alex's therapy against formal definitions of torture: both the United Nations Convention Against Torture and the U.S. penal code's statutory definition of torture, formally adopted in 1990, include mind- and personality-altering practices, such as the treatment inflicted on Alex in the film.[15] The second question is addressed in the final section of this chapter, which compares *ACO* to recent feature films and documentaries that condemn the use of torture against terrorism suspects. These texts are unambiguous exposés of injustice that use the stock character of the innocent victim to distinguish good from evil; as a result they avoid confronting the more vexing question of how to deal with the violent, morally repugnant terrorist. At a time when Jack Bauer, the fictional counterterrorism hero of the hit television show *24*, provides the answer for millions of viewers and a legion of fans, including at least one U.S. Supreme Court justice,[16] we await a film of *ACO*'s artistic caliber to condemn the use of torture on anyone, whether wicked or blameless, in the war on terror.

By combining textual analysis with an historicist perspective,[17] I approach *ACO*'s depiction of torture with three objectives: first, to situate the text in the context of the late 1960s and early 1970s, when concerns mounted over the penal-welfare complex, and when allegations of covert U.S. security experiments and operations involving torture emerged; second, to consider how the troubling use and legal justifications of state torture in the context of the war on terror reframe *ACO*'s possible readings; and third, to compare how recent documentary and feature films pose the same question about what sacrifices liberal democracies are prepared to make in the name of security.[18] Kubrick is dead, but *ACO* retains its capacity to speak in a new time of torture.

Text and Context

Stanley Kubrick earned his reputation as an auteur soon after his entry into feature films. In the 1950s he was something of a talented enfant terrible, drawn to subjects that pushed the viewing public's tolerance, particularly on questions of sex and politics. In *Lolita* and in the darkly satirical *Dr. Strangelove* two years later, his screenplay adaptations of novels combined stylized visual effects with verbal and musical humor targeting bourgeois hypocrisy and political chauvinism.[19] So in 1962, when Kubrick read Burgess's slim novel (what the *Times Literary Supplement* famously termed "a nasty little shocker"), he found it inspiring but focused on other projects.[20] By the time he turned to the novel's adaptation, his public stature had overshadowed Burgess's, and *ACO*'s filmic identity overtook its original form. Avant-garde cineastes eagerly anticipated Kubrick's latest work, wondering what might follow his war epics, westerns, sexual melodramas, political satires, and science fiction. Most who admired *ACO* were drawn to its artistry: "It is brilliant, a tour de force of extraordinary images, music, words and feelings, a much more original achievement for commercial films than the Burgess novel is for literature," Vincent Canby declared at its New York opening.[21] There were other admirers as well, more politically oriented, who read the film as Kubrick saw it—as a timely warning against authoritarianism.

ACO unfolds in three acts, with the first being the source of the censorship row. McDowell's voice-over narrates the opening scene, in which Alex DeLarge and his band of "droogs" sit in the bizarre Korova Milk Bar, preparing themselves for a night of mayhem by downing drafts of hallucinogenic drugs. McDowell is clearly older than Burgess's fifteen-year-old Alex, yet he convincingly portrays mindless juvenile rebelliousness and narcissism, with sex appeal that matched that of Mick Jagger, who was originally considered for the part. When Alex asks, "What's it going to be then, eh?" the answer is "a bit of ultraviolence." Kubrick retained Burgess's invented language of Nadsat, but by adding electronic musical counterpoint, plus low and wide-angle shots and extreme close-ups, he produced sensory disorientation, particularly in the scenes that follow Alex on his criminal adventures. The droogs taunt and beat an elderly drunk beggar, they clash with a rival gang, and they speed through the countryside to "HOME," a secluded house occupied by a writer and his wife. In the film's most notorious scene the gang kicks the man of the house down the stairs and rapes the woman, while Alex delivers a jubilant rendition of "Singin' in the Rain." His criminal thirst quenched he returns to his bleak estate where his parents—an infantile mother and a milquetoast father—greet him fearfully, willfully blind to their son's nightlife of brutality.

The crime that leads Alex to prison follows this orgy of violence. When they next meet he forces his droogs into committing a robbery at a health farm, and he beats and humiliates them along the way to remind them "who was master and leader." A frenzied cat-and-mouse encounter ensues as Alex, disguised in a grotesque mask and codpiece, circles his victim, a middle-aged woman whose house is filled with pornographic imagery, including a gigantic plastic phallus. Kubrick's quick cuts and handheld shots, overlayered with Rossini's *La Gazza Ladra* overture, bring the scene to a horrific climax, when Alex wields the phallus as a weapon and impales the woman. This murder and the earlier rape scene were cited in early feminist film criticism as paradigmatic celluloid misogyny.[22] Even now, its retro pop-art aesthetic retains the capacity to shock, since Kubrick presents sexual violence from the exuberant rapist and murderer's perspective without inducing sympathy for his victims.

The film's second half, which shifts to the state's violence toward Alex, has a contrasting sombre tone. Kubrick sets up the transition with flat lighting, dialogue delivered in conventional speech, and a style generally consistent with cinema verité and social realism, rather than the garish visuals and topsy-turvy stylizations of the opening act. There are aural cues as well, as silence abruptly follows after forty minutes of Wendy (then Walter) Carlos's synthesized music. The film encloses the audience, along with Alex, in a spare interrogation room—whitewashed walls, a scratched wooden table, and chairs. Police detectives try to beat a confession out of him, but the suspect remains cocky until his school guidance counselor, Mr. Deltoid, arrives. At this juncture cat turns into mouse as the blandest of social welfare bureaucrats, clad in a beige trench coat, toys with his prey. When Deltoid informs his "hard case" that he will face a murder charge, the camera slants down on Alex, closing in as he crouches in the corner. Alex nervously protests his innocence and fights back with a civil rights abuse accusation: "This must be some new form of torture: say it, brother, sir!" Deltoid holds his ground and defends such threats as character forming. He positively relishes the thought that Alex's crime might haunt him: "It will be your own torture. I hope to God it will torture you to madness!"

With this pivotal shift in point of view, Kubrick places the viewer in the position of the taunted suspect. The violence done to Alex, both physical and psychological, is depicted in real time, adding to the cinematic realism in the film's second act. Kubrick's camera tilts up toward Deltoid as the man spits in his hard case's face, and the detectives consider this an invitation to egg him on: "If you'd care to give him a bash in the chops, sir, don't mind us. We'll hold him down. He must be a great disappointment to you, sir." Deltoid calmly declines. He has accomplished his purpose and has taken his twisted pleasure, which requires no physical violence, only intimidation.

The young man's outrageous criminal behavior is a disappointment for the welfare state of which Deltoid is a chilling representative, and Alex's defiance becomes impotent.

ACO's prison chaplain, in contrast, is the voice of reason and humanity who questions the intent behind Alex's treatment at the hands of the state. Perhaps a remnant of Burgess's Catholicism, Kubrick's "Father" is the film's moral pole star, a believer in God, but more importantly, a believer in the necessity of "man" making his own moral choices. Initially, Alex is sentenced to fourteen years' imprisonment for the murder of the health-farm woman, and he encounters the chaplain in a classic nineteenth-century penitentiary—big, stark, and ruled by a sergeant major–style warder. Prisoner 655321 is stripped of his name, his bowler hat, his codpiece and carnivalesque makeup, then handed a drab uniform. The violence here is short and sharp but largely avoidable, so Alex tows the line, refashioning himself into a manipulative model prisoner in search of an early release. When the minister of the interior visits the prison to recruit volunteers for a new correctional program, Alex sees his chance. The smarmy politician announces the government's intention to incarcerate fewer ordinary criminals in order to free up prisons for the government's political enemies. The plan sounds simple: "Common criminals like these are best dealt with on a purely curative basis. Kill the criminal reflex, that's all." Suspicious that anything other than self-reflection and "trust in the Lord" can effect moral transformation, the chaplain warns Alex to resist the call for volunteers in the minister's experimental cure program: "The question is whether this technique *really* makes a man 'good.' Goodness comes from within. Goodness must be chosen. When a man can't choose, he ceases to be a man." But Alex has no appreciation for high-minded moral philosophy and no desire to be a man. All he wants is freedom.

In "the Torture Chair"

After the film's first act establishes Alex's capacity to harm by indulging his inclination toward violence, the second focuses on the harm produced in the name of doing social good. The chaplain is the voice of evangelical penal reform, the early nineteenth-century movement that regarded penitence as the cure for criminality and the key to salvation. By the 1970s this once-progressive discourse had acquired a quaint tone, and a dark one as well, in the eyes of postwar critics of liberal democracy. For Michel Foucault control of the criminal and fallen, not concern for their souls, instigated the historic shift from sovereign justice, with its public rituals of violence, to new disciplinary techniques reliant on hierarchical observation and the judgment of individuals against norms. Alex's transfer from penitentiary to medical center plays out like a scene from *Discipline and Punish*,[23] the book Foucault published in 1975 after a decade of fierce academic and political battles in France against authoritarianism. He traced the origins of the disciplinary society to the birth of the prison, "a laboratory; it could be used as a machine to carry out experiments, to alter behavior, to train or correct individuals. To experiment with medicines and monitor their effects."[24] As if springing to life from the pages of Foucault's book, the unsuspecting Alex, reclassified as the ward of a therapeutic correctional apparatus geared to normalize the deviant, is marched from the penitentiary yard to the adjoining clinic. Prisoner 655321 enters modern punishment's laboratory and becomes a docile body, subjected to a secret psychological and pharmaceutical experiment.[25]

The penitentiary's spit-and-polish male warder is replaced by the treatment center's medical expert—a middle-aged woman adorned with the white coat of scientific authority. The friendly Dr. Branom is reassuringly warm, and her maternal manner sooths Alex into compliance: "You're a very lucky boy to have been chosen," she murmurs as she slips a hypodermic needle into his vein. Once drugged he will watch some films, she tells him, and her promise elicits a childish response: "You mean like going to the pictures?" The infantilized Alex is vulnerable, and the viewer shares his suspense. What chemicals course in his veins? What films will he watch, and why?

In Kubrick's depiction of the Ludovico Treatment his "visionary warning against 'the Establishment'" finds its clearest image.[26] The drugged subject is led to a theater, empty save for Dr. Branom and her clinical partner, Dr. Brodsky, who sit up top in a control booth. Alone in the front row Alex is strapped in a seat, his head immobilized and eyelids clamped open so that he must watch everything before him, while electrodes attached to his scalp track his physiological responses. The results are encouraging: beatings and acts of sexual violence that once gave Alex pleasure have begun to produce the opposite effect. When he complains of pain and nausea Dr. Brodsky tells him his reaction is normal: "One of our early test subjects described it as being like death, a sense of stifling or drowning. And it is in this period, we have found, that the subject would make his most rewarding associations between his catastrophic experience of violence and the violence he sees." Under pressure from the government's expectation that "this vicious young hoodlum will be transformed beyond all recognition," the scientists are confident that they can deliver.

Alex faces a difficult choice: to remain in the program and become "a free man in a fortnight's time," or face his full sentence in the penitentiary. He decides to stay but soon regrets his choice. The second film he is made to watch features Nazi war atrocities, scored to his favorite piece, Beethoven's Ninth Symphony. When he realizes that "lovely Ludwig Van's" music has become tainted, along with the violence he once enjoyed, his initial distress turns to panic. Forced to listen as well as watch he sits in "the chair of torture" while the blasting music produces excruciating pain. The clinicians discover an unanticipated benefit: the symphonic track heightens Alex's anguish and doubles the expected curative effects. "The governor ought to be pleased," Dr. Brodsky smiles, as he turns up the volume.

The Ludovico Technique's efficacy is publicly demonstrated in the final scene of the second act, in which experts and bureaucrats are assembled to observe the cured criminal's conditioned responses. Subjected to two tests (a staged confrontation with a smart-mouthed man spoiling for a fight, and an encounter with a nearly naked woman, used to bait his rapacious urges) Alex is shown to be incapable of responding as he once did. He cannot make sense of his altered feelings: "The horrible killing sickness had whooshed up, and turned the like joy of battle into a feeling I was going to snuff it." The interior minister beams because the "young hoodlum" has become "as decent a lad as you would meet on a May morning." The prison chaplain is the only one who challenges the result. If Alex "ceases to be a wrongdoer," it is simply because he "ceases to be a creature capable of moral choice," acting only from a fear of pain. To the padre's ethical challenge the minister provides a utilitarian response: "We're not concerned with motives, with the higher ethics. We are concerned only with cutting down crime!" The experimental treatment is good because "it works."

In the remainder of the film, comprising the final thirty minutes, Alex is released only to find himself unwanted and out of place in his old world. His parents reject him, the tramp he thrashed in an earlier scene jumps him with a pack of beggars, and his former droogs, now clad in police uniforms, exact revenge on their former leader by beating and abandoning him. A desperate Alex, bleeding and bruised, stumbles back to the first sanctuary he finds, which turns out to be the "HOME" where he had committed his brutal crimes. But Alex has forgotten this and the wheelchair-bound owner, writer Frank Alexander, cannot recall the previously masked criminal.

Instead he recognizes Alex as the government's poster boy for its social control program. Alexander is all sympathy: "Are you not the victim of this new horrible technique?" he asks his guest. The host then launches into a textbook condemnation of behavior modification and the supposedly democratic government that authorizes it: "[A] debilitating and will-sapping technique of conditioning . . . oh, we've seen it all before in other countries. The thin end of the wedge. Before we know where we are we'll have the full apparatus of totalitarianism. . . . This young boy is a living witness to these diabolical proposals. The people, the common people, must know, must see. There are traditions of liberty to defend. That tradition is all." Because the liberal Alexander believes that the minister's law-and-order government has turned Alex into its fascistic political tool, he describes the Ludovico Treatment as abuse ill-befitting a democracy: "Tortured in prison, then to be sent out to be tortured by the police, my heart goes out to you, poor, poor boy."

But in an instant Alexander transforms from a sentimental liberal into an agent of sadistic retributive justice. Once he hears Alex reprise a rendition of "Singin' in the Rain," he recognizes the "vicious young hoodlum" who raped his wife and crippled him. Filled with rage and a surging desire to make the criminal suffer, Alexander plots his revenge. Rather than send Alex on his way or order his burly assistant to attack him, Alexander opts for an impromptu session of the Ludovico Technique. With Alex locked securely in a third-story room, Alexander plays a recording of Beethoven's Ninth Symphony at ear-splitting volume, knowing that the music will torture his prisoner. Alexander's no-touch technique works perfectly, forcing Alex to seek his escape by leaping from a third-story window.

In the final scenes the minister reappears, trying to save face after Alex's suicide attempt provokes inquiries into the secret experiment. The government, which had expected positive coverage of Alex's transformation, suddenly finds itself ducking reports of the debacle:

> Government Accused of Inhuman Means in Crime Reform—Boy Attempts Suicide
> Minister Is Accused of Inhuman Cure—Alex Driven to Suicide by Scientists
> Government Is Murderer—Doctors Charge as Alex Recovers
> Storm Over "Crime Cure" Boy—Doctors Blame Government Scientists for Changing Alex's Nature
> Alex's Death Bid Blamed on Brain Men—Minister Under Attack
> Treatment Torture . . . Brainwashing Responsible for . . .

Kubrick's rapid montage of accusatory headlines reinforces the Foucauldian and Szaszian insight: the clinic and the prison are interlocked in the modern welfare state. Experts, bureaucrats, and politicians are framed. None can escape blame.

The Ludovico Warning

By comparing the political concerns that drove Burgess and Kubrick in the 1960s and '70s to those that have emerged in light of reports of government-sanctioned torture in the war on terror, significant connections become apparent. In some ways much has changed. Human rights organizations and investigative journalists have subjected the mistreatment of detainees to greater scrutiny than those who tried in the 1970s to expose the use of torture by the CIA and U.S. troops.[27] And official justification of the use of torture, even in sanitized language, is more forthright now than it was in the days when it was touted as therapeutic for prisoners, or when its Cold War and Vietnam War applications were covered up. Yet there are surprising similarities as well. Disillusionment over the West's backslide toward torture in the fight against terrorism, as expressed by leading thinkers in publications such as the *Index on Censorship*,[28] parallels the distrust of the establishment that marked the 1970s.[29] Beginning at its radical and youth-based fringe, wariness of institutionalized power in government, military, and medical hands reached such mainstream venues as the *New York Times* and Congress around the time of *ACO*'s release. Peace activists and civil rights protestors were the most visible opponents of government-sanctioned violence, but criticism of its experimental and secret uses gained momentum as well by the mid-1970s. Disenchantment with the rule of law, far from a recent phenomenon, as Richard Sherwin claims,[30] was as much a mark of the era in which *ACO* was produced as it is a feature of the 2000s.

By presenting Deltoid, the representative of the social welfare state, as perhaps the film's cruelest character, Kubrick added his voice to a growing chorus of concern in the late 1960s and early '70s about correctional practices that coerced "cases" into compliance.[31] Welfarist approaches to criminality fell under a two-flanked attack: libertarians proposed radical new schemes based on social justice models of crime reduction and decarceration, while law-and-order advocates called for a return to deterrence. The reintroduction of the death penalty in the United States in 1976 (after a brief period of abeyance) and an ever-expanding carceral regime signaled that the search for security would ultimately trump the preservation of liberty in the so-called free world.[32] Youth violence rose in the 1950s and '60s, along with general rates of interpersonal violence in industrialized affluent societies, and the get-tough approach triumphed by the 1970s, leaving radical voices and provocative works of art, like *ACO*, to play a significant role in questioning abuses of state power.

When Richard Nixon won the presidency in 1968 by promising to govern on behalf of the "silent majority," his Cold War message comforted those who feared communists and troublemakers of all sorts, yet it deeply disturbed New Left and old-line libertarians who read his election as a shift to authoritarianism after the liberal reforms of the late 1950s and early 1960s. Experts in the medical profession, most prominently psychiatrist Thomas Szasz, began to campaign publicly about the abuse of pharmacological programming, shock therapy, and lobotomies, all justified as modern means to control misfits and others at the social margins. Within mainstream politics distrust of the government and willingness to question mounted as well, especially in the realm of foreign relations. By the mid-1970s Senate inquiries and CIA reviews were following up fragmentary evidence that the United States used torture, perfected with the assistance of university-based medical researchers and in contravention of the country's avowed adherence to the Geneva Conventions.[33] Burgess's book and Kubrick's film were products of that same moment, when left-leaning critics asked how torture could ever be justified, especially by the self-appointed leader of the free world. *ACO* was an artistic expression of a minority, though strongly held, view that governments that valued order over freedom risked sinking into totalitarianism.

Perhaps the most forthright acknowledgment of the film's redeeming qualities came from the British Board of Film Classifications in 1971. Although it imposed an X rating, the board's decision to allow circulation of *ACO* without cuts hinged on what it considered to be the film's *antiviolence* message: "Disturbed though we were by the first half of the film, which is basically a statement of some of the problems of violence, we were, nonetheless, satisfied by the end of the film that it could not be accused of exploitation: quite the contrary, it is a valuable contribution to the whole debate about violence."[34]

Pauline Kael was no fan of the film but she accurately summed up its content: "For most of the film we see [Alex] tortured and beaten and humiliated."[35] Nevertheless she denied that *ACO* could serve any moral purpose, since McDowell masterfully portrayed the charming criminal and since Kubrick presented him in a far more appealing light than either his victims or his captors. Her moral doubt raises critical aesthetic and ethical questions: Do sympathetic depictions of tortured perpetrators endorse their actions? Is victimhood necessarily a zero-sum proposition?

While most reviewers in the early 1970s believed the film inured viewers to violence (one likened it to battle-conditioning films), some intellectuals and artists agreed that it raised worthwhile questions about violent state practices, including those that were touted as therapeutic. Evidence of mind manipulation was not hidden but openly proclaimed at conferences and in academic publications.[36] *ACO* was not the only contemporary artistic work to express concern over science's capacity to program human behavior. In 1962, the same year Burgess published his novel, Ken Keasey published *One Flew Over the Cuckoo's Nest*,[37] made into a feature film in 1975. Both works presented pharmacologically and surgically designed conformity as a dangerous assault on individual liberty and free will. Jeffrie G. Murphy, philosopher and critic of the penal-welfare complex, concurred from a Kantian point of view. Punishing an offender for doing wrong is dignified, he argued, because it respects the individual and "leaves one's status as a moral person intact." With psychological or pharmacological therapy, in contrast, "one here gets not what one deserves but, rather, what one (in some paternalistic sense) needs—perhaps a total restructuring of one's personality." Writing six months after *ACO* was released, Murphy cited Keysey's novel and Kubrick's film as significant artistic expressions of the same argument.[38]

Chemical and surgical interventions to alter personalities were not just fantasy-film fodder when *ACO* was released. Some experts, such as the scientists who met at a "behaviour control conference on physical manipulation of the brain" shortly after the film's release likened the Ludovico Treatment to the new scientific techniques used to control the deviant, the criminal, and the mentally ill.[39] A debate flared up in *Science News* in 1972 over penal and medical experiments similar to those portrayed in *ACO*, and Kubrick could have inserted the title of one article, "A Clockwork Orange in a California Prison," and its subheading into his montage of Ludovico exposé headlines: "Ethical debate is brewing over recently revealed experimental brain surgery on prisoners and a possible resurgence in the use of lobotomy and psychosurgery to control violent persons."[40] The report revealed the wide range of experimental brain research programs then underway in the United States. Some were designed to relieve pain and anxiety, but many experiments funded by the Department of Justice were undertaken to reduce prison populations. These programs were staged with negligible ethical guidelines, and treatments like Alex's were frequently imposed without prisoners' consent or full knowledge.[41] Outspoken critics within the field of neuroscience worried that too little was known about the brain to meddle with it. And worse, to some it seemed that state-funded psychological and pharmacological research was "leading to a technologic totalitarianism of the future."[42]

In the 1970s the use of psychosurgery and shock therapy garnered the greatest criticism from within the psychiatric and legal professions, but less invasive means of behavior modification began to fall into disrepute as well.[43] Yale scientist José M. R. Delgado, author of *Physical Manipulation of the Brain*,[44] was well funded for his experimental research that involved "implanting electrodes to stimulate various pleasure (and pain) centers in the brain" until his support suddenly dried up in 1973.[45] The National Institute of Health pulled Delgado's funding, a policy change that had been sparked, Delgado complained, by baseless fears that his treatment "could introduce the nightmare of mass control over man, overriding and overpowering individual self-determination."[46]

ACO was not responsible for cutting support for such programs, since well-publicized court cases on the use of psychosurgery, chemical castration, and abusive shock treatment both preceded and followed its release.[47] But the film touched a growing current of concern that brainwashing, conditioning, and chemical and surgical alterations were not just the weapons of Soviet agents or Vietcong insurgents: they were tools used by liberal democracies searching for new scientific means to impose order within and to fight foreign agents without. Even the Senate began to follow up allegations that CIA operations and experiments had involved the use of torture, and mainstream media, including the *New York Times*, published the little information the agency was prepared to divulge in the early 1970s.[48] In this sense *ACO*'s notoriety accomplished at least as much or more than Congress to encourage vigilance over the collusion between science and the security-seeking state.[49] When the *Times* education editor accused Kubrick of presenting humanity as inherently evil, and thus in need of control imposed by a police state, the director shot back: "So far from advocating that fascism be given a second chance, [my film] warns against the new psychedelic fascism."[50]

ACO presented a nightmarish vision of a possible future, when torture might become a tool of liberal democratic rule, and it combined that projection with an awareness of the darkest moments in recent history.

Kubrick liked to quote a Catholic film reviewer who endorsed *ACO* and referred to the Ludovico Treatment as precisely "the sort of weapon that totalitarians in state, church or society might wish for an easier good, even at the cost of individual rights and dignity."[51] *ACO* dramatized the harm caused by techniques whose rationale, as the minister of the interior and the Ludovico doctors confirmed, was socially beneficial; more profoundly, it challenged the use of torture against any individual, on any grounds.

Awaiting a New Kubrick?

In Britain, where *ACO* was rereleased in 1999, almost thirty years after Kubrick restricted its circulation, its reappearance led, not surprisingly, to a new round of discussions about the film's place in the history of sexual violence, obscenity, and censorship.[52] This angle of analysis did not incorporate *ACO*'s capacity to raise important questions about the potential abuses of state power at a time when torture has become a counterterrorism tactic in countries avowedly committed to respecting human rights. The world-shifting events of 2001 and the subsequent war on terror have transformed the film's possible readings, lending it fresh currency in public debates about torture's recrudescence.

Films, like all texts, have the potential to assume a variety of meanings in distinct historical moments, and this is especially true of controversial works of art.[53] Like a notorious criminal case, a film of *ACO*'s notoriety can be read for the ways in which it exposes the "shared, conflicted and newly emerging beliefs, values and expectations" of its time.[54] One way to trace meaning-making shifts is to examine remakes of films, such as J. Lee Thompson's *Cape Fear*,[55] updated in 1991 by Martin Scorcese;[56] another is to move from one historical moment to another, comparing films that explore similar themes. This latter strategy, applied to films critical of torture in liberal democratic states, reveals that recent major films follow considerably more conventional narratives of injustice than Kubrick explored forty years ago.

New viewers of *ACO* and old reviewers inevitably see a different film than the one that screened in the early 1970s. As literary theorist Stuart McDougal argued in 2003, "For many viewers, the incarceration and treatment of Alex by the state constitute the most dangerous violence in the film."[57] This interpretation has become more plausible in light of recent investigations into prisoner abuse, some of them involving explorations of official memoranda and hidden reports. Journalists have probed into the political authorization of detainee abuses and have traced how legal, medical, and psychiatric experts have justified various forms of torture as extraordinary but necessary measures.[58] If Kubrick's critics were correct to accuse him of having it both ways, creating a stylish sociopath whose treatment by the state is morally repugnant, then *ACO* is a model of moral clarity compared to the statements of White House lawyers and psychiatrists, who have tiptoed around the "t-word." Does placing individuals in stress positions or hooding or waterboarding them constitute torture? Government-appointed legal experts hired to advise federal authorities obediently replied in the negative. Their Orwellian memos on the matter gave the Bush White House what it wanted: definitions of enhanced interrogation practices that twisted the strict legal definition of torture.[59] Despite the production of documents that have proved executive endorsement of torture against terror suspects, it appears that none of the torture apologists will be held accountable.[60] In Peter Brooks's opinion these legal advisors' justificatory memos are masterpieces of arbitrary or "phony" interpretation that have corrupted "plain meaning." Against this venal casuistry, he pleads, the humanistic tradition of "responsible reading" has a critical role to play.[61] Art plays a role as well, but creative works inevitably inspire multiple readings, especially when they experiment in style and form and challenge audiences to question, rather than provide clear moral resolutions.

Recent feature films and documentaries have condemned this moral drift by depicting the stories of torture's innocent victims.[62] New images of a new war tell an old and uncontroversial moral tale: innocent people do not deserve to face punishment. Filmmakers, particularly producers of feature films, have far greater license than investigative journalists, Congressional questioners, or Amnesty International spokespeople to dramatize the brutality of interrogators and the dehumanization of detainees, and Michael Winterbottom and Matt Whitecross used that license liberally in *The Road to Guantánamo*.[63] A standout example of experimentation, it mixes documentary footage, reenactments, and dramatizations in a hybrid "factional" form. The film pits President Bush's famous 2003 claim about terror detainees ("The only thing I know for certain is that these are bad people") against the testimony of the "Tipton Three," a trio of young British Muslim men detained for two years and released without charge. Although several reviewers criticized the film for allowing the detainees' accounts of events to go unchallenged, and for reinforcing their claims by intercutting testimony with harrowing portrayals of their torture, *The Road* won the Silver Bear Award for direction, and its reception has been overwhelmingly positive.

As much an "innocents abroad" film as an indictment of state-authorized torture—in it carefree lads from the Midlands knocking about in Pakistan are wrongly imprisoned for their alleged terrorist links—it manages to condemn interrogators and guards by encouraging the viewer to identify with young, smart-mouthed Muslims. This is what America, the standard bearer of freedom, has sunk to: painful and degrading abuse. What's worse, these captives could be you or me—innocents.

Less experimental post–September 11 political thrillers and truth-seeking documentaries have produced liberal moral outrage by conforming to the category of "film as judgment."[64] Following a linear narrative technique *Rendition*,[65] starring a roster of Academy Award and BAFTA winners, is based on the experience of Khalid El-Mazri, who was tortured as the result of an identity mix up that began with a spelling error on a CIA report. Critic Roger Ebert (who denounced *ACO* in 1972 because it "pretends to oppose the police state and forced mind control, but all it really does is celebrate the nastiness of its hero, Alex") described *Rendition* as "valuable and rare . . . a movie about the theory and practice of two things: torture and personal responsibility. And it is wise about what is right, and what is wrong."[66] In contrast documentary filmmaker Alex Gibney's *Taxi to the Dark Side*[67] uses no stars and relies on conventional documentary techniques to uncover the truth and to expose the injustice of torture. Again we encounter the "innocent citizen," a taxi driver who is killed while in American custody at Bagram Air Force Base in 2002, as the victim/hero. Like *The Road to Guantánamo*, this film's condemnation of America's use of torture in its detention and interrogation policies is unmistakable, and approval of *Taxi*'s moral stance, at least in the professional film community, earned it the Academy Award for Best Documentary Feature in 2007 along with the New York Film Critics Award the same year. These recently lauded films position the filmmaker as judge and constitute the audience as jury, encouraging the viewing public to condemn democracies willing to abrogate human rights in the name of order and security. They do not, however, ask the audience to consider how rightfully accused terrorists ought to be interrogated.

Kubrick rejected the wrongfully accused, wrongly punished narrative formula on which recent "wise and right" films depend for their critical and popular appeal. *ACO* certainly sanitised Burgess's Alex, as many critics have noted, and feminist criticism of the film's misogynistic viewpoint is unassailable. Yet the film makes no secret of Alex's criminality and it does not absolve him of responsibility with welfare-speak. *ACO* took a far bolder stance, anchored in the period's disillusionment with liberalism's limits, to criticise the welfare state's preparedness to violate the rights of the guilty in the name of the greater good. Even "bad art," Iris Murdoch argues, serves a noble purpose when it addresses the immorality of "terrible human fates," among which is torture.[68]

ACO takes on a new valence as the balance between fear and security tips in response to a different era's real and imagined threats. Kubrick's 1971 artwork now circulates in DVD format, fictional portrayals of torture in film and television inspire interrogators,[69] and Web sites provide images (of beheadings, for instance) that far exceed the repulsiveness of the Ludovico Treatment. When *ACO* was rereleased in 1999 in Britain, the guardians of morality failed to rally against the film, and a new wave of droog-inspired crimes never appeared. In this new mediascape sexually violent material that would have received an X rating in 1971 shows on free-to-air television, while the video game market has stymied efforts to police who gets to see what.[70] The sex wars of the 1970s and '80s have subsided, and feminist criticism of pornography and sexually violent imagery has become fragmented and marginal. In contrast a new generation of medical and legal experts, most famously law professor Alan Dershowitz, followed by the infamous drafters of torture memos, have formulated ways to legalize torture, while leading liberals, notably Michael Ignatieff, stand accused of becoming apologists for lesser evils perpetrated in the fight against terrorism, this epoch's great evil.[71] Film texts, alongside investigative journalism and human rights workers, may play as great a role as lawmakers in questioning the conduct of coalition partners in the war on terror, but they do not need to be new films or remakes to do so. *ACO* continues to be shown at Kubrick and McDowell retrospective film festivals, and the film still asks, in regard to torture, "What's it going to be, then, eh?"

NOTES

An earlier version of this chapter appeared as "Stanley Kubrick's *A Clockwork Orange* as Art Against Torture" in *Crime Media Culture* 6, no. 3 (December 2010): 267–84; reprinted with permission.

1. Anthony Burgess, *A Clockwork Orange* (New York: Norton, 1962).
2. Stephen Prince, *Savage Cinema: Sam Peckinpah and the Rise of Ultraviolent Movies* (Austin: University of Texas Press, 1998); J. David Slocum, "Violence and American Cinema: Notes for an Introduction," in *Violence and American Cinema* (New York: Routledge, 2001).

3. Garth Jowett, *Film—The Democratic Art: Social History of American Film* (Oxford: Focal Press, 1976).
4. *Midnight Cowboy*, directed by John Schlesinger (Los Angeles: United Artists, 1969); *Medium Cool*, directed by Haskell Wexler (Los Angeles: Paramount Pictures, 1969); *Bob and Carol and Ted and Alice*, directed by Paul Mazursky (Culver City, Calif.: Columbia Pictures Television, 1969).
5. *2001: A Space Odyssey*, directed by Stanley Kubrick (Burbank, Calif.: Warner Bros., 1968).
6. *A Clockwork Orange*, directed by Stanley Kubrick (Burbank, Calif.: Warner Bros., 1971).
7. *Dirty Harry*, directed by Don Siegel (Burbank, Calif.: Warner Bros., 1971); *The French Connection*, directed by William Friedkin (Los Angeles: Twentieth Century Fox, 1971); *Straw Dogs*, directed by Sam Peckinpah (Culver City, Calif.: Screen Gems, 1971).
8. Pauline Kael, "Stanley Strangelove," *New Yorker*, January 1, 1972, 50–53.
9. Susan Rice, "Stanley Klockwork's 'Cubrick Orange,'" *Media and Methods* 8, no. 7 (1972): 39.
10. Kubrick's nominations were for best picture, best director, best adapted screenplay, and best editing.
11. Janet Staiger, *Perverse Spectators: The Practices of Film Reception* (New York: New York University Press, 2000); Susan Carruthers, "Past Future: The Troubled History of Stanley Kubrick's *A Clockwork Orange*," *National Forum: Phi Kappa Phi Journal* 81 (2001): 29–34; Stuart Y. McDougal, *Stanley Kubrick's "A Clockwork Orange"* (Cambridge: Cambridge University Press, 2003).
12. Carruthers, "Past Future," 29–34.
13. Philip Strick and Penelope Houston, "Modern Times: An Interview with Stanley Kubrick," *Sight and Sound* 42, no. 2 (1972): 44–46.
14. Orit Kamir, "Why 'Law-and-Film' and What Does It Actually Mean? A Perspective," *Continuum: Journal of Media and Cultural Studies* 19 (2005): 255–78.
15. The U.S. penal code defines torture, among other things, as: "(1) . . . an act committed by a person acting under the color of law specifically intended to inflict severe physical or mental pain or suffering (other than pain or suffering incidental to lawful sanctions) upon another person within his custody or physical control; (2) 'severe mental pain or suffering' means the prolonged mental harm caused by or resulting from—(A) the intentional infliction or threatened infliction of severe physical pain or suffering; and (B) the administration or application, or threatened administration or application, of mind-altering substances or other procedures calculated to disrupt profoundly the senses or the personality."
16. Jane Mayer, "Whatever It Takes: The Politics of the Man Behind *24*," *New Yorker*, February 19, 2007, http://www.newyorker.com/reporting/2007/02/19/070219fa_fact_mayer (accessed December 12, 2009); Scott Horton, "Nino Scalia: Holly-

wood's Justice," *Harper's Magazine*, June 2007, http://www.harpers.org/archive/2007/06/hbc-90000302 (accessed March 20, 2010).
17. Harold Aram Veeser, ed., *The New Historicism* (London: Routledge, 1989).
18. Alfred W. McCoy, *A Question of Torture: CIA Interrogation, from the Cold War to the War on Terror* (New York: Holt, 2006); Jane Mayer, *The Dark Side: The Inside Story of How the War on Terror Turned Into a War on American Ideals* (New York: Doubleday, 2007).
19. *Lolita*, directed by Stanley Kubrick (New York: Samuel Goldwyn, 1962); *Dr. Strangelove or: How I Learned to Stop Worrying and Love the Bomb*, directed by Stanley Kubrick (Culver City, Calif.: Columbia Pictures, 1964). On Kubrick's auteur signature effects in *ACO*, see Thomas Allen Nelson, *Kubrick: Inside a Film Artist's Maze* (Bloomington: Indiana University Press, 1983), 142–43.
20. Blake Morrison, introduction to *A Clockwork Orange*, by Anthony Burgess (London: Penguin, 1996), vii–xxiii; Carruthers, "Past Future," 29–34.
21. Vincent Canby, "*A Clockwork Orange* Dazzles the Senses and Mind," *New York Times*, December 20, 1971, http://movies.nytimes.com/movie/review?res=9A02E1D61038EF34BC4851DFB467838A669EDE (accessed December 12, 2009).
22. Beverly Walker, "From Novel to Film: Kubrick's *A Clockwork Orange*," *Women and Film* 2 (1972): 4–10; Joan Mellen, *Women and Their Sexuality in the New Film* (New York: Horizon, 1973); Marjorie Rosen, *Popcorn Venus: Women, Movies and the American Dream* (London: Avon Books, 1973); Molly Haskell, *From Reverence to Rape: The Treatment of Women in the Movies (Chicago: University of Chicago Press, 1974)*.
23. Michel Foucault, *Discipline and Punish: The Birth of the Prison*, trans. Alan Sheridan (New York: Vintage, 1995).
24. Ibid., 203.
25. Pat J. Gehrke, "Deviant Subjects in Foucault and *A Clockwork Orange*: Congruent Critiques of Criminological Constructions of Subjectivity," in *Depth of Field: Stanley Kubrick, Film, and the Uses of History*, ed. Geoffrey Cocks, James Diedrick, and Glenn Perusek (Madison: University of Wisconsin Press, 2006).
26. Kael, "Stanley Strangelove," 50–53.
27. McCoy, *A Question of Torture*.
28. In February 2005 criminologist Stanley Cohen guest edited an edition of *Index on Censorship* in which Conor Gearty, professor of human rights law at the London School of Economics, contributed an essay that accused Michael Ignatieff of having become a liberal apologist for "Rumsfeldians" actually willing to implement torture. Ignatieff resigned from the editorial board rather than responding. In 2008 Igantieff became leader of the Liberal Party of Canada and leader of the opposition.
29. Laurie Taylor, "No More Mr. Nice Guy: Laurie Taylor on Mr. Ignatieff," *New Humanist* 120 (2005): 5, http://newhumanist.org.uk/1299/no-more-mr-nice-guy-laurie-taylor-on-michael-ignatieff (accessed March 20 2010).

30. R. K. Sherwin, *When Law Goes Pop: The Vanishing Line Between Law and Popular Culture* (Chicago: University of Chicago Press, 2000).
31. Jeffry Heller and John Kiraly Jr., "Behavior Modification: A Classroom Clockwork Orange?" *Elementary School Journal* 74 (1974): 196–202.
32. David Garland, *Punishment and Welfare: A History of Penal Strategies* (Aldershot, UK: Ashgate, 1985).
33. Alfred W. McCoy, "Cruel Science: C.I.A. Torture and U.S. Foreign Policy," *New England Journal of Public Policy* 19 (2004): 209–62.
34. British Board of Film Classification secretary Stephen Murphy, quoted in James C. Robertson, *The Hidden Cinema: British Film Censorship in Action, 1913–72* (London: Routledge, 1993), 147.
35. Kael, "Stanley Strangelove," 51.
36. A. D. Biderman and H. Zimmer, *The Manipulation of Human Behavior* (New York: Wiley, 1961); Christopher Simpson, *Science of Coercion: Communication Research and Psychological Warfare* (Boston: Unwin Hyman, 1994).
37. Ken Keasey, *One Flew Over the Cuckoo's Nest* (New York: Signet, 1963).
38. Jeffrie G. Murphy, "Moral Death: A Kantian Essay on Psychopathy," *Ethics* 82, no. 4 (1972): 291.
39. Bruce Hilton, "Mind Manipulation," *Hasting's Center Report* 2, no. 1 (1972): 11.
40. Robert J. Trotter, "*A Clockwork Orange* in a California Prison," *Science News* 101 (1972): 174.
41. Hilton, "Mind Manipulation," 11.
42. Trotter used this quote from the work of Washington, D.C., psychiatrist Peter R. Breggin, author of "The Return of Lobotomy and Psychosurgery," unpublished at the time of Trotter's *Science News* article. Trotter, "*A Clockwork Orange* in a California Prison," 174–75.
43. James J. Gobert, "Psychosurgery, Conditioning, and the Prisoner's Right to Refuse 'Rehabilitation,'" *Virginia Law Review* 61 (1975): 155–96.
44. José M. R. Delgado, *Physical Manipulation of the Brain* (New York: Hastings Center 1973).
45. Trotter, "*A Clockwork Orange* in a California Prison," 175.
46. Robert J. Trotter, "A Shocking Story," *Science News* 105, no. 15 (1974): 245.
47. Simpson, *Science of Coercion*, 1994; Roy G. Spece, "Note, Conditioning and Other Technologies Used to 'Treat?' 'Rehabilitate?' 'Demolish?' Prisoners and Mental Patients," *Southern California Law Review* 45 (1972): 616–84.
48. J. Marks, *The Search for the "Manchurian Candidate": The CIA and Mind Control* (New York: Times Books, 1979); McCoy, "Cruel Science," 209–62.
49. Stephen Farber, "The Old Ultra-Violence," *Hudson Review* 25, no. 2 (1972): 287–94.
50. Stanley Kubrick, "Kubrick Fights Back," *New York Times*, February 27, 1972, Section 2, 1, 11.
51. Ibid.
52. McDougal, *Stanley Kubrick's "A Clockwork Orange."*

53. Staiger, *Perverse Spectators*, 95.
54. Sherwin, "When Law Goes Pop," 171.
55. *Cape Fear*, directed by J. Lee Thompson, (Universal City, Calif.: Universal, 1962).
56. Gerald Thain, "Cape Fear—Two Versions and Two Visions Separated by Thirty Years," Journal of Law and Society 28 (2001): 40–46.
57. McDougal, *Stanley Kubrick's "A Clockwork Orange,"* 6.
58. Carolyn Strange, "The 'Shock' Over Torture: An Historiographical Challenge," History Workshop Journal 61 (2006): 135–52; Mayer, *The Dark Side*.
59. Karen J. Greenberg and Joshua L. Dratel, eds., *The Torture Papers: The Road to Abu Ghraib* (New York: Cambridge University Press, 2005). Boalt Law Professor John Yoo prepared exculpatory memos for the Office of Legal Counsel. See in particular Jay S. Bybee (assistant attorney general, Office of Legal Counsel) to William J. Haynes II (general counsel, Department of Defense), "The President's Power as Commander in Chief to Transfer Captured Terrorists to the Control and Custody of Foreign Nations," memorandum, March 13, 2002, and to Alberto R. Gonzales (counsel to the president), "Standards of Conduct for Interrogation under 18 U.S.C. §§ 2340–2340A," memorandum, August 1, 2002.
60. Dahlia Lithwick, "Torture Bored: How We've Erased the Legal Lines Around Torture and Replaced Them with Nothing," *Slate*, February 22, 2010, http://www.slate.com/id/2243737 (accessed March 1, 2010); Mayer, *The Dark Side*; McCoy, *A Question of Torture*.
61. Peter Brooks, "The Humanities as an Export Commodity," *Profession* 7 (2008): 33–39. I am grateful to Russell Smith for drawing my attention to this source.
62. Critical representations of torture have been slower to make their way into popular television series. See Human Rights First's list of programs that question torture, "Primetime Torture," http://www.humanrightsfirst.org/us_law/etn/primetime/index.asp (accessed July 15 2009).
63. *The Road to Guantánamo*, directed by Michael Winterbottom and Mat Whitecross (Los Angeles: Roadside Attractions, 2006).
64. Kamir, "Why 'Law-and-Film' and What Does It Actually Mean?" 255–78.
65. *Rendition*, directed by Gavin Hood (Los Angeles: New Line Cinema, 2007).
66. Roger Ebert, review of *A Clockwork Orange*, Warner Bros., *Chicago Sun Times*, February 11, 1972, http://rogerebert.suntimes.com/apps/pbcs.dll/article?AID=/19720211/REVIEWS/202110301/1023 (accessed May 17, 2009), and review of *Rendition*, New Line Cinema, *Chicago Sun Times*, October 19, 2007, http://rogerebert.suntimes.com/apps/pbcs.dll/article?AID=/20071018/REVIEWS/710180307 (accessed December 20, 2009).
67. *Taxi to the Dark Side*, directed by Alex Gibney (New York: ThinkFilm, 2007).
68. Iris Murdoch, *Guide to the Metaphysics of Morals* (New York: Allen Lane, 1992), 93.
69. Mayer, "Whatever It Takes."
70. Steven Vaughan, *Freedom and Entertainment: Rating the Movies in an Age of New Media* (Cambridge: Cambridge University Press, 2006).

71. Conor Gearty, "With a Little Help From Our Friends: Torture Is Wrong and Ineffective So Why Is It Making a Comeback?" *Index on Censorship* 34 (2005): 46–53. Kenneth Roth, executive director of Human Rights Watch, has defended Ignatieff against the charges; however, he adds: "I myself would not always agree with the lines that Ignatieff draws." David Usborne, "Michael Ignatieff: Under Siege," *Independent*, January 21, 2006, http://www.independent.co.uk/news/people/profiles/michael-ignatieff-under-siege-523915.html (accessed May 15, 2010).

FURTHER READING

Burgess, Jackson. Review of *A Clockwork Orange*, Warner Bros. *Film Quarterly* 25, no. 3 (Spring 1972): 33–6.

Cockburn, Alexander and Jeffrey St. Clair. *Whiteout: The CIA, Drugs, and the Press*. New York: Verso, 1988.

Danner, Mark. "Torture and Truth: America, Abu Ghraib, and the War on Terror." *New York Review of Books*, June 2004. http://www.nybooks.com/articles/17150 (accessed December 12 2009).

Hechinger, Fred M. "A Liberal Fights Back." *New York Times*, February 13, 1972.

Johnson, Rebecca and Ruth Buchanan. "Getting the Insider's Story Out: What Popular Film Can Tell Us About Legal Method's Dirty Secrets." *Windsor Yearbook of Access to Justice* 20 (2001): 87–110.

Jowett, Garth. "'A Significant Medium for the Communication of Ideas': The *Miracle* Decision and the Decline of Motion Picture Censorship, 1952–1968." In *Movie Censorship and American Culture*, edited by Frances G. Covares, 258–76. Boston: University of Massachusetts Press, 2006.

Roszak, Theodore. *The Making of a Counter-Culture*. Garden City: Doubleday, 1969.

PART III

Confronting the Legacies of Torture and State Terror

Zulu Love Letter, 2004

8

"Accorded a Place in the Design"
TORTURE IN POSTAPARTHEID CINEMA
Elizabeth Swanson Goldberg

To discuss torture as it is represented in postapartheid South African films or in U.S. films about South Africa means discussing the South African Truth and Reconciliation Commission (TRC), for the TRC is the elephant in the living room of testimony, an obstacle to the process of remaking South African society after the devastation wrought by apartheid and by colonialism before it. This chapter, then, must grapple with the TRC in the process of considering the representation of torture in postapartheid South African cultural production, as well as in U.S. movies made after the era of protest/solidarity films such as *Cry Freedom* (1987), *Cry the Beloved Country* (1952, 1995), *A Dry White Season* (1989), and *Sarafina* (1992). In spite of its de rigueur address to the monumental testimonial spectacle, however, this chapter is not about the TRC; rather it is about torture, about tracking the path of torture's destruction as it snakes through all aspects of South African life—family, work, media, community, culture, economics, politics—and as it is picked up and illuminated in the cinematic stories circulated in and outside of South Africa, set during and after the apartheid era.

The fact that it is impossible to consider the brutality of the apartheid regime or the shape of postapartheid society without explicitly referencing the TRC is constitutive of the most forceful critiques of that endeavor. The TRC's status as the first act of the Interim Constitution, mandated at the highest levels of the new government as the vehicle for nationbuilding and the prevention of civil war, meant that it was incorporated as something like a monopoly, gobbling up or closing out competitors in the form of community-based, grass-roots, nongovernmental groups (not to mention alternative visions of justice, including redistributive and retributive ones), and asserting its mode of truth-telling and testimony, healing and conciliation, and an acceptance that in some cases neither of these were, nor would be, forthcoming.[1]

To discuss representations of torture in postapartheid film also necessitates a return to J. M. Coetzee's important essay "Into the Dark Chamber: The Writer and the South African State,"[2] which poses urgent questions attending the representation of that "extreme human experience" in the specific context of South African apartheid and that have much broader implications (ibid., 363). No romantic, Coetzee; he acknowledged nearly a decade before the transition to democracy that "revolution will put an end neither to cruelty and suffering, nor perhaps even to torture" (ibid., 365). The crux of Coetzee's argument is not its examination of the ethical problems of representing torture (the eroticization of pain, the spectacularization of violence, the appropriation of others' experiences and voices), but rather in the claim that the writer (or, for our purposes here, the filmmaker) who would try to represent torture is irreparably aligned with the state that tortures. A careful reading of the essay reminds us that it is precisely the nature of the TRC as part of a state apparatus—new as it may have been—that potentially compromises its standing as a forum for healing and restoring the dignity of those most harmed by the apartheid system.[3] In turn this understanding of the situated sanctioning of the TRC sheds light on the differential treatment it receives in postapartheid films made in South Africa and in the United States, respectively. A study of strategies for representing torture in postapartheid South African films such as *Forgiveness* and *Zulu Love Letter*, in comparison with U.S. films such as *In My Country*, *Catch a Fire*, and the documentary *Long Night's Journey Into Day*, must apprehend why U.S. films consistently focus on the TRC as a spectacular (in both senses of the word) vehicle for redemption, forgiveness, and (re)conciliation, while South African films often tell stories of post-apartheid working through in the shadows of the TRC, outside the circle of light cast by international media attention and inside other individual or communal spaces: the home, the workplace, schools, and burial grounds and other sacred memorial spaces.

There Is No Outside: The TRC and the State

Coetzee's "Into the Dark Chamber" ruminates on the ethics of representing torture, essentially posing the question, "To represent or not to represent?" In response to the problem of representing the "pornographic" enterprise of torture, Coetzee identifies two options, each with its own hazards: first, represent torture as a means of protesting it, and fall prey to reproducing the terror designed by the state to repress its other(s), and second, choose *not* to represent torture, also as an act of protest, and risk silence and complicity with its institutional practice. "For the writer the deeper problem is *not* to allow himself to be impaled on the dilemma proposed by the state, namely either to ignore its obscenities or else to produce representations of them. The true challenge is: how not to play the game by the rules of the state, how to establish one's own authority, how to imagine torture and death on one's own terms" (Coetzee, "Into the Dark Chamber," 366).

Coetzee's essay concludes somewhat ambiguously by asserting that the writer's dilemma will be resolved when "humanity will be restored across the face of society, and therefore when all human acts will be returned to the ambit of moral judgment" (ibid., 368). How this restoration of humanity within the structures of society will occur is left open—but as noted above, Coetzee retains no illusions that it will manifest through political revolution. The question for Coetzee, then, is not how to bring about a utopian end to the use of torture, but rather how to reposition torture as an act situated within the sphere of moral judgment from which it had been wrenched by the apartheid government, with its state apparatus as perpetrator and its judiciary providing elaborate legal justifications for such practices.

Given this emphasis, one might be forgiven for imagining that, according to Coetzee's argument, the TRC could be the vehicle par excellence for just such a restoration of humanity, just such a return of state-sanctioned torture and cruelty to the arena of moral judgment. With its quasi-religious, quasi-juridical status the TRC combined the three great sources of social authority—the state, the law, and the church—in setting forth its mandate: "The Constitution states that there is a need for understanding but not for vengeance, a need for reparation but not for retaliation, a need for *ubuntu* but not for victimization."[4]

Its purpose, then, was to hold the brutal truths of the past up for public scrutiny and to pass not only legal but also moral judgment on those truths without regard for the racial or gendered identities of perpetrators, victims, survivors, and bystanders. In this context that meant neutralizing the charges of any of the former moral universes inhering in the dark matter of the apartheid state: the "morality" of the South African police, or "Third Force," enforcing the law of the land, fighting the threats of "terrorism" and "communism" in the names of capitalism, democracy, and Christianity;[5]

the morality of the freedom fighter struggling against the total oppression and brutality that was apartheid.[6]

In spite of its moral weight, resting on the outsized shoulders of Nelson Mandela and Desmond Tutu, and in spite of its laudable and innovative ethical goals, the TRC, now twelve years on from its *Final Report*, arguably failed to meet its extremely ambitious goals, not only the "restoration of humanity across society" via "the return of all human acts to the ambit of moral judgment," but also the generation of a healing force capable of carrying an authentic conciliation past its borders of place and time (1996–1998) and into the fabric of the new South Africa. While there is a great deal to be said for the achievements of the TRC—not least its status as an international model for postconflict resolution capable of forestalling the worst-case scenario, which is civil war—most assessments by scholars, activists, and even survivors resonate with the conclusion drawn by Kay Schaffer and Sidonie Smith that, "despite its valiant attempts at reconciliation, in the end the TRC could not manage all the uncertainties that lay ahead in the journey toward social, economic, and political reconstruction."[7] As Schaffer and Smith's evaluation indicates, the TRC's shortcomings sprang at least in part from its ambitions, its illusions about the degree of healing and restoration it could achieve, that ended up producing the kind of coercive (non)consensus that Jean-François Lyotard warned about in *The Postmodern Condition*. Lyotard identifies the aspiration to consensus not as an authentic agreement by equal partners in any discourse community, but rather as "a component of the system, which manipulates it in order to maintain and improve its performance."[8] While a full examination of this theorization of consensus in relation to the TRC remains outside the scope of this chapter, I would call attention to Lyotard's assertion that in the postmodern era "consensus has become an outmoded and suspect value. But justice as a value is neither outmoded nor suspect. We must thus arrive at an idea and practice of justice that is not linked to that of consensus."[9]

Lyotard's redirection from consensus to justice as the objective of community dialogue bears significantly on the South African case, in which the "trade" of justice for truth is precisely the sacrifice lamented by many who criticize the institutionalization of forgiveness and reconciliation as the end goals of the TRC. While it must be recognized that the imposition of something like consensus about procedures and methods for transition was necessary for the sake of expediency, forestalling potential violence, and even ensuring the survival of the fledgling democratic state, the critique of the homogenization of ideas about, approaches to, and language employed in the address of past atrocities remains germane, particularly in the context of relatively static conditions of material life in the postapartheid era. This issue of consensus as a kind of "terror"[10] perpetrated by the TRC, which was meant to provide the "bridge" from the "past of a deeply divided society to a future committed to human rights, democracy, and peaceful coexistence,"[11] relates to the TRC's problematic status as an organ of the state, and therefore to its production of narratives that serve the project of nation building, or at least of shoring up the (new) state.

And the doubled heart of the problem is not just that the TRC *was* the state but also that it arguably attempted to control the terms of representation of atrocity. In his important empirical study of survivor perspectives of the TRC hearings, Hugo van der Merwe finds that "the TRC attempted to engage survivors of human rights abuses in a process of restorative justice through storytelling, public accountability, and reparations. . . . The way that the TRC discounted retributive demands and misrepresented survivors' views about justice are, however, very disquieting, as it presents a false sense of what was achieved and marginalizes discordant voices that did not buy into the process."[12]

Those marginalized voices, along with the demands for justice via the concrete avenue of the law, as opposed to within the liminal space of the TRC, continue to echo in public discourse through the work of groups such as the Khulumani Support Group, whose mission is "to build an inclusive and just society in which the dignity of people harmed by apartheid is restored through the process of transforming victims into victors."[13]

The experience of the TRC by many South Africans as another state apparatus in the particular historical lineage of the colonial and then authoritarian apartheid states is one way to think about the relocation in South African films such as *Forgiveness* and *Zulu Love Letter* of the scene of testimonial, forgiveness, reconciliation, and healing outside the frame of the TRC and their identification of alternative modalities for addressing these needs in community structures and interactions. Conversely, the sustained focus on the TRC by U.S. feature films as a model vehicle for addressing a violently racist past may reveal more about the avoidance in the U.S. social imaginary of its own history—and the displacement of a real working through of that history and its ongoing legacies onto a fantasy of nonviolent redemption and reconciliation in which forgiveness translates more accurately to absolution for the sins of the past, even as they remain largely unconfessed—than it does about a dispassionate interest in the workings of the TRC.[14] Significantly, the only film in the U.S. context to attempt to make an ethical case for a square reckoning of the United States with its own version of apartheid is the documentary *Long Night's Journey Into Day*, and even then only in the film's pedagogical apparatus rather than overtly in its content.[15]

Representing Apartheid- and Transition-Era Torture in South African Cinema

Two thousand four was a banner year for cinematic production about the aftermaths and legacies of apartheid: two major films on the subject were released in South Africa and three in the United States. Six years had passed since the publication of the *TRC Final Report*, a sufficient amount of time to allow for substantial evaluations of its outcomes and efficacy, the cultural work it performed, and the actual state of the new South Africa it claimed a central role in bringing into being. Both South African films—Ian Gabriel's *Forgiveness* and Ramadan Suleiman's *Zulu Love Letter*—tell the kinds of stories characteristic of the TRC; however, each film sets the operations of reckoning—testimonial and truth-telling, requests for forgiveness, desires for retribution, gestures toward closure and healing—entirely outside the space of the TRC. Indeed, in both cases the TRC is portrayed at the least neutrally, and at worst negatively, having failed to generate the healing and reconciliation it seemed to offer or, much more consequentially, having created the conditions for violent retribution by perpetrators in an attempt to silence victims prepared to testify against them (*Zulu Love Letter*).

In these films guilt and forgiveness are neither individualized nor constructed through discrete speech acts or gestures with clear political consequences in the manner of the TRC; rather, exploration of these issues is diffused over time and broadened to include much larger life matters of family, work, and community. Cinematic space is widened from the TRC, which serves as a kind of vanishing point whose limits are more apparent than its substance. In *Forgiveness*, for instance, former South African Police officer Tertius Coetzee is apparently left unsatisfied after his encounter with the TRC, in spite of having been granted amnesty for the murder of student and antiapartheid activist Daniel Grootboom, among other crimes, because the TRC did not mandate an encounter with the family.[16] Coetzee's unassuaged guilt compels him to confront the family in a bid for the forgiveness that they "withheld" by refusing to be present for or participate in the TRC proceedings.[17] While the setting of the film's exploration of forgiveness outside the space of the TRC and the strategic use of melodramatic and western generic formulas provide important supplements to the valorization of the TRC as keeper of processes related to forgiveness and absolution, the film rather egregiously depicts the perpetrator as more human—indeed, humanist—than Daniel's family, who are thick with denial and violent rage, and who initiate a deadly retributive process against Coetzee, who in effect becomes a martyr in his own right. In the encounter, which takes place in Daniel Grootbroom's Western Cape coast family home, we witness the perpetrator's emotional agony at the memory of his crimes, his desire to set things right, and his embrace of his victim's cultural traditions—he gathers shells and places them on Daniel's grave when he learns that the fishing community of Paternoster considers them to be "flowers" of the sea, appropriate for memorializing.[18] In the end he is even credited by Daniel's mother for "bringing the fish back" after many seasons of a steadily declining catch. For all his atrocities, Coetzee's presence is depicted as *restoring* a way of life and a family's bonds as opposed to audiences' official reading of him as *taking* a life—and here I refer both to his murder of Daniel Grootbroom and to the community's initial presumption that Coetzee is a real estate developer who has come to the town of Paternoster to meet with the Grootbrooms in order to try to snatch their oceanfront property, exchanging it for cash and effectively putting an end to their community and way of life.

These representations of the perpetrator in *Forgiveness* are particularly problematic given the grounding of the film in a series of documentaries by Mark Kaplan that "explore the history of Siphiwo Mthimkulu, tortured and murdered by security policemen in the early 1980s, and the subsequent interaction between Gideon Nieuwoudt, one of the perpetrators, and the Mthimkulu family during the Truth and Reconciliation Hearings."[19] The documentaries intersperse footage of interviews with Nieuwoudt (also implicated in the death of South African Black Consciousness leader Stephen Biko), Joyce Mthimkulu (mother of the victim, Siphiwo), and others who knew Siphiwo with voice-over narration of Siphiwo's affidavits describing his experience of torture while in detention. Nieuwoudt expresses no real remorse for his crimes, nor does he seek forgiveness except via the most banal, abstract Christian rhetoric based on his alleged religious conversion while serving time in prison. Significantly, Nieuwoudt approached the filmmaker, Kaplan, directly to arrange the meeting with the Mthimkulu family. In contrast with the documentaries the feature film transposes the Christian-confessional framework of the TRC onto the story, offering a protagonist who is consumed with remorse to the point of addiction, despair, and at times, near insanity, a setting in a town named Paternoster ("our father"), and an intermediary who is a priest rather than a filmmaker.

In the original documentaries Siphiwo's torture is reconstructed through voice-over narration based on actual affidavits, read to dramatic visual reconstructions of those torture scenes interspersed with photographs of Siphiwo taken near the time of his death. The film shifts between Siphiwo's official testimony and an interview with Gideon Nieuwoudt at Siphiwo's gravesite. In her reading of the film Lesley Marx describes a "note of pride, even boasting, becom[ing] even more pronounced, accompanied by a glimmer of a smile, as he adds, 'If these walls could speak at this moment, there's no words to explain the situation, of what effect this special branch were at this stage, how effective we were.'"[20] In *Between Joyce and Remembrance* Kaplan himself reflects on Nieuwoudt's demonstrable lack of remorse: "'Looking at him, I see no signs of remorse. What strikes me most is how remote he seems, but perhaps this is merely the outward sign of someone suddenly powerless now trying to hold things together, while living a nightmare.'"[21]

In *Forgiveness* the pride and boasting are shifted from the torturer's description of skill at his craft to the victim's heroic fortitude in not speaking—had he spoken, the security police officer informs Daniel/Siphiwo's horrified family, the torture would have ended. This valorization of the hero who does not betray his comrades reifies an integral aspect of the structure of torture itself, as Jean-Paul Sartre so powerfully described in his introduction to Henri Alleg's memoir of detention and torture by the French during the Algerian war: "The purpose of torture is not only to make a person talk, but to make him betray others. The victim must turn himself by his screams and by his submission into a lower animal, in the eyes of all and in his own eyes. His betrayal must destroy him and take away his human dignity. He who gives way under questioning is not only constrained from talking again, but is given a new status, that of a sub-man."[22]

Sartre's analysis of the specious construction of the one who withstands torture without betraying self or other as a hero—which, by implication, renders those who were unable to "hold up" under interrogation as traitors—has particular relevance to the issues of race at play in the South African case.[23] Coetzee's testimony to Daniel's silence may perversely be read in this context as a sign of the new South Africa, in which the racism of the old regime is replaced by recognition of the humanity of all members of "the Rainbow Nation." Additionally, Coetzee's acknowledgment of Daniel's heroism as part of his testimony to the act of Daniel's torture and murder renders Coetzee a sympathetic character inasmuch as he—again, rather perversely—"gives credit where credit is due," lauding his former enemy, the son, the student, the freedom fighter who died honorably, if honor can be measured within the twisted system of torture by the state.

In spite of director Ian Gabriel's protestations that *Forgiveness* is a composite tale of many TRC stories, its direct reference to an event in the Mthimkulu case captured in *Between Joyce and Remembrance* makes it impossible not to analyze the two films together: the smashing of a vase (or a teapot, in the case of the feature film) over the perpetrator's head by one of the deceased's family members (his son, Sikhumbuzo, in the documentary; his brother, Ernest, in the feature). The differential treatments of this event in the two films reveal striking contrasts in their goals and objectives: in the documentary, whose substance and editing clearly cue a sense of sympathy with Siphiwo's surviving family, as opposed to the perpetrator, the capturing of this moment of spontaneous rage provides a moment of audience catharsis and "throws into disarray the mandate (and the official miracle narrative) of the TRC."[24] The feature, by contrast, provides the occasion for that miracle narrative to surface. When Ernest smashes the teapot over Coetzee's head, his father instructs Ernest's sister, Sanni, to ride with Coetzee to the hospital. The scene cuts to the car ride, with Sanni reaching over the backseat to salve Coetzee's wounds, a moment that provides the first human encounter with the perpetrator and that ultimately opens space for, first, her identification with him; next, her forgiveness of him; and finally, her defense of him against the retributive murder plot that she has initiated with Daniel's comrades.

In the documentary Sikhumbuzo throws the vase after a series of *denials* by Nieuwoudt that he was actually responsible for Siphiwo's death (he claims that he killed Siphiwo's friend, Topsy Madaka, but that another security police officer killed Siphiwo); in *Forgiveness,* by contrast, the teapot is thrown during Coetzee's *testimony* to his torture of Daniel. In the one case it is the refusal to accept responsibility that triggers the violent act on the part of the survivor, while in the retooled feature the (good) perpetrator shows no reticence in accepting responsibility, and so the violent response has its source in the verbalization of the horrifying truth and in the rage of the survivor. As Lesley Marx has pointed out, the decision to deliver the testimony of torture by way of the perpetrator in *Forgiveness* mirrors the structural scene of the torture chamber as described by Elaine Scarry, wherein the perpetrator's voice engages in an act of world making, co-opting the prisoner's voice and, in the process, destroying the prisoner's sense of self and world. In its eagerness to invoke the TRC "miracle narrative" of the perpetrator's remorse, this representational decision—essentially to present a lie, as measured against the documentary "facts" of the case—ends up "playing the game by the rules of the state," as Coetzee warned against in "Into the Dark Chamber," thereby trapping the film within the original representational dilemma.

In contrast Ramadan Suleiman's *Zulu Love Letter* innovates in its representation of the torture of protagonist Thandeka, a journalist who was deeply engaged in the struggle. A survivor, she also witnessed the murder of Dineo, a young antiapartheid activist killed by security police, whose remains were never recovered. The film is set in the transition era, and the action centers on a request from Me'tau, Dineo's mother, that Thandeka help find her daughter's bones so that she can give her a traditional Zulu burial. In the process Thandeka and Me'tau seek out information from one of the perpetrators, a black police officer during the apartheid era who now runs a local store in the Soweto community near where Me'tau lives. Capturing the phenomenon of perpetrators and victims/survivors sharing community space in the transition and postapartheid eras, the film explores the legacies of apartheid and, perhaps more significantly, given its relative invisibility in public narrative, the impact of participation in the struggle on antiapartheid activists, their families, and their communities.

In the process of facing this history and working through the transition from apartheid, Thandeka confronts her own legacy of torture, which, we discover, is responsible for the deafness of her thirteen-year-old daughter, Mangi, as Thandeka was pregnant while in detention. Audiences learn about Thandeka's torture tangentially, through flashback scenes that arise amid the material and psychological stresses of transition and the challenge of facing the past posed by the impending presence of the TRC. Each flashback is presented through Thandeka's memory as part of her own larger process of working through her experience, which is, indeed, a communal and community process, as opposed to the individual reconstruction of Daniel's torture and death in the heavily confessional *Forgiveness*.

Suleiman employs surrealist cinematography in order to reconstruct three torture-execution scenes witnessed or imagined by Thandeka, and each is carefully woven into the plotline featuring the convergence of personal, familial, community, and national recovery and reconciliation in the posttransition period. The use of surrealism as a mode for the visual reconstruction of torture scenes suggests the convoluted psychological frameworks of traumatic memory and healing, as opposed to the prescribed linear testimonial framework embraced by the TRC. Significantly, however, Thandeka's memory of her own torture is presented to audiences only at the end of a long journey of reconstruction, during which she remembers the execution of Dineo at point-blank range in an alley in Soweto by the South African Security Police. Remembering this event as part of the process of working through the past so as to move back into her role as mother and professional in a new and suddenly unfamiliar South Africa, Thandeka then imagines the torture of Michael, the photographer who captured the moment of Dineo's execution in a photograph carried around by another survivor, Thandeka's now perpetually drunken former colleague Bouda'D. The imagined reconstruction of Michael's death takes place at a farm that evokes Vlakplaas, the "counterinsurgency base" used to torture and murder antiapartheid activists. Incidents in this scene bear striking similarities to some of the most horrifying testimonies from the TRC, including the practice of Third Force operatives barbequing their dinners on one fire and burning the dismembered bodies of antiapartheid activists on another (indeed this was the scenario reported by Gideon Nieuwoudt and his colleagues in their testimony to the murder and disposal of Siphiwo Mthimkulu and Topsy Madaka). The flashbacks to both atrocities are filmed out of focus, with jagged film speed and disjunctive material and symbolic elements, mirroring the surreal dream state of recovered memory or the horror of imagining, as a survivor, the torture and murder of a comrade/loved one. Thandeka's memories are triggered by everyday encounters with family and community members as she seeks to create a life after the struggle.

Thandeka's experience as survivor is, then, secondary in the film's schema to her role as witness. Indeed the film is instructive in portraying the complexity of negotiating these dual roles so common to those who have been active in political struggle, but so often misunderstood in human rights circles. The roles are those of survivors testifying in the first-person voice to their own experiences of abuse and third-party/third-person witnesses to violations against others, the latter including journalists, activists, aid workers, and academics. The film is also instructive in demonstrating how witnessing atrocity, particularly as the witness is implicated in the torture of others as a participant in political activities against the state, can cause as much psychic damage, if not perhaps even more, than experiencing one's own torture.

The revelation of Thandeka's personal experience of torture is finally prompted by the murder of her ex-husband, Moola, by former Security Police officers who run his car off the road as a warning to Thandeka not to testify before the TRC. In the aftermath of the accident, with Mangi missing from the accident site, Thandeka forces her way into the home of a former comrade who is currently a politician in the new ANC government, demanding that he help find her daughter. The scene serves two purposes. First, it emphasizes one of the film's messages with regard to the legacies of torture used by the South African apartheid state: that survivors are everywhere in the new South Africa, living out a range of effects from their detention. Second, it underscores the sense among many in the new South Africa that the comrades who made their way into the government after the transition have benefited from their status and position without instituting the material changes fought for in the struggle. In both senses the survivor/government official has his foil in Bouda'D, Thandeka's comrade, another journalist who survived torture only to stay permanently drunk as a way to avoid remembering; as he tells Thandeka, "I would rather hear the bells in my glass than the wind in my head," with the wind signifying not only his memories of torture but also the spirit of resistance driving the antiapartheid struggle. This spirit is made evident in the chanting of a struggle song by Thandeka and Bouda'D: "Where does the breeze begin to blow, my brother? Where does the breeze begin to blow, my sister?" as they toyi-toyi in the street, reliving shared memories of the struggle.[25] The scene is an important one, revealing the same pattern of witness preceding testimony as Bouda'D tells Thandeka, on the heels of a drunken exhortation to demand reparations from the TRC, "We will freeze his face in our minds. The mother of all pictures. One click and all hell broke loose. All Mike ever wanted to be was a photographer. And when he finally took the picture that mattered, our lives were in tatters."

To return to Coetzee's thesis, situated in the context of apartheid state censorship of images of South African prisons, if even representations of the external *structure* of the prison must be censored under the apartheid regime, then the image of Dineo's extrajudicial execution—the cycle of resistance/repression/death frozen in its frame, verifying that which the state would violently disavow—could only set in motion the corresponding censure of those journalists involved in producing it. This censure too, of course, remained hidden from view—inasmuch as it took place on the farm that in both geographical and political senses lay "outside the ambit of moral judgment" (Coetzee, "Into the Dark Chamber," 68), indistinguishable from any other South African landscape, as Bouda'D emphasizes when Thandeka asks if he can remember the farm where they were tortured and identify it in testimony to the TRC: "Fuck [Thandeka], I remember fuck all, man. All I remember are the trees that would go on forever and the breeze that would blow and blow and blow."

Bouda'D's street "testimony" to Thandeka continues with the revelation of two secrets regarding possible betrayal under torture: "Can I tell you two secrets? *Number one*: those shits were fucking me up so bad I wanted to tell them where you were, but I didn't know. *Number two*: they were fucking you up on the same farm where they were fucking me up in the first place." As in many postapartheid films, the secret of state-sponsored torture is revealed to be not only the disgrace of its application on the detainee but also the lethal manipulation and corruption of interpersonal and community ties by the security police. As Bouda'D "confesses" to Thandeka his desire to reveal her whereabouts to the security police in order to stop his own torture, the brutal irony is that the great heroism of his holding out is nullified in the context of an interrogation that was actually an end in itself, a surreal language game in which "the answer" that justifies the torture is predetermined and "the question" has always already been an exercise in the absurd.

The remains of state-sponsored torture in the form of broken relationships, shameful secrets, and traumatized people are scattered everywhere in the new South Africa, and *Zulu Love Letter* is at pains to show the pervasive—if unrecognized—presence of the survivor at every level of society. Significantly, Thandeka's appeal to her former comrade who is now a politician is based precisely on his experience as a survivor—"You were an activist—you were detained." While this shared experience could potentially provide some platform of solidarity, the gulf between them is as wide as the difference between the safety of his family behind a barbed-wired, fenced-in home and the vulnerability of her Soweto and urban Johannesburg communities. This too, the film seems to say, is a betrayal—and perhaps the one with the most enduring consequences for those members of the antiapartheid movement who did not find themselves at the head of the new dispensation, and who represent the material gap between rich and poor that stands also as a temporal blockade, thwarting passage to a discernibly *post*apartheid era.

It is the comrade/politician's platitude, "The truth will out, my sister," in response to Thandeka's calls that he do something to bring her daughter home that finally prompts her testimony about her own torture, couched in an emphatic rejection of the TRC trade of justice for truth—"Fuck the truth. The only truth I know is what I felt with my entire body"[26]—and visualized in a flashback remembrance of the prison cell where she was held and the experience of being tortured while pregnant. In addition to illuminating the psychological processes of reconstruction that finally lead to Thandeka's reluctant testimony, the representational choices in this scene explore the ethical condition of a protagonist testifying to her own experience while, significantly, emphasizing the corporeal effects of torture by locating the loaded postapartheid signifier "truth" in an embodied memory. Thandeka forces her interlocutor to recognize the gendered experience of pain by holding his hand to her abdomen while describing the fear she felt for her unborn child as she was being beaten by security police.

If audiences learn of Thandeka's torture only as secondary to her witnessing of the torture and murder of others in the struggle, they also understand her memory of it only as one small part of the process of regeneration she undergoes in trying to work through the effects of the political transition, part of which means reconciling with her adolescent daughter, who grew up largely in Thandeka's parents' care while she was engaged in the struggle. We learn about Thandeka's torture as a way of understanding more deeply her alienation from Mangi, signified in the film by her refusal to learn sign language in order to communicate with her. The fact that Mangi's deafness was caused by Thandeka's torture does not mitigate our sense that Thandeka ought to learn sign language in order to be able to fully communicate with her daughter, a position disapprovingly articulated to Thandeka by Mangi's teachers; however, it does provide a deeper sense of the cost of Thandeka's activism and a partial response to those members of Thandeka's family—her parents, Mangi, and even her ex-husband—who resent her absence from family structures and responsibilities because of her work as an antiapartheid activist.

Indeed *Zulu Love Letter* illuminates the intrusion of the political into all other arenas of life during the time of the struggle, representing it as uncontainable in Thandeka's life in a way that mirrors the excessiveness of traumatic memory, spilling into her family and work relations. At the newspaper where she works she angrily accuses her white boss of betrayal in turning the photographer, Mike, over to the security police, in a statement that reveals the source of her mistrust of the law that extends from the apartheid era straight through to the present day in the new South Africa: "Your files were subpoenaed. The best you can do is to hide behind your legalities." At home Thandeka interrupts a loving moment in which her mother is talking with Mangi about the symbolic significance of colors, angrily correcting her mother: "If there's one thing the black consciousness movement taught us, it's that black is beautiful and white is far from pure."

The tension between the political interpretation of color and the warm familial teaching of aesthetics highlights the intrusion of the political as a disruptive term in family life—both "readings" of color are right and good, however incompatible. Audiences encounter Thandeka as alienated from her family and, indeed, from herself as she struggles to understand and fulfill the competing roles of political activist, professional woman, and family member. Her family feels some lingering resentment; as her father reminds her, "While you were out toyi-toying, we brought [Mangi] up."

To be sure, one element shared by the South African films *Forgiveness* and *Zulu Love Letter* is an emphasis on the costs of participation in the struggle in terms of community connections and family ties. In *Forgiveness* we learn that rather than considering Daniel a hero because he was a freedom fighter, his father has chosen to accept the official security police story that Daniel was killed in a carjacking. This state of denial is attributed to the sense of shame that the alternative would bring on the family—appearing before the TRC and acknowledging Daniel's antiapartheid activities, which made him a terrorist in the eyes of the state.

Such representations may come as something of a surprise to international audiences familiar with films about the TRC and the legacies of apartheid, and who view antiapartheid activists largely as unmitigated heroes for their personal sacrifices and devotion to freedom, while the complexity of the effects of such activism on their families and communities is left unexamined. In U.S. films on the subject, such as *In My Country*, antiapartheid activists are known through TRC testimony (their own or that of their loved ones, in the cases of those who did not survive) about the violation of their rights at the hands of security police, which leaves the question of the effect of activism on families and communities unaddressed, reducing these human beings to the mere facts of their ill-treatment or death.

Change of Venue: Addressing Apartheid Outside the Bounds of the TRC

U.S. films about the South African transition from apartheid to democracy seem to universally embrace the dicta of forgiveness and reconciliation advanced by the TRC as organ of the new state apparatus, so that what viewers learn about torture under apartheid is gleaned through the narrative of a seemingly preordained forgiveness of the torturer by the survivor or by the victim's family—regardless of the perpetrator's request for forgiveness or expression of remorse, or lack thereof. While the excessive romantic melodrama of *In My Country* is the antithesis of the raw documentary footage presented in the acclaimed *Long Night's Journey Into Day*, both films select only cases that ultimately show forgiveness and reconciliation—even if it is reluctant, as in the case of the mothers of the Gugulethu Seven (seven young activists set up and killed by security police), who at first refuse to forgive the black police officer who asks to meet with them to express remorse for his part in their sons' deaths and to ask their forgiveness, but who then reconsider after one of the mothers reminds them all of Jesus' forgiveness of those who killed him, reinforcing the persuasiveness of the Christian framework articulated by TRC chair Archbishop Desmond Tutu. The shift of the narrative at the crossroads where political action merges with an unlikely act of forgiveness reinforces the consensus that forgiveness is the great—perhaps the *only*—story to tell about the South African transition, and that that forgiveness, which in turn promises a fabled reconciliation, is exclusively bound to the institutional platform provided by the TRC.

It is this circularity that *Zulu Love Letter* disrupts, locating the TRC as just one site—and a profoundly fraught one at that—and forgiveness as just one outcome among many venues and methods for postapartheid address, redress, healing, mourning, and reconciliation. In a reading of the TRC that both acknowledges its limitations and analyzes its radical accomplishments, well beyond the mythical miracle narrative so frequently circulated in the global sphere, Mark Sanders advances the idea that one of the most significant—and least discussed—parts of the TRC's work was to "take the place of the other . . . to assume . . . the unacknowledged responsibility of the perpetrator for the deeds of the past . . . [to function] as a national clearinghouse between victims and perpetrators, even if it did not often arrange actual meetings between them."[27] In a chapter entitled "Remembering Apartheid," Sanders asks what apartheid was and, in a convincing reading of witness testimony before the TRC, concludes that "what we hear when we listen to those witnesses is this: apartheid was a proscription on mourning, specifically of the other" (ibid., 35). Sanders' work in this chapter focuses on the problem of lost or hidden remains of bodies, and of bodies denied a proper burial, which is also the engine for action in *Zulu Love Letter*, inasmuch as the film revolves around Dineo's mother's search for her daughter's remains so that she can be put to rest in the Zulu tradition and restored to the company of her ancestors. Sanders claims that one significant function of the TRC was to act as "proxy for the perpetrator," especially when "faced with the reality that perpetrators would not come forward en masse to make good for what they had done" (ibid., 9). When considered in light of Coetzee's argument about the representational dilemma imposed by the state, this proxy status on the part of the TRC becomes more interesting: the TRC, part of the new ANC-led democratic government, was not the perpetrator of the crimes under examination in its hearings; however, its "innocence" was good only for the infinitesimal moment of its coming into being. As soon as the new state was formed, coterminous with the formation of the TRC, it began to accrue symbolic capital as a real, not proxy, perpetrator. This shift in status resulted partly from the state's position as guarantor and agent for the TRC's recommendations about the reparations that were so central for the healing process—not least because, had they been substantial enough, reparations may have instituted some shift out of the material condition that Sanders refers to by what he calls a "deliberate oxymoron": "the *enduring violence* of the past" (ibid., 13; italics are mine).

And herein lies the problem. In addition to lingering critiques that the South African government mobilized the TRC's coerced consensus to produce a unified narrative of forgiveness and reconciliation that would serve to legitimate its status, it also instituted broadly neoliberal policies encouraging foreign direct investment and rejecting large-scale redistribution of land and resources, such that the material conditions that prevailed under apartheid have not been substantially (or even, arguably, minimally) transformed. As Sanders notes in his chapter on reparations, the TRC turned over its recommendations for reparations to the government, but in monetary terms, the government had fallen "well short of [its] figure" (ibid., 115). The government also "opposed suits for reparations filed in the United States by declaring that [it] would not be party to any such [international] matters" (ibid.).

The South African government's refusal to cooperate with alternative paths to political and economic justice on the basis of national sovereignty and its decision to reject calls for a more radical redistribution of wealth, and even for the larger reparations recommended to it by the TRC, arguably contribute to the "enduring violence" of material conditions for the majority of black people in South Africa. The fact that the political miracle remains unaccompanied by substantial material and economic change informs the sense that the apartheid past survives in the ongoing economic deprivation of nonwhites, rendering the ANC-led government another kind of state perpetrator and informing the need of the people to "go outside" the TRC/state for the mourning, condolences, and healing that Sanders considers to be a major function of the TRC's "symbolic reparations" and its laudable status as proxy for the perpetrator.

It is important to remember here that in his analysis of state censorship of images of the prison in "Into the Dark Chamber," Coetzee shows how this censorship is of a piece with the "hiding away" of the poor. His definition of apartheid has less to do with the proscription against forming social bonds (Sanders) and more to do with understanding the inseparability of economic from racial segregation: "Is apartheid about segregation of blacks or segregation of the poor? Perhaps not an important question, when blacks and the poor are so nearly the same" (Coetzee, "Into the Dark Chamber," 362). Certainly, the democratic South African government is no longer in the business of hiding the (black) poor from a white electorate in homelands and townships that whites avoid (though whites do still avoid the townships); however, the state in the postapartheid era may be considered not just a proxy for the perpetrator but also an agent in ongoing economic warfare, representing the apartheid past that persists in material, corporeal form into the democratic present. It is precisely because of the problem of economic reparations that the characters in *Zulu Love Letter* refuse to participate in the TRC as their space for working through the past; as Bouda'D tells Thandeka, "You and I came back so we could spook those bastards [their torturers]. We will sue the damn state for reparations because reparations are a must. Or else we look like fools in front of the Truth and Reconciliation Commission. You and I, we will always remember, and fuck reconciliation." Notice the refusal of the reconciliatory narrative of the TRC, the demand for justice, the emphasis on reparations that were in fact not delivered. *Zulu Love Letter* concludes with a scene of community healing, in which Dineo's life is celebrated and her soul is put to rest, that is completely outside the frame of the TRC, immersed as it is in Zulu cultural traditions represented by the beaded quilt, the "Zulu love letter" of the film's title.

Such "turning outside" the TRC for testimony and mourning provides a cinematic escape from Coetzee's double bind of representation: how to represent the experience of torture without capitulating to the state that has sanctioned and then disavowed it, thereby taking it outside the "ambit of moral judgment." The film's pointed rejection of the state—represented by the TRC—as an adequate space within which to recollect and represent the experience of apartheid-era torture and its legacies simultaneously implicates the state apparatus and refuses its claims to authority. Reconstructing the experience of torture and the processes of mourning outside the purview of the TRC, the film pushes representation beyond merely reproducing the "gorgon's head" of state-sponsored torture or, just as unsatisfactorily, remaining silent, opening a cinematic space in which, as Coetzee so tentatively and ambivalently anticipated in 1986, "even the torture chamber can be accorded a place in the design."

NOTES

I am grateful to the Babson College Faculty Research Fund, which provided generous support for this project, and especially to Susan Chern for her assistance.

1. I use the term "conciliation" here to acknowledge the point made by Daniel Herwitz, among others, that "the very idea of *reconciliation* in South Africa, of reconciliation as process and as goal or ideal, is, strictly speaking, a fiction.... Reconciliation implies that beings were once one, came apart, and are now back together again. This is hardly, from the historical point of view, the case." Herwitz, *Race and Reconciliation*, 41.
2. Coetzee, "Into the Dark Chamber," hereafter cited in text. While Coetzee's essay is about the ethics of representing torture in the novel, the occasion for its inquiry is the apartheid state proscription against visual images of the prison (photographs, drawings); I take the liberty here of applying Coetzee's arguments about the novel to narrative cinema.
3. Of course, the opposite case may also be argued: that without legitimization as part of the new majority representative government, without the imprimatur of state power and its formal recognition of the crimes of the past, the TRC would have been a relatively inconsequential body. I acknowledge this double-bind of the TRC, and follow scholars such as Mark Sanders in acknowledging what the TRC was able to achieve while also assessing its limitations as the mark of any human action taken in the wake of such a brutal history, which can never be made right by any/body, with or without the seal of the state.
4. Republic of South Africa, *Promotion of National Unity and Reconciliation Act*. See Sanders, *Ambiguities of Witnessing*, 24–33, for an extended discussion of the concept of "Ubuntu" and issues related to its translation from Zulu into other languages: "*Ubuntu*, variously determined as a theological, moral, political, and juridico-legal concept, also informs the thinking of those who promoted the idea of a truth commission.... *Ubuntu* can be understood, provisionally, as a notion of reciprocity: a human being is a human being through other human beings. One is, it follows, responsible for the other, in a way that, according to constitutional jurists, regulates and limits the rights of the individual in favor of the collective" (24).

5. See Ellis, "The Historical Significance of South Africa's Third Force," for an excellent analysis of the violent operations of those networks within and without the security forces that have become known collectively as the "Third Force" (261) during the transition period.
6. This equalizing was a particularly bitter pill for many ANC/MK and PAC members; see *Long Night's Journey Into Day* for coverage of the amnesty hearing for Robert McBride, former MK cadre convicted in 1986 for the Magoo's Bar bombing. Appearing before the TRC voluntarily after having served a six-year sentence, McBride expressed indignation at the absence of any distinction made between freedom fighters and apartheid operatives, observing, "I don't believe an Allied soldier would appreciate being compared with a Nazi."
7. Schaffer and Smith, *Human Rights and Narrated Lives*, 70.
8. Lyotard, *The Postmodern Condition*, 60.
9. Ibid., 66.
10. The term is Lyotard's description of the institutional drive to consensus. Ibid., 63.
11. Minow, *Between Vengeance and Forgiveness*, 53.
12. Van der Merwe, "What Survivors Say About Justice," 44.
13. Le Roux, "Activities," Khulumani Support Group South Africa. Khulumani describes its advocacy services precisely as a response to exclusion from the TRC: "The TRC failed to address the consequences of political violence and human rights violations for many people. 90% of Khulumani's members who are gross human rights survivors were not included in the processes of the TRC."
14. To date there has been one Truth and Reconciliation Commission in the United States to address the shooting death of four Communist Workers' Party members and one supporter on November 3, 1979, during a confrontation with members of the Ku Klux Klan at a public march. The Greensboro Truth and Reconciliation Commission was brought into being by the Greensboro Truth and Community Reconciliation Project, which cites the South African TRC as a major inspiration, but which also imagines the Greensboro TRC as just one piece of a much deeper investigation into the racist violence in U.S. history: "What if America's cities—especially Southern cities—stopped ignoring the skeletons in their closets? What if they were inspired by the potential of the truth & reconciliation model as demonstrated in South Africa, Peru, and elsewhere, to help them seek life-affirming restorative justice and constructively deal with past incidents of injustice?" Home page, Greensboro Truth and Community Reconciliation Project Web site, http://www.gtcrp.org/. See also Greensboro Truth and Reconciliation Commission, http://www.greensborotrc.org/.
15. See, for example, the contribution by Nesbitt, "Using *Long Night's Journey Into Day* to Confront Issues of Race," in which Nesbitt asserts that "the United States, as a nation, still hides its painful racial history and avoids long-term, structural solutions to its ongoing racial crises. *Long Night's Journey into Day* is a poignant excla-

mation point that the US has a long-overdue need for an in-depth process of truth finding, followed, one hopes, by reconciliation."
16. Given its reference to events depicted in the documentary *Between Joyce and Remembrance*, the perpetrator in *Forgiveness* is based on Gideon Nieuwoudt, a colonel in the Security Police, while his victim in the film is based on Siphiwo Mtimkhulu, leader of the Congress of South African Students (COSAS), who was murdered and burned in 1982.
17. In actuality, Nieuwoudt and his colleagues successfully mounted legal challenges to the testimony of Siphiwo's mother, Joyce Mthimkulu, before the original TRC hearing in Port Elizabeth, April 1996, such that she was only belatedly permitted to testify in June 1996. See Philips, "The Student, the Mother, and the Security Policeman"; and Sanders, *Ambiguities of Witnessing*, for two important analyses of the hearing.
18. The relocation of the story from the Mthimkulu's home in the politically radicalized Eastern Cape to the symbolically significant fishing town of Paternoster ("Our Father") in the Western Cape contributes to the film's commitment to the Christian ideal of reconciliation associated with Archbishop Desmond Tutu, chair of the TRC.
19. Marx, "Cinema, Glamour, Atrocity," 44. The names "Siphiwo" and "Mthimkulu" are spelled inconsistently in source materials. I join Mark Sanders and others in following the spelling found in Joyce Mthimkulu's testimony in the *TRC Final Report*.
20. *Between Joyce and Remembrance*, quoted in Marx, "Cinema, Glamour, Atrocity: Narratives of Trauma," 30.
21. Ibid., 33.
22. Sartre, "Introduction: A Victory," 30–31.
23. See also Scarry, *The Body in Pain*, especially chapter 1, "The Structure of Torture," for an analysis of the notion of self-betrayal through interrogation as a structural component of the act of torture.
24. Marx, "Cinema, Glamour, Atrocity," 34.
25. Toyi-toyi is a traditional dance used during antiapartheid marches. As Lisa Nevitt writes, "From protests to celebrations, the chants capture the emotions of joy, pain, encouragement, heartbreak and solace. Toyi-toyi is a powerful and infectious statement, by which the oppressed may voice their grievances to the government." Nevitt, "What's the Deal with Toyi-toyi?"
26. It is perhaps not incidental that in his spontaneous street testimony in the earlier scene, Bouda'D responds to the idea of testifying before the TRC with the imperative, "Fuck reconciliation." Here those marginalized perspectives refusing the ideals of forgiveness and reconciliation empirically documented by Van der Merwe in his study of torture survivors are articulated in concise fashion in a film that situates the painstaking process of building truths outside the bounds of the TRC and the state.
27. Sanders, *Ambiguities of Witnessing*, 19. Hereafter cited in text.

WORKS CITED

Between Joyce and Remembrance. Directed by Mark Kaplan. Johannesburg: Grey Matter Media, 2004.

Coetzee, J. M. "Into the Dark Chamber: The Writer and the South African State." *Doubling the Point: Essays and Interviews.* Edited by David Attwell. Cambridge, Mass.: Harvard University Press, 1992.

———. *Waiting for the Barbarians.* New York: Penguin, 1982. Reprinted 1999.

Cry Freedom. Directed by Richard Attenborough. Universal City, Calif.: Universal Pictures, 1987.

Cry the Beloved Country. Directed by Darryl Roodt. New York: Miramax, 1995.

A Dry White Season. Directed by Euzan Palcy. Century City, Calif.: MGM, 1989.

Ellis, Stephen. "The Historical Significance of South Africa's Third Force." *Journal of Southern African Studies* 24, no. 2 (June 1998): 261–99.

Forgiveness. Directed by Ian Gabriel. Johannesburg: Dv8 Films, 2004.

Foster, Dan, Paul Haupt, and Maresa De Beer. *The Theatre of Violence: Narratives of Protagonists in the South African Conflict.* Capetown: Human Sciences Research Council Press, 2005.

Gordimer, Nadine. *Burgher's Daughter.* New York: Penguin, 1980.

Greensboro Truth and Community Reconciliation Project. Home page. http://www.gtcrp.org/.

Greensboro Truth and Reconciliation Commission. http://www.greensborotrc.org/.

Hemer, Oscar. "Fiction's Truth and Social Change: Preliminary Outlines for an Investigation of Fiction as a Research Method and a Means of Communication for Social Change." Paper prersented at the Rethinking Communication for Development conference at University of Queensland, Brisbane, Australia, July 5–7, 2006.

Herwitz, Daniel. *Race and Reconciliation: Essays from the New South Africa.* Minneapolis: University of Minnesota Press, 2003.

In My Country. Directed by John Boorman. Culver City, Calif.: Columbia TriStar, 2004.

Kozain, Rustom. Review of *Complicities: The Intellectual and Apartheid*, by Mark Sanders. *H-Net Reviews*, March 2005, http://www.h-net.org/reviews/showrev.php?id=10294 (accessed September 2, 2010).

Le Roux, Pierre. "Activities." Khulumani Support Group South Africa. Last modified March 18, 2011. http://www.khulumani.net/khulumani/about-us/item/4-activities.html.

Long Night's Journey Into Day. Directed by Deborah Hoffman. Berkeley: Iris Films, 2000.

Lyotard, Jean-François. *The Postmodern Condition: A Report on Knowledge.* Translated by Geoff Bennington and Brian Massumi. Minneapolis: University of Minnesota Press, 1984. Reprinted in 1993.

Marx, Lesley. "Cinema, Glamour, Atrocity: Narratives of Trauma." *Social Dynamics* 32, no 2 (2006): 22–49.

Minow, Martha. *Between Vengeance and Forgiveness: Facing History After Genocide and Mass Violence*. Boston: Beacon Press, 1998.
Nesbitt, Prexy. "Using *Long Night's Journey Into Day* to Confront Issues of Race." In *"Long Night's Journey Into Day":Facilitator Guide*. Edited by Pamela Harris. Berkeley: Iris Films, 2000. http://newsreel.org/guides/longnight.htm#Nesbitt.
Nevitt, Lisa. "What's the Deal With Toyi-toyi?" *Capetown Magazine* Online. http://www.capetownmagazine.com/whats-the-deal-with/Whats-the-Deal-With-Toyitoyi/125_22_17384.
Philips, David. "The Student, the Mother, and the Security Policeman: Truth and Reconciliation in the Siphiwo Mtimkhulu Case?" *London Grip International Cultural Magazine*. http://www.londongrip.com/LondonGrip/SouthAfrica_TRC(3)_by_David_Philips.html
Robbins, Tim and Robyn Slovo. "'Catch a Fire': New Film Depicts Life of South African Freedom Fighter Patrick Chamusso." By Amy Goodman. Pacifica Radio. *Democracy Now: The War and Peace Report*. October, 16 2006. http://www.democracynow.org/2006/10/13/catch_a_fire_new_film_depicts.
Sanders, Mark. *Ambiguities of Witnessing: Law and Literature in the Time of a Truth Commission*. Stanford: Stanford University Press, 2007.
——. *Complicities: The Intellectual and Apartheid*. Durham and London: Duke University Press, 2002.
Sarafina! Directed by Darrell Roodt. New York: Miramax, 1992.
Sartre, Jean-Paul. "Introduction: A Victory." *The Question*, by Henri Alleg. New York: Braziller, 1958.
Scarry, Elaine. *The Body in Pain: The Making and Unmaking of the World*. New York: Oxford University Press, 1985.
Schaffer, Kay and Sidonie Smith. *Human Rights and Narrated Lives: The Ethics of Recognition*. New York: Palgrave, 2004.
South Africa, Republic of. *Promotion of National Unity and Reconciliation Act*. 1995. http://www.doj.gov.za/trc/legal/act9534.htm (accessed 25 August 2010).
Urquhart, Troy. "Truth, Reconciliation, and the Restoration of the State: Coetzee's *Waiting for the Barbarians*." *Twentieth-Century Literature* 52, no. 1 (Spring 2006): 1–22.
Van der Merwe, Hugo. "What Survivors Say About Justice: An Analysis of the TRC Victim Hearings." *Truth and Reconciliation in South Africa: Did the TRC Deliver?* Edited by Audrey R. Chapman and Hugo van der Merwe. Philadelphia: University of Pennsylvania Press, 2008.
Zulu Love Letter. Directed by Ramadan Suleiman. Paris: Films Distribution Mercure International, 2004.

Waltz with Bashir, 2008

9
Confessing Without Regret
AN ISRAELI FILM GENRE

Livia Alexander

> "You felt guilty at the age of 19. Unwillingly, you took on the role of the Nazi. You were there, firing flares, but you didn't carry out the massacre."
> —Therapist to Folman's character, Waltz with Bashir

The international success of Ari Folman's animated mockumentary *Waltz with Bashir* (*Valts im Bashir*) (2008) brought to the forefront a genre dominant in Israeli filmmaking: confessional cinema. First emerging during the time of the first intifada (1987–1994) and focused on addressing the actions taken by Israeli soldiers against their perceived Palestinian and Lebanese enemies, Israeli confessional cinema was initially heavily preoccupied with the moral dilemmas and self-questioning triggered by the outbreak of the first intifada, with films like *Testimonies* (*Eduyut*) (1991) and *What Happened* (*Ma Kara*) (1988). The evolution of the genre through the post-Oslo years, the outbreak of the second intifada (September 2000–2004), the Second Lebanon War (July 2006), and continuing today mirrors the changes that took place in the broader Israeli society and its perceptions of itself and those it considers its enemies. These perceptions are not unproblematic, because the way the confessional films perceive these others—as enemies (or victims, as the scholarly literature on confession would have it)—is symptomatic of an issue at the heart of Israeli confessional cinema: that the films disregard other ways of collectively describing or imagining Palestinians in relation to Israel (e.g., as colonized or oppressed people, or as fellow citizens).

Beginning by questioning the effects that the suppression of the first intifada had on the moral conduct of Israeli soldiers, Israeli confessional cinema shifted to a focus on anger at the Palestinians and Lebanese for forcing Israelis to compromise their humanity, and then began to vindicate and validate the actions of Israeli soldiers amid growing international criticism. It is a genre in which confessing Israeli soldiers perceive and promote themselves as the actual victims, and in which Palestinian and Lebanese civilians and fighters have no presence. Palestinians and Lebanese have consistently challenged the Israeli narrative concerning acts of violence, but Israelis generally, and Israeli cinema more specifically, have by and large excluded them from the discourse. The continuing conflict and Israel's state of war with Arab nations have stood in the way of a Zionist vision that never included the Palestinians. This point is typical of most settler colonial nationalisms and their disavowals of prior presence, as is explicitly evident in our discussion of the absence of Palestinians in confessional films. The fact that one cannot erase the Palestinian presence from the land despite the desire to never include them—as demonstrated by Meron Benvenisti's study, *Sacred Landscapes*, and Sandi Hilal, Alessandro Petti, and Eyal Weizman's architecture collective, Decolonizing Architecture Art Residency[1]—is a useful insight for the films under review here. While these voices remain absent, it is perhaps most productive to study the limits, shape, and construction of that absence rather than imagining if there "should" be a presence. In other words it is in keeping with Zionist discourse that Palestinians not appear in films as victims or visible subjects who might trouble the anxiety being expressed on the part of confessional soldiers. But in fact, these absences constantly "speak" to the presence of Palestinians.

Confession and forgiveness in this genre of Israeli cinema take place outside the official space of state practice and institutional structures. Confession unfolds between individuals and the recording lens of the camera, between former soldier and filmmaker, and finally, between the latter two and audiences. The prominence of soldiers' confessions in Israeli cinema suggests the prevailing belief in both the political and moral powers of telling as healing, as studies on torture and reconciliation demonstrate, underscoring the presumption that once a confession is made, nothing more is needed for both perpetrators and victims to "move on," politically as well as personally.[2] Yet, as scholars such as Leigh Payne point out, rather than closing a chapter, in fact one is opened, linking the past to the present and opening up a debate over signification and interpretation of these past acts and violence. However, for individual confessing soldiers engaged in the cinematic medium as part of a familiar effort to leave a troubled past behind, the Israeli context bears a typography that departs from most critical scholarly engagements with questions of confession, reconciliation, and forgiveness rooted in post-conflict peace-building efforts.[3] Thus while the individual acts of confessing soldiers might be set in the past, the Israeli collective engagement with its occupation of the Palestinian Territories, its animosity toward its Palestinian citizens, and its military excursions in Lebanon, are ongoing. A second disjuncture is at play between the soldier's own authoritarian position over the civil population under his or her jurisdiction while in active military duty and Israel's self-perception as "the only democracy in the Middle East."

Within this context of ongoing occupation and conflict, the debate unfolding in Israeli cinema over the nature of confession, forgiveness, and regret has an urgency that is very much based in ever-evolving debates about Israel's view of itself in light of increasing international criticism. Ironically, this focus on confession gives undue political power to the perpetrators of military crimes. For Payne, perpetrators' confessions interpret the past and by so doing advance political debate and consequently democratic discourse, or what Payne refers to as "contentious co-existence."[4] However, the emphasis of Israeli cinema on the tortured soul of the confessing soldier as the victim of his own act leaves that promise unmet. Instead the space opened up by the cinematic field of public confession offers a forward-moving moment of absolution and cleansing so that the repenting soldier can find personal redemption and seek reintegration into Israeli society, and humanity at large. It is a process that strikingly excludes victims and concerns itself with appealing to Israeli audiences, or at most, the international community. Here, however, it is worth considering the ways in which Palestinians or Lebanese in these situations might be better characterized than merely as victims. Rather than shoehorn Lebanese and Palestinians back into these Israeli narratives as victims, I would like to extend the range of possible discourses here. The discourse of victimhood is less politically useful since it accepts the dichotomous terms of colonization, even if it does so in a concerned, liberal kind of way. I do not mean to suggest, as others might, that there is some heroic resistance that means Palestinians are never victims, but rather that there is something about the liberal victor-victim discourse that reinscribes a Zionist narrative of Israeli exceptionalism.

Despite changing circumstances over the years, an ever-shifting blend of victimhood and entitlement continuously informs and shapes mainstream Israeli discourse, anchored in the experience of the European Jew as a victim of pogroms and the Holocaust on one hand, and in the Zionist enterprise on the other—an enterprise fashioned according to the governing principles of European colonialism, which placed the rights and interests of European powers over those of indigenous populations and allowed for the appropriation of land and natural resources. Israeli scholars such as Ilan Pappe and Avi Shlaim, known as "the new historians," have examined this official Zionist historiography, critically assessing Zionism's colonial roots in the British Mandate period and the ethnic cleansing and injustices it brought about.[5] In cinema too, a growing number of filmmakers, primarily documentarians, have taken on a more critical examination of the Zionist narrative and its outcome in films such as *Have You Ever Shot Anyone? (ha-im Yarita Pa'am be-Mishehu?)* (1995) and *For My Children (la-Yeladim sheli)* (2002) by Michal Aviad; Yulie Cohen Gerstel's trilogy, *My Terrorist (ha-Mehabel Sheli,* 2002), *My Land Zion (Zion admati)* (2004), and *My Brother (ha-Akh sheli)* (2007); and Amit Goren's *Another Land (Eretz Aheret)* (1998), among many others. Yet despite the growing number of films, questions of guilt, regret, and accountability remain unaddressed for the most part in a cinema that portrays its makers and subjects as tragic victims caught up in existential moral dilemmas. It is a discourse that by and large prompts mainstream Israeli public opinion to resort to accusations of anti-Semitism in response to critiques of Israeli official policies and avoid a fuller engagement with questions of power and policy between an occupying Israeli army and the occupied Palestinian population.[6] In *My Terrorist* Israeli director Yulie Cohen Gerstel follows Fahad Mihyi, a Palestinian who in 1978 carried out an attack against an El-Al flight crew in London in which she, a young flight attendant, was lightly injured. Years later Gerstel decides to seek him out in his prison cell in England as part of her critical reevaluation of the Zionist ideology she was brought up with. Gerstel refers to him throughout her film as a terrorist to whom she grants her forgiveness for the attack. Gerstel has grown to accept that the Zionist project has dispossessed Palestinians, but does not take the next leap to frame Fahad's act as a struggle for his country and people, as opposed to merely being a terrorist attack (suggesting his were irrational acts motivated by blind hatred and not the result of critical independent thought). She has the power to effect Fahad's release from prison, which fails to resolve the imbalance in their power relationship. She seeks his release because of what she perceives as his redemption, not hers. He has changed his ways; he understands now that what he did was wrong. Both narratives of perpetrator and victim, forgiver and forgiven, articulated by Gerstel, are mediated and framed by and within an Israeli-Zionist framework at the core of her study, and refrain from a critical engagement with questions of victimhood and forgiveness. Here again is where we can productively consider alternatives to the discourses on victimhood that emerge in Gerstel's narratives. In other words, are there other political alternatives that might emerge from Gerstel's film that move us beyond that dichotomy, one which merely replaces an Israeli victim with a Palestinian one? Can the issue be reframed to show that what she leaves out is politics, occupation, colonialism, and racism, among others? Thinking about the situation in those terms, I argue, gives a different kind of critical purchase on an issue that is not so much about personal agency and culpability and suffering as it is about larger and more complex narratives and causes.

Israeli films are not alone in their depiction of the victimization of Israel's soldiers and an absent enemy. As David Desser shows in his discussion of American Vietnam War movies, this is an ideological tendency characteristic of war films, be they Israeli, American, Japanese, or German.[7] As in American Vietnam movies such as *Apocalypse Now* (1977), *Platoon* (1986), and *Full Metal Jacket* (1987), Israeli soldiers/protagonists appear as little more than victims of outside forces beyond their control.[8] However, unlike other cinemas discussed by Desser, Israeli films attempt to engage a reality in which war is not fought against a distant enemy in a foreign land but between two interacting societies in close proximity. Furthermore Israeli films advocate or lament the lack of coexistence, while concomitantly failing to step out of their national boundaries to achieve an understanding of the broad historical complexities of the conflict. Afflicted with political blindness, these films focus initially on what they regard as the deterioration of Israel's ideals and then later on the country's assumed moral superiority, and they offer a monopolitical track of inquiry from an Israeli-Zionist perspective. There is no recognition that the ongoing conflicts Israel is embroiled in are the culmination of a long historical process, rather than just an arena for national accidents, bad leadership, and a trigger for abnormal situations—as I will discuss further. Israeli confessional films, much like American films about the Vietnam War, are, as Michael Klein dubs them, "films of closure," disentangling themselves from their perceived enemies both epistemically and spatially.[9]

First Intifada: "Shooting and Crying"

The outbreak of the first Palestinian intifada in December 1987 brought to the surface some of the underlying ideological tensions in Israeli society.

196 CONFRONTING THE LEGACIES OF TORTURE AND STATE TERROR

To the Israeli public, accustomed to continually seeing itself as the victim, the army's harsh repression of the intifada triggered a principled dilemma over what it perceived as the moral deterioration of Israeli society. In contrast to previous wars, during which Israel fought other armies, the country now engaged a new kind of enemy, civilians, in most cases children. Taught to believe in Israel as a humanist, peace-seeking nation, the Israeli public faced reports and television clips of soldiers mercilessly beating and shooting "legions" of stone-throwing children. The brutality was encapsulated by Yitzhak Rabin, then defense minister in Yitzhak Shamir's national unity government, who, in reference to the Palestinians, ordered Israeli soldiers to "break their bones."

Because it forced Israelis to deal with Palestinian demands for the establishment of an independent state, the intifada also sparked a fierce debate over the future of the Occupied Territories. Secular and religious nationalist parties of the Israeli right regarded any concessions to the Palestinians as a betrayal, and advocated the use of force to suppress the uprising, a complete separation from Palestinians, or, alternatively, the transfer of Palestinians to neighboring Arab countries. These seemingly deep differences did not, however, break down the boundaries of Israeli national political consensus regarding the conflict. Both main political camps agreed that Palestinians, as demonstrated by the intifada, represented a threat to the Jewish national project; they differed only in the methods they preferred for dealing with the threat.

For some filmmakers the first intifada raised issues that represented an extension of the moral dilemmas they faced earlier that decade, when the Israeli army invaded Lebanon in June 1982.[10] Because most filmmakers preferred to distance themselves from the political realities around them, only a relatively small number feature films engaged the first intifada directly, and even then, only during the first few years of the uprising. Such films include *What's Wrong?* (*Ma kara?*) (1988), *The Cage* (*ha-Kluv*) (1989), *Green Fields* (*Sadot yerukim*) (1989), and *Outlook* (*Nekudat tatspit*) (1990). Other films explore it only tangentially, and include *One of Us* (*Ehad mishelanu*) (1989) and *A Deserter's Wife* (*Isha zara*) (1992). According to Israeli film scholar Shmulik Duvdevani, the general silence and political disengagement characterizing Israeli cinema during the time of the first intifada can be attributed to confusion felt by filmmakers who were baffled by images of armed soldiers fighting stone-throwing children, even as their films marked how unviable peace—promoted in Israeli cinema of the 1980s—had become.[11] These films therefore convey much about Israelis' attitudes about themselves, the conflict, and Palestinians. They depict the Israeli man in uniform as a tortured soul—a soldier who bemoans the immorality of shooting at civilians while all the same carrying out what he regards as his patriotic duty to his nation. These films belong to what has become known in Israel as the "shooting and crying" syndrome, coined after a song by a famous Israeli pop singer, Ci Heiman.

Film as a Courthouse: *One of Us*

Many of the first intifada films dealing with Israeli occupation conclude with a confession of the murder of a Palestinian (as often happens in real life—the killing of the boy Muhammad Durra in 2000, for example). The murder victim is usually an innocent passerby, a woman or a child or, as in the case of *One of Us*, a "terrorist"—although the act of violence is never dramatized. In *What's Wrong?* the father of the main character, Gai, cannot sleep at night, worrying about his son, a young soldier on military duty in the Occupied Territories. At first relieved to see Gai waiting for him as he arrives at work, he notices his son's grim expression. "Dad, I killed a woman today," he spits out in agony. The frame freezes on the soldier's tormented face before fading in a slow superimposition to a blatantly clichéd and romantic portrayal of a Palestinian woman: an abstract character, nameless and faceless, she has no history or story. In *Outlook* an Israeli soldier avenges the death of a young Palestinian boy he had grown fond of as he watched the boy's family from his literal and metaphorical position at a military observation point. In his anger the soldier shoots the Palestinian man responsible for the boy's death. In *One of Us* an audiotape discloses an officer's implication in the murder of a Palestinian prisoner, but he stores the incriminating tape with his girlfriend instead of destroying it.

In first intifada films an apparently nonnormative action, such as the killing of a woman in *What's Wrong?* or of a child in *A Deserter's Wife*, appears as a "mistake" or, as in *Green Fields*, the result of temporary insanity and an "abnormal situation" into which a normal family has been thrown.[12] These films offer dovish solutions that have to do with restoring whatever moral strength Israelis imagine themselves as having had in the past. "It's an image of a confused, crazed, desperate nation that has rid itself of its past ideals but has found nothing to replace them [with]," reads one critic's view of the vision of Israel in *Green Fields*.[13] The unchallenged depiction of Israel's "past ideals" notwithstanding, the predominance of confession suggests that by the act of pleading guilty to a "mitigated" murder, order, and normalcy can be restored. As Peter Brooks puts it: "Confession of wrongdoing is considered fundamental to morality because it constitutes a verbal act of self-recognition as wrongdoer and hence provides the basis for rehabilitation. It is the precondition of the end to ostracism, reentry into one's desired place in the human community."[14]

Many have pointed to the narcissistic essence of the confession genre, from Augustine to Rousseau to Dostoevsky's fictional characters. Confession, Dennis Foster argues, "requires that a private knowledge be revealed in a way that would allow another to understand, judge, forgive, and perhaps even sympathize."[15] In addition to these films constituting an expression of remorse and a search for redemption, at some level, in their relationship with the viewer, they also act as a courtroom in which the audience members serve as judges. Using Bakhtinian language, Brooks argues that the confession, even if it comes in the form of a monologue, always has a built-in listener, which makes the confession dialogic. The reaction of the listener, even if silent, is factored into the confessant's address. Indeed, Brooks adds, "the listener's response is in a deep sense what the speech is all about."[16]

The direct dialogue between confessant and audience-as-judge transfers the confession from a private to a public act and the accused from the filmic text to society at large, implicating the audience in both the confessant's sense of guilt and in the confession's possible redemptive qualities. As Brooks argues, those who stand accused are everyone and at the same time no one, reflected in a mirror the confessant holds out to his contemporaries.[17] At the same time confession suggests a division between the remorseful and those without remorse. By confessing Israelis on the left believe that they hold the moral high ground while right-wing factions, who see no need for such expressions of culpability, are regarded by them as bearing the responsibility for the conflict even more than Palestinians.[18]

Uri Barabash's *One of Us* exemplifies the use of the dual principles of redemptive and legal confession.[19] Based on a play written by the filmmaker's brother, Benny Barabash, the film opened about a year after the first intifada broke out in the Occupied Territories. Adapted to the screen, *One of Us* is one of the first Israeli films to touch on the effects of the occupation on Israeli soldiers. The film, which deals with an investigation of an elite military unit suspected of the murder of a Palestinian prisoner, opened in the theaters the same week that four soldiers of Giv'ati, an elite army team, were pardoned for the charge of beating a Palestinian to death. They were acquitted on the grounds that convicting them would negatively affect the sense of solidarity and morale necessary for soldiers to carry out their duties.[20] This political context made the film especially relevant.

In the film an army investigator, Rapha' (Sharon Alexander), arrives at a military base in the Occupied Territories to inquire into the death of a Palestinian prisoner detained there. Upon his arrival Rapha' is surprised to find that the commander of the suspected unit, Yotam (played by Alon Aboutboul), is a former friend and colleague from basic training. A third friend, Amir (Dan Toren), was killed by the slain Palestinian. The main question Rapha' faces is whether to expose the truth about the circumstances surrounding the death of the Palestinian prisoner, who was tortured and eventually shot, or maintain his loyalty to his old friends and approve their version of the story. Torn between his understanding of the truth and the solidarity of the army unit, Rapha' expands his investigation to reexamine his relationship with the group.

Rapha' functions as both interrogator and confessor. His forgiveness and dismissal of the falsified file will allow Yotam, the defendant/confessant, to rejoin society and will clear him, and the Israeli mainstream, of culpability in the unjust actions of the Israeli occupation. On many levels the film functions as a public courtroom, in which Yotam, while addressing Rapha', concomitantly addresses a second, extratextual interrogator/confessor, the audience. In one scene a symbolic courtroom is created in the same place where Amir was killed. After much prodding from Yotam, Rapha' begins to recount in legal language the offenses Yotam's unit committed against the local Palestinian population: "On the night between August 1 and 2 you assembled all of the residents of the refugee camp in the main market square. Then you made them crawl on the ground." Yotam, in response, becomes a defendant, explaining the motives behind his actions. Rapha' is positioned with his back to the camera at the corner of the frame, while Yotam addresses him and the audience at the center of the frame. As the scene reaches its climax Yotam narrates the events leading to Amir's death.

The film, however, constructs a specular image reflected in the affinity between the investigator and the subject of his investigation. It places different values on the life of an Israeli soldier and the Palestinian he killed—a noncharacter, but the only Palestinian in the film. He is consistently referred to as a terrorist, and references to his acts reflect the film's image of Palestinians in general. Yotam, though eventually confessing to his complicity in the murder, does not experience moral remorse for his acts; his only regret is that he was caught. The dilemma the film presents does not center on the morality of Yotam's actions, but on how they affect the long-standing relationships that sustain this microcosm of Israeli society. The death of the Palestinian prisoner has no meaning other than as a trigger for this principled debate.

The film is open-ended, offering no clear solutions. Barabash avoids bringing the events to their dramatic conclusion. Some of this ambivalence can be attributed to the intervention of the military in the making of *One of Us*. In exchange for providing one of its bases for location shooting, the army demanded certain changes be made in the film to fit with military views. For example, the military objected to the ending of the story in the original script, which suggested that Yotam murders Rapha'. A second objection related to Rapha's destroying the evidence once he discovers the truth. The army's disapproval led to a compromise, the ambivalent shot at the end of the film in which it is unclear whether Rapha' has burned the incriminating investigation file. Army officials also demanded that the tone of the scene in which Rapha' is brutally beaten by the soldiers of the platoon under investigation be softened, to defuse any possible critique or negative portrayal of the army. To create an additional barrier between the film and the reality to which it supposedly alludes, *One of Us* opens with a statement by the Israeli military spokesman denouncing any connection between reality and the events in the film.

The film's ambivalent ending avoids any judgment of the characters, who all withdraw into themselves, reflecting the response of certain segments of Israeli society to the first intifada. For mainstream Israeli society, the audience for all of these first intifada films, the military suppression of the uprising was another milestone in Zionism's fall from grace and a sign of the country's moral deterioration. Even if people chose to distance themselves from politics, they were not abandoning the basic assumptions of Zionism, of Jews' right to a national homeland in Palestine. On the contrary, they were concerned only that the moral high ground was lost. Such a view is one of the highly problematic aspects constitutive of liberal Zionist discourse, which never took into account, or preferred to ignore, the fact that a successful fulfillment of its vision meant dispossession and tragedy for the people already living in Palestine.

The first intifada dramatized the inherent contradictions, biases, and iniquities of Zionism. In the face of these contradictions many of Israel's so-called liberals choose to avoid confronting this unpleasant reality altogether by assuming the privilege of withdrawing into their private lives. As attempts to regain this false innocence through admission of guilt fail, confession becomes a goal in and of itself, after which there is nothing.

Normalcy is not restored and escapism and detachment become the alluring alternatives.

Second Intifada and Beyond: "Shooting and Laughing"

Israelis who sought a peaceful settlement welcomed the signing of the 1993 Oslo Accords with great euphoria, regarding it as the end of a century-old conflict. As Amnon Raz-Krakotzkin points out, the accords did not signal a change in Israeli attitudes toward Palestinians; they reflected the desire to preserve Israeli-Zionist identity and goals.[21] The end of the conflict could ultimately bring the final realization of the Zionist dream: normalcy. This dominant word in the Israeli discourse rests on the Zionist ethos of ending Jews' abnormal status in the diaspora and making them into a nation among nations by establishing a Jewish national state in the biblical land of Israel.[22]

The outbreak of the second al-Aqsa intifada in September 2000 abruptly ended the discussion of normalcy through the Oslo Accords' proposed separation and the two-state solution as a means to ending the conflict, evident in important shifts that have occurred in confessional cinema since 2000. While the dominance of confession in the first intifada films suggests a heavy sense of guilt in Israeli society, by the time of the second intifada the onus of responsibility for these acts often shifts to Palestinians and Lebanese. The guilt expressed in these films shifts to anger and blame at what "the situation" makes innocent Israeli soldiers do, and then to a feeling of righteousness and vindication for any acts of violence carried out by the Israeli military, an attitude condemned in one instance by Palestinian MP Dr. Jamal Zahalka, who called it "shooting and laughing."[23] The ensuing blanket condemnation of Zahalka in the Israeli press notwithstanding, his comments point to important changes in the practices and prevailing discourse of the Israeli military. Uri Blau, writing in *Haaretz*, discusses t-shirts printed for Israeli soldiers graduating from military training programs. The slogans printed on these t-shirts reflect the blatant racism and brutality that have become rampant among soldiers. One shirt, ordered by a sniper unit, includes an image of a pregnant "Arab woman" clad in a stereotypical veiled dress, and is captioned, "One shot kills two," celebrating the accomplishments of a successful sniper.[24] The banality that came to characterize Israeli occupation and the everyday conduct of IDF soldiers was further expressed in the public uproar surrounding pictures posted by a former female soldier, Eden Aberjil, on her Facebook page in the summer of 2010. Having completed her military service as a warden in one of Israeli's military prisons in the Occupied Territories, Aberjil shared photographs taken during her military service on Facebook. Against captions like "the most beautiful time of my life," Aberjil is seen smiling into the camera while a number of Palestinian men sit just behind her, blindfolded and handcuffed. The exchange between Aberjil and her friends is no less revealing than the images themselves. One remark includes a crude sexual innuendo about Arab men's alleged enhanced sexuality—"He has an erection because of you, for sure." Another sarcastically says, "I wonder if he has a Facebook page! I have to tag him in the picture," alluding to the practice of tagging the names of people in photographs posted on Facebook, inadvertently emphasizing the anonymity of the Palestinian prisoners captured by Aberjil's photographs.[25] While the Israeli military denounces such activity as extreme nonnormative behavior, and Israeli liberals condemn it as further evidence of the corrupting power of the occupation, only a few dare to examine the underlying dual premises of Zionism—victimhood and entitlement—and its colonial underpinnings in order to fully engage the moral trajectory of Israel's evolution as a nation.

The films do not offer a direct engagement with military acts of violence, remorse, or either the challenges that come with guilt or the political analysis that might come with the passage of time. Some films, such as *Wasted* (*Mevuzbazim*) (2006), *The Alpha Diaries* (*Shalom pluga alef*) (2007), *Every Mother Should Know* (*Teda kol em ivriya*) (2008), and *My First War* (*Hamilchama Harishona Sheli*) (2008), have begun to blame the Israeli government and the military leadership for inept management of the recent wars. At the center of the political debate that followed the Second Lebanon War in the summer of 2006, and reflected in *Every Mother Should Know* and *My First War*, was the Israeli public's critique of what it perceived as the political and military leadership's failures. The debate was less over whether the war was justified and more over the concern that soldiers had been sent to carry out an ill-planned and badly executed war campaign. Here soldiers were portrayed in the media, popular culture, and film as victims of a reality stronger than them, rather than as active agents shaping society and responsible for electing its leadership.[26] The films of this period engage with trauma and provide a healing platform for former soldiers to share the scars left by their military experiences. Israeli confessional films repeatedly iterate the idea of insanity and a hallucinatory reality that takes over as one leaves the boundaries of Israel for the Occupied Territories and Southern Lebanon. "Sometimes I feel a little crazy," says one of the female soldiers in *To See If I'm Smiling* (*Lir'ot im ani mehayehet*) (2007). "I have these memories of things that are unrelated to reality and maybe never happened. But I know they did happen, as I feel them so intensely." The tension between amnesia and remembrance is implicit in the filmmaking process. As the soldiers seek to forget, the act of narrating to the camera reactivates their memories. The impulse to forget seems to kick in only after military service is over, in hindsight.[27]

Most of the recent confessional films reiterate the soldiers' lack of agency and depict them as innocently carrying out orders delivered from above, victims manipulated by unidentified callous politicians. They describe a sense of fear, trauma, horror, and being under attack. The enemy in these films remains invisible, and the consequences of these soldiers' actions remain absent; the soldiers cope with a reality that is imposed on them, but not one in which they are active participants. By the time of the second intifada, post–September 11 discourse also begins to permeate the narrative landscape, in which Israel's battles are seen as embroiled in the global war on terror. Soldiers repeatedly label Palestinian and Lebanese fighters as terrorists, and any acts against civilians are justified by their harboring terrorists. Given that these fighters emerge from and are integral to the fabric of their respective societies, and that they represent a popular resistance against Israel, the failure to distinguish combatants from noncombatants only serves to further justify Israeli military attacks against civilian targets.

Filmmaker as Healer: *Waltz with Bashir*

Waltz with Bashir is perhaps the quintessential and most internationally known confessional film in Israeli cinema of the 2000s. It seeks to engage with an earlier trauma, experienced by director Ari Folman as an IDF soldier during the First Lebanon War in 1982, that culminated with the Sabra and Shatila refugee camps massacre, where thousands of Palestinians were killed by Maronite Phalangists, then under Israeli military control. It shuttles in time between past and present, where Folman's character, through the process of making the film, tries to make sense of his traumas and recover erased memories of former comrades, friends, psychologists, and other key figures involved in the war. The fictional narrative of the film is based on documentary-style interviews, but Folman uses animation to illustrate the stories of those he speaks with as a means to reactivate his buried past. He creates a complete story about his alleged comrades during the war, drawing on testimonies of former soldiers who responded to his newspaper ad inviting interviewees to give testimony to their experiences of the war. Various critics have taken issue with the film's animated format as an inappropriate form for the harsh and tragic issue at hand. Joshua Simon argues that the film (as well as another Israeli film made at that time, Eran Rikli's *The Lemon Tree* [2008]) demonstrates that "the only way that contemporary Israeli cinema is able to deal with politics is to make a children's movie."[28] For Yitzhak Laor the film's comic book style has a reductive effect that estranges and distances the viewer. For him nothing in the film is linked to reality and actual memory, as opposed to manipulated memory. One could argue, however, that it is precisely because the film addresses "unspeakable" events to recover a traumatic past that the choice of animation reactivates suppressed memory while commenting on the subject's inner state of mind. The film's stunning visual style allows viewers to empathize with its protagonists, not as heroes but merely as sensitive individuals. Folman's choice to animate his film obviously breaks any pretense of the indexicality of footage and reality. One could further argue that his choice to animate is a deliberate attempt to cast doubts on the already illusive nature of memory and emphasize the subjective nature of its depiction of the war. The recorded interviews of actual people provide the voice-overs for the animated figures, and the real individuals are mixed with fictionalized characters, further blurring the distinction between reality and imagination.

Waltz with Bashir claims to reveal the folly of war in general, the wasted human life, the insanity of battle, and the pain it inflicts on those participating in it.[29] The film animator, David Polonsky, said in an interview that one of the most important things for him in animating the film was not to introduce the soldiers as children and victims. "They are not shooting and crying. There is no romantic glory and forgiveness in war. [The film offers] a clear and simple message that war is a terrible thing. We made a great effort not to pass the message that war is something heroic and that soldiers are . . . heroes and . . . role model[s]." Folman adds, "[The film] lacks the Israeli military sheen, glorification of the soldiers. Everyone in the film is an anti-hero."[30] *Waltz with Bashir* then, according to its makers, represents another milestone in the trajectory of political films released since the first intifada, depicting the ongoing transformation of the hero in Israeli cinema as a reflection of the loosened grip of Zionist mythology (though not necessarily its underlying ideological principles) over the country's society. Following Israel's near defeat in the 1973 War and the controversy over the First Lebanon War, the heroic figure of the nationalist era was transformed first into a man crippled by the trauma of war and then into the "shooting and crying" character of the intifada era. Films of the 1990s such as *Burning Memories* (*Resisim*) (1989), *The Deserter's Wife* (1991), *Real Time* (*Zman emet*) (1991), and *Time for Cherries* (*Onat ha-duvdevanim*) (1991) all depict the Israeli soldier as disturbed, crippled, or paralyzed by the experience of war, be it the Lebanon War or the intifada. The futility of war marks the protagonist as a victim and stands as a barrier between him and a peaceful existence.

While Folman battles with amnesia and lost memories of his own wartime actions, another strand of pervasive memory invades the film's landscape—that of the Holocaust. The film synthesizes imagery and key concepts that are iconic in Israel's official discourse about the Holocaust. Consequently, the film shows how the Jewish state's assumed duty to "never forget" shapes and informs its present engagement with its enemies, and how Folman's own family legacy as a son of Holocaust survivors connects him to the collective memory institutionalized by the state. *Waltz with Bashir* is replete with visual references that have become synonymous with the memory of the Holocaust, such as the little boy raising his hands at the Auschwitz concentration camp, and the skeletal figures of the young men emerging from the sea in Folman's hallucination scene—his only memory of the Sabra and Shatila massacre. The latter scene is pivotal to my analysis of the confessional particularities of the film, a primal moment of purity and sublime transformation, where the naked soldiers emerge from the purifying sea to don their combat fatigues and engage in the messy business of war. The young men submerged in the calm baptismal waters rise— innocent, puzzled, and confused—gazing at Beirut burning in front of them. They put on their uniforms as they slip into their new role as soldiers, transplanted into this new context almost by divine intervention, suggested by the bloody orange sky and rising dawn. The young soldiers appear perplexed, out of place, silent witnesses as they stare at the anonymous and uniformly clad sea of women passing by them. The repetition of this scene throughout the film marks it as a primal moment of prebirth, a cleansing moment before and outside of time, that provides Folman the necessary space where absolution and healing can take place. Shuttling between his moments of amnesia and hallucination, the film ultimately creates an extratemporal space where characters can escape responsibility.

In the soldiers' discussions of memory, Folman's absence in the narrative space further serves to absolve him—and by extension audiences identifying with the main character—from responsibility for the crimes addressed in the film. The making of the film as a therapeutic process relieves the protagonists not from a sense of guilt over the war's dead victims, as Udi

Aloni points out, but from the unpleasant images of war.³¹ What the film consciously and deliberately aims to do is to break down reality into little pieces of torn memory, fragments of memories loosely pieced together. It is that deliberate insistence on incomprehension and amnesia that ultimately absolves the characters not only from the past but also from their present lives as compromised individuals crippled by their past traumas. Folman's traumatized character shifts the victimhood from the camps survivors of the massacre to the witness cooperating with the perpetrators. The actual casualities are not shown in the film, except for an allegorical reference in the opening scene, where a herd of angry dogs shot by an Israeli soldier during the war comes back to haunt him in his dreams. Against this substitution of Palestinian or Lebanese enemies with dogs stands, therefore, the Israeli humanist soldier who agonizes over having shot dogs, suggesting the overall superiority of Israeli soldiers and their moral quandaries.³² The dogs, as a reference to Palestinians, function as a catalyst that triggers the suppressed memory for the traumatized Israeli soldier, who is stuck between a faceless enemy and a reckless leadership.

The film's kindly protagonist, Folman, is haunted by what he saw as a witness to the massacre, which triggers his amnesia of the war. It is only in the last few minutes of the film that Folman presents actual footage of the massacre and anchors the bloody story of the war squarely outside the boundaries of Israel and its actions, limiting all blame to blood-thirsty Phalangists seeking to revenge the death of their leader, Bashir Gemayel. Such a strategy overlooks the heavy Israeli shelling of densely populated cities and towns that lead to the deaths of thousands of civilians.³³ The film ultimately reduces the First Lebanon War to the massacres of Sabra and Shatila. Israeli critics of the film have pointed to the ultimate responsibility of the Israeli leadership, and more specifically of the then minister of defense, Ariel Sharon, for the massacres of Sabra and Shatila, and accused the film of deflecting both individual and collective responsibility for the incidents. Folman looks to these massacres not as a way of addressing guilt or individual accountability but in order to depict the trauma of war. The absolution offered by the confessional genre becomes in *Waltz with Bashir* a purging of the personal and collective responsibility of Israeli society (as opposed to the Israeli leadership). As Folman says in the film, "It's not in my system," and in an interview in the Israeli press: "A massacre is not on the radar of people like us. You don't even conceive that people are slaughtered for three days. You don't put the pieces together."³⁴ Yet the making of the film took place when Ariel Sharon, who was condemned for his role in the Sabra and Shatila massacre, was elected again as prime minister. The film itself was released in Israeli theaters during the Israeli attack on Gaza in December 2008, when over a thousand Palestinian civilians died, including hundreds of women, children, and the elderly, invoking scenes that according to Israeli critic Gideon Levy were not that different from those portrayed in *Waltz with Bashir*.[35] Folman's overall emphasis on the folly of war in general, as opposed to its specific instances, disables any critical engagement with real wars. Ultimately, *Waltz with Bashir* is skillfully punctuated by absences: It's not me. It's not a war movie. It's not our massacre. I have no memory.

Questions of Accountability: *Z32*

Documentary filmmaker Avi Mograbi's *Z32* was released at about the same time as *Waltz with Bashir*. Although it did not get the same international attention as Folman's film, *Z32* presents an intellectually far more sincere and in-depth engagement with the question of Israeli military violence, guilt, and responsibility. The film tells the story of a young Israeli and former soldier in a military elite unit, identified as Ronnie, who is haunted by his guilt for partaking in the killing of two innocent Palestinian policemen in an army revenge operation. The film is named after the file belonging to the Israeli human rights group Breaking the Silence that documents the incident on which the story is based. It revolves around the soldier's attempts to absolve himself and seek forgiveness from his girlfriend and from the world more broadly. The actual incident, which lasted about twenty minutes, is told and retold throughout the film, conveying the soldier's almost obsessive insistence on forgiveness, as if the mere repeating of the story could suffice to bring absolution.

As with most of his previous films, Mograbi structures *Z32* along parallel narratives that link his engagement as a filmmaker with the documentary subject of the film itself and integrates fictionalized segments that serve as a commentary on the documentary footage, accentuating the discursive nature of documentary filmmaking. Here he interjects Brechtian musical interludes that expose his own process of questioning and his struggles in making the film: Is he helping to harbor a murderer, while scraping together another film out of the situation? Can this person be forgiven? As Ginsburg has pointed out, Mograbi "insists that the process of making a documentary is one of the crucial, if not the most crucial aspects of the reality depicted and that, therefore, the process should be included in the documentary."[36]

Mograbi intentionally avoids asking his protagonist about his motivations. He is solely focused on the act around which the film is centered. Thus Mograbi avoids discussing with Ronnie his guilt in order to avoid subjecting himself to the soldier's desire for forgiveness and becoming Ronnie's judge and prosecutor, redeemer and forgiver. It is Ronnie's girlfriend who fulfills those functions. Mograbi also seeks to avoid developing any relationship with the soldier because, he says, he felt that might create unavoidable empathy.[37] The question of empathy is treated as a gendered matter, whereby the soldier's girlfriend is assigned the role of caregiver and forgiver. Sheltered from his violence and alluded to as having not served in the military, she offers the insights of an outsider, interrogator, and confessant, but is treated as ultimately incapable of understanding the soldier's plight. Equally, the director's wife struggles to comprehend the director's desire and need to engage with this confessing soldier's need for redemption. Both women, in their disparate roles, have difficulty understanding, and are passively positioned outside the masculine dichotomy of violence and empathy at the heart of this film. This depiction begs the question about Israeli women's role as active participants in national violence, portrayed in films like *To See If I'm Smiling*.

Mograbi is preoccupied with the question of violence in Israeli society, a thread that runs throughout his films. This violence, in Mograbi's opinion, is far from limited to the confines of the Israeli-Palestinian conflict and war zones with neighboring Arab counties and seeps into every aspect of Israeli daily life—in interactions on the street and in parliament, as well as inside homes. In *Z32* Mograbi's own living room functions as a central arena where the questioning of morality and accountability plays out, a space where Ronnie's confession is recorded, where Mograbi's orchestra convenes to accompany Mograbi's contemplative singing. It is a space where Mograbi collapses Israeli society's insistence on the dichotomous landscapes between "here" and "there," between high morals represented within the boundaries of Israel proper and the actions of those easily dismissed as wild weeds generated by Israel's engagement in the Occupied Territories. Mograbi sarcastically crones, "It happened somewhere out there, don't bring it over here. . . . It's a story about a soldier who was raised to be one of the hot shots. Who was cultivated to wait until they let him . . . charge."

Self-reflexively, Mograbi then analyzes the effect of this violence on his fictionalized self—the filmmaker in the film. In *Z32* the performance of the confessional act is expanded beyond the scope of the soldier narrating and repeating his story to include the filmmaker himself. In the fictionalized scenes Mograbi's character enters into a performative duo with the confessing soldier. In a sense this dialogical performance with the confessant extends Mograbi's underlying premise that as a filmmaker he cannot avoid becoming implicated in the same violence that his film seeks to explore. The camera is not only a recorder of violence, but also precipitates it. Thus, in contrast to *Waltz with Bashir*, here society, filmmaker, and camera are all generators and active participants in acts of violence, not merely passive consumers or observers of it. Ginsburg asked whether these reenactments, ironic as they are, function to reveal or in fact to mask the filmmaker. It is that tension that Mograbi seeks to play on.

Mograbi's camera, which in earlier films served as a witness, reporter, and opposition activist, opens up a space of reflection and debate in *Z32*. The violence permeating every scene in films like *August (Ogust)* (2002) and *Avenge But One of My Two Eyes (N'qam ahat mi-shte' enai)* (2005) now occupies a new space, configured as a postclimactic arena, a theraputic space. Except for the thread that follows Ronnie and Mograbi's return to the scene of the crime to reconstruct the events surrounding the killings, all other scenes take place in closed private spaces: the filmmaker's living room, Ronnie and his girlfriend's apartment, a hotel room in India where the couple is staying. The filmmaker's living room workspace, populated by characters, is also the director's own private space and comfort zone, into which his wife walks in one of the scenes. Ronnie's apartment, where he has soul-searching conversations with his girlfriend, is also the space where he carries on with his everyday life, as reflected in a sequence that takes place while the couple are eating their lunch. The camera in *Z32* takes on a dominant role as if it were one of the characters in the film, seeking a final and ultimate space where engagement and healing can be explored. The film opens with Ronnie and his girlfriend as they switch on the camera, getting ready to engage each other as witness and confessant, and the camera plays a crucial role. "Is it rolling? . . . Do you think the frame looks good? . . . Okay, talk," the girlfriend tells Ronnie. At first they address their awkwardness speaking to the camera, acknowledging its presence. By the end of the film, however, the camera becomes the final witness, as the exasperated couple reach the limit of their exchange, and words can no longer provide the necessary shield and relief. When language fails, an awkward silence falls as they gaze into the recording lens and finally decide that nothing has really been resolved and there is nothing left to do but turn it off.

Ronnie is incapable of making the ultimate confession—I am a murderer. Instead he is focused on, and even obsessed with, his personal redemption and ability to reintegrate into society and resume his "normal" life.

After a long exchange with his girlfriend—in which she struggles to understand his predicament and clearly exclaims that what he was engaged in was murder—Ronnie does not even pause, ponder or reflect, but immediately bolts out, "And do you forgive me?" His actual engagement with the implications and meanings of his actions is limited to his own absolution. He then continues, in an accusing tone, "You know, it calls for some kind of forgiveness or acceptance." The reconciliation he wants is with his own people, society, and life partner, not with his victims and their families, as is so strikingly evident in the reenactment scenes of the crime, where the Palestinian victim is absent. Mograbi's return to the scene of the crime with Ronnie to reconstruct the details of the event is similar to the parallel scene in *One of Us*; here the scene becomes the ultimate courtroom where Ronnie must confront his crime. But while in *One of Us* the courtroom scene is aimed at excavating a hidden truth, in *Z32* that truth has already been told, and it is its interpretation that is being contested. The issue of responsibility is at the heart of Mograbi's exploration, not only the soldier's personal responsibility for his actions, but also the responsibility of a society whose culture makes such actions possible. In some respects Mograbi is inadvertently exonerating the soldier and absolving him of his own responsibility by putting the onus on a society that makes good people do bad things.[38] The film is further centered on what Israelis could argue is an extreme event: a revenge operation carried out in response to the Palestinian killing of six Israeli soldiers. As it is an extreme event, Mograbi is able to offer a clear moral dilemma for Israeli audiences who view the occupation as a necessary measure to guarantee their security.

Throughout his work Mograbi is highly conscious of the implications of Zionism and Israel's presence for Palestinians. While Mograbi is critical of the Israeli state, he does not necessarily address Zionist ideology more specifically as a possible starting point to critically examine and evaluate Israel's current violence. Furthermore his films, *Z32* included, focus primarily on the consequences of Israel's control of Palestinians for Israelis, and Palestinians are absent from *Z32*'s landscape. One can attribute that absence to Ronnie's disregard for Palestinians, most strikingly evident in the reconstruction scenes, where he completely ignores the presence of any Palestinians passing through the frame as he retells his story of the killing. But Palestinians and the Palestinian presence are generally absent from Mograbi's films as a whole, punctuating the lingering effects of their presence, and mirroring their absence from Israeli society. Mograbi leaves Palestinian agency to Palestinians and focuses his discussion on the conflict as an internal Israeli issue. The unifying core space of most of his films, a critical engagement with his own living room, so to speak, remains largely off limits. It is a site that, while representing his internal struggles vis-à-vis the outside world gone mad, remains a space of civility. Perhaps not coincidentally, Mograbi's musical references to Bertold Brecht, which annotate and comment on the crumbling world outside, are most strongly associated with the perceived high values of the European culture of early Zionism and, with his own home at the center of Tel Aviv, reflect that culture's precarious position in contemporary Israeli society.

Waltz with Bashir and *Z32* were developed and released around the same time, yet offer dramatically different approaches to the question of accountability. Both films reflect on a soldier's trauma during military service, but neither shows us archival or documentary footage of the events addressed. Both films offer distinct styles to address this visually inaccessible past, infusing theatricality and drama into the narrative elements, whether recreating a past and evoking an emotional reaction to it through visual (*Waltz*) or musical (*Z32*) elements. Both films strive to make illustrative or cognitive associations between image, sound, and testimony. While Folman opts for highly deft animation to present his characters, Mograbi chooses to put a digital mask on the face of his character to disguise his identity. The brilliant execution of the masking may leave viewers wondering if they are privy to the soldier's actual facial characteristics. Throughout the film Mograbi reminds us of the mask in shots that tease out its presence. This technique allowed Mograbi to retain access to the soldier's facial expressions as an important element of his character, while allowing the soldier to hide his identity to avoid any legal liability. While Mograbi strives to remove barriers between viewer and character, Folman's decision to animate his film seems to indicate a pull in the other direction, providing his characters a shield behind which they can stand and act. Yet the film's lack of emotional depth leaves viewers with a sterile sense of the horror of war and the moral dilemmas the film wants to address. The choice of animation and disguise emphasize what has already become an accepted truism about subjectivity and the active role of narrative in documentary films.

Both films are framed by a particular set of musical references that signify the filmmakers' respective struggles with the declining ideals of and challenges to Zionist Israel's Ashkenazi Jewish elite. The European cultural heritage of the Viennese waltz provides the frame in *Waltz with Bashir*, as does the music of Wiel and theater of Bertold Brecht in *Z32*. It is a tradition now punctured by the rhythm of gunshots, as the Israeli soldier waltzes in the midst of a street battle to the whistle of bullets shooting by; it crescendos with soul-searching Brechtian music and lyrics sung by Mograbi as he contemplates military morality and the responsibility of Israeli society.

In *The Politics of Regret* Jeffrey Olick addresses how the rise of individualism, increased division of labor, and the growth of polyglot modern societies effects a greater need for forgiveness as a means to regulate and maintain social order.[39] Within such dense networks of relations any one action triggers a wide circle of implications. Israel was a polyglot society from its inception, and its binding glue has been the firm hold of Zionist ideology. The internal and external political-existential challenges to the Israeli state, as evident in Israeli confessional cinema, coupled with the rise of individualism and a consumer society in the 1990s, have loosened the threads binding Israel's people. The main question now is, what part of itself does Israeli society hope to regulate in the making of these confessional films? The discourse is internal, aimed in most instances (*Z32* being the exception) at healing and restoring to Israeli society its moral image of itself, but also international, as Israel seeks to maintain its image as "the only democracy in the Middle East" in the face of growing international criticism. Ultimately, the act of confession implies a desire for forgiveness, an acknowledgement of wrongdoing, and penance. Because the majority of Israeli films do not really address guilt or responsibility, they confess without regret toward their victims. In the absence of engagement with the direct victim in the epistemological space of confession, reconciliation cannot realistically be the intended outcome of the confessing Israeli perpetrator/soldier; rather, what we witness as viewers is the desire to confess in order to forget.

NOTES

1. Meron Benvenisti, *Sacred Landscapes* (Berkeley: University of California Press, 2002).
2. Leigh A. Payne, *Unsettling Accounts: Neither Truth nor Reconciliation in Confessions of State Violence* (Durham: Duke University Press, 2008), 1; Daniel Levy and Nathan Sznaider, "Forgive and Not Forget: Reconciliation Between Forgiveness and Resentment," in *Taking Wrongs Seriously: Apologies and Reconciliation*, ed. Elazar Barkan and Alexander Karn, 84 (Palo Alto: Stanford University Press, 2005), 84.
3. In addition to the references listed in notes 1 and 2, there has been extensive literature on this subject, including Mark Gibney, *The Age of Apology: Facing up to the Past* (Philadelphia: University of Pennsylvania Press, 2008); Jennifer M. Lind, *Sorry States: Apologies in International Politics* (Ithaca: Cornell University Press,

2010); Melissa Nobles, *The Politics of Official Apologies* (Cambridge: Cambridge University Press, 2008); and Jeffrey K. Olick, "Times for Forgiveness: A Historical Perspective," in *Considering Forgiveness*, ed. Aleksandra Wagner (New York: Vera List Center for Arts and Politics, New School, 2009), 85–92.
4. Payne, *Unsettling Accounts*, 13.
5. Works on this subject include Ilan Pappé, *The Making of the Arab-Israeli Conflict, 1947–51* (London: Tauris, 1992), and *The Israel/Palestine Question* (London: Routledge, 1999); Avi Shlaim, *The Politics of Partition: King Abdullah, the Zionists, and Palestine, 1921–1951* (New York: Columbia University Press, 1990); and Benny Morris, *The Birth of the Palestinian Refugee Problem, 1947–1949* (Cambridge: Cambridge University Press, 1987).
6. Following the international criticism of Israel's attack on the flotilla to Gaza in May 2010, for example, Israeli public opinion turned against Turkey. Previously, Israelis had regarded Turkey as their only Muslim ally in the region and a popular tourist destination for cheap vacations; however, they now heavily criticize Turkey for its long-standing brutal suppression of Kurdish human rights. The UN and its various agencies, once regarded as a source of support, are now frequently criticized for their one-sided condemnation of Israel. While obviously other instances of international human rights violations are strongly condemnable, this attitude among Israelis avoids and seeks to deflect attention from and engagement with Israel's violation of human rights and international law.
7. David Desser, "Charlie Don't Surf: Race and Culture in the Vietnam War Films," in *Inventing Vietnam: The War in Film and Television*, ed. Michael Anderegg (Philadelphia: Temple University Press, 1991), 88.
8. This point about Vietnam movies is made by Tony Williams, "Narrative Patterns and Mythic Trajectories in Mid-1980s Vietnam Movies," in Anderegg, *Inventing Vietnam*, 125.
9. Michael Klein, "Historical Memory, Film, and the Vietnam Era," in *From Hanoi to Hollywood: The Vietnam War in American Film*, ed. Linda Dittmar and Gene Michaud, 22 (New Brunswick: Rutgers University Press, 1990).
10. Michal Bat-Adam as quoted in Hagai Levy, "Mehakim li" [They Are Waiting for Me], *Hadashot*, May 28, 1993; Amit Goren as quoted in Yael Israel, "ha-Ehad me'orav ha-sheni lo" [One Is Involved, the Other Is Not], *Al ha-Mishmar*, July 14, 1989.
11. Shmulik Duvdevani, *Guf Rishon, Matzlema: Kolno'a Ti'udi Ishi be-Israel* [First-Person Camera: Documentary Filmmaking in Israel] (Jerusalem: Keter, 2010), 86.
12. Shlomo Papirblat, "Kesheata tofes."
13. Dan Fainaru, "Frittered 'Fields.'"
14. Peter Brooks, *Troubling Confessions: Speaking Guilt in Law and Literature* (Chicago: Chicago University Press, 2000), 2.
15. Dennis A. Foster, *Confession and Complicity in Narrative* (Cambridge: Cambridge University Press, 1987), 2.

16. Brooks, *Troubling Confessions*, 163. A similar argument is made by Michel Foucault in *The History of Sexuality: An Introduction*, trans. Robert Hurley (Harmondsworth, UK: Penguin, 1981), 59–62.
17. Brooks, *Troubling Confessions*, 164.
18. Various Israeli films reflect this attitude; one can find it in *Palestine Circus (Kirkas Palestina)* (Eyal Halfon, 1998), and more so in documentaries such as *119 Bullets and Three (119 kadurim ve-shalosh)* (Yeud Levanon, 1996), *Inside God's Bunker (be-Tokh ha-bunker shel elohim)* (Micha Peled, 1994), and *Reflection: A Diary of a Reserve Soldier 1989 (Hishtakfut: yomanu shel hayal milu'im 1989)* (Yishai Shuster, 1991).
19. Barabash, more than any other Israeli filmmaker, directly engages problems of contemporary Israeli society. In his best-known film, *Beyond the Walls*, and its sequel, *Beyond the Walls II*, he examines Arab-Jewish relations within an Israeli prison. In his next film, *Dreamers (ha-Holmim)* (1987), an English-language epic, he focuses on an early community of Jewish settlers in Palestine. *One of Us (Ehad mi-shelanu)* (1989) signals the beginning of Barabash's interest in various aspects of the Israeli army. Together with his brother—scriptwriter, former military lieutenant colonel, and Peace Now activist Benny Barabash—he developed this theme in films like the musical *Strawberries (le-Lakek ta 'tut)* (1992), focusing on a military musical troupe, and the television series *Basic Training (Tironut)*, which has aired on Channel 2 since 1998.
20. Calev Ben-David, "Ambiguities in Khaki," *Jerusalem Post*, October 20, 1989.
21. See Amnon Raz-Krakotzkin, "A Peace Without Arabs: The Discourse of Peace and the Limits of Israeli Consciousness," in *After Oslo: New Realities, Old Problems*, ed. George Giacaman and Dag Jørund Lønning, 60 (London: Pluto Press, 1998).
22. As Tom Segev points out, what constitutes normal and abnormal can be debated. For him the impoverishment of most countries in the non-Western world is actually "normal." A state to which only members of one particular religion are allowed to immigrate while its indigenous people are denied similar rights is "abnormal." Tom Segev, "Mekhonit Folsvagen ba-kibbutz, nani'ah" [Let's Suppose, a Volkswagen in the Kibbutz], in *Sefer Haaretz: ha-shana ha-75* [*Haaretz*: The Seventy-fifth Year], ed. Yehoshua Knaz, 173–76 (Tel Aviv: Shukan, 1996).
23. "Ha-hak-im neged Zoabi: Mehuma, klalot ve-kim'at Makot," [MPs Against Zoabi: Chaos, Curses, and Almost Hitting], Ynet.co, http://www.ynet.co.il/articles/0,7340,L-3898005,00.html.
24. Uri Blau, "Korbanot Ofna: Ha-Hedpesim shs-al Hultzut Yehidot Tahal: Hereg Tinokot ve-Nashim be-Herayon" [Fashion Victims: Prints on IDF T-shirts: Killing of Infants and Pregnant Women], *Haaretz*, March 20, 2009, http://www.haaretz.co.il/hasite/spages/1072299.html.
25. Aberjil's Facebook photographs generated a heated discussion in the Israeli press. See, for example, Uri Misgav, "ha-Banaliyut shel ha-Kibush" [The Banality of Occupation], *Yediot Aharonot*, August 20, 2010; *Haaretz*, "I would gladly kill

Arabs—even slaughter them," August 10, 2010, http://www.haaretz.com/news/national/i-would-gladly-kill-arabs-even-slaughter-them-1.309031.

26. This sentiment was epitomized in a speech given by renowned Israeli writer David Grossman, who lost his son Uri during the last day of the war; he gave a strong voice to the Israeli leftist elite in debates on the war as well as the IDF and government leaderships' abandonment of soldiers on the battlefield.

27. But, as Israeli critic Yitzhak Laor considers in his critique of *Waltz with Bashir*, do these films ultimately serve to protect their audiences from the memory of the war, in this particular instance the massacre of Sabra and Shatila? "Is the director's amnesia in the film providing a cinematic space for audiences to keep a safe distance from its horrors, from actually remembering it?" Yitzhak Laor, "Dor Shalem Doresh Tashlum," *Haaretz*, February 27, 2009, http://www.haaretz.co.il/hasite/pages/ShArt.jhtml?itemNo=1067189.

28. Joshua Simon, review of *Valtz im Bashir* (*Waltz with Bashir*), by Ari Folman, *Maaravon*, no. 5 (Summer 2009): 4.

29. In an interview with Terry Gross on *Fresh Air*, on NPR, December 23, 2008, Folman kept claiming this universal kind of message, dodging any further talk about the barely discussed specifics of the Lebanon War itself. See http://www.npr.org/templates/story/story.php?storyId=98634515.

30. *Haaretz*, June 6, 2008, www.haaretz.com/hasite/spages/990093.html.

31. Adam Horowitz, "Israeli Filmmaker to Jerry Seinfeld: 'Don't Cooperate with the Occupation,'" *Mondoweiss*, September 22, 2009, http://mondoweiss.net/2009/09/israeli-filmmaker-to-jerry-seinfeld-dont-cooperate-with-the-occupation.html.

32. The image of dogs also triggers Israeli associations with the Holocaust, as testimonies by Holocaust survivors often described the ways in which the Nazis used dogs against Jews in the camps. The association between dogs and Nazis is also referenced by the dog in the German porn movie one of the Israeli soldiers watches during the film. In a piece commissioned by the Sharjah Biennale in 2009, artist Agnes Janish created "Man to Man," a claustrophobic maze that references the dog kennels at Auschwitz, where the food, conditions, and health care were comparatively better than those endured by human prisoners at the camp. In the artist's commentary about the piece in the biennale's catalog, Janish references the legacy of this experience and its emotional impact as it relates to the Israeli-Palestinian context. See *Provisions*, Sharjah Biennale catalog, (Sharjah: Sharjah Art Foundation, 2009), 249–56.

33. According to Human Rights Watch, 1,125 Lebanese died during the 2006 Lebanon War, as well as 119 Israeli soldiers and 40 civilians. See Human Rights Watch, *Why They Died: Civilian Casualties in Lebanon During the 2006 War*, Vol. 19, no. 5(E), September 2007.

34. Rogel Alper, "Tzayer li Zva'a: Re'ayon im Ari Fulman" [Draw Me a Nightmare: An Interview with Ari Fullman], MaarivNRG, www.nrg.co.il/online/5/ART1/742/935.html.

35. Gideon Levy, "Ezor ha-Dimdumim-Valtz im Bashir," Haaretz, February 27, 2009, www.haaretz.co.il/hasite/spages/1065537.html.
36. Shai Ginsburg, "Studying Violence: The Films of Avi Mograbi," Zeek, October 24, 2009, http://zeek.forward.com/articles/115717/.
37. Avi Mograbi, interview with the author, New York, September 14, 2009
38. In her introduction to Evil to the Core, an exhibition presented at the Digital Center in Holon, Israel, in 2009, curators Galit Eilat and Ran Kasmy Ilan reference a variety of works by behavioral psychologists, philosophers, and artists who sought to examine similar issues of docility, social conformity, morality, authority, and obedience, and perhaps most importantly, questions of disobedience and its contested relationship to loyalty and patriotism, especially in the Israeli context. See http://www.digitalartlab.org.il/ExhibitionPage.asp?id=372&path=level_1.
39. Jeffrey K. Olick, The Politics of Regret (New York: Routledge, 2002).

PART IV

Torture and the Shortcomings of Film

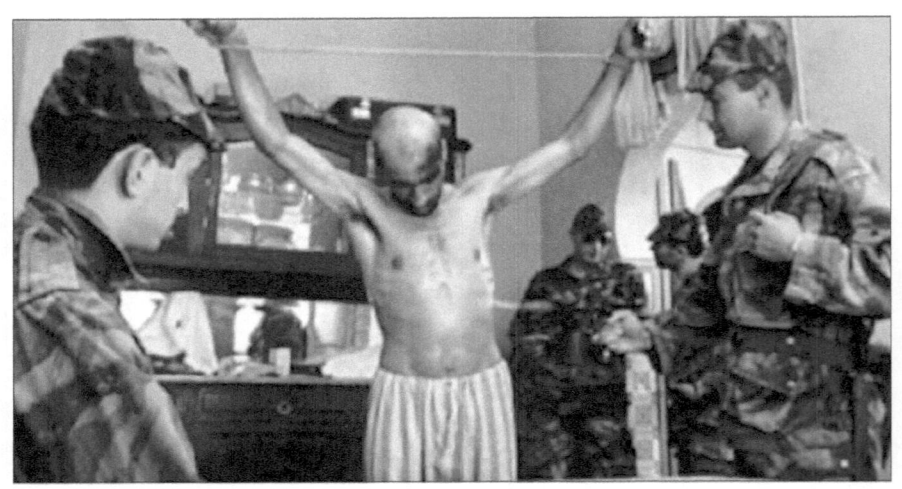

The Battle of Algiers, 1966

10
Movies of Modern Torture as Convenient Truths

Darius Rejali

Torture movies purvey convenient truths. But I don't mean here to document conscious misdirection or blissful ignorance. Rather, in life people make certain misrepresentations that are convenient, even when they should know better. Convenient truths, like urban legends, don't respect political boundaries. They can be found equally on left and right, among policy makers, academics, reporters, artists, and directors. I'll identify what makes a truth convenient, but those interested in further evidence for my claims may refer to *Torture and Democracy*, an 850-page sourcebook on how torture technology works.[1]

Here I'll map how convenient truths circulate, and how movies convey this thoughtlessness. After some preliminaries I'll focus on two theses about torture. One is sometimes called torture's oldest urban legend, namely, that torture works. The other is the belief that a single universal distributor (Evil Devices R Us) is the source of all modern tortures. Each thesis leans heavily on convenient truths, and often that is why people cite these theses thoughtlessly.

Convenient Truths

Two tired students, Bob and Ann, meet in a library lobby one night. Ann complains, "I've been here since 10 A.M." "Tell me about it!" says Bob; "I've been here since 7 A.M.," or "Yeah, I've been here every day this week till 2 A.M."

Libraries are for studying, as everyone knows. But some students, budding social scientists, wonder what their peers actually do in libraries. They observe students talking to friends, sleeping at desks, texting, eating furtively, doodling, and many other activities that don't involve studying. They administer a library survey, asking how much time a student spends on each activity. They discover that poor students have no private quarters, so they study in libraries. But most use libraries mainly to socialize. Libraries help them cultivate social networks they use for fun, opportunity, and employment.[2]

Now Bob and Ann could have been telling the truth. But the odds are that most such chats are status games. In these games students use the notion that "libraries are for studying" to generate a convenient truth, that the time spent in library *is* time spent studying. Some students then use their clocked time to outdo each other. They would be bothered by a sociological study that raises doubts about whether they are the workers they claim to be. Students would label the student-sociologist a nerd, and then resume the status game.

Forging convenient truths is a process by which people habitually pass off one activity or situation as another.[3] Library time is study time, for instance. So life can go on we are going to proceed in *this way*. People misrecognize such claims for truth because they are invested in particular ways of thinking about themselves and others. To proceed otherwise would be unthinkable or, at least, deeply disconcerting. Convenient truths lie at the border of consent and coercion. Students don't punch the library clock to win a status game, but how long they spend in the library is an important talking point. And people partner in confirming each other's misrepresentations, even if one of them is worse off as a result. Students who lose the status game still participate in it; who wants to be the nerd?

Like urban legends, convenient truths are difficult to correct when they involve things that can't be seen or easily verified. Imagine three professors complaining about how hard they work. Office time *is* work time; who will dare check up on professors in their offices? Still, challenging urban legends doesn't offend people. Challenging convenient truths does, because it questions the way people present themselves.

Convenient truths are socially maintained. People collaborate with each other in misrepresentations. This phenomenon differs from false consensus and pluralistic ignorance, where individuals judge what others think incorrectly and act accordingly.[4] Yet convenient truths aren't simply lies we share. Students in libraries study some of the time; they just don't keep track of how much time. People recruit others into sharing convenient truths, and thus misrepresenting the world. University administrators, for example, may participate in the students' misdirection. Repeating how much time students spend in the library recruits paying customers, reinforces one's scholarly reputation, and justifies financial investments. But convenient truths aren't worldviews. Ideologues can cite them, but opposing ideologies can share the same misrepresentation.

Torture, Movies, and Convenient Truths

Commonly, when people ask me about torture movies, they are asking about *why* people do evil, and the stories we tell about them. I discuss this elsewhere,[5] so I will pass over the *why* of torturers and consider the *how* of torture. Most people don't really know how torture works, that is, the techniques, their genesis, and their effects on human beings. Hell in torture is in the details. People forge convenient truths often by ignoring details. In turn noting details offers a good way to understand how people forge and circulate convenient truths. Once one pays attention to how torture works, certain accounts of why torture happens become implausible.

Why, for example, did soldiers take the Abu Ghraib photographs? Historically, soldiers have taken torture photographs for many local reasons. For example, battlefield trophy photography is a genre. The explanation that captured the most attention came from Seymour Hersh, the prize-winning journalist. According to Hersh, soldiers took the photographs in order to blackmail prisoners to give information on the insurgency.[6] Now if you were blackmailing prisoners, would you put bags over their heads and *then* take pictures? Would you take pictures of their torsos, the backs of their heads, and their buttocks?

Like students discussing their library work, Hersh isn't exactly lying, even though he has seen the photographs that undermine his explanation. Many others have repeated this convenient truth (Abu Ghraib photographs equal blackmail plan) because it fits into a broader notion of why torture happened there. Suggesting something is planned means someone higher up ordered it. The blackmail story conveniently fits the story of centrally organized torture.[7] No one attends too much to torture's details, the *how* of torture, in this case the photographs. When someone points to them, then everyone feels uncomfortable. The photographs violate a deep norm: don't blame the troops; blame the higher ups. Supporting the troops is an unspoken journalistic norm, and these photographs do not fit the story of centrally organized torture, the story many peopled wanted to hear.

Like reporters, moviemakers relate convenient truths. However, movies show whereas news articles tell. Telling in this case means providing statements that can be critically evaluated. When something is shown it can more easily escape evaluation. As the convenient truth forms the film's background, viewers affirm it carelessly. For example, movies show torture machines with dials and levers. This suggests a scale of pain. It fits a folklore on pain that teaches that more injury produces more pain. Moving the dials leads to more pain, which causes the prisoner to scream, confess or lie, and that's enough to keep the story going. Stories must keep the viewer's attention. But in reality pain is not composed of discrete units that one can add up, and more injury often produces less pain, especially during long interrogation (Rejali, *Torture and Democracy*, 447–53). The torture dial is a convenient truth, and only a torture expert ruins the fantasy for everyone by exposing it as false.

Some torture techniques take days, and it is challenging to depict the pain they cause. Directors seem to prefer electricity as a torture tool. It is dramatic, fast, and seemingly scientific. They can show technology (dials and levers) and can reference the folklore on pain as well as a familiar iconography to keep the story moving. Actors know how to portray electroshock artistically. Bodies thrash uncontrollably. Chests heave forward. Eyes bulge and look up. Even cartoons use this iconography, as when Syndrome electrotortures Mr. Incredible in *The Incredibles*.

But electrotorture causes other symptoms for which directors have no patience (ibid., 131–32, 136–38). During repeated electroshock, muscles contract. As they contract, bones break—like a rubber band tightening at both ends of a stick. Spines, arms, and legs snap. Jaws lock, making it impossible to speak. If one's tongue is in the way, one will bite it off. Torturers sometimes have to perform laborious massage, even stroking the jaws so victims can answer their questions. Electroconvulsive therapy resembles the accepted iconography even less. The body doesn't go into seizures. Doctors anaesthetize patients, and then they administer muscle relaxants to prevent fractures and other drugs to avoid seizures.

Actors sometimes ask me how to portray real electrotorture as they prepare for plays like Martin McDonagh's *The Pillowman* (2003). I advise them to stick to what audiences imagine electrotorture to be, since otherwise people wouldn't recognize or appreciate what they were doing. Everyone knows Rambo didn't have any trouble moving or speaking after repeated electrotorture in *First Blood II* (1985). And frankly, the story wouldn't move forward if Mr. Incredible couldn't speak immediately after receiving one hundred thousand volts in *The Incredibles*.

In short convenient truths enter movies by showing, not telling, by using an accepted iconography, and by referencing a folklore on pain. These truths fit what a story formally requires to keep it moving. They are information shortcuts that are real enough. Audiences accept these cinematic features as substantive truths about torture, and they don't think too hard about them. "Real enough" fits certain understandings we have of the world. Don't ruin the movie for everyone. When this is done well, movies achieve semidocumentary status.

An Algerian Story

Can torture be selectively, scientifically, professionally administered, yielding accurate information in a timely manner? Specialized studies have long suggested that torture doesn't work in this way. Nevertheless policy debates focus instead on personal testimonials and historical cases. "The Battle of Algiers" and "the Gestapo" stand for memories, movies, and stories "we all know."

For example, after the Algerian War, French generals described the battle of Algiers like this: a colonial paramilitary force used torture selectively to win a tactical victory against the FLN, a national revolutionary organization, in a city quarter called the Casbah. The movie *The Battle of Algiers* (1966) adopts the same story. Yet oddly, Gillo Pontecorvo was a left-wing director; Yacef Saadi, the FLN guerilla, advised him; and the movie played to audiences who cheered for the FLN. The film offers only one caveat to the French story: torture works in the short run and not in the long run. But the real battle bears little resemblance to the French story (ibid., 480–93, 160–65). I will focus here on three points.

First, the French army had an awesomely efficient informant system. This included loyal Algerian block wardens and former FLN operators, including the former FLN chiefs for both East and West Algiers. These double agents were responsible for most of the critical arrests shown in the movie. They helped corner the FLN leader Yacef Saadi and tracked the new FLN bomb squad chief and his military deputy. Loyal block wardens led the French *paras* (paratroopers) to the safe house where they found the FLN leader Ben M'Hidi in pajamas. And informers revealed the location of the last FLN refuge, where Ali la Pointe, Hassiba, and twelve-year-old "Petit" Omar, snipping paper cut outs as usual, lay hidden for hours. These double agents also planted documents on dead accused traitors implicating loyal leaders as traitorous informers. The movie glosses over this uncomfortable two-year period when the FLN severed its own limbs in nasty political infighting, and instead shows crowds suddenly emerging shouting for the FLN a few years later.

Second, if we go through the Battle of Algiers event by event, considering the known historiography, we find only two instances in which torture might have generated true, timely information, and how one judges what success means in these cases is open to considerable interpretation (ibid., 491). No rank-and-file soldier has related an incident in which he personally, through timely interrogation, produced decisive information that stopped a ticking bomb from exploding.[8] That always happens elsewhere and involves things any given soldier has only heard about.[9] In fact key FLN members were never tortured, and some betrayed the FLN without any torture. By contrast, four important FLN prisoners were tortured, but they surrendered nothing other than their identities. A few FLN small fry were more pliable under torture, but this is a dismal record. Lastly, the FLN had instructed its members that, if tortured, they should give up the names of their counterparts in a rival organization, the more accommodationist MNA (National Algerian Movement). Not very knowledgeable in the subtleties of Algerian nationalism, the French helped the FLN liquidate their rivals. In the final scenes of the film, the crowds chant, "Long live Algeria! Long live the partisans!" identifying the FLN with Algeria, though this was in large part because the FLN made sure they were the only ones left standing. The movie doesn't even mention the MNA.

Third, torture in the Battle of Algiers was wholesale, not retail, terror. General Massu's strategy wasn't to go after the (at most) 1,400 FLN operatives in the Casbah. He identified and disabled anyone who was even remotely associated with the FLN. Torture was not selective. The Casbah's population was 80,000. Minimally, Massu detained 24,000 people, including 30 to 40 percent of all males, and most were tortured. This excludes many who were detained extrajudicially, including the 3,024 people who disappeared. Massu did win the Battle of Algiers, but he did not win because of coerced information. His victory followed from three factors, though weighing their importance is difficult. Arresting one-third of an entire city quarter in just nine months—a remarkable feat under any circumstances—creates a general feeling of terror that is hard to discount. Persistent selective violence (e.g., death squads) powerfully deters populations, as other studies have demonstrated. Lastly, the informant system led soldiers to many critical arrests.

The real Battle of Algiers doesn't resemble the self-congratulatory accounts of the French generals, accounts even General Massu came to regret in later years.[10] But telling the story in this way suits both sides of the conflict well. The revolutionary organization held the view that it was the people, as the movie repeatedly reminds the viewer, and that it had no rivals. If it lost the battle despite such popular support, it must have been because torture worked. That is the convenient truth: "the French won" equals "torture worked." French veterans also cling to the notion that they applied torture selectively and saved lives. Otherwise they would have to acknowledge that they committed massive war crimes. Both sides of this conflict are deeply invested in the story that tells how professional, controlled torture delivered final victory to the French.

Indeed, the movie shows how torture led to all the critical arrests. It opens with a torture victim revealing Ali la Pointe's hideout, when in fact informants had already revealed this last FLN refuge. Pontecorvo does not give informants a big part in the movie, gesturing briefly to a bartender and a hooded Cagoulard at a checkpoint. He doesn't show the serious FLN defections or how the notorious informer Ourhia the Brown, the jilted wife of an FLN fighter, tracked down the last FLN leader in Algiers. That, not Ali la Pointe's death, was the battle's last major event.

The Battle of Algiers glosses over the betrayals, the key informers, the nationalist rivals, and the popular anger against the FLN. Unlike the movie, which portrays the Algerian population as united behind the FLN and assumes that torture is why the French won the battle, the real Battle of Algiers was a story of terror, collaboration, and betrayal by the local population. It was "a population that was cowed beyond belief and blamed the FLN leadership for having brought them to this pass."[11] As for torture, the French story of efficient, selective, professional torture was fictional. You will only find it in the movies.

Pauline Kael, the noted film critic, rightly described *The Battle of Algiers* as one of the finest propaganda films ever made, in the same class as Leni Riefenstahl's Nazi classic, *Triumph of the Will*.[12] Pontecorvo successfully enlists the self-congratulatory French story to polish and sell the FLN's revolutionary image. The best convenient truth is one that even your enemies, for their own reasons, collude with you to promote. And so it is today. Everyone watches *The Battle of Algiers*, even the staff of the Pentagon. For apologists the movie shows that torture worked. For critics it shows that torture failed in the long run. Each side draws its own convenient moral. No one wants to discuss whether torture worked even in the short run. Questioning the movie's misleading history might involve reading French, and that's a tiring thought.

Gestapo Stories

During the Algerian War, a French torturer sighed wistfully about the Gestapo: "Them at least, they knew how to work; they weren't amateurs."[13] Many since then have referenced how effective Gestapo torture was. For example, recently Alan Dershowitz dismissed those who argue that torture doesn't work with what he appeared to think was historical fact. "This is simply not true, as evidenced by the many decent members of the French Resistance who, under Nazi torture, disclosed the locations of their closest friends and relatives."[14]

But the Gestapo was no less an exception to the dynamics of torture and policing than the French *paras*. Even Hitler's notorious secret police got most of their information from public tips, informers, and interagency cooperation (Rejali, *Torture and Democracy*, 493–96). That information was more than enough to help the Gestapo decimate anti-Nazi resistance in Austria, Czechoslovakia, Poland, Denmark, Norway, France, Russia, and the concentration camps.

Yes, the Gestapo did torture people for intelligence, especially in later years. But this reflected not torture's efficacy but the loss of many seasoned professionals in war, increasingly desperate competition for intelligence among Gestapo units, and an influx of less disciplined younger members. Why do serious, tedious police work when you have a uniform and a whip? Torture has a well-known deprofessionalization effect (ibid., 454–58, 485–86, 494–95 [on the Gestapo in particular], 500–503).

In fact it is surprising how unsuccessful the Gestapo's brutal efforts were. They failed to break senior leaders of the French, Danish, Polish, and German resistance movements. *Torture and Democracy* collects all the known Gestapo torture "successes"; the number is small and the results pathetic, especially compared with what informers achieved (ibid., 496–99).

For example, in 1942 the Czech resistance assassinated Reinhard Heydrich, Reichsprotektor of Czechoslovakia. The Gestapo found the three assassins, but to get these men, they arrested, tortured, and killed 7,545 people, and in the process annihilated two villages (ibid., 497–98). They also caught about one hundred resistance members for whom they weren't searching. These results are typical, comparable to other cases like the Battle of Algiers. And in fact what broke the case was not Gestapo torture but Karel Curda, a Czech resistance member who betrayed everyone.

The curious question is why so many people want to believe that Gestapo officers were master torturers. After the Allied victory in Europe everyone wanted to identify with the winners. One corollary was this: as the Gestapo tortured "us," we resisted, all of us. This story of widespread resistance reinforced the myth of torture's effectiveness. If entire populations were resisting Nazis, and if entire resistance networks were compromised, this had to be because Gestapo torture was so efficient. People had no other choice.

The myth of Gestapo torture's effectiveness then dovetails with the darkest chapter of European history: the extent of European collaboration with Nazi governments. Betrayal equals effective Gestapo torture. Like every other successful police force, the Gestapo received far more assistance than anyone wanted admit after the war. It was more politic to present the Gestapo as a frighteningly efficient machine that beat the truth out of anyone.

Ticking Time-Bomb Stories

Soon others found reason to repeat this collaborator's story. For instance, French soldiers sometimes embraced the Gestapo's reputation to portray themselves as master torturers.[15] And then in 1960 a war journalist and former paratrooper, Jean Lartéguy, wrote *Les Centurions*, a novel about French paratroopers during the Franco-Algerian War.[16] The novel's protagonist is Boisfeuras, a paratrooper tortured by Nazis and again by the Vietcong, who learned during those ordeals the real meaning of strength and weakness. As a result of these experiences, Boisfeuras is born again as an effective torturer of Algerians. He can defend democracy because liberalism has not made him weak.

Torture seems to always work for Boisfeuras and his *paras*. In one scene Major Glatigny brutally and repeatedly slaps the beautiful Aicha in order to learn the location of bomb detonators. "I love you and hate you," Aicha says afterward. "You've raped me and I've given myself to you; you are my master and I shall kill you; you hurt me terribly and I want to start all over again."[17] The torturer is the real man.[18] In another scene Arouche, a dentist, plants fifteen bombs to explode in crowded stores the next morning. Esclavier tortures Arouche after first describing his own torture by the Gestapo, and Arouche reveals everything.[19]

Many things in the novel happen as the *paras* wished they had. In the real battle, for example, General Aussaresses strung up and hanged with his own hands Si Millial/Ben M'Hidi, the FLN's leader in Algiers; in the novel Si Millial/Ben M'Hidi slits his wrists in despair. Arab women fall in love with Frenchmen after torture. And Boisfeuras and his soldiers apply torture morally and selectively to stop ticking bombs just hours after extracting true confessions—though even those who have seen the famous movie of the battle and accept it at face value know that no event like this occurred.

Les Centurions substitutes the symbolic violence of the ticking time-bomb scenario for the messy, wholesale process of torture during the Algerian war. It sold half a million copies, a privilege no book on the real

Algerian war can claim. Columbia Tristar adapted it for a major Hollywood movie, *Lost Command* (1966), releasing it the same year as *The Battle of Algiers*. The bomb scenario has also appeared in many TV shows and movies—most recently in *24* and *NYPD Blue*. And always producers frame torture and terrorism around the theme of manliness. In *24*, for example, tough experts advise an insecure, antitorture vice president who has been forced to take power after the strong, protorture president was seriously hurt. They give him spine, while down the ranks Kiefer Sutherland has the kind of success with torture most torturers can only dream of.

Such shows express values that have been more or less explicit in American newspapers since September 11, as pundits express deep doubts about American civilization. "Radical terrorists will take advantage of our fussy legality, so we may have to suspend it to beat them. Radical terrorists mock our namby-pamby prisons, so we must make them tougher. Radical terrorists are nasty, so to defeat them we have to be nastier."[20] Behind this attitude is the same raw anxiety that drove Lartéguy's novel: the fear that we have become sissies and our enemies know it.

And Lartéguy's story fills one with reassurance. Real men will have the courage to torture. Among Americans today, as among Frenchmen fifty years ago, Lartéguy's thought experiment is a rite of manhood, a test of moral character. That is why many soldiers, lawyers, and professors—usually all men—are drawn to it. Only real men will say yes to the question, will you torture in this case? affirming it with their lives. It is true that such scenarios are extremely rare, arguably nonexistent. And many thoughtfully reject torture in these cases. But these answers don't take hold because the scenario is rooted in modern democratic anxieties about manhood. Any answer other than yes—no matter how smart the no might be—reveals one to be a sissy, and so, by definition, an inadequate moral agent. What Boisfeuras achieves, and what every American who embraces the time-bomb scenario wants, is to be recognized for making the manly decision and so being a proper moral agent in democratic life.

I have argued elsewhere that torture does not make the man.[21] But if Nazis are to be our security models, let's consider a Nazi answer. A reader, a refugee from Nazi Germany, once told me that the original time bomb story appeared in Karl Ritter's *Verräter* (1936). *Verräter* (*Traitors*) describes how two spies, Morris and Geyer, seek plans for a new German dive-bomber. To this end, they blackmail Fritz Brockau, a civilian engineer, and Hans Klemm, a tank officer. Although Klemm informs his superiors, spineless Brockau reveals what he knows as he dies. Police foil the plot.

The movie conveys urgency: Foreign spies are at work! Be vigilant! The movie does not show a time-bomb scenario, much less torture. In fact it makes a different point: without public cooperation, the police are relatively helpless. Real men count on loyal citizens and noncoercive interrogation. Heinz von Pannwitz, from the Gestapo's antisabotage unit, knew this (Rejali, *Torture and Democracy*, 497). Hans Scharff, the Luftwaffe's crack interrogator, used it to devastating effect on Allied POWs.[22] They, at least, weren't amateurs.

Huge government studies—American, English, and Canadian—have confirmed that without public cooperation, the chances that a crime will be solved fall to less than 10 percent.[23] Public cooperation works well even when time is short. Not only is torture the clumsiest method, it also undermines what we know works.[24] Ironically, a melodramatic Nazi movie conveys this better than decades of French and American homophobic fantasies.

Altering Origins

Let me turn to a different convenient truth, one that doesn't concern whether torture works, but rather where torture comes from. In the 1980s Americans flocked to movies featuring Rambo, the tormented Vietnam veteran played by Sylvester Stallone. In *First Blood: Part II*, Lt. Colonel Podovsky and Captain Vinh subject Rambo to electrotorture in Vietnam.[25] The irony in Rambo's electrotorture is that it was American, French, and South Vietnamese torturers who used the technique in Vietnam. The movie points away from where this modern torture originated.

The convenient truth here is that modern torture equals authoritarianism; democracies did not originate modern torture. But most modern techniques did not originate with fascists, Stalinists, or inquisitors. What has driven torture technology turns out to be something that would seem completely unrelated to torture, namely, international monitoring and democracy.

To be specific, one can distinguish between two types of torture techniques, those that leave marks and those that don't. Over the past two centuries scarring techniques have been disappearing worldwide. On the other hand, clean techniques are spreading.

Electrotorture, for instance, was relatively unknown for most of the twentieth century (Rejali, *Torture and Democracy*, 123–66). Americans practiced electrotorture first, as early as 1910, in police stations throughout the United States. U.S. Marines practiced electrotorture by field telephone in Haiti in 1919, and the French did the same in Indochina in 1931 (ibid.,

144–48).²⁶ Electrotorture did not appear in Europe until 1942, in the hands of Vichy police in southern France. The Gestapo picked it up, using it mainly in France until the German defeat three years later (ibid., 111–16, 149–50). Electrotorture was rare in the Communist world between 1950 and 1980. It spread in the free world after the 1960s, and then the contagion effect was huge (ibid., 167–224).

What makes clean techniques like electrotorture valuable is that allegations of torture are simply less credible when there is nothing to show for it. In the absence of visible wounds or photographs, whom are you going to believe? Clean torture breaks down a victim's ability to communicate with the wider community. And stealthy tortures are calculated to subvert this relationship, which is why they appeared first in democracies and then become more common as human rights monitoring spread. Whenever we watch, torturers become sneaky, and so clean tortures appeared in American hands in Vietnam. Modern tortures are democratic tortures. When we watch Rambo's torture, we are watching ourselves through a mirror darkly.

Altered States

In 1953 Chinese communists released films in which American pilots held prisoner in Korea made unbelievable confessions, apparently voluntarily. For many Americans these were terrifying movies, and movies like *The Manchurian Candidate* (1962) fed that terror. Americans came to fear that an evil scientific genius invented modern torture. One story names I. P. Pavlov as this genius; his behavioral control experiments showed the Soviets how to brainwash prisoners, and Communist agents spread it around the world (ibid., 87–90, 542–43). Another story names Dr. Ewen Cameron as the evil genius; his experiments combined electroconvulsive therapy (ECT) machines with sensory deprivation (SD) boxes, and CIA agents spread these around the world (ibid., 139–42, 256, 370–71, 376–77, 445, 467, 542–43). In both stories an irresponsible scientist gives unscrupulous politicians a science of torture, corrupting freedom everywhere. Contemporary torture documentaries reference both stories. *The Ghosts of Abu Ghraib* (2007) and *Taxi to the Dark Side* (2007) connect American torture to CIA-funded SD and ECT experiments, while *Torturing Democracies* (2008) characterizes Guantánamo torture techniques as "stolen Soviet techniques" and "psychological techniques of the Korean war."

If a science of torture exists, one would expect to see it all over the world, and if not in squeamish democratic states then at least in authoritarian states. But the evidence on the ground is otherwise. Torturers use low-tech, not high-tech devices. All the techniques used at Abu Ghraib and other American facilities belong either to tortures that descend from old Western European military and police punishments or they descend from the pre–World War II practices of French colonialism. All these tortures existed long before the CIA and the Soviet Union, and they have not changed in their particulars (ibid., 378).[27]

Faced with all this, many observers connect the dots speculatively. Any sign of electrotorture must be evidence of CIA ECT experimentation. Any waterboarding has to be related to John Lilly's fearsome sensory deprivation water tank. "Sensory deprivation" is equated with any stress (standing, forced postures, freezing, and hot boxes), disorientation (hooding, sleep deprivation), debility (being deprived of food and water), overstimulation (loud noises), and isolation (solitary confinement in a small cell). It even expresses a full doctrine of statecraft, "the shock doctrine."[28]

Only someone unfamiliar with torture would think SD and ECT devices are great ways of making people talk (Rejali, *Torture and Democracy*, 138–43, 373–84). Cameron's specific approach produced retrograde amnesia, useful for "brainwashing" perhaps, but hardly useful if the interrogator was hoping to get information about the previous six months to ten years. It is seriously questionable why police officers seeking accurate information would use machines that induce confused judgment, inaccurate perceptions, and amnesia about recent events, including one's own torture! SD white noise reduces one's capacity to feel pain, so why would one use it to torture? And why would police buy expensive devices with control panels that resemble the space shuttle's flight deck when stun guns and plastic bags are cheap, easier to use for torture, and leave no marks?

CIA reports single out Lilly's water tank as being particularly effective in generating stress and anxiety.[29] Of all the high-tech techniques mentioned, only Lilly's water tank transitioned to everyday use, though not for torture (Rejali, *Torture and Democracy*, 369–73). Lilly found that his water tank was profoundly relaxing. He also experienced altered states of consciousness that he attributed to it. Indeed he abandoned the tank after consulting with three extraterrestrial beings within it; they suggested he work with dolphins. Lilly's pioneering work on dolphin intelligence was subsequently portrayed in *The Day of the Dolphin* (1973), with George C. Scott as Lilly. Paddy Chayefsky explored Lilly's mind-altering journeys in his novel, *Altered States* (1978), which subsequently became a movie of the same name (1980).

In 1972 Glenn Perry, a shy computer programmer at Xerox, approached Lilly about building his own tank. Perry used the tank to overcome his shyness, and together they started a company, Samadhi, to sell the tank commercially.[30] This tank, and Lilly's books on it, became a New Age phenomenon. Today wellness retreats throughout the world have Lilly tanks, using them to treat pain and insomnia as well as for meditation, self-analysis, and transcendental experiences. Scientists know that SD effects vary depending on how one conceives of the situation. It is unlikely that even they imagined that the most fearsome SD box would be a popular home relaxation device.

Since Orwell we have feared that torturers might harness the powers of science. Indeed they have, but not in the way Orwell imagined. Torturers like devices that cause intense pain or save them labor. But there is no science of torture yet, and it is unlikely this will ever happen unless the nature of pain itself changes (Rejali, *Torture and Democracy*, 447–50). The belief that torture is becoming ever more scientific is rooted in general preconceptions about technology and progress, not in the empirical study of torture instruments. Torturers may cloak themselves in the mantle of science, but this does not make their methods scientific any more than wearing a white lab coat makes one a scientist.

Orwellian Shortcuts

Orwellian stories feed the myth that torture works. After all, there is no such thing as a science that does not work. If it does not work, it is not a science. Not surprisingly, many who favor torture prefer describing it as a scientific way of getting at the truth, implying control and accuracy where little of either exists. At the same time Orwellian stories conveniently dovetail with stories describing how Bush lawyers authorized torture. After all, a science of torture means that someone high-up had to organize it. Orwellian stories force moral blame upward, from the lower ranks to the higher-ups. And so others, even strong political opponents, partner in telling Orwellian stories because they fit what each wants to believe.

Take the Oscar-winning documentary *Taxi to the Darkside*. *Taxi* documents how American soldiers killed Dilawar, a taxi driver in Bagram, Afghanistan. It connects the dots from Bagram prison to the White House. It shows how the top is responsible, while patriotically exculpating those at the bottom who tortured. And to this end it also describes a CIA science of torture.

The problem is that Dilawar's death is a poor example. While we are years away from any adequate account of recent American torture, we know enough to doubt that his death reveals the existence of scientific torture. Dilawar died as his arms were cuffed to the ceiling ("high cuffing"). Soldiers repeatedly struck him in the upper thighs with their knees (the "common peroneal strike") until his bones became jelly. The common peroneal strike is a long-standing military compliance technique.[31] High cuffing, too, is an old military technique. American military prison guards legally high cuffed during World War I, applying this old slave torture to pacifists. The War Department banned it in December 1918, but soldiers and police quietly passed it on down the decades unchanged.[32] High cuffing and the common peroneal strike are not among known SERE techniques, much less sensory deprivation techniques.[33] Nor do Bush lawyers list these among authorized techniques in their memos.[34] But they are the techniques that killed Dilawar.

Taxi tells a different story. It connects the military techniques that killed Dilawar to a long-hidden CIA science of torture. It also accepts unquestioningly his killers' stories that they did only what real men do in emergencies. And it suggests that they tortured because Washington ordered them to. White House bureaucrats didn't simply justify torture; they caused it. Oddly, these views fit Alan Dershowitz's view that lawyers can and should regulate coercion for soldiers, and soldiers should do what they must in emergencies.

The problem is that U.S. Army figures show a 75 percent drop in casualties in the last half of 2002 when Dilawar was detained. In fact during his actual detention (November-December 2002), the U.S. Army records that one soldier died and eight were wounded in Afghanistan.[35] If the situation was urgent when Dilawar died, if scores of soldiers were dying in ticking time-bomb situations, army figures didn't record it. Moreover American soldiers began torturing prisoners in Afghanistan in February 2002.[36] February 2002 is an inconvenient date. It is six months before the Bybee memo authorizing the CIA to torture (August 2002), almost a year before the Rumsfeld-Haynes memo authorizing Guantánamo interrogators to torture (December 2002), and long before U.S. Army memos authorizing torture reached the battlefront (mid-2003).[37]

In short it appears soldiers tortured and killed Dilawar in nonemergency conditions and using ordinary military techniques, ones that Americans were using in Afghanistan before Washington drafted a single known torture memo. This isn't surprising. Lawyers usually come after torture has begun, covering up, justifying, and organizing its future implementation. For all this they are culpable. But there is little evidence to support the odd notion that torturers wait for lawyers to tell them what to do (Rejali, *Torture and Democracy*, 526–32). Usually, ordinary situations lead people to torture, and often have.[38]

Torture is a social practice, not a legal policy. It lives in society, not in a CIA vault guarded by lawyers. And torture returns with decommissioned soldiers, soldiers like Dilawar's murderers. They become police and private security guards, and they get ahead using techniques they know. This has happened twice already in American history.[39] And it's likely this war's tortures will be coming to a neighborhood near you. When these former soldiers torture, they will choose clean low-tech procedures they can transmit easily through backroom apprenticeships. Low-tech torture thrives on ignorance, custom, rumor, selective memory, poverty, and media publicity. It lives off the violence in stockyards, schools, barracks, and homes. These are less sensational sources of evil, but far greater dangers to life and limb today than sensory deprivation or ECT machines.

Imagining Futures

We generate convenient truths because we can imagine things differently than they are. Living without convenient truths would mean life without imagination. And without imagination our lives would be unbearable. Imagination sustains our families, protects our political beliefs, and makes our workplaces tolerable. Without it we also wouldn't be able to leave our boxes and change our lives at all. Still we have to be ready. People everywhere prefer imagining torture in ways that leave their lives unchanged and their politics untouched—this is the torture talk we Americans, from left to right, want. Until we want to change, see you at the movies.

NOTES

1. Darius Rejali, *Torture and Democracy* (Princeton: Princeton University Press, 2007); hereafter cited in text.
2. For a study like this, see Pierre Bourdieu and Monique de Saint Martin, "The Users of Lille University Library," in *Academic Discourse*, ed. Pierre Bourdieu, Jean-

Claude Passeron, and Monique de Saint Martin, 122–33 (Stanford: Stanford University Press, 1994).

3. Pierre Bourdieu, *Outline of a Theory of Practice*, trans. Richard Nice (Cambridge: Cambridge University Press, 1989), 21–22, 195–96; Pierre Bourdieu and Loïs Wacquant, *An Invitation to Reflexive Sociology* (Chicago: University of Chicago, 1992), 167–68.

4. Both of these phenomena also characterize the American torture debate. See Paul Gronke and Darius Rejali, "U.S Public Opinion on Torture, 2001–2009," in "PS Symposium: Torture and the War on Terror," ed. Jim Piazza and Jim Walsh, *PS* (July 2010): 437–44; Darius Rejali, "Torture and Democracy: What Now?" in *Torture, Democracy, and the Human Body*, ed. Shampa Biswas and Zahi Zalloua (Seattle: University of Washington Press, 2010).

5. Darius Rejali, "Why Do People Do Violence?" in *Approaches to Violence* (Princeton: Princeton University Press, 2008).

6. Seymour Hersh, "The Gray Zone," *New Yorker*, May 24, 2004, 42.

7. See, for example, "10 Questions for Andrew Sullivan," *New York Times* online, January 27, 2005, http://www.nytimes.com/2005/01/27/books/sullivan-questions.html.

8. More torturers and those proximate to torture have written and spoken about what they did during the Algerian conflict than virtually any other. The current record includes thirteen autobiographies, two collections of interviews, and a collection of psychiatric reports. For a complete list, see Rejali, *Torture and Democracy*, 749n5.

9. The most extreme example is Ted Morgan (see Morgan, *My Battle of Algiers* [New York: Harper Collins, 2005]). His only personal account involves killing the man he was interrogating, (91–92) but this does not prevent him from repeatedly affirming torture's efficacy (xix, 151) and accepting at face value descriptions of cases in which he did not participate. For other examples, see Rejali, *Torture and Democracy*, 753n132.

10. When asked whether torture was indispensable in wartime, General Massu replied in 2000: "No, when I think back about Algeria, it grieves me. We could have done things differently." Beauge Florence, "Le général Massu exprime ses regret pour la torture en Algérie," *Le Monde*, June 22, 2000.

11. Edward Behr, *The Algerian Problem* (London: Hodder and Stoughton, 1961), 118.

12. Pauline Kael, *5001 Nights at the Movies* (New York: Holt, 1982), 54. See also Rejali, *Torture and Democracy*, 545–50.

13. Jean-Pierre Cômes, *"Ma" guerre d'Algerie et la torture* (Paris: L'Harmattan, 2002), 70.

14. Alan Dershowitz, "Democrats and Waterboarding," *Wall Street Journal*, November 7, 2007, A23.

15. For various French uses of the Nazi metaphor, see Rejali, *Torture and Democracy*, 165–66.

16. Jean Lartéguy, *The Centurions*, trans. Xan Felding (New York: Dutton, 1962). See also Rejali, *Torture and Democracy*, 548–49.
17. Lartéguy, *The Centurions*, 470.
18. For similar torrid scenes in other novels of this period, see Pierre Vidal-Naquet, *Torture*, trans. Barry Richard (Harmondsworth, UK: Penguin Books, 1963), 146.
19. Lartéguy, 481.
20. Anne Applebaum, "The Torture Myth," *Washington Post*, January 12, 2005, A21.
21. Darius Rejali, "Torture Makes the Man," *South Central Review* 24, no. 1 (Spring 2007), 151–69, and *Torture and Democracy*, 548–49.
22. Raymond Toliver, *The Interrogator*, with Hanns Scharff (Fallbrook, Calif.: Aero, 1978).
23. David Bayley, *Police for the Future* (Oxford: Oxford University Press, 1994), 8.
24. Ibid., 474–90.
25. Sylvester Stallone and James Cameron, *Rambo: First Blood, Part II, Final Shooting Script*, Daily Script, http://www.dailyscript.com/scripts/rambo_first_blood_2.html.
26. My thanks to Professor Alejandra Bronfman, who has uncovered incidents of U.S. marines using electrotorture techniques in a two-thousand-page U.S. Senate report, *Inquiry into the Occupation of Haiti and Santo Domingo*, 67th Congress, 1st session (1921–1922) (e-mail correspondence with the author, November 15, 2009).
27. For their particular histories, see chapters 4–18 of Rejali, *Torture and Democracy*.
28. Naomi Klein, *The Shock Doctrine: The Rise of Disaster Capitalism* (New York: Metropolitan, 2007).
29. Central Intelligence Agency, *Kubark Counterintelligence Interrogation* (CIA Training Manuals, National Security Archive, George Washington University, Washington, D.C., July 1963), 87–90; Central Intelligence Agency, *Human Resource Exploitation Training Manual* (CIA Training Manuals, National Security Archive, George Washington University, Washington, D.C., 1983), K.6–7. Both manuals are available at http://www2.gwu.edu/~nsarchiv/NSAEBB/NSAEBB122/.
30. "Samadhi Flotation Tank Home," Samadhi Tank Co. Inc., http://www.samadhitank.com.
31. Joshua E. S. Phillips, *None of Us Were Like This Before: How American Soldiers Turned to Torture* (New York: Verso, 2010), 40.
32. Rejali, *Torture and Democracy*, 306–11, and "Ice Water and Sweatboxes: The Long and Sadistic History behind the CIA's Torture Techniques," *Slate Magazine*, March 17, 2009.
33. For a complete list of known SERE techniques, see Rejali, *Torture and Democracy*, 431–32; For a list of sensory deprivation techniques, see ibid., 368–83.
34. For a list of these, see Gronke and Rejali, "U.S Public Opinion on Torture, 2001–2009," 439, also available as a white paper at www.tortureanddemocracy.com.
35. See Phillips, *None of Us Were Like This Before*, 38.

36. See, for example, Laurel Fletcher and Eric Stover, *Guantánamo and Its Aftermath* (Berkeley: Human Rights Center and International Human Rights Clinic, University of California, 2008), 19–24, http://hrc.berkeley.edu/pdfs/Gtmo-Aftermath.pdf; the case of Guantánamo detainee Abdul Rahim Al Ginco in Abdul Rahim Abdul Razak al Ginco v. George W. Bush et al, CV 05-1310-RJL, "Declaration of Darius Rejali" (submitted December 22, 2008); and Phillips, *None of Us Were Like This Before*, 18–50.
37. For the precise time frame of the Rumsfeld/Haynes memo, see Philippe Sands, *Torture Team* (New York: Palgrave Macmillan, 2008). For other memos, see David Cole, ed., *The Torture Memos* (New York: New Press, 2009).
38. For other American examples, see Rejali, *Torture and Democracy*, 70–74, 172–78, 240–42, 581–91. For a general explanation using Abu Ghraib as an example, see Philip Zimbardo, *The Lucifer Effect: Understanding How Good People Turn Evil* (New York: Random House, 2007.)
39. Rejali, "Torture and Democracy: What Now?" and *Torture and Democracy*, 436.

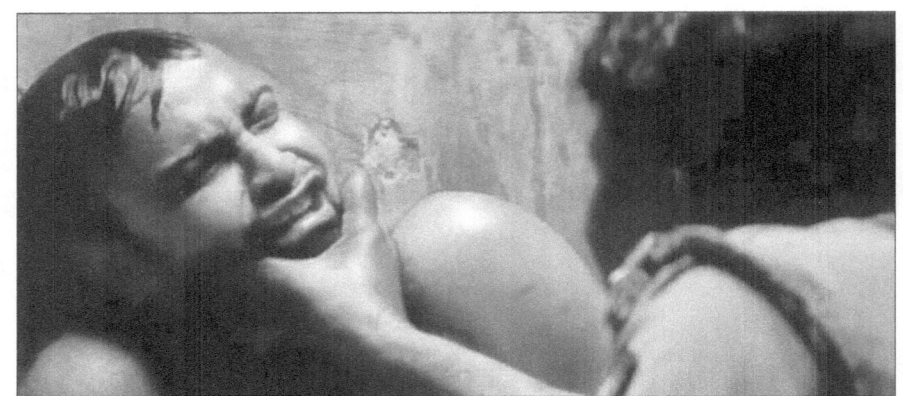

Black Friday, 2004

11
Torture at the Limit of Politics
Faisal Devji

In his classic work on the emergence of modern regimes of punishment in Western Europe, Michel Foucault points out that those who supported such apparently humane forms of imprisonment and correction wrongly identified the corporal exactions of the past as torture.[1] Inflicting pain on the bodies of suspects and criminals in earlier times, he argues, was not simply a barbarous and inefficient use of discipline, but represented rather a different order of truth. For the confessions and recantations extracted from prisoners served not as information in the modern sense but rather as demonstrations of the triumph of truth over falsehood. The chastised and broken bodies of heretics and criminals were in this way presented to the view of ordinary men and women as examples of falsehood, and their injuries was meant to signal the restoration of virtue while at the same time serving as a deterrent for others. These bodies had a metaphysical status, and their degradation illustrated falsehood just as the dignity of the martyr's body, or the incorruptibility of the saint's cadaver, demonstrated truth. But with the rise of regulative institutions in modern times, the body lost its metaphysical status and became part of a "humanitarian" machinery of correction, according to Foucault. Prior forms of punishment were now defined as torture and considered irrational or unproductive, while the link between suffering and truth was broken, with the latter being relegated to the statistical patterns and other abstractions of institutional knowledge.

As we know, however, these now illicit forms of torture managed to survive the new regulative regimes that Foucault has so masterfully described.[2] Indeed they are even to be found at the heart of these regimes, where such abuse is still linked to truth in an obsessive way, since the ability of suffering to elicit truth has come to serve as its unique justification. Although such truth has lost its metaphysical character and been reduced to information, the fact that it is still seen as taking refuge in the bodies of individuals means that this information does not yet belong to the rationality of institutions—for which knowledge is only possible in the abstract form of data. The archetypal Hollywood torture scene is one in which some agent of evil must be physically chastised, so that the information he finally discloses might allow the hero to save his country or even the world, usually just in the nick of time. Nothing about this scene belongs to Foucault's world of discipline and regulation, though the whole thing might well occur within an institution like a prison. If it is not to be defined merely as a historical artifact, then torture both as representation and reality must disturb if not entirely derange the logic of institutions, by which I mean not simply Foucault's idea of that logic but also our received sense of what counts as rational and legitimate action.

It is of course impossible to speak about torture in its own right in its postmetaphysical mode, for it possesses no autonomy and can only be described either as the hidden supplement for legitimate procedures of politics and policing or, on the contrary, as the violation of such practices by those acting under secret orders and to pursue their own sadistic pleasures. Perhaps the best example of this inability to speak of torture in its own name is the discussion in the United States about legalizing waterboarding and other modes of physical distress for those held on terrorism charges after September 11. What is interesting about this debate is its entirely utilitarian nature, with proponents of the measure holding that, properly managed, torment serves as the necessary supplement of a politics dedicated to safeguarding a world in which torture is unthinkable, and opponents saying that, in addition to possessing no proven advantages, such practices cannot be used to defend a politics they violate. In either case torture is seen as a supplement of rational and legitimate action and defined entirely in its terms, while managing at the same time to remain outside them. In no case was a purely moral stance taken on the issue, even though this is a commonplace in debates about practices such as abortion. So while the term possesses a range of meanings, both legal and moral, and in the conventions of international organizations refers only to practices condoned or carried out by states and would-be states, I will treat as torture any physical exaction that functions as a supplement and whose purpose is to defend a political order that operates by denying such practices.

Rather than seeing in torture's supplementary character a demonstration of political rationality run wild—once it is unchained from the conventions and regulations that govern the behavior of states—I want to make the opposite case, that abuse actually illustrates the limits and anxieties of its dominion. By this account the legal conventions on torture should not be thought of as limiting political action, but instead as protecting its methods from such disruptive practices, whose focus on individual bodies inevitably runs the risk of becoming gratuitous sadism or pleasurable fetishism, and thus exiting the generalized logic of any institution. This fear of being seduced by the victim's body is so important that even those like the American constitutional lawyer Alan Dershowitz, who would justify some abuses in the fight against terrorism, are careful to state that the information obtained by such procedures should not be used against the individuals from whom it was coerced.[3] In doing so Dershowitz and his colleagues separate suffering from the confessions and other judicial forms that defined torture in times past, which had focused on the body of the victim in moral and metaphysical ways. For now the infliction of pain can only be justified by reference to knowledge of a more abstract and disembodied kind. Indeed the obsessive attention paid to information in these justifications of physical chastisement, as in the celebrated ticking time-bomb scenario so beloved of Hollywood, serves to shift our gaze from the body of the would-be terrorist to the threat he or she poses those citizens whose lives are managed by the generalized rationality of institutions.

Only by such procedures of evasion can torture be prevented from falling into forms of personal pleasure or revenge, as well as from tumbling headlong into the realm of moral life, for which the focus on particular individuals and their acts is a requirement. Revenge is after all a moral sentiment, and one that does not always require the law for justification. Like torture, however, morality, too, must forsake its autonomy if it is to serve as a supplement to the rationality of political institutions, which is increasingly the case in secular discussions of ethics. Other modes of evasion include protecting the structures of a disciplined society from the supplementary logic of torture, for example by the Bush administration's creation of anomalous legal sites like Guantánamo Bay and categories of persons like enemy combatants. But by engaging in a public debate that confuses the already subtle relationship between regulation and its supplement, the defenders of corporal punishment may have done nothing more than expose the instability of political rationality itself. In this chapter I will look at the way in which representations of torture on film foreground this instability, and by making visible the supplementary logic of abuse in a structural rather than directorial way, I will place it beyond the rationality of institutional politics, alongside morality. The melodramatic role of moral choice in such films illustrates the possibility of life outside the regulative institutions of modern politics.

An Empty Craft

In perhaps the most detailed study of modern torture yet published, the political scientist Darius Rejali describes how "clean," or nonscarring, techniques of physical distress originated in Western democracies and were exported to the rest of the world during the last century, quickly becoming the commonest form taken by the state's illegal infliction of pain on the bodies and minds of individuals, practices that are imitated even by groups and individuals not connected to any democratic order. Typical of such practices, for example, are those captured by the famous digital photographs from Abu Ghraib that emerged in 2003, depicting American soldiers abusing Iraqi prisoners. Rejali argues that it is the relatively transparent politics of democratic states, and the accountability of their leaders before courts of justice as much as public opinion, that makes such stealthy practices necessary. And though he recognizes that this great transformation of torture is not always uniform, nor its techniques always concealed, as the images from Abu Ghraib demonstrate such forms of torture emerge in response to the monitoring and regulative functions of democratic institutions, according to Rejali. He has more difficulty explaining why governments in undemocratic countries should take up these techniques, and can only account for this by invoking their fear of international repercussions and loss of domestic prestige. The quotation that follows serves as an instance of his reasoning on this question:

> Consider, for example, the case of an officer in Mobutu's Zaire who stopped his soldiers from beating a prisoner with sticks saying, "It will leave scars and we will get complaints from Amnesty International." It is unlikely this officer had any direct connection to Amnesty. It's possible he knew his immediate superior didn't want a mess, or that he had a circular directly from Mobutu's office on the subject or that he was in touch with the local CIA adviser who told him to cool it. The truth is we are unlikely ever to know. All we can say for certain is that *he* cared about international monitoring. It's possible other

people around him did too, but who more so than others is anyone's guess (ibid., 14).

There is no doubt a great deal of truth in Rejali's argument that clean forms of torture are linked to democratic institutions, but rather than deriving them directly from the tormentor's fear of discovery and prosecution—which reduces publicized acts of torture like those at Abu Ghraib merely into illustrations of some breakdown in the structure of concealment—it might perhaps be more productive to view the modernity of these practices from another angle. Is it possible to say that the rationality of democratic institutions is so dependent on the absorption of everything that is visible into its own logic that it disallows traditional forms of torture on principle rather than simply because such practices are now offensive to public opinion? The exhibition of broken bodies, in other words, offends not only the sentiments of ordinary citizens but also the very rationality of modern institutions, as that rationality is founded on statistical abstractions. The spectacle of suffering must therefore be hidden from the state's own modernity, not out of fear so much as in order to escape its rationality, or at least to avoid confounding it in the most damaging way. Surely this account is better able to explain the adoption of modern techniques of torture by undemocratic regimes than any argument founded on considerations like fear and embarrassment, neither of which seemed to occupy governments such as Mobutu's in other aspects of their behavior.

Visibility is crucial to the institutional rationality of modern politics, whose great models, after all, are the freedom of debate and transparency of elections. And it is because of this rationality that torture must remain hidden even if it is known to occur. Foucault insists on this logic, which would also shift legitimate practices like judicial execution from their traditional form as spectacles into acts of silence and concealment, not least because they might compromise the abstract knowledge of modern institutions by bringing to the fore individual bodies and the moral narratives that attend on them. In the case of torture, of course, the silence has to be more profound still, for in addition to inspiring a very understandable caution among those who deploy it, the practice's illegitimacy allows it to become a perfect supplement to the rationality of institutional discipline, a function that such techniques can only perform from the outside, by evacuating themselves of all autonomy and indeed ontological weight. Again, in this way torture joins morality as a supplemental aspect of modern politics. Rejali himself goes some way toward recognizing this role when he notes that clean forms of torture end up depriving suffering of a visible home in the body, and thus "tangling the victims and their communities in doubts, uncertainties, and illusions" (ibid., 31). Indeed it is precisely because "the spaces in which we can appear before each other in our pain have become more scarce" (ibid.) that Rejali dedicates his book to giving this pain its own visibility and status.

Absorbed as it otherwise is in the supplementary logic of modern politics, torture can only exist as a craft far removed from the disciplined behavior bred by institutional rationality. So Rejali marshals an extraordinary amount of information to point out that despite the language of professionalism in which its apologists describe the modes of corporal chastisement, these practices are in fact invariably amateurish, undisciplined, difficult to oversee, and destructive of institutional politics. This is so much the case that even those who approve of torture as a legally limited and professionally regulated activity are unable to codify its practices and therefore to learn from their own experiences. However, Rejali again attributes all of this—from the lack of proper instruction manuals to the informal and craftlike nature of torture—to the fear among its perpetrators of being held responsible for abuse. Whatever the case, his descriptions of modern torment do little more than illustrate its supplementary logic with regard to the practices of institutional rationality, of which the following passages from *Torture and Democracy* are indicative: "Torture increasingly takes in more suspects than those approved, leads to harsher methods than are authorized, and leads to greater bureaucratic fragmentation" (ibid., 24). "To think professionalism is a guard against causing excessive pain is an illusion. Instead, torture breaks down professionalism. Professionals become less disciplined, more brutal, and less skilled while their organizations become more fragmented and corrupt. Usually, organizations and interrogators are worse off than before they started torturing despite their best intentions, an interesting demonstration of counter-finality" (ibid., 454).

Indeed it is difficult for us to think of torture as an institutionalized form of rationality, representations of which are generally available to us only in the comic form of the mad scientist, whose progenitors are all, of course, medical doctors, from Frankenstein to Jekyll, and whose epigones include the slightly ridiculous figures who play the villains in James Bond films. It can even be argued that truly "scientific" modes of torture are only represented in science fiction. But what about the undeniably serious form that the mad scientist takes in the person of Dr. Mengele, to say nothing of the famously disciplined way in which the Nazis tortured and tried to exterminate populations like the Jews in wartime Europe? One of the great virtues of Darius Rejali's book is its demonstration that the image of "scientific" torture, whether negatively associated with regimes like Nazi Germany and the Soviet Union or positively with countries like the United States, is not much more than a myth. Notwithstanding exceptions here and there, as a rule both clean and scarring forms of torture are demonstrations of craft rather than science and tend in general to use crude, ordinary, and easily available tools, whose often multipurpose character allows for the disavowal of abuse. Despite the existence of national and regional patterns of torture, moreover, its techniques cannot be identified with any political or ideological order, these practices being freely adopted from one group by another, even by the bitterest enemies. While the sheer scale of state violence in Nazi Germany might have been unprecedented, its rationality was all too familiar. Nothing illustrates this so much as the fact that the Nazis insisted on legalizing even the most egregious forms of discrimination and oppression in recognized ways, thus making sure that the institutional rationality of modern politics was maintained alongside the supplementary logic of abuse that still required concealment.[4]

The Morality of Images

Torture must stand outside the institutional rationality of politics while at the same time paying homage to it, a function that is rehearsed over and over again in filmic representations of abuse like the popular American television show 24, which in the post–September 11 period depicted its hero using illegal force to prevent various terrorist acts. What is interesting about this plotline is that by standing outside the discipline of any institution, the hero takes on the most weighty moral responsibility, to the extent of putting his own life and career on the line when making decisions to break the law, if only in order to fulfill it in a paradox common to melodrama. It is the very vulnerability of this otherwise powerful figure, in other words, that makes a moral actor of him, but only on condition that he stand outside the regulative order. More than representing some romance of the outsider or frontiersman, this role is a structural one bringing suffering and morality together as they were in times past. Like many commentators, however, those accused of abuse in real life are often unwilling to recognize the moral character of their acts, being desperate rather to link these back to the world of institutions, generally by attributing them to the orders or at least the approval of superiors, as was the case with the soldiers tried for tormenting inmates at Abu

Ghraib. And while such approval might well have been forthcoming, the obsession with discovering a "chain of command" seems to indicate nothing so much as an effort to insert torture within the logic of institutions, either as their secret truth or tragic violation. Yet the morality of torture refuses confinement within the plots of films and television shows, even making an appearance in a U.S. Department of Defense report on detentions and the deployment of torture in Afghanistan and Iraq:

> A morally consistent approach to the problem would be to recognize there are occasions when violating norms is understandable but not necessarily correct—that is, we can recognize that a good person might, in good faith, violate standards. In principle, someone who, facing such a dilemma, committed abuse should be required to offer his actions up for review and judgement by a competent authority. An excellent example is the case of a 4th Infantry Division battalion commander who permitted his men to beat a detainee whom he had good reason to believe had information about future attacks against his unit. When the beating failed to produce the desired results, the commander fired his weapon near the detainee's head. The technique was successful and the lives of US servicemen were likely saved. However, his actions clearly violated the Geneva Conventions and he reported his actions knowing he would be prosecuted by the army. He was punished in moderation and allowed to retire.[5]

Not only does the scenario described above represent the ideal form of torture's supplementary logic, it recognizes that morality, too, lies beyond the bounds of institutional regulation and thus makes each act of abuse an ethical test in which every tormentor has the potential to become a moral hero. This curious situation is, I think, most fulsomely explored in film, which merely by depicting torture reconstitutes an arena outside political rationality where suffering lies alongside morality. But why should it be the torturer rather than his victim who comes to embody the success or failure of a moral sensibility in film? I shall address this question and its implications by looking at a popular and critically acclaimed Hindi film called *Black Friday*, directed by Anurag Kashyap and released in 2007, having been held up for two years while court cases relating to its subject were being tried.[6] The film deals with the serial bombing in 1993 that caused death and devastation across Bombay (now Mumbai). Set off by elements of the city's Muslim underworld, probably with help from Pakistan, these bombs were intended as retaliation for the extensive riots of 1992 in which

Muslims had overwhelmingly been the victims of Hindu mobs. These Hindu crowds were celebrating the destruction by their coreligionists in northern India of a sixteenth-century mosque, allegedly built on a temple marking the birthplace of the divine incarnation Rama.

Like the book on which it is based, S. Hussain Zaidi's *Black Friday: The True Story of the Bombay Bomb Blasts*, Kashyap's film remains faithful to the facts of the traumatic events it depicts while at the same time weaving them into a plot that is literary rather than documentary in character. And though this tends to be true of all filmic narratives, *Black Friday*'s openly aesthetic approach allows it to place the blasts within a moral arena, one that I will argue is no longer available, or at least not convincingly so, in the world of political rationality. The film tells the story of the Bombay blasts and the investigation that followed through the lives of two main characters, Badshah Khan (Aditya Srivastava), one of the terrorists who turns out to have been a dupe of handlers in Dubai and Pakistan, and Rakesh Maria (Kay Kay Menon), the district police commissioner in charge of the investigation. Following the destruction of his timber business in the Hindu-Muslim riots, a gangster named Tiger Memon (Pavan Malhotra) seeks the help of Dawood Ibrahim (Vijay Maurya), the Dubai-based boss of Bombay's largest criminal syndicate, to exact revenge while at the same time demonstrating the power of his gang. Ibrahim turns to the Pakistani secret service, which assists with training and equipment that includes the RDX used to set off bombs across the city. A number of Muslim men in Bombay, roused to action mostly out of shame and vanity, are taken to Pakistan for training and payment, and are guaranteed a quick exit from India following the operation, whose frequently shambolic nature is often on view in the film. Having been abandoned by his handlers after the blasts and gone on the run, Badshah Khan is eventually tracked down by Rakesh Maria and, after repenting and turning to religion while in prison, becomes part of the latter's investigation, which results in the capture and trial of all the operation's foot soldiers, but none of their handlers or paymasters.

Black Friday opens with a scene of torture. A Muslim man is strung up and beaten in a Bombay police station for unknown reasons, the suggestion being that this is simply one instance of a rather routine practice. Though the Muslim is unable to provide any useful knowledge during his ordeal, once at ease he tells the police that something big is about to happen in the city, but is ignored, and shortly afterward Bombay literally explodes. A few more scenes of abuse follow, as policemen try to piece together what happened, but only one produces any reliable information, and the others engage in mishaps of various kinds. Thus a Hindu businessman with links to the underworld is threatened by the police and ends up committing suicide, while in another powerful scene the wives and daughters of imprisoned Muslim suspects are manhandled and possibly raped by policemen in front of their jailed relatives, though no new information is extracted from the prisoners as a result. And in all this it is Rakesh Maria, the police officer conducting the investigation, who is portrayed as behaving dispassionately and even with a sense of rueful resignation about what he sees as his extralegal duty. This duty, of course, consists in condoning torture at some risk to his career even though he has no liking for it.

Unlike the terrorists in the film, who are depicted as being motivated by revenge, the desire to recover Muslim prestige—or in the case of the foot soldiers eventually betrayed by their leaders, a mixture of blackmail and manipulated sentiments—the police officer who is the film's hero turns out to be its moral center as well. By assuming complete responsibility for the forbidden practice of torture, after all, he operates outside the world of institutional regulation and is thus a free moral agent. Moreover, unlike the terrorists' personal investment in and even enjoyment of their crimes, to say nothing of the pleasure that Rakesh Maria's subordinates take in tormenting their suspects, Maria is repulsed and even tormented by these actions that have his full approval, thus claiming the very suffering of his tortured victims for himself. And yet Maria is not the film's only moral actor. One of the arrested terrorists, Badshah Khan, turns informer not because he has been tormented but due to his rediscovery of Islam in prison, while the mastermind Tiger Memon's brother returns from Dubai to voluntarily give himself up, as indeed was the case in reality. In fact the reformed terrorist is easily the most sympathetic character in the film, an incompetent if genial figure with whom the audience comes to identify.

Apart from being a complex work in which physical chastisement does not play the usual Hollywood role of ensuring the world's salvation in a ticking time-bomb scenario, and where indeed it is shown as being a ritualized but largely ineffective practice, Kashyap's film breaks ground in other respects as well. For one thing it belongs firmly to the period of India's economic liberalization, which, beginning toward the end of the 1980s, saw the state retreat from certain sectors of the country's social life. In times past the duty of a government expected to promote religious harmony and maintain social stability would have entailed banning such a film, depicting as it did a traumatic event that was part of India's contemporary politics.

Unlike earlier generations of Hindi films, whose more stylized portrayal of violence belonged in the autarkic world of India's closed economy, *Black Friday* belongs to the era of economic liberalization insofar as it participates in the international conventions of filmic realism. In earlier times, after all, suffering bodies had represented old-fashioned metaphysical qualities and were very explicitly endowed with divine fortitude or demonic frenzy, as the case might be, and sometimes even called forth miracles of various kinds.[7] But of course this shift from one way of portraying torture to another is not the one described by Foucault in *Discipline and Punish*, if only because Indian modes of punishment had already been modernized in the nineteenth century, however uneven this process might have been. The film is not merely catching up to historical reality but rather posing it an important question. Aside from its functions of social control and power projection, all of which could be secured in other ways, does torture possess any specific task, given what I have described as its ritualized and largely ineffective practices?

Perhaps this question should be posed from the other side: if the suffering body no longer represents morality in the form of heroism, martyrdom, or even demonic possession, what then does its portrayal indicate? Have such bodies become merely human, reduced to objects and made available only for victimization? This of course would be a classic humanitarian situation, in which moral agency is seen as belonging either to the perpetrator of violence or to the savior of its victims. And in our case it would mean that the moral dimension of pain, both inflicted and endured, belongs to the torturer who now occupies the same structural position as the humanitarian, that is to say, someone who must choose between those who are to be saved and others who may be sacrificed. Indeed the torturer is even more of a moral presence than humanitarian figures like the relief worker or aid giver, because in addition to escaping the victim's objectification, he invariably operates illicitly and outside the rationality of institutional regulation. Having been expelled from the rationality of modern politics, then, morality seems to have taken refuge in the person of the torturer as much as the humanitarian, since only the former's behavior will determine whether suffering remains supplementary to formal politics or becomes gratuitous and so personal. For unlike many other Hindi films, in which a personal relationship can be established between the vengeful policeman and his evil enemy, who might be killed in violation of the law as in a form of divine retribution, in *Black Friday*'s international style morality is manifested by the absence of such relations. It is instead the purity of motive that counts, where the policeman serves the law while breaking it at some risk to himself.

Despite its impersonal nature, however, the torturer's discipline is not bureaucratic or institutional but voluntary in a way that implies his accepting a great amount of personal responsibility, and so moral freedom, for his actions. This practice is thus oddly traditional, moral in essence, and the very reverse of bureaucratic procedures, being defined by an identification with the law from outside its demesne. Such discipline without institutional regulation represents therefore the fidelity precisely of a supplement. Like the Nazi Eichmann's infamous identification with the law in Hannah Arendt's account of his trial,[8] the tormentor's obedience to his discipline is Kantian, but in an even truer sense than was the Nazi's, since it is after all seen as being freely given rather than required by some institution. Perhaps it is the fate of moral freedom to live at the edges of legality in an age of institutional rationality. Whatever the case, I have suggested that the filmmaker's depiction of torture cannot belong in the world of regulation, not only because such abuse is in fact unregulated, but also because representation ends up robbing it of any supplementary function by the very fact of making it visible beyond the rationality of institutions. The depiction of torture points to the limits of political rationality rather than demonstrating its hegemony. Even more than in feature films and other fictional forms, these limits can be seen in what might be called torture's self-representation, to whose gruesome images I now turn.

Outside the Confessional

Among the most celebrated self-representations of torture in our time are of course the images that emerged from Abu Ghraib, which I want to argue indicate much more than the "permission" supposedly given American soldiers to do what they liked with inmates, or indeed their turn to sadistic and other fantasies in the trying circumstances of wartime Iraq.[9] The narratives of accountability indulged in by those accused of abuse, who tried to fit their acts into the stereotyped mold of the political supplement, as well as the tales of responsibility deployed by their critics to similar purpose, conceal the fact that these performances were far removed from any institutional rationality and entailed establishing direct relationships with the victims of torture outside the prison's regulatory regime. Indeed the creation of a visual record and the circulation of its images not only deprived these acts of their supplementary logic, it also made of the soldiers a moral community defined by mutual complicity, each having become the other's hostage by means of the photographs they all possessed. More than stupidity, in other words, the rendering visible of abuse brought its perpetrators together because of their shared vulnerability, thus giving them a private identity outside military discipline and even against it. In fact distinctions between friend and enemy at Abu Ghraib seem to have collapsed, for despite the violence exercised against them, its prisoners were sometimes seen by the soldiers as sharing a common status as victims, while the army itself was frequently viewed as a mutual enemy.[10] Darius Rejali seems to concur with and lend historical weight to this account of identification when he points out that torturers often submit their victims to procedures they have endured themselves, or to situations that had frightened them in childhood (Rejali, *Torture and Democracy*, 19).

The confessional nature of the torturer's self-portrayal shares a great deal with that made available by martyrdom videotapes and other militant images. Both kinds of confession are concerned not so much with the admission of guilt as with a display of vulnerability, since we know that it is often on the basis of such images that arrests are made and sentences handed down. Recorded well before the attacks they seek to commemorate, martyrdom videotapes, especially once they have been mailed out to media outlets, serve as the militant's point of no return, immediately transforming him into a marked man. But what about the coerced confessions of captives like the American journalist Daniel Pearl, whose recording was followed by his brutal beheading in 2002 by militants in Pakistan? Here, too, there is a strange homology between terrorist and victim, with the latter's confession implying his identification with the former's cause. And rather than detracting from the truth of that cause, it is almost as if the forced character of this confession accentuates it, since the victim's admission is made in the face of certain death, when he has nothing more to fear or hope for. These confessions seem to play the old metaphysical role of recantations, whose truth is guaranteed rather than falsified by their forcible extraction from a victim, one whose impending death can only dignify his last words with a veracity that has nothing to do with the banality of information. In this sense such performances are quite unlike the show trials of the Nazi or Stalinist past, whose confessions Hannah Arendt has described as providing proof of the "logic of history" that underlay the ideologies of fascism and communism, a logic that required the emergence of enemies and traitors from within as part of a historical dialectic.[11]

But there is no historical dialectic in militant Islam that requires enemies to demonstrate its truth, a fact that is only emphasized by the absence of any judicial forms in videotapes of confessions and beheadings. For even the accusations that are often read out by militants in these gory performances tend to refer not to the victim of impending execution but to abstractions like the "Crusader-Zionist Axis." Is this why the most horrifying part of such videotapes is also its least institutional? Departing from the conventional ways in which hostages have been executed in the past, by shooting for instance, the beheadings that became fashionable among militants in Iraq, Pakistan, and Afghanistan during the early years of the war on terror have few if any links with legal forms of punishment. In fact beheading, itself a traditional judicial form, is not an appropriate term for these acts, which involve not the chopping of heads but the cutting of throats. Not only is the act done in a way similar to the ritually sanctioned slaughter of animals for food, it is often even called by the same name. But apart from dehumanizing them, this execution method would make the victims of beheading into sacrificial innocents, of which Jesus' comparably "dehumanized" figure as the Lamb of God provides the most potent example. Such victims are perhaps to be seen not as criminals, therefore, but as those who have repented and identified with their killers to become willing sacrifices, equivalent in this respect to the suicide bombers and others among the terrorist fraternity who deploy the language of martyrdom.

Naturally, these claims can only remain speculative, though I would like to press the point that suffering in such depictions no longer belongs to the supplementary logic of torture, because it has broken faith with institutional regulation and come to occupy an arena that is increasingly available only outside the institution's procedures. So it is clear that the confessional forms defining this arena have little if anything in common with that technology of the self whose disciplinary history, from the rituals of the Catholic Church to those of psychoanalysis, Michel Foucault has so famously analyzed in his work.[12] Perhaps the most important conclusion to be drawn from the visibility of torture in our times, whether it is deemed to be clean or scarring, is that it breaks with the old logic of the political supplement by its very nature, because abuse cannot be represented in media like film without questioning the integrity of modern institutions. For the more rational these institutions become, with procedures meant to create and circulate data, the more disruptive supplementary forms like torture become, as the breakdown of military discipline occasioned by the abuse at Abu Ghraib makes clear. Is this why depictions of torture on film can only reconcile its practice with institutional rationality by invoking the melodramatic contradiction between duty and morality, and in effect lending torture an ontology of its own once it has exited the supplement's realm of rumor and disbelief to become something visible? If anything this seems to indicate that far from cannibalizing all that it comes across, the regulative rationality of such institutions limits its own procedures, and in fact weakens its hold on society the more highly developed it becomes. Of this situation nothing is more emblematic than what I have been describing as the reunion of suffering and morality in the criminal act, which is capable of making even the torturer into a moral hero.

While torture in our time is constantly being attached to political institutions, most commonly thought of as resulting from a chain of command, it is in fact forever dropping out of the political. Because it is disavowed, the act of torture cannot possess any sovereignty even when it is illicit and involves great risk, since without visibility the torturer's decision can only be a moral one. Part of a judicial fantasy involving the extraction of information, torture in its conventional narrative plays the role of a mere supplement to politics, one that lacks any ontology of its own. The confession or resistance of the tortured victim is also therefore nonpolitical, though its difficulty in achieving moral status often results in such status being transferred to the torturer, who is seen as the only one with the luxury of choice. In *Black Friday*, for instance, the terrorist's confession can become a moral act only when it is separated from the coercion of torture and made freely. And yet this freedom remains nonpolitical, with the repentant bomber retiring into a moral life. Rendering torture visible, then, results merely in the destruction of its supplemental role and does nothing more than expose the limits of political rationality.

The militant who dies or kills on a videotape, however, belongs to a different regime of visibility. His spectacular gestures become meaningful as sacrifices and are therefore sovereign in a fundamentally political way, though outside the purview of statelike institutions. In the militant's contempt for torture's instrumental narrative of information that needs to be retrieved, the shock and awe inspired by such acts might even represent the breakdown of statist sovereignty and its fragmentation within a global arena. Like Abraham's willingness to sacrifice his son in Kierkegaard's retelling of the tale, the militant's act neither supplements politics nor degenerates into a practice of moral choice, but rather involves the "ethical suspension of ethics."[13] That is to say, it occurs in the absence of a common moral understanding and is therefore fully responsible for itself. And in fact the language of global Islamic militancy, against which the torture narratives of Guantánamo and Abu Ghraib are set, is clear about the difference between the two. So while every other act of militant violence is deliberately disclaimed as being the mirror image of Western practices, a response that discounts any ontology these acts may have, martyrdom is the unique gesture for which responsibility is claimed. Its sovereignty might therefore belong to a politics beyond institutional limits, one appropriate to a global arena that possesses as yet no political institutions of its own.

NOTES

1. See Michel Foucault, trans. Alan Sheridan, *Discipline and Punish: The Birth of the Prison* (New York: Vintage, 1995).
2. For the way in which torture evades Foucault's disciplinary logic, see Darius Rejali, *Torture and Modernity: Self, Society, and State in Modern Iran* (Boulder: Westview Press, 1994).
3. Darius Rejali, *Torture and Democracy* (Princeton: University Press, 2007), 37; hereafter cited in text.
4. The most celebrated argument about the "banality" of Nazi practices is undoubtedly Hannah Arendt's *Eichmann in Jerusalem: A Report on the Banality of Evil* (New York: Penguin, 1977).
5. Mark Danner, *Torture and Truth: America, Abu Ghraib, and the War on Terror* (New York: New York Review of Books, 2004), 401.
6. For an analysis of this film and its social context, see Vyjayanthi Rao, "How to Read a Bomb: Scenes from Bombay's *Black Friday*," *Public Culture* 19, no. 3 (Fall 2007): 567–92.
7. For the metaphysical element in Hindi cinema, see Rachel Dwyer, *Filming the Gods: Religion and Indian Cinema* (New York: Routledge, 2006).
8. See Arendt, *Eichmann in Jerusalem*, 135–37.
9. I make this argument at greater length in Faisal Devji, *The Terrorist in Search of Humanity: Militant Islam and Global Politics* (New York: Columbia University Press, 2008), chapter 5.
10. For details of the relations that developed between prisoners and soldiers at Abu Ghraib, see Philip Gourevitch and Errol Morris, *Standard Operating Procedure: A War Story* (London: Picador, 2008).
11. For a summary of her argument, see Hannah Arendt, *The Origins of Totalitarianism* (San Diego: Harcourt, 1979), 472–73.

12. See especially Michel Foucault, *The History of Sexuality: An Introduction*, trans. Robert Hurley (New York: Vintage, 1990).
13. For a lengthier discussion of Kierkegaard's *Fear and Trembling*, see Faisal Devji, *Landscapes of the Jihad: Militancy, Morality, Modernity* (New York: Cornell University Press, 2005), 118–23.

The Ghosts of Abu Ghraib, 2007

12

Doing Torture in Film

CONFRONTING AMBIGUITY AND AMBIVALENCE

Marnia Lazreg

Apologies for torture, whether in print or speech, follow a familiar pattern whereby the practice is acknowledged as being extreme and unusual, even evil, before being hailed as necessary and mandatory under exceptional circumstances. Written defenses of torture usually rest on its effectiveness and are generally based on fictitious, hypothetical emergency situations such as the ticking time-bomb scenario.[1] Unlike the printed or spoken word, the representation of torture in films appears to be either emphatic about the barbarity of torture as a tool in the hands of discredited political systems or more ambiguous about its meaning. Television shows occasionally contain more or less explicit scenes of physical torment of abducted individuals. But representations of torture in the context of political crises, including war, are the stock-in-trade of spy and anti-Nazi thrillers, such as the 1947 feature *13, Rue Madeleine*, starring James Cagney, and *Marathon Man*, a 1976 film starring Dustin Hoffman.

Since September 11 the authorized use of torture by the Bush administration in the aftermath of the invasions of Afghanistan and Iraq has lent a new urgency to the exploration of the theme of torture in film, but has also thrown the occasional director willing to address the issue into a quandary about how to best depict torture. U.S. involvement in Afghanistan and Iraq also revived interest in the 1965 feature film *The Battle of Algiers*, which dramatized an episode in the Algerian War during which torture was systematically used in the dismantling of an urban guerilla network operating out of the Casbah, the old city. This chapter focuses on the uncertainties and silences surrounding the filmic treatment of torture, as well as its garbled or ambiguous meanings as conveyed in *The Battle of Algiers* and the documentaries *Standard Operating Procedure* and *Taxi to the Dark Side*.[2]

Torture in *The Battle of Algiers*

Under the leadership of Donald Rumsfeld the Pentagon held a screening of *The Battle of Algiers* before an audience comprised of military officers and civilians.[3] At first glance it might seem that the benefit from viewing this film was dubious, since France lost Algeria in spite of nearly eight years of intense military action. Yet the Pentagon made the right choice. Like Afghanistan and Iraq, the Algerian War took place in a predominantly Muslim country where an underground decolonization movement using guerilla warfare tactics faced a professional army. Although the title of the film was a misnomer in that the episode it depicted was not, properly speaking, a "battle" but a sustained assault on a dense neighborhood in the city of Algiers by paratroops,[4] it drew attention to the minutia of urban guerilla warfare. Most importantly, it evoked torture. The film opens with a shaken man who has just been tortured; a French colonel puts a hat on the victim's head in a patronizing gesture, apparently in generous recognition that the man has undergone an ordeal. The victim is driven to a house in the thick of the Casbah, where he points to a hideout concealed behind a wall. Two active members of the special urban guerilla organization for Algiers, La Zone Autonome, as well as a boy will be blown up in their hideout after refusing to surrender. Torture works. Its effectiveness is framed as part of the dogged, painstaking work of military intelligence officers who piece together every bit of information extracted from various individuals picked up in city sweeps or by militants who break under torture. Intelligence is represented as being a function of method, patience, and the use of torture. Names (foreign to the French officers' ears) are carefully jotted on flow charts, the cell structure of the urban guerilla organization is reconstructed, militants are one by one neutralized, and the leader of the organization, Saadi Yacef, who played his own role in the movie and on whose memoirs the film was based, is captured.[5] Bombs will stop going off in public places, and peace will descend on the troubled city, at least for a while. The systematic use of torture by paratroops is alluded to in one scene where bodies are shown hanging from beams, faces contorted by pain as a blowtorch scorches someone's chest. Depictions of the cruelty of torture, however, are overshadowed by the overall effectiveness of the military's repressive methods of hunting down urban guerillas.

The history of the dismantlement of the FLN political organization in the Casbah has yet to be fully documented and analyzed, although many authors have told it in various ways.[6] The memoirs of special operations intelligence officer Paul Aussaresses, published thirty-six years after the making of *The Battle of Algiers*, reveal how common torture was in Algiers. They also reveal how FLN leaders, including Larbi Ben M'hidi, who is portrayed in *The Battle of Algiers*, were murdered in cold blood after being interrogated. More important, a rejoinder to Aussaresses' memoirs by Benyoucef Benkhedda, a former president of the FNL's government in exile,[7] tells a far more gruesome story than either *The Battle of Algiers* or Aussaresses' book. Benkhedda points out that torture was inflicted on innocent men and children in their Casbah homes with portable equipment. In addition an enlisted paratrooper, Pierre Leulliette, reports in his own memoirs that armed soldiers stormed baths used by women ostensibly to search for the guerillas.[8]

Given that *The Battle of Algiers* focuses on an extraordinary episode meant to highlight the severity of the war of decolonization, it is bewildering why the film did not examine the use of torture in more detail. Admittedly, the film was based on Saadi Yacef's memoirs, which provide just one view of the attack on the Casbah. However, the film does dwell on the method military intelligence officers used to reconstruct the FLN urban organizational structure, even if it does not look at the role of torture in it. Although Colonel Mathieu is shown lecturing his troops with visual aids about the nature of guerila warfare, including how to do searches in order to spot FLN operatives on the street, he does not lay out the fundamentals of counterinsurgency warfare in which torture plays a strategic role. Yet paratroops in Algiers and elsewhere in the country were implementing a well-thought-out military doctrine in which torture figured prominently. In the 1950s a group of French officers, veterans of World War II as well as decolonization wars in Madagascar and Vietnam, set out to formulate a new war doctrine. They studied the Chinese Revolution, Mao Zedong's military writings, and the methods used by the Vietminh to explain why professional armies might not decisively defeat insurgents. This task was all the more urgent given that ill-equipped guerilas defeated the French Army at Dien Bien Phu in May 1954. The officers concluded that war in the aftermath of World War II is of a new kind, "revolutionary" and subversive, carried out by highly mobile bands of armed men using the population as a refuge as well as logistical support in a hit-and-run strategy. Dubbing this new war *guerre révolutionnaire*, theorists devised a doctrine according to which professional armies could best fight such a war by adopting the organizational, operational, and psychological methods of their opponents. This counterinsurgency doctrine, also referred to as the French school,[9] rested on two principal tenets: first, counterinsurgency war must take place in and against the population defined as friend-enemy; second, intelligence is key to swift military action. In this view torture helps to extract actionable intelligence and thus becomes the "antidote to terrorism."[10] Torture helps to screen the population and distinguish the friends from the enemies. The colonial army during the Algerian war taught *guerre révolutionnaire* theory and doctrine to its troops, including the use of torture. They specifically taught that to be "humane" torture should not leave traces or be carried out by a person of rank or in the presence of young soldiers, and it should stop as soon the victim talks.[11]

Given this background it is unclear why *The Battle of Algiers* did not include a discussion of torture in Colonel Mathieu's lecture on FLN guerilla warfare. Assuming that the specifics of French counterinsurgency doctrine were not known to the director of the film or to Saadi Yacef, who advised him, the routine use of torture during the war called for more than a few scenes about the subject matter. The half-hearted, perfunctory representation of torture in the film further manages to elide the significance of the practice for FLN militants. No dialogue between FLN militants alludes to torture. No psychological preparation to torture is alluded to before the women are handed bombs to place around the city. It is as if torture was not an issue for the guerilas. Yet memoirs written by former FLN militants indicate that torture was a nagging preoccupation. One man worried that he might be castrated under torture, and was glad that he already had children. He even implied that he agreed to cooperate with the French military after he was captured because he dreaded torture.[12] Remarkably, at least two of the female guerillas featured in the film had been tortured, Djamila Bouhired and Djamila Boupacha. Yet torture in the film targets only men. The film is ambiguous about the capture of Saadi Yacef and his female companion. Were they tortured? In personal conversations former militants point out that Saadi was not tortured, but made a deal with his captors, giving them information about his comrades. The film also fails to capture the climate of terror that torture creates. Instead it focuses on the terror caused by the bombings conducted by both the FLN and the French Right extremist underground. But no matter how frightening these explosions were, they did not occur every day or everywhere in the country. By contrast torture was inflicted in detention centers, military posts, and police stations throughout the country, and its secrecy ensured its terror effect. Torture often resulted in the "disappearance" of its victims, which, along with the exposure of dead bodies and public summary executions, enhanced the climate of terror. Finally, torture was also used as a prelude to brainwashing, causing severe behavioral problems in its survivors.[13] By focusing on the terror caused by explosions, the film dramatizes the effectiveness of torture, since these bombings were brought to an end as the FLN organization in the Casbah was dismantled. It is true that the last scene in the Casbah drama, depicting a defeated Saadi Yacef being driven in a military vehicle after his capture, is followed by footage of spontaneous mass demonstrations of the Algerian people in support of their independence. However, torture and other abuses continued between the dismantling of the FLN in 1957 and the onset of the demonstrations in 1961. Admittedly, the ultimate message conveyed by the film is that torture did not work. However, it is not clear whether it was the ineffectiveness of torture that caused the demise of colonial rule. From a narrow military perspective, in fact, torture did work.

Clearly, neither the director, Gillo Pontecorvo, who was known for his progressive political views, nor Saadi Yacef meant to condone or dismiss torture's role in wars of decolonization. However, by representing torture as just one aspect of the French military's conduct of the war, the film minimizes its centrality to the war while creating uncertainty about its meaning for the guerillas and the French intelligence officers. Given the systematic character of torture during the war, *The Battle of Algiers* could not avoid bringing it up. But having failed to appreciate the strategic role that torture played in the French counterinsurgency doctrine, the film deals instead with clichés such as the idea that torture targets men, not women, that it can be effective in dismantling an elaborate underground organization, that it is not a major preoccupation of those it targets, and that it is not terror producing, unlike explosions. In the end torture as a military strategy and an experience eludes the film. This form of filmic amnesia, which views torture as a formal attribute of a war of decolonization but ignores the insidious manner in which it actually pervaded everyday life for the colonized, as well as the special power it conferred on the military, is not accidental. It is a significant aspect of the political, psychological, emotional, and cultural matrix in which the idea of torture is ensconced. Torture is a "limit experience," to quote Michel Foucault. It is an extreme experience that people living in industrial liberal democratic societies agree, at least theoretically, is politically abhorrent, as it connotes the arbitrariness of the power that orders or condones it. Torture is also ominous in its suspension of the civil rights protections that citizens value, even when some of them argue in favor of the exceptional circumstances under which torture is permissible. Psychologically, torture confronts the individual with his or her vulnerability. No one is immune to torture. Consequently, torture makes us uneasy even when the pain it inflicts on those deemed deserving of it seems just. The prevailing culture, in its secular or religious form, stresses punishment and discipline as normative. The torture matrix is unstable and leaves us with a residual uncertainty about the ultimate legitimacy of the practice. How should a moviemaker represent torture? Should he dwell on its cruel side and run the risk of activating the unsettling character of torture in his audience? Should he hint at its occurrence in a few images and move on to the rest of his subject matter? When making *The Battle of Algiers*, the director undoubtedly felt that he had done enough by inserting scenes depicting the gruesome side of torture, with hanging bodies and blowtorches. But the phenomenal side of torture was left to the imagination. From the perspective of its makers, the film was not about torture even though torture was central to the war. Herein lies the conundrum of torture in commercial films. How is one to represent torture without exploring its fundamental inhumanity as experienced by its victims or invoking their terror, as well as the discomfort of those in the audience who dread it? Torture is palatable only when represented partially, so as to elide the truth of its existence: that it reveals the fragility of the political culture that claims to protect the inviolability of the individual.

However, some representations of torture appear to be more palatable, such as the photographs from Abu Ghraib. These widely disseminated pictures of bodies in various stress positions represent sexual torment, which in the mind of the average viewer is not quite torture. They have a titillating character that makes them acceptable for display on magazine covers and in newspapers. They do not depict "pain" since the faces of the detainees are covered. The victims are faceless, anonymous, and seem more like exhibitionists than suffering victims. If pain was involved, viewers assumed it was sexual and thus not quite the pain of torture. In these pictures, Iraqi prisoners tethered to electrical wires look like scarecrows with arms outstretched and heads bagged. The torture inflicted on the detainees was concealed by all of the sexual and farcical camera effects. Arguably, the Abu Ghraib pictures were discreet, leaked to the press as iconic representations of what soldiers might get up to in an occupied land. They were not part of a structured story told by a muckraking filmmaker. Presumably, a documentary film that focuses on torture at Abu Ghraib, such as *Standard Operating Pro-*

cedure, would avoid the problems of representation that trouble *The Battle of Algiers*.

Standard Operating Procedure

Errol Morris's *Standard Operating Procedure*, released in May 2008, forty-three years after *The Battle of Algiers*, is on the face of it rather graphic in its depiction of torture at Abu Ghraib. It revisits the photographs of sexual torture, to which it adds brief scenes of dogs charging detainees and a male victim tied up in a shower stall (one of the torture methods used) from which he will not emerge alive. We see the body of the dead man being wrapped in ice, his eyes fixed in a blank stare. Since the public had already seen many of these pictures, the film focused on making them intelligible by having the torturers explain themselves. The documentary focuses on the small group of lower-ranked men and women involved, supplemented by interviews, including one with Janis L. Karpinski, former brigadier general in Iraq, under whose watch the torture took place. There is little narration to provide a context for the sequence of torturers' monologues, which were presumably answers to questions posed by the filmmaker. To its credit, *The Battle of Algiers*, on occasion, contextualizes scenes that might have been confusing (such as the killing of pimps or the mistreatment of alcoholics by the native population) by narrating the FLN policy of "cleansing" society of drug use, alcoholism, and pimping. By contrast *Standard Operating Procedure* leaves it up to each participant to create his or her own context for explaining the torture. For example, Specialist Sabrina Harman, Sergeant Javal Davis, and Private First Class Lynndie England evoke the devastation and grim conditions they experienced in Fallujah, where the U.S. Army battled insurgents—the unnerving sounds of explosions, helicopters going up in flames overhead, a nightly curfew, and a diffuse fear mixed with anger resulting from all this—as factors that presumably conditioned them to later torture detainees with impunity. The implication is that torture would have happened even if it had not been condoned, or ordered by General Miller, as Karpinski emphasizes; the environment made it possible.

If Errol Morris wished to emphasize the ordinariness of the people who engage in torture, or the rationalizations that torturers dream up in order to explain their unsavory acts, he only half succeeded. By letting the soldiers present their views unchallenged, he allowed them to minimize the importance of torture as a violation of the law. Characters wondered out loud whether enforced nakedness, masturbation, or even walking a naked man on a leash were really torture. In this they echo a sentiment shared by the common man. The investigator in the film points out that the culprits have done "something stupid" by taking pictures. He has twelve CDs documenting the time and date of the torture episodes, which would be taken as evidence of wrongdoing. To get away with torture one must keep it secret. As one protagonist says, "A picture is worth a thousand words." Soldiers in the film are not asked why they do not consider sexual torture, or torture in the shower, to constitute real torture. Harman feels that sexual torture is "molestation," although she likens the torture pose of one detainee to that of Jesus Christ. Yet she fails to compare the pain experienced by Christ to the pain that the detainees experienced while shackled and tied to windows in stressful positions or choking to death in a shower. Similarly, Specialist Megan Ambuhl finds the methods of torture "unorthodox." These euphemisms, typical among torturers, are all the more remarkable in that they put a spin on the pictures, which are interpreted variously by those who took or performed for them.

The presence of women among the torturers in the film highlights the ambiguity of the meaning that the director imparts to torture. The women minimize their roles in Abu Ghraib by portraying themselves as bewildered spectators who sensed that the mistreatment of detainees was wrong, but went along with it anyway. Sabrina Harman, like so many young French soldiers during the Algerian War, took pictures of tortured victims as proof to show others at a later date. She does not bring up the plight of Iraqi female detainees. Lynndie England's monologue best captures the symbolic transformation of torture into the victimization of women in the military. England dismisses her involvement in the humiliation of the Iraqi detainee she walked on a leash by claiming that she "never" dragged him. As she sees it, her boyfriend, Specialist Charles Graner, had already leashed the detainee. Besides, "every woman was there [at the torture scenes] because of a man." The military being a "man's world . . . you need to stack up." To be one of the guys a woman must go along with the guys. If men torture, women should join in order to stack up. Torture is the mechanism by which women in the military acquire status as soldiers. Not only does Morris allow such an interpretation of the role of women in the military to go unchallenged, but he also presents the torturer as the victim of torture. This psychological trope was used by torturers during the Algerian War, who argued that by being made to carry out orders to torture they were themselves the real victims of the practice: they had to inflict pain and suffering on command whether they liked it or not.[14] Responsibility for torture is imputed not to the torturer but solely to those who issued orders, looked the other way, or purposely gave vague instructions about the manner in which interrogation was to be implemented.

The centrality of torture at Abu Ghraib (and in other jails throughout occupied Iraq) further recedes from the viewer's consciousness as torture becomes tangled up in a tale of unrequited love. As England sees it, she was "blinded by being in love with a man" who did not deserve her love. Not only did this female soldier commit a dishonorable act in order to acquire acceptance from fellow male soldiers, she also fell in love with her superior, with whom she had sex in violation of Army rules. England glosses over the sordid character of the tale as her resigned and bitter face fills the screen. She is pitiful, and may even win some viewers' sympathy. Torture is thus relative; its cruelty becomes a function of the place where it occurs and the people who commit it. Abu Ghraib is far away, in a country the public knows little more about than they do its former leader and his disreputable acts. Morris's foregrounding of the female soldiers at Abu Ghraib creates a cultural imbalance: what about the Iraqi women held at Abu Ghraib? Yet before the film was made the Taguba report[15] mentioned that a woman had been raped, and Iraqi parents and relatives of imprisoned women had staged a demonstration outside Abu Ghraib. The exclusion of Iraqi women who were among the victims of torture reinforces the gender prejudice (which also plagued *The Battle of Algiers*) that only men are tortured. Besides, no male victims of torture are given the opportunity to talk in the film. Their inclusion in the documentary would have undoubtedly caused the monologues of the torturers to sound more disingenuous, and would have undermined the justifications they presented. In the end this film about torture succeeds in making torture a failure of character in some of the perpetrators; it also turns the act of torture into a sad commentary on love and betrayal. Torturers even appear to have redeemed themselves, as some of the guards went after a few adult detainees for having raped teenage boys held in their cells. Once more the experience of torture and its meaning for the victims and for the political system that made it possible are not portrayed. An exception is one picture of ants tormenting detainees in a cell, which gives an inkling of the squalor and cruelty of detention. Perhaps the title of the documentary, *Standard Operating Procedure*, was meant to highlight the acceptance of torture by the army. But this only helps to relativize torture, since the majority of the people interviewed were lower-ranked soldiers. Their narratives of what they did or did not do are a ploy for not confronting the act and experience of torture.[16] Although the film manages to provide little information about the sociocultural background of the torturers, their speech patterns betray their social origins: they represent the common man. Torture may be ordered or condoned by the top brass, but the common man/soldier is all too happy to oblige. Given the relatively light sentences that the torturers received, the implication is that engaging in torture is like committing a minor crime. The film holds in abeyance the future of this practice.

Taxi to the Dark Side

Unlike *Standard Operating Procedure*, Alex Gibney's 2007 documentary, *Taxi to the Dark Side*, presents a balanced view of the use of torture in Afghanistan, Guantánamo Bay, and Iraq. The film is unabashedly against torture, but gives advocates of the practice (including former vice-president Cheney and former president George W. Bush) the opportunity to voice their opinions. The narration provides a framework within which to understand the sequence of events since September 11 that led to the capture, incarceration, and torture of detainees; it also details the manipulation of the law that helped to legalize torture in violation of the Geneva Conventions as well as rights, such as habeas corpus, guaranteed by the Constitution. The narration, supplemented by interviews with civil and military lawyers, gives the audience a basis for determining the validity of the arguments put forth in favor or against torture.

More important, the film includes three elements that were missing from both *The Battle of Algiers* and *Standard Operating Procedure*: first, it portrays the effects of torture on its victims; second, it delineates the process by which torture evolves; third, it sheds light on the constellation of antecedents that give torture its ultimately unreliable as well as arbitrary character. The film begins by tracing the death under torture of a taxi driver, Dilawar, who was driving passengers to the town of Yakubi in Khost Province when he was arrested by U.S. troops on a tip provided by an Afghan commander. It later appears likely that the commander used Dilawar to cover up his own tracks as an "insurgent" who launched rocket attacks on a U.S. Army base. Dilawar was an innocent young man subjected to several torture techniques, including isolation in an airlock spiked with concertina wire, sensory deprivation, forced nudity, hooding, shackling, and standing in stress positions, as well as having a fierce dog over his head. Unable to bear his pain, he started to scream and fidget. To quiet him down, his torturers repeatedly struck the sides of his thighs with their knees so that "his lower limbs [looked] as if he had been run over by a bus." Had he survived, his legs would have been amputated. In one episode, in addition to the strikes to his thighs, four MPs stood on him, gave him kidney blows, and jumped up and down on his back. As a slight, one-hundred-twenty-two-pound man, Dilawar could not survive the severity of the torture he sustained. Oddly, one of his torturers complained that his knees were tired from striking him. Dilawar is hardly an isolated case of an innocent man subjected to death by torture. Rather his story typifies the effect of torture when used as military strategy in counterinsurgency warfare.

Another detainee, Moazzam Begg, was luckier than Dilawar: he survived torture and was able to tell his story. He was picked up from his home in Islamabad, Pakistan, by security forces, covered with a garment from head to foot, goggled, hooded, shackled, and airlifted in a stressful position to Kandahar and then Bagram before winding up at Guantánamo Bay. He, too, was accused of acts of terrorism he had not committed. His story reveals the pressure that intelligence officers and other security personnel were under to make detainees admit to their participation in al-Qaeda and the Taliban movement. Confessions, the veracity of which could not always be ascertained, appeared to be the goal of torture. Begg was subjected to all the techniques of torture used on other detainees. At Guantánamo he was held in isolation in a six-foot by eight-foot cell for twenty months, threatened with execution several times, and denied access to a lawyer. The inclusion in the documentary of two victims of torture, one whose death was recounted by several people, among them investigative reporters, the other speaking in his own voice, allows the audience to enter the murky world of torture created by an avowedly democratic state, to get a sense of the meaning of torture for the military, as well as to assess the consequences of torture for its victims.

The depiction of how a detainee met his death under torture demystifies the commonly held notion that torture is a practice of last resort targeting individuals known to have information that can save lives. In *Taxi to the Dark Side* various reporters, lawyers, and members of the military clearly indicate that torture, once started, acquires a life of its own. Inflicting pain and suffering on Afghan, Iraqi, and Pakistani prisoners became a violent sport. Torturers jeered and laughed at their victims; as more detainees arrived and cells were filled, abuse embedded itself in the texture of everyday life. Knee strikes, for example, became an "amusement." Regardless of whether torture was ordered, or carried out in violation of the Army Field Manual, it was part of a larger pattern of human degradation in which cultural, religious, and political prejudice trumped the search for actionable intelligence. American troops were told that Afghans were their enemies, sworn to seek their destruction. The fact that al-Qaeda had initially operated out of Afghanistan provided additional fodder to enmity for the average Afghan regardless of guilt or innocence. The culture of the enemy, which the average soldier knows through stereotypes, plays a role in the dehumanization of the detainees. When Dilawar cried out in pain, he was labeled "combative." A mentally challenged detainee was perceived as a con man trying to hide his guilt. Since no detainee could be believed, torture could never elicit usable, reliable, truthful intelligence. Torture became a way of dealing with otherness; it became a method for assuaging fear and a means of exacting revenge for the attacks of September 11. Dilawar's death was ruled a homicide; torture became a method of killing. The routinization of torture divorces the practice from its purported goal of intelligence gathering. About 90 percent of detainees at Bagram (and at Guantánamo) in the aftermath of the invasion of Afghanistan were arrested by Afghan warlords in exchange for monetary rewards paid by the United States or Pakistani bounty hunters. Consequently, interrogators knew all too well that their captives might have been brought in for the wrong reasons, which included not only money but also the settling of scores between tribal leaders and neighbors. In this context the twin pressures to produce intelligence and project power identified by the film were a rationalization for interrogators to engage in the systematic abuse of detainees belonging to a different culture and holding different worldviews.

In addressing the routinization of torture and providing information about the context that made it possible, *Taxi to the Dark Side* sheds light on an important aspect of torture: it is not reducible to one technique. On the contrary, detainees were subjected to a combination of techniques that included stripping, hooding, shackling, isolation, exposure to specially trained dogs, etc. In addition, in between torture sessions they were subjected to insults, jeering, laughing, as well as kicking, knee strikes in their thighs, and other forms of abuse. The film helps the viewer see that torture is a holistic phenomenon structured in such a way as to keep physical and psychological pain constant to an extent that drives its victim close to madness or can result in his death.[17] The film conveys not only the cruelty meted out to individuals who had no information to give but also the torturers' utter disregard for the pain experienced by their victims. Protagonists in the film suggest the lack of training in interrogation was the cause of deaths that occurred under torture, some of which were ruled homicides (including Dilawar's). They also point to sadism as playing a role in torturers' disregard for their victims. Although plausible, such explanations are not compelling. French torturers who were experts in torture techniques still killed their victims.[18]

In reality, the torturer is not concerned with the humanity of his victim. He is engaged in a contest of wills and wants to break the victim. To achieve his goals he uses a combination of techniques regardless of whether they will be tolerated by his victim. Even when doctors lend their expertise to torturers, victims still die or survive maimed. The film presents copies of logs kept by intelligence officers, some of which indicate that a detainee was given an enema, another violation of bodily integrity. At any rate *Taxi to the Dark Side* makes it clear that torturers behave with all the aggressiveness and psychological detachment that the power they hold over their victims allows. The power that the torturer enjoys is rarely limited by moral restraint or rules of procedure. A female soldier featured in the film, Salceda, was irate that a detainee she attempted to break by exposing herself to him, thus violating a cultural taboo, would not look her in the eye. As a result he was grabbed by the shirt and knocked against the wall multiple times. Torture as a pain-producing practice is not easily checked, and once torture has become synonymous with the interrogation of "enemies," defined as terrorists, it cannot be controlled. It was not controlled during the Algerian War; it was not controlled in Iraq or at Guantánamo Bay. The routinization of torture as depicted in *Taxi* was sustained by a common language understood by torturers, guards, and other military personnel on hand. Labels used to refer to detainees changed in ways that did not affect torture. For example, NEC (Non–Enemy Combatant) and NLEC (No Longer an Enemy Combatant) were confusing acronyms that left uncertain whether the changing status of detainees was the result of torture. Was torture used as a method of screening detainees in a manner consistent with French counterinsurgency warfare?

Unlike written depictions, films dealing with torture betray greater ambivalence about how to portray this practice. Arguably, it would be bad taste for film directors to reconstitute the full range of torture techniques as they are applied to detainees. Were they to do so, they would run the risk of trivializing torture or making its techniques knowable and repeatable by those willing to engage in them. These considerations may be incidental to the films covered in this chapter, since torture is either unavoidable or central to them. The differences in how torture is portrayed in the three films reflect ambivalence about either the effectiveness of torture in reaching its apparent goal of extracting actionable intelligence or about accountability for its occurrence

When torture is confronted directly, from the standpoints of its advocates as well as its victims, its reality acquires more sharpness, and the viewer is allowed to form an opinion. By providing background information about the use of torture in counterinsurgency war under the Bush administration, and tracing how torture resulted in the death of one victim, *Taxi* demystifies the prevailing notion that torture is a method of last resort used to save innocent lives. Representations of torture in films need to be clear about the arbitrariness of torture, its routinization, as well as the hollowness of its political justifications. They can do so only by being clear about the illegality of torture and by depicting its consequences for the victims, who must be allowed to present their experiences of psychological and physical pain and degradation. Perhaps the documentary film is best suited for exposing viewers to the unjustifiable character of torture, arguing for accountability, and unambiguously calling for its eradication. Documentaries can succeed in this effort as long as they are conducted in a factual and dialogical manner.

NOTES

1. See, among others, Michael Walzer, "Political Action: The Problem of Dirty Hands," in *Torture*, ed. Sanford Levinson (New York: Oxford University Press, 2005); and Michael Ignatieff, *The Lesser Evil: Political Ethics in an Age of Terror* (Princeton: Princeton University Press, 2004).
2. A recent Swedish television series on torture (*Tortyr*) aired in November 2009. It features a number of experts, including psychologists, as well as Henri Alleg, a French journalist who was tortured in 1957 for his sympathies for the Algerian Front of National Liberation. A dramatization of Henri Alleg's experience, *La Question*, was written and directed by Laurent Heynemann in 1977. It details the arrest and torture of both Alleg (named Henri Charlègue in the film) and Maurice Audin (renamed Oudinot), a young professor of mathematics who died under torture. This film makes explicit torture techniques as well as their effects on the victims of torture.
3. See Michael T. Kaufman, "What Does the Pentagon See in Battle of Algiers?" *New York Times*, September 7, 2003, http://www.rialtopictures.com/eyes_xtras/battle_times.html, (accessed January 23, 2010).
4. Henri Alleg makes this point in his *Retour sur la question* (Bruxelles: Editions Aden, 2006), 19.

5. A better-known leader, Larbi ben M'hidi, was also captured by accident, and later murdered by Paul Aussaresses, General Jacques Massu's sidekick. Aussaresses confessed to the use of torture in *The Battle of the Casbah: Counterterrorism and Torture* (New York: Enigma Books, 2002–2006).
6. See, for example, Alistair Horne, *A Savage War of Peace* (New York: New York Review of Books, 2006).
7. This was the Gouvernment Provisoire de la République Algérienne (known by the acronym GPRA).
8. Pierre Leulliette, *St. Michael and the Dragon: Memoirs of a Paratrooper* (Boston: Houghton Mifflin, 1964), 282.
9. See Marie Monique Robin, *Les escadrons de la mort: L'Ecole française* (Paris: La Découverte, 2004).
10. Roger Trinquier, *Guerre, subversion, révolution* (Paris: Robert Laffont, 1968), 70.
11. See Marnia Lazreg, *Torture and the Twilight of Empire: From Algiers to Baghdad* (Princeton: Princeton University Press, 2008), 115.
12. Béchir Boumaza et al., *La gangrène* (Ryad El Feth, Alger: Editions Rahma, 1992), 42.
13. See Frantz Fanon, *The Wretched of the Earth* (New York: Grove, 1963), appendix.
14. See Lazreg, *Torture and the Twilight*, 116.
15. Antonio Taguba, *Article 15-6 Investigation of the 800th Military Police Brigade* (U.S. Army, 2004) 16. https//.www.agonistorg/annex/taguba.htm (accessed November 16, 2011).
16. By contrast the series *Tortyr* foregrounds the inadmissibility of torture under any circumstance (see endnote 2).
17. During the Algerian War some victims of torture were driven to madness.
18. General Paul Aussaresses describes how he killed an Algerian when he waterboarded him. See Aussaresses, *The Battle of the Casbah*.

Standard Operating Procedure, 2008

13

Documenting the Documentaries on Abu Ghraib

FACTS VERSUS DISTORTION

Stjepan G. Mestrovic

I was appointed as an expert witness in sociology for the defense teams of three of the soldiers, so-called "rotten apples," involved in the abuse at Abu Ghraib: Javal Davis, Sabrina Harman, and Lynndie England. In the process of fulfilling my role as an expert witness, I had the opportunity to observe and interact with the remaining convicted soldiers, Charles Graner, Ivan Frederick, and especially Jeremy Sivits and Megan Ambuhl. Simply hanging out at the courthouse gave me the opportunity to conduct participant-observation research with scores of other soldiers who were witnesses, observers, and in other ways participants in this drama. While I will be concentrating on Abu Ghraib in this chapter, and especially on two film documentaries about Abu Ghraib and some of the soldiers I came to know, it is important to note that I also served as an expert witness in the courts-martial pertaining to the Operation Iron Triangle killings of 2006 and the Baghdad Canal killings of 2007. Several distinct and interesting patterns emerged in these cases regarding torture, abuse, killing, and the treatment of prisoners. The common strand that binds these cases together is that of a scientifically designed stage for sadism established by the government, followed by an equally scientific system designed to shift blame onto the lowest-ranking soldiers while protecting the power elite. In other words the military deliberately trains its soldiers to behave like abusive and killing machines, and when that abuse is exposed, it just as deliberately throws accused soldiers into a machinelike legal process designed to produce convictions and scapegoats. But the culture industry, as Theodor Adorno called it, similarly dehumanizes its subjects, which are used for news and entertainment, and it uses machinelike techniques to entertain and inform the masses.[1]

A reader may suspect that my advocacy for some of the soldiers may cloud my judgment or introduce bias into this discussion. However, my views on the military's stance regarding abuses were vindicated in 2008, when the U.S. Senate Armed Services Committee issued the Levin-McCain Report.[2] The report exonerated the soldiers who had been convicted and scapegoated during courts-martial in 2004 and 2005 for the abuses at Abu Ghraib committed in 2003. It was not a true vindication, because no one in the government, media, or American society as a whole looked back at the Abu Ghraib "experience" to apologize, expiate, or redress the wrongs that were committed against these soldiers or the Iraqis they abused. Nevertheless the Levin-McCain Report established and documented at least two uncontestable facts, among others. First, that the torture and abuse at Abu Ghraib had been planned and orchestrated from the White House and traveled down the chain of command to the lowest-ranking U.S. soldiers at Abu Ghraib. Second, that the torture and abuse at Abu Ghraib were part of a widespread policy that made use of similar "techniques" at Guantánamo, in Afghanistan, at other sites in Iraq, and at black rendition sites.

However, metaphorically the Levin-McCain report is a giant dangling participle in history that makes no difference in the comprehension, expiation, or correction of America's cultural turn toward "the dark side."[3] This is because the government and culture media's success in painting the "rotten apples" at Abu Ghraib as sadists and the ones solely responsible for the abuse makes it difficult for most people to digest the import of the Levin-McCain report. The culture media played on the most simplistic—and false—explanation possible: photographs show that sadism occurred, so sadists must have committed it. Nevertheless it is a fact, documented in sworn testimony at the trials, that none of the convicted soldiers were sadists. I am certain of this fact because I testified on this issue using their results from psychological tests, and because I came to know them. It is more important to know that all of the soldiers suffered from Post-Traumatic Stress Syndrome (PTSD), anxiety, depression, and various symptoms of combat stress. The culture industry failed to report these facts, which emerged in testimony by different expert witnesses. In other words the more accurate assessment of the situation is that the army scientifically created a sadistic social climate that harmed its own soldiers as well as the prisoners. The so-called "rotten apples" should be more accurately understood as psychiatric casualties of a very deliberate and harmful policy of torture.[4]

Why is it so difficult for this documented, verifiable truth to emerge in the culture industry's depiction of Abu Ghraib?

Studying the Captains of the Culture Industry

It is useful to conjoin Thorstein Veblen's term for latter-day barbarians in the business world, whom he called the "captains of industry," with Adorno's culture industry.[5] The interplay of these two corporate industries, and their mutual relationship with the government, leads to new insights regarding a topic that most people assume they understand, namely, the abuse at Abu Ghraib as purportedly caused by abusive and sadistic individuals.

Many definitions of sadism exist, but I find Erich Fromm's understanding of the term to be most helpful.[6] Fromm regarded control as the essence of sadism, such that the sadist seeks complete control of the other, including the right to inflict physical as well as psychic pain and humiliation. Sadism includes efforts to prevent the other from being able to defend his or her self or to escape the intolerable situation. Fromm's understanding enables one to shift the focus from sadistic persons or acts to sadistic systems, programs, and social institutions—including the information media and documentary films.

Regarding the mechanization and systematization of sadism at Abu Ghraib, the reader need only concentrate on facts exposed by Levin-McCain and other reports that demonstrate that the military and the CIA designed a cold, calculating, and scientific approach toward interrogating and "softening up" prisoners that completely ignored the humanity of the torturers and victims alike.[7] The soldiers were regarded as interchangeable assets and the prisoners as nameless detainees. It is illogical and simply impossible to conclude rationally that these soldiers invented the torture and abuse on their own during the night shift, given that the precise methods they used were found at Guantánamo, Bagram Air Force Base in Afghanistan, other sites, and of course in the pages of the Levin-McCain report.

The torturers at Abu Ghraib developed PTSD—a fact that was disclosed in testimony, but not disclosed widely in media reports and documentaries—in line with mountains of research that shows that it is not human nature to inflict pain on others. Nothing is known formally of the PTSD or damage caused to the Arab victims.

In this chapter I will focus on two documentaries pertaining to Abu Ghraib: Errol Morris's *Standard Operating Procedure (SOP)* (2008) and

Rory Kennedy's *The Ghosts of Abu Ghraib* (2007). However, my analysis is informed by experience and knowledge gained through observing and interacting with journalists as well as other filmmakers regarding the aforementioned additional sites of sadism and abuse. My overall finding is that these captains of the culture industry perceive news and information as valuable commodities to be sold for a profit, and that they seek as much control as possible and compete fiercely with each other for access to these commodities. While I was able to establish rapport with most participants in this drama, it was almost impossible to establish rapport with journalists and filmmakers. This may be because the captains of the culture industry have a seemingly omnipotent ability to cut, edit, and frame their commodities in a manner that they believe will appeal to their audiences. I have been able to describe the emotions, thoughts, and inner psychic worlds of the soldiers because they made themselves available to empathetic understanding. But the captains of the culture industry behaved, in my view, as if they "had the upper hand," and made it impossible to penetrate their inner worlds.

Journalists and filmmakers struggled to get the soldiers to agree to interviews, especially ones on film, following their release from prison. The social positions of the soldiers were precarious. Although some of them had served their sentences and were dishonorably discharged, others were still in the army. The army would choose the date when it would formally sever all ties with the released soldiers. Moreover, in some cases the soldiers' appeals process continued throughout their imprisonment and even after they had been released from prison. From the perspective of their defense attorneys, the legal cases of some of these soldiers were still "live" even after their release. However, the attorneys for Sabrina Harman, Megan Ambuhl, and Javal Davis wanted their clients to appear in documentaries and, in general, to tell their stories to the media on the grounds that such appearances would help their clients, but they allowed their clients to make their own decisions. Because I had established genuine rapport with these soldiers, some of them turned to me for advice, and also insisted to the documentary producers that I be consulted or even be present during the filming.

For the soldiers the decision to appear in the documentaries came down to an issue of trust. They did not trust the media in general or the documentary producers in particular. The soldiers were well aware of the negative ways they were depicted in the media and were hurt by these depictions. Several of them acquired "bad apple" tattoos as a sort of symbolic defiance of the media and the government. For example, the first words uttered by Javal Davis upon his release from prison were, "I am not a rotten apple." On the other hand, they did want to give their versions of what happened and their roles in the Abu Ghraib fiasco.

Journalists, as I observed, did not attend the trials from 8 A.M. to 5 P.M. They came and left at random hours, but mostly did not return after 1 P.M., which is when they filed their reports for the day. There were only two exceptions to this rule: Debbie Stevenson, who wrote for the local newspaper, the *Killeen Daily Herald*, and Joanne Wypijewski, a freelance writer. These two journalists saw and heard everything that I saw and heard in the courtroom—although they were not permitted to speak with the soldiers.

In summary, the values, beliefs, and norms for the captains of the culture industry I observed seem to come down to the following: time is money. The low-ranking soldiers on trial were not as educated as they were and definitely did not belong to the same social class. The journalists and filmmakers were "entitled" to get information and to edit it according to their rules. The persons they depicted in their stories and films had absolutely no right to edit, censor, question, or even know how they would be depicted by the culture industry. News and documented information are commodities that bring profit. One must beat one's competitors in seizing some of these commodities and then in packaging and sending them out for consumption.

Interacting with Rory Kennedy and Errol Morris

Errol Morris and Rory Kennedy were competing with each other. Kennedy's *Ghosts of Abu Ghraib* premiered on January 19, 2007, and *SOP* premiered in the spring of 2008. The assistants for both filmmakers contacted me in August and September of 2006, and both were scrambling to get the female "rotten apples" on film, namely, Sabrina Harman, Megan Ambuhl, and Lynndie England. A film composed of exclusively male talking heads plus the one female, Janis Karpinski, would seem out of sync with contemporary society.[8] Only three out of about 150 soldiers at Abu Ghraib were female, but society demands a more equal representation of the sexes in its image of the military and in general. England was still in prison in September of 2006, so that all their efforts at that time went toward securing Ambuhl and Harman. I had been in contact with Ambuhl and Harman since the trials. Morris had filmed both of them as of August 2006, and they were very unhappy with their on-camera interviews. They felt that they were being humiliated and did not believe that their genuine views would be aired. They consented to the interviews because Morris also filmed the defense attorney, Frank Spinner, and they trusted Spinner. But Spinner was cut from *SOP* and does not appear in the released version of the film.

At first Ambuhl and Harman refused to be in Kennedy's film. They felt traumatized by the experiences of Abu Ghraib, the trials, and other journalists and filmmakers. Nevertheless they insisted to Kennedy that they might participate if I were present during the filming, and if my views were also included in the film. Kennedy's assistant e-mailed me and stated that Ambuhl and Harman wanted me to be present during negotiations and possible filming. I agreed to fly to Washington, D.C., on September 9, 2006, to meet with Kennedy, Ambuhl, and Harman in Senator Edward Kennedy's office. The two female soldiers and I were told that we would meet with Senator Kennedy. I spoke with Rory Kennedy prior to the trip and tried to convey to her the two factual pillars that would later appear in the Levin-McCain report. It was as if she did not hear me. She made it clear that she wanted Ambuhl and Harman in the film because they were female.

I arrived in Washington, D.C., on the evening of September 9. The two female soldiers met me at the hotel at 8 A.M. and we spoke until 11 A.M. They told me they wanted to convey what the three of us already knew, but the world did not know, namely, there were JAG officers at Abu Ghraib who knew of and approved the abusive techniques. There were scores of commissioned officers who approved and ordered the abuse, and who were never even mentioned at the trials. These women wanted to convey that the abuse had been normalized at Abu Ghraib, and that they had been powerless to stop it. Their lives had been shattered by the trials and their aftermath. They were trying to cope with their PTSD and were not receiving any treatment.

When we arrived Rory Kennedy explained that her uncle, Senator Kennedy, was not available to see us, but that we could convey our concerns to his assistant. The situation was tense. Ambuhl did most of the talking, because Harman is very shy. During the conversation Ambuhl tried to convey to the assistant and to Rory Kennedy her frustrations about the wrongful convictions of the soldiers. The assistant did not make any promises and repeated that the army has appeal, clemency, and parole procedures that must take their course. The two female soldiers were disappointed, but Rory Kennedy invited us to lunch at an expensive restaurant on the Potomac River.

We hailed a taxi, and I noticed the chasm in social class between Kennedy, the two soldiers, and myself. Kennedy's clothing seemed so stylish and expensive that the three of us came across as commoners going to lunch with royalty. At the restaurant the situation was more edgy than it had been in the senator's office. Ambuhl and Harman could not conceal their disappointment and reluctance to be in the film. The two female soldiers concluded that they would participate in Kennedy's film only if I were present and if Senator Kennedy or Rory Kennedy took concrete, helpful steps to help them. Both women felt that they were being exploited and wanted something tangible in return for their participation—they did not want money, but did want legal assistance to have their names cleared.

A month later I heard from Ambuhl. She said that they showed up for the filming expecting me to be present, and were surprised that I was not there. For my part, I did not know when they would be filmed and had not been invited, even though I kept e-mailing Rory Kennedy's assistant for information. The two female soldiers never received any of the legal assistance they had requested. They felt betrayed, but were also fatalistic about the situation.

In summary, I have nothing to report on the feelings, motivations, or aspiration of Morris and Kennedy, despite my interactions with them. Their mode of interaction with me was such that they were in charge, they were in the know, and they would decide what the story of Abu Ghraib would be—not what it was or might be. I felt very uncomfortable, as if they had reduced me to the role of a pimp in delivering soldiers and information to them—which I refused to do. It was obvious that I was supposed to be impressed with the Kennedy mystique and with Morris as a genius, but they did not seem to be interested at all in the very real and very human stories of the soldiers.

Standard Operating Procedure Analyzed

The film begins with a disclaimer from Sony Corporation claiming that this film "is for entertainment only," and that the views contained therein do not represent the views of Sony. It is odd, in a Baudrillardesque sort of way, for a documentary to begin with the claim that its sole purpose is entertainment. Janis Karpinski appears in the visual context of the famous playing cards that were used to identify high-value targets in the war on terror, and she says that there was tremendous pressure on her and the military "to find Saddam." A letter appears on the screen, accompanied by the voice of Sabrina Harman, whom Morris does not identify. She reads her own letter, which conveys that she had a "bad feeling" about Abu Ghraib from the moment she arrived. In the first few minutes of the film, the viewer is disoriented: one does not know who is speaking or why, and there is no narrator or other device that would enable the viewer to discern a pattern in what has been presented. In its own subtly subversive way the film opens up the way a standard interrogation method begins: the aim of both is to isolate the "target" (suspect or viewer) from all that is familiar and expose that target to new, unfamiliar, and seemingly random stimuli that actually have been orchestrated meticulously. In short the film "softens up" the viewer.

Javal Davis appears on the screen, and he, too, is not identified. He speaks about the stench of feces and daily mortar attacks at the prison. He adds that he and the other soldiers also lived in prison cells. He says that he inquired why the Arab prisoners were naked, and that he was told, "That's MI [military intelligence]." Lynndie England appears on the screen, and she is identified immediately. Why are some of the participants identified while others are not? Why are some identified immediately while others are identified much later in the film? England says that she thought the setting was "weird and wrong." Harman appears again, and states that she started taking photographs on October 20, 2003, in order "to record" and to "prove" what was happening.

Megan Ambuhl appears, unidentified in the film at this point. She states that in the infamous photographs of England and "Gus," England was not dragging the unnamed Arab prisoner. There is no mention of the fact that he had been nicknamed "Gus" by the soldiers, and in the film—as in the prison as well as the trial—his real identity is not given. An unidentified male states that criminals typically do something stupid, and that "taking photographs was stupid." But the viewer has just learned from an unidentified Harman that she took the photographs in order to document the abuse. Who is this unknown male who implicitly discredits her version of events? One learns far into the movie that he is a former civilian "contractor" who interrogated prisoners at Abu Ghraib.

Another unidentified male talks about the need to separate one's emotions and polemics in trying to understand the abuse at Abu Ghraib. He speaks about the need to determine how much effort the soldiers put into the abuse, and to determine precisely who was involved. He is identified later in the film as Brent Pack, and labeled as a former Army CID (Criminal Investigation Division) agent. But the film never mentions the important fact that Mr. Pack testified as an expert witness for the government, and against the accused soldiers. Furthermore he testified only in the court-martial of Lynndie England. One should ponder the following points about

Pack's role in the film: He is the only expert witness of any sort interviewed in the film, and he represented the prosecution. Morris spends considerable time in the film on Pack's explanations of how he calibrated and matched the clocks on various cameras to determine the exact time that each photograph was taken. But these efforts are nullified by the simple fact that—as the film later shows—the army allowed the several hundred other soldiers at Abu Ghraib who possessed photographs or films of the abuse to erase the material from their computers or discard the material during a specified period of "amnesty." It is possible that the army engaged in a cover-up and obstructed justice by enticing soldiers to destroy evidence.

Pack's testimony during England's court-martial was short and its impact negligible. But Pack's role in Morris's film is disproportionally large, measured in minutes devoted to him and the many reenactments of the "science" that went into his calculations. The viewer does not learn anything substantive about the abuse at Abu Ghraib in either case. Incidentally, the most explosive part of Pack's testimony was his disclosure during the trial that over 16,000 photographs were analyzed. I informed Mr. Morris of this fact, but he chose not to use it in the film. This fact begs the obvious question: what was the content of the more than 16,000 photographs that were never released and will probably never be released to the public?

England talks about her problems with Graner as a "man"—"It's a man's world," she says. The effect on the viewer is akin to experiencing gossip among girlfriends who are talking about their relationships. This is a far cry from expert witness Dr. Xavier Amador's detailed testimony at England's trial, in which he argued that she complied with Graner's orders as a way to cope with her PTSD, anxiety, and depression. But Morris does not show any of the soldiers disclosing or discussing their formally diagnosed PTSD, which has easily recognizable symptoms. Dr. Amador is not in the film. All the soldiers I interviewed who had contact with Abu Ghraib in any way spoke readily about their sleeplessness, nightmares, anxiety, phobias, and other symptoms. Morris completely edits the reality of their mental states out of his documentary.

Before the viewer can have a chance to digest the significance of the observations made by Javal Davis, Harman appears on the screen to talk about how completely dark the prison was at night, and about ant attacks on juvenile prisoners. One of the previously unidentified males in the film, Tim Dugan, is finally identified as one of the "civilian contractors" at Abu Ghraib. He explains that Arab prisoners were stripped naked to break them down by using their culture against them, and that female soldiers were present to heighten the humiliation for the males. It was an "Arab culture thing," Dugan states. On the contrary, it was an "American culture thing" to scientifically study Arab culture with the aim of using it as a weapon against Arabs.

Ken Davis is identified by name when he appears on screen, but not by his heroic and important function at the prison, namely, that he was the most important whistleblower. The film makes no mention of the fact that the Army "rewarded" Ken Davis for his moral conscience by pressing charges of abuse against him, which were later dropped. The film fails to mention that he did not abuse anyone, but confronted many people about their abuse, and reported the abuse all the way up the chain of command to the U.S. Congress. The film fails to mention that he suffers from extreme PTSD. He is shown stating that no one was hiding the abuse, and that he said to some of his comrades, "I had enough," and left a scene of abuse.

The seemingly random pastiche of clips and sentences continues relentlessly: Karpinski states that the interrogators put on a "dog and pony show" whenever the generals visited Abu Ghraib. Javal Davis confirms that there were "ghost detainees" who were never listed officially as being at Abu Ghraib. Two more unidentified males talk about the "cover-up" involved in the death of Iraqi general Al-Jamadi. Harman says, "There is no way he died of a heart attack." I recognized the rotten apple Jeremy Sivits, who was sent to prison for a year for taking just one photograph. He said, "I'm a nice guy, so I took it." Taken out of context, this remark might be construed by an uninformed viewer as mere rationalization. But after speaking with Sivits for many hours, I am convinced that Sivits was indeed a "nice guy," and took the photograph because he thought it was the right thing to do. Sivits was a mechanic at Abu Ghraib, and is undoubtedly the most innocent scapegoat among the soldiers who were convicted. Frederick asked him to take a photograph—and Sivits did, in order to comply. The film makes no mention of the fact that Sivits was the first to be convicted because the army made a deal with him: he would serve no more than one year in prison in exchange for his testimony against his comrades. Morris completely overlooks the army's scientific method of intimidating soldiers in order to shore up weak cases against them.

Morris offers a series of reenactments of various episodes of abuse that have been edited into a montage of photographs and film clips of actual abuse. There is no way for a nonexpert to distinguish the simulated depictions from the real ones. Karpinski claims that there was a "cover-up." England says that "everybody knew" about the abuse. Javal Davis describes the amnesty period ordered by Colonel Pappas, in which evidence was willfully destroyed. Logically, this means that the only photographic evidence that the army had available were the photographs that were not destroyed. Javal Davis is undoubtedly correct when he states in the film that the army decided to "sacrifice the little guys," namely, the seven rotten apples who did not take advantage of the amnesty program. Did Morris miss the obvious fact that this contradicts Tim Dugan's rationalizations for the photographs? Will the viewer, confused by a pastiche of unidentified and partly identified "actors," notice the discrepancy? Pack comes on again: "Photographs depict what is." Anybody who has followed all that has been presented in the film will find that statement unintelligible.

Javal Davis states that the real torture occurred in the interrogation rooms, where no one was taking photographs. Dugan also says that there was a cover-up. The film ends with Dugan describing a poetic moment he had at Abu Ghraib, when he realized that the birds could fly away but that he and the other civilians, soldiers, and agents could not.

Rory Kennedy's *Ghosts Of Abu Ghraib*

Morris begins and ends his film with clips of the civilian interrogator, Tim Dugan, and his seemingly poetic observations on death and birds. Kennedy begins and ends her film with clips of Stanley Milgram's famous experiments on "obedience to authority." Like Morris, Kennedy is capricious in deciding which "actors" who appear on screen will be identified and when. They both use Javal Davis, Ken Davis, Sabrina Harman, Megan Ambuhl, Janis Karpinski, and Lynndie England. Whereas Morris relies on Tim Dugan and Brent Pack as his "experts" to make sense of the events, Kennedy uses John Yoo, Alberto Mora, Scott Horton, Mark Danner, and Alfred McCoy. But these experts in law and human rights are not experts on Abu Ghraib. Moreover she equalizes them, so that an uninformed viewer will not be immediately aware that John Yoo was a White House lawyer who actually drafted the so-called torture memos, whereas Alfred McCoy is a distinguished author and critic of these same memos. Both Morris and Kennedy omit any mention or use of the distinguished attorneys who defended the rotten apples, including Paul Bergrin and Frank Spinner. Both Morris and Kennedy omit any mention or use of the expert witnesses who testified in the defense of the convicted soldiers, including Dr. Xavier Amador, Philip Zimbardo, and me. Thus while the two films differ slightly with regard to some of the interviewees, overall they follow a similar formula: focus on the available convicted soldiers, completely ignore all the distinguished attorneys and experts who defended them at their trials, and use experts who mainly make the case for the prosecution.

After showing clips of Milgram's experiment, Kennedy shows Javal Davis saying that he had "become a robot" at Abu Ghraib. Israel Rivera is shown describing the abuse. Harman states that "you'd go crazy if you don't adapt." Javal Davis says, "Somebody has to pay." A clip of former president George W. Bush is shown in which he says, "Smoke them out." We then see a clip of America's attack on Afghanistan in 2001. Expert Horton says that up to World War II, the U.S. held itself to standards higher than the Geneva Conventions. Yoo is shown saying that the Geneva Conventions do not apply to al-Qaeda. Danner says that Yoo's opinion is "unprecedented." A clip shows former secretary of defense Donald Rumsfeld saying that the detainees in the current war "are not POWs." Danner appears citing the United Nations Convention Against Torture. Yoo says that these various conventions "do not say what is severe pain and suffering," and are "ambiguous." Immediately after, Danner says that the U.S. government embarked on a program to "redefine torture." A clip of Rumsfeld from March of 2003 shows him saying that the U.S. is following the Geneva Conventions. Javal Davis then says that Abu Ghraib was like a "Mad Max movie," and that when he got there, he said to himself, "Wow, I'm at war."

Ken Davis appears on the screen and says: "I need to know the ROE [Rules of Engagement]." He says that his superiors told him the ROE were as follows: "If it looks like the enemy, shoot it." Davis says, "Everything looks like the enemy to me out here." The remarks by Ken Davis are highly significant, in that they connect the unlawful, or "loose," ROE at Abu Ghraib with similar rules that were used at the massacres at Operation Iron Triangle and the Baghdad Canal. However, the film does not explain how the issue of ROE relates in any way to the preceding discussion among the experts on the Geneva Conventions. Kennedy shows experts disagreeing with each other as to the meaning of torture, whereas ROE involve rules for killing a perceived enemy, not interrogating that enemy. The experts in the film say nothing about ROE. On the other hand, the soldiers and interrogators say nothing about the Geneva Conventions. It is not at all clear whether Kennedy was trying to make connections between these seemingly disconnected claims.

Former MI (Military Intelligence) officer Tony Lagouranis says that prisoners were rounded up based on "rumors and hunches." An Iraqi man named Mohamed Tatul says that he was arrested, and that soldiers took his gold and money. MI Roman Krol says, "The place was horrible." Javal Davis talks about Hussein's death chambers at Abu Ghraib and how he felt "lost souls were walking around here." He describes the temperature being over 130 degrees, and the odor of sweat, trash, feces, and urine. Abu Ghraib was a "nasty, dark, haunted place" according to Javal Davis. Former MI Sam Provance continues the theme that Abu Ghraib had "ghosts," and that it was "surreal," like "*Apocalypse Now* meets *The Shining*."

Javal Davis says that upon entering the prison, the soldiers were ordered to put their weapons away. He continues by saying that Abu Ghraib was the most attacked site in Iraq, and that it came under mortar attack every day. "You definitely did not feel safe." The road to Abu Ghraib was the most dangerous road in Iraq. "I wouldn't wish it on my worst enemy." Javal Davis and other soldiers gave similar testimony at the courts-martial, but expert witnesses at the trials made the connection that the constant threat of mortar attacks and fear of dying—such that soldiers were never sure they would wake up alive—contributed to combat stress for all the soldiers, which in turn made them more compliant to MI demands that they abuse prisoners. Kennedy conspicuously does not make this obvious and important connection in the film. To her credit she films Javal Davis accurately describing the dangerous situation the army failed to correct. But the connection to PTSD, and the conclusion that the soldiers were psychiatric casualties of war, is not going to be obvious to the average viewer, even if it was obvious to experts who testified at the trials.

Harman appears and says that "they needed females in 1-B." The full context for her remark—never made or implied in the film—is that the military deliberately, systematically, and scientifically used female U.S. soldiers to degrade and humiliate Iraqis. Ambuhl says that there were six or seven guards on any given shift in 1-B for one thousand prisoners. Javal Davis says that he was led to believe that the inmates had killed American soldiers. Ambuhl says they were told that the prisoners were "the worst of the worst." Karpinski says that the prisoners were simply in the wrong place at the wrong time, and that 80 percent of them had no information to give. Lagouranis says that "we were frustrated" and "got nothing" in terms of intelligence from the prisoners. An Arab named Omar Rashid tells us that he was imprisoned for seven months at Abu Ghraib "for nothing." Danner says General Geoffrey Miller was chosen to "Gitmoize" Abu Ghraib because he had a reputation (albeit, false) for "getting results."

Alfred McCoy makes the poignant observation that Abu Ghraib was an "ad hoc behavioral laboratory." I agree with McCoy, and believe that his comments should have been used to frame the film. But under Kennedy's editing, McCoy's accurate observation comes across as disconnected from the way she frames the drama under Milgram's studies of obedience to authority. The important point is this: Abu Ghraib was not an ad hoc experiment in obedience to authority but was an experiment in using stress to break down prisoners so that they would give information. The absurdity of this experiment is that the prisoners had no information to give, that the stress broke down the soldiers as well as the prisoners, and that there is no orthodox scientific theory or finding to support the hypothesis that stress makes people remember or talk.

McCoy lists some of the methods that were used in the "laboratory" that was Abu Ghraib, including the use of solitary confinement, stress positions, induced phobias, and sexual humiliation. He makes another poignant assessment in claiming—and I think correctly—that the psychic trauma caused by these and other methods is far more damaging than the physical traumas. I should add that the army uses each and every one of these same methods listed by McCoy on its own soldiers during interrogations. The Reid Technique is just one small aspect of a much larger methodology of deliberately inducing stress in suspects and prisoners that amounts to systematic sadism.

Kennedy uses film clips to show that Rumsfeld sent Major General Miller to "Gitmoize" Abu Ghraib. Karpinski says that Miller instructed subordinates to treat prisoners like dogs. McCoy tells us that General Sanchez issued orders for extreme techniques. Yoo says that all of these techniques were in compliance with the Geneva Conventions as he interpreted them. Kennedy then shows a clip of Sanchez rescinding some of the extreme techniques. MI Krul is shown saying that the techniques were "confusing." Ken Davis says, "It was never clear to me what was allowed and what was not." Javal Davis says, "Why are all these people naked with panties on their heads?" The viewer is supposed to connect the fact that putting panties on the heads of nude prisoners was a "technique" authorized by Sanchez (in fact, it was). Rivera says that "no one raised objections" to the nudity. Ambuhl says that "every day there was nudity and shackling." A compilation of interviews with several former Arab prisoners from Abu Ghraib shows them stating that they were forced to be naked for days or months at a time.

Then Kennedy zeroes in on Harman and the reasons why she was smiling in the photographs. It is important to note that Harman is shown on screen holding photographs of herself smiling during scenes of abuse.

There is something humiliating and sadistic about the film director forcing Harman to display herself in this manner to the camera. Harman tries to explain herself on camera: "If I saw something, I take a photo, and if I'm in a photo, I smile. It's stupid, but it happened." The important point is that Harman cannot explain why she smiled. It requires an expert witness to connect the dots, namely, that Harman is not sadistic according to her psychological tests; that she was anxious, depressed and suffering from PTSD; and that her smiling was a coping mechanism. I testified to this at her trial, and the jury seemed to accept the explanation. But Kennedy does not attempt to explain Harman's smile. Rather she tries to force Harman to explain her smile, knowing that Harman cannot do so.

Kennedy returns to Harman, who is now holding up a photograph of herself smiling over the dead body of General al-Jamadi. It is extremely important to know, for the sake of context, that she had no role whatsoever in his death. After Kennedy shocks the viewer with the out-of-context juxtaposition of Harman and al-Jamadi, she does allow Ken Davis to say on camera that Harman was charged with a crime for being in photographs, but not that particular photograph, and that no one was charged with al-Jamadi's murder. Ken Davis adds, "This says 'cover-up.'" Harman says, "I always smile," and, "I didn't know he was just murdered." There is something odd in Kennedy filming Harman holding a photograph of herself next to a murder victim whose killers were never prosecuted, with full knowledge that Harman was not charged with any crime in relation to that photograph or murder. How can the uninformed viewer of the film possibly know all this context and background? The government did not bring up that photograph at Harman's trial because it did not want to open the door to questions about al-Jamadi's death. In its own way the government's cover-up is comprehensible. But Kennedy brings up that particular photograph by having Harman hold it, not to open the door to questions about al-Jamadi's death or murder at Abu Ghraib, but merely to focus on Harman.

Toward the end of the film the soldiers come closest to stating the real state of affairs regarding the investigations and trials. Ken Davis says that the army was embarrassed by the photographs documenting the abuse, "and the army got back at them." I agree with Ken Davis that under the guise of supposedly fair and impartial trials, the government was taking vengeance on the soldiers who documented the abuse. Javal Davis says that had there been no photographs, there would have been no investigations and no trials. In his poignant quip he says, "No photos—whatever."

I agree with Javal Davis. The assessments by these two soldiers stand in sharp contrast to the many other contradictory assessments of the role of the photographs found in both documentaries: that it was stupid for the soldiers to take the photographs, that the images were evidence, that other photographs were destroyed, that they were part of the alleged "Animal House" atmosphere.

The film ends with another film clip of Stanley Milgram's famous experiment, and the line that the cruelty depicted in his experiment as well as at Abu Ghraib is part of "human nature." Milgram and Kennedy should not have the last word on what constitutes human nature. There exist many diverse perspectives on what constitutes human nature.

Both films are open to diverse interpretations, especially from the dominant, default perspectives of modernity and postmodernism. Neither perspective is entirely satisfactory. A modernist would look for signs of firm referents, clear boundaries, names, central arguments, and balanced perspectives in each film. I have already pointed out that both films fail to meet even the most elementary criteria for a modern documentary. The names and identities of the persons in the film are haphazardly presented at best and disorienting to the viewer at worst. So many different perspectives and arguments are presented that it is almost impossible to find one or two that are central. As for balanced perspectives, one should note that the voices of advocacy for the convicted soldiers are completely silenced in both films. None of the defense attorneys and none of the expert witnesses for the defense are represented, even though some of them were filmed or could have been filmed. Both films privilege the voices of government officials, interrogators, and witnesses for the prosecution. One may be tempted to conclude that both films merely promulgate the standard government and media interpretations of Abu Ghraib.

From the postmodernist perspective it is noteworthy that the "voices" of human rights activists such as Horton, Danner, and McCoy are put on an equal plane with the architects of torture policies such as Yoo, the interrogators, the prosecution's expert witness Brent Pack, and various purveyors of "conscious disinformation." It appears that no one's point of view is privileged, in accordance with postmodernist tenets of deconstruction. The overall effect may be interpreted as a display of the postmodernist goal: many diverse voices are heard, there is no privileged or central voice, and the net result is noise. Who should be believed in all this diversity of opinions? It is entirely possible to argue that the films have achieved the "implosion of meaning" that Baudrillard and other postmodernists have explained, demonized, mocked, and simultaneously lauded.[9]

A third interpretation is that these two documentaries, as well as the abuse at Abu Ghraib, exemplify a disturbing trend in contemporary American society toward control and the mechanization of emotions, whose effects result in what I have termed elsewhere a "postemotional society."[10] In particular both films display what might be called postemotional sadism in the way they depict sadism. By postemotional sadism I mean that cruelty, control, and lack of empathy are systematized and stylized to such an extent in the films that one's human reactions to the sadism are neutralized. In both cases—regarding the actual site of abuse at Abu Ghraib, and the two films—one feels as if one belongs to a helpless "society without opposition." If Fromm is correct that the essence of sadism is control, including the fact that the sadist's victim is rendered helpless to resist the control, it is possible to characterize the contemporary style of documentary films as sadistic. Of course, I am not claiming that the film producers or directors are sadistic individuals. I am referring to the sociological implications of numerous aspects of the documentary film in general, and these two films in particular, that may be understood as sadistic: The director has complete control over what will be edited and cut, and the participants have no input into this decision. Some of the participants in these documentaries were pursued like prey and expressed the opinion that they felt humiliated. These documentaries offer no signs of rapport, empathy, or dialogue with their participants. As I have already noted, the style of the documentaries—which may be misconstrued easily as "postmodern"—bears an uncanny resemblance to cruel and unlawful interrogation techniques. Lack of empathy toward the participants is revealed by the complete absence of any context, history, or life-story of any of the participants.

Above all, the documentaries exhibit signs of mechanized techniques that are characteristic of the culture industry as a whole and that are uncomfortably similar to interrogation techniques. For example, in *Ghosts Of Abu Ghraib* the participants were isolated from each other—no group discussions were filmed—and the director, Kennedy, forced England and Harman to comment on photographs of themselves. With few exceptions, one searches in vain in both films for moments in which the filmed participants express spontaneous emotions through smiling, weeping, sighing, or other easily recognizable signs. Instead most of them are reduced to the status of talking heads. It is human to ask, who or what took away the humanity of these people?

The documentaries on Abu Ghraib exhibit a double irony. First, they fail to document the central findings of the Levin-McCain Report and other respected reports on what really happened at Abu Ghraib and why, namely, that abuse was the result of sadistic government policies that scientifically induced abuse by dehumanizing soldiers and prisoners alike. Second, and more disturbing, the films mimic the mechanization of these methods of abuse. The viewer becomes the victim of carefully managed "theming," which includes manipulation, deceit, the elimination of alternative explanations, and other standard techniques whose aims are destructive. Old-fashioned interrogators told me that the best way to get information out of someone is to be kind to them, give them a Coke to drink, and establish genuine rapport. In the words of Erich Fromm, relatedness—as opposed to narcissism—is the state of being "actively concerned with the other person's growth and happiness; I am not a spectator. I am responsible, that is, I respond to his needs, to those he can express and more so to those he does not or cannot express."[11] The entire Abu Ghraib drama, from its origins in the White House memos to the film documentaries, illustrates the failure of relatedness and the triumph of systemic sadism. By turning us into helpless spectators the government and the culture industry have obfuscated the simple truth that we are all responsible for the abuse at Abu Ghraib.

NOTES

1. Theodor Adorno, *The Culture Industry* (London: Routledge, 1991).
2. U.S. Senate, Committee on Armed Services, *Inquiry Into the Treatment of Detainees in U.S. Custody*, 110th Congress, 2nd session (Washington, D.C.: Government Printing Office, 2008), http://www.democrats.com/senate-armed-services-committee-report-on-torture.
3. Jane Mayer, *The Dark Side: The Inside Story of How the War on Terror Turned into a War on American Ideals* (New York: Doubleday, 2007).
4. I document my reasons for these claims in Stjepan Mestrovic, *The Trials of Abu Ghraib* (Boulder: Paradigm, 2007), *Rules of Engagement?* (New York: Algora, 2008), and *The Good Soldier on Trial* (New York: Algora, 2009). Space does not permit a discussion of Philip Zimbardo's contribution to this discussion, although I address his work in the aforementioned publications. In summary, I agree with Zimbardo that the abuse occurred as a result of the "situation" and not the alleged sadism of the participants. But I believe that his famous Stanford prison experiment, which he uses as his paradigm to explain the abuse at Abu Ghraib, is flawed in that Zimbardo acted as the prison warden (as he admits), and thereby created the conditions for sadism to ensue. I differ from Zimbardo in maintaining the boundaries

of my role as researcher, and in focusing upon the psychological breakdown of the participants in the abuse prior to their commission of the abuse.
5. Thorstein Veblen, *The Theory of the Leisure Class* (New York: Penguin, 1899).
6. Erich Fromm, *The Anatomy of Human Destructiveness* (New York: Holt, 1977).
7. Stephen Strasser, *The Abu Ghraib Investigations* (New York: Public Affairs, 2004).
8. Janis Karpinski, *One Woman's Army* (New York: Hyperion, 2005).
9. Jean Baudrillard, *America* (London: Verso, 1986).
10. Stjepan Mestrovic, *The Postemotional Society* (London: Routlege, 1997).
11. Erich Fromm, *The Sane Society* (New York: Fawcett, 1955), 38.

Contributors

Livia Alexander is executive director of ArteEast, an international nonprofit organization that supports and promotes artists from the Middle East and its diasporas by raising awareness of their work through public events, exhibitions, film screenings, and a resource-rich Web site. She has curated and consulted on numerous film festivals focusing on the cinemas of the Middle East, including Music on the Nile: Fifty Years of Egyptian Musical Films, Debating Center and Margin: Minorities in the Middle East, and Crossing Borders: From Algerian to Buer Cinema. She has a PhD in Middle Eastern cinemas from New York University and is currently completing a book manuscript on Israeli and Palestinian cinemas between the two intifadas.

Chris Berry is professor of film and television studies and codirector of the Goldsmiths Leverhulme Media Research Centre at Goldsmiths College, University of London, and author of many books, including *Postsocialist Cinema in Post-Mao China: The Cultural Revolution After the Cultural Revolution*.

Phil Carney is a lecturer in criminology at University of Kent, England, and author of the forthcoming *The Punitive Gaze*.

David Danzig is project director for the Primetime Torture Project at Human Rights First and coproducer of the documentary *Primetime Torture*.

Faisal Devji is University Reader in Modern South Asian History at Oxford University and sits on the editorial board of the journal *Public Culture*. Devji is the author of two books, *Landscapes of the Jihad: Militancy, Morality, Modernity* and *The Terrorist in Search of Humanity: Militant Islam and Global Politics*, and is currently writing a book on the emergence of Muslim politics and the founding of Pakistan.

Michael Flynn is associate professor of psychology at York College, City University of New York, and associate director of the Center on Terrorism at John Jay College of Criminal Justice, City University of New York. He is the coeditor of *Globalizing the Streets: Cross-Cultural Perspectives on Youth, Social Control, and Empowerment*; *Trauma and Self*; *Genocide, War, and Human Survival*; and *The Year 2000: Essays on the End*.

Elizabeth Swanson Goldberg is professor of English at Babson College and author of *Beyond Terror: Gender, Narrative, and Human Rights*.

Marnia Lazreg is professor of sociology at the Graduate Center, City University of New York, and author of several books, including *Torture and the Twilight of Empire: From Algiers to Bagdad*.

Alfred W. McCoy is J. R. W. Smail Professor of History, University of Wisconsin, Madison, and author of many books, including *A Question of Torture: CIA Interrogation, from the Cold War to the War on Terror*.

Stjepan G. Mestrovic is professor of sociology at Texas A&M University and author of several books, including *The Trials of Abu Ghraib: An Expert Witness Account of Honor and Shame*.

Lee Quinby is Distinguished Lecturer of English and American Studies at Macauley Honors College, City University of New York, and author of many books, including *Millennial Seduction: A Skeptic Confronts Apocalyptic Culture*.

Darius Rejali is professor of political science at Reed College and author of *Torture and Democracy*.

Fabiola F. Salek is associate professor and chair of humanities and foreign languages and coordinator of the women's studies program at York College, City University of New York, and research associate at the Center on Terrorism at John Jay College of Criminal Justice, City University of New York. She has published articles on gender, human rights, and film.

Carolyn Strange is senior research fellow at Australia National University's College of Arts and Sciences and author of *True Crime, True North: The Golden Age of Canadian Pulp Magazines*.

Index

Aberjil, Eden, 201–2, 214n25
Aboutboul, Alon, 199
Abu Ghraib prison, 6–7, 13, 122, 133, 254, 288–90; American public's reaction to, 131; as behavioral science laboratory, 285–86; as breakdown in structures of concealment, 243; "civilian contractors" at, 281; "clean torture" and, 242; culture industry depiction of, 273–75; description of conditions at, 285; "ghost detainees," 282; "Gitmoization" of, 285, 286; government cover-up about, 287; interrogators at, 22, 29; moral responsibility and, 245–46, 250–51; photogenic torture at, 105; political aftermath of, 112; reasons for photographs taken at, 221; revelations of abuse at, 24–25; sexualized torture at, 113–14, 124, 262, 263; Sontag's story about, 109–10; in *Standard Operating Procedure*, 262–66; systematization of sadism at, 275;
torture images from, 94, 134n4; unreleased photographs from, 281; victims' suffering and experience, 14; worldwide protests over, 123
Abu Zubaydah, 125–26, 132
Academy Awards, 36, 158
action-thriller genre, 42, 47
Adorno, Theodor, 95, 273, 275
aesthetics, 4, 181
Afghanistan war, 6, 257, 266, 284; CIA torture of prisoners during, 54–55; detainees arrested by warlords, 268; Geneva Conventions and, 122, 246; al-Qaeda and, 268
African National Congress (ANC), 178, 183, 186n6
Alexander, Livia, 12, 14
Alexander, Sharon, 199
Algerian War, 112, 174, 223–25, 257; centrality of torture to French counterinsurgency, 14, 261, 262; comparison with Iraq and Afghanistan, 258, 264, 269
Ali la Pointe, 223, 225
Alleg, Henri, 174, 270n2

Aloni, Udi, 205–6
Alpha Diaries, The [Shalom pluga alef] (2007), 202
Altered States (1978), 231
Amador, Xavier, 281, 283
Ambuhl, Specialist Megan, 264, 273, 276, 278–79, 283, 285
Améry, Jean, 9–10
Amnesty International, 157, 242
Ang, Maria Elena, 120–21
Another Land [Eretz Aheret] (1998), 194
Anthony, Marc, 59, 60
Anti-Defamation League, 39
anti-Semitism, 37, 39–40, 41, 194
Antonioni, Michelangelo, 94
apartheid, 14, 168, 180; addressed outside boundaries of TRC, 181–85; legacies of torture, 176, 178; torture and, 169
Apocalypse Now (1977), 195, 285
Apocalypto (2006), 13, 36, 37, 46; evil sovereign in, 43, 45; Gibson and audiences for, 41; purification by pain in, 44, 45; symbolic function of blood in, 49; violence as spectacle, 47
Arendt, Hannah, 14, 250, 251
Army, U.S., 29, 233, 263; Criminal Investigation Division, 110, 280; Field Manual, 267; interrogation doctrines of, 112; possible Abu Ghraib cover-up by, 281; Special Forces, 28
Ashcroft, John, 123
audiences/viewers: attractions of film viewing, 4, 5; catharsis and, 175; in China, 73, 76–79, 88; empathy for torturers, 2, 61; of Gibson movies, 42, 50n10; graphic violence and, 11; identification with torture victims, 4; of Israeli cinema, 192; popularity of 24, 25; in position of protagonist, 97–98; "real enough" representations of torture and, 222–23; voyeurism of, 95–96
Audin, Maurice, 270n2
August [Ogust] (2002), 209
Augustine, Saint, 198
Aussaresses, Gen. Paul, 227, 259, 271n5, 271n18
authoritarianism, 146, 149, 153; of apartheid state in South Africa, 171; obedience to authority, 283, 286
Avenge But One of My Two Eyes [N'qam ahat mi-shte' enai] (2005), 209
Aviad, Michal, 194
Azalea Mountain [Dujuan Shan] (1974), 80

Background Paper on CIA's Combined Use of Interrogation Techniques, 125
"bad guys," 11, 23, 35
Baghdad Canal killings (2007), 273, 284
Bagram Air Force Base (Afghanistan), prison at, 6, 158, 267, 275
Bailey, David, 93
Barabash, Benny, 198, 214n19
Barabashi, Uri, 198
Bar at the Folies Bergère (Manet), 99–100
Baroque aesthetic, 115
Basic Training [Tironut] (Israeli television series), 214n19

Bataille, Georges, 74, 75, 83
Bates, Norman (fictional character), 96, 98, 102
Batman, 12
Battle of Algiers, The (1966), 4, 14, 218, 257–58, 266; real battle of Algiers compared with, 223–25; torture scenes in, 258–63
Baudelaire, Charles, 113
Baudrillard, Jean, 95
Bauer, Jack (fictional character), 21–22, 27, 31, 127–28; appeal to viewers, 24–25; Bush compared to, 132; copied by real-life interrogators, 23; critics of, 26; erotic dimension of torture and, 128; real-life interrogators compared with, 29, 30; Scalia's defense of, 22, 128, 145; torture used by, 23–24. See also *24* (television series)
Beaver, Lt. Col. Diane, 6, 7, 23, 24
Beccaria, Cesare, 10
Begg, Moazzam, 267
beheadings, by Islamic militants, 252
Benjamin, Walter, 100
Benkhedda, Benyoucef, 259
Ben M'hidi, Larbi, 259, 271n5
Benvenisti, Meron, 192
Bergrin, Paul, 283
Berry, Chris, 12, 13
Bertolucci, Bernardo, 71
Bethesda's Brink (video game), 129
Between Joyce and Remembrance (Kaplan), 174, 175
Beyond the Walls (1984), 214n19
Beyond the Walls II (1994), 214n19
Big Road/The Highway [*Da Lu*] (1934), 81, 86

Biko, Stephen, 173
Bin Laden, Osama, 30, 132
biopower, 43, 48
Black Friday (2004), 14, 238, 246–50, 253
Black Friday: The True Story of the Bombay Bomb Blasts (Zaidi), 247
Blau, Uri, 201
blood, 11, 43, 48, 56; purity of bloodlines, 44; symbolic function of, 45, 47
Blowup (1966), 94, 95
Blue, Gregory, 74, 75, 79, 82
B movies, 95
Bob and Carol and Ted and Alice (1969), 143
Body of Lies (2008), 3
Boehm, Carl, 98
Bond, James (fictional character), 55, 74, 129–30, 244
Boorstin, Daniel, 95
Bouhired, Djamila, 260
Boupacha, Djamila, 260
Bourgon, Jérôme, 74, 75, 79, 82
Bourne Ultimatum, The (2007), 3
brainwashing, 117, 144, 151, 230, 231
Braudy, Leo, 56
Braveheart (1995), 13, 36, 37, 50n1; evil sovereign in, 43, 45; purification by pain in, 42, 44, 45; sexualized gender dualism and, 48; violence as spectacle, 47
Breaking the Silence (Israeli human rights group), 207
Brecht, Bertolt, 211
Britain, 144, 156
Brokeback Mountain (2005), 88
Brook, Timothy, 74, 75, 79, 82
Brooks, Peter, 10, 157, 198

Brown, Jeffrey A., 48
Buñuel, Luis, 127
bureaucracy, 23, 64, 147, 150, 152, 250; escape of torture from controls of, 118; fragmentation of, 244; science of torture and, 233
Burgess, Anthony, 143, 146, 148, 153
Burning Memories [*Resisim*] (1989), 205
Bush, George W., 122, 123, 127, 157, 266, 284
Bush administration, 6, 7, 46, 157, 257; Abu Ghraib scandal and, 131–32; counterinsurgency war under, 270; extraordinary rendition program and, 55; Geneva Conventions and, 22, 122; lawyers of, 232, 233
Bybee, Jay, 122–23, 133

Caballero, Sgt. Florencio, 119
Cage, The [*ha-Kluv*] (1989), 196
Cagney, James, 257
Cai Chusheng, 86
Cameron, Ewen, 230, 231
Camp X-Ray, 94, 105
Canby, Vincent, 146
Canetti, Elias, 58
Cape Fear (1962, 1991), 156
capitalism, 4, 53, 95, 169
Carlos, Wendy (Walter), 147
Carney, Phil, 13–14
Casino Royale (2006), 3, *108*, 129–30
castration, 101–2, 115, 130, 155
Catch a Fire (2006), 168
Catholicism, 8, 39, 43, 59, 62; in *A Clockwork Orange*, 148; rituals of, 252; *supplice* torture in tradition of, 75; Traditionalist, 44–45
celebrity, culture of, 93, 94, 99

censorship: in China, 76, 78, 90n14; of *A Clockwork Orange*, 144, 156; in South Africa, 178, 184
Centurions, Les (Lartéguy), 227–28
chain of command, 7, 122, 123, 246, 253
Chang, Eileen (Zhang Ailing), 77, 78
Chayefsky, Paddy, 231
Cheney, Dick, 7, 123, 266
Cheney, Liz, 133
Chen Guofu, 89
Chen Huaikai, 84
Chen Kaige, 82
Chi, Robert, 76, 81, 82
Chien Andalou, Un (1929), 127
children, 59, 62, 63–64, 65
China: Cultural Revolution, 80, 82, 83; democracy movement (1989), 88; KMT (Kuomintang) Nationalists, 72, 79, 87; People's Republic (PRC), 72, 73, 76, 78, 82, 84; polarized reactions to *Lust, Caution*, 76–78; Qing state, 75; sex and torture in cinema, 84–86; stereotyped as "land of a thousand cuts," 72, 74–76; torture scenes on film, 79–84, *80*, *81*; War of Resistance against Japan, 71
Chow, Rey, 88
Christianity, 169, 182
Christians, evangelical, 37–38, 47, 50n2
CIA (Central Intelligence Agency), 114, 133, 152, 234; "black sites" (secret prisons) of, 7, 122, 125, 132, 133, 274; Bush administration and, 122–25; "clean torture" and, 61, 242; former agents of, 11, 12; history of torture used by, 13;

intelligence failures of, 54; in *Man on Fire*, 2, 55, 59, 64; MKUltra program, 116, 135n18; partisan politics and, 132; psychological torture and, 116–19, 230–31; science of torture and, 232, 233, 275; sexualized torture in the Philippines and, 119; in *Taken*, 55, 56–57; in *Unthinkable*, 55, 58; U.S. interrogation doctrine and, 112
Cinematic Body, The (Shaviro), 102
cinema verité, 147
Circus of Horrors (1960), 94, 95
Citizen Kane (1941), 96
civil society, 12
Clinton, Bill, 22
Clockwork Orange, A [ACO] (1971), 4, 13, *142*, 152; antiauthoritarian and antitorture message of, 144–45, 146, 153; critical reviews, 153–54, 156, 158; cult status of, 144; debates over behavior modification treatments and, 154–56; "Ludovico Treatment," 143–44, 149–52, 154, 156, 159; rerelease (1999) and new viewers of, 156–59; text and context, 145–48; violence of, 143–44; X rating of, 144, 153, 159
Clockwork Orange, A (Burgess novel), 143, 146
Clooney, George, 129
Cochran, Bob, 26
Coetzee, J. M., 168–69, 176, 183, 184, 185
Colby, William, 118
"cold cell," 54
Cold War, 8, 53–54, 112, 152
colonialism, 194, 195, 231
Columbo (fictional character), 29–30

communism, 112, 120, 169, 230, 251
Communist Party, Chinese, 79, 80, 84–85
confessional cinema, 191–92, 202
confessions, 3, 9, 253, 267; confessional nature of torturers' self-portrayals, 251; false, 64; historical uses of torture to obtain, 114; myth of truthful confessions under torture, 10, 56, 227; narcissism of confession genre, 198; orders of truth and, 239
Constitution, U.S., 12, 266
consumerism, 93, 94, 98, 105
Cooley, Charles H., 101
counterinsurgency: of apartheid state in South Africa, 177; of French in Algeria, 14, 259, 260, 269; science of terror and, 103; of United States in Iraq and Afghanistan, 15, 267, 270
Counter-Reformation, 115
Craig, Daniel, 129, 130
criminals/criminality, 3, 11, 148, 152–53, 154; organized crime, 61, 63, 65; public cooperation in solving of crimes, 229
Crouching Tiger, Hidden Dragon [*Wo Hu Cang Long*] (2000), 73, 88
Cry Freedom (1987), 167
Cry the Beloved Country (1952, 1995), 167
Cui Wei, 84
culture industry, 95, 273–77, 289, 290
Curda, Karel, 226
Cuse, Carlton, 27, 28

Dalí, Salvador, 127
Damon, Matt, 129

Danner, Mark, 283, 284, 288
Danzig, David, 12
Dark Knight, The (2008), 3, 10
Davis, Sgt. Javal, 263, 276; as "bad apple," 273, 277; in *Ghosts of Abu Ghraib*, 283–85, 286, 287–88; in *Standard Operating Procedure*, 280, 282–83
Davis, Ken, 282, 283, 284, 286
Day of the Dolphin, The (1978), 231
death and killing, 3, 62; biopower and, 43; choreographed, 97, 98; death anxiety of torture survivors, 10; death under torture, 264, 267, 268–69, 271n18; trauma survivors and, 9; victims seeing their own death, 99
Death and the Maiden (1994), 4
Death by a Thousand Cuts (Brook, Bourgon, and Blue), 74, 79
death squads, 53, 61, 224
Debord, Guy, 50n12, 95
Decolonizing Architecture Art Residency, 192
Delgado, José M. R., 155
democracy, 53, 88, 148, 151, 155, 267; "clean torture" and, 229, 242–43; in Israel, 212; in South Africa, 168, 169, 171; torturers as defenders of, 227; torture viewed as abhorrent, 261
Democratic Party, 37
Dershowitz, Alan, 159, 226, 233, 241
Deserter's Wife, A [*Isha zara*] (1992), 196, 197, 205
desire, 94, 98, 100, 101–5
Desser. David, 195
Destro, Robert, 29
detentions, illegal, 6

Devane, William, 1
de Villeneuve, Justin, 93
Devji, Faisal, 14
DIA (Defense Intelligence Agency), 32
DiCaprio, Leonardo, 10
Dien Bien Phu, French defeat at, 259
Dilawar (Afghan torture victim), 232–33, 266–67, 268, 269
Ding Mocun, 77
Dirty Harry (1971), 4, 143
disaster films, 56
Discipline and Punish (Foucault), 66, 149, 249
dismemberment, 11
disorientation, 231
Dr. Strangelove (1964), 146
documentaries, 3, 13, 15, 175, 275; antitorture, 145; criteria for, 288; as entertainment, 279
dogs, used in torture, 110, 124, 215n32, 263, 266, 268
Dolce Vita, La (1960), 94, 95
domination, 7
dominatrix imagery, 109, 123
Donovan, Terence, 93
Dostoevsky, Fyodor, 198
Dreamers [*ha-Holmim*] (1987), 214n19
drugs/drug therapy, 13, 116–17
Dry White Season, A (1989), 167
Dugan, Tim, 281–82, 283
Durbin, Sen. Richard J., 131
Durra, Muhammad, 197
Duvdevani, Shmulik, 196

Ebert, Roger, 158
Edelstein, David, 3
Edward I, King of England, 36
"ego down" tactic, 124

Eichmann, Adolf, 250
Eisenhower, Dwight, 117
electrical torture, 57, 116, 119; at Abu Ghraib, 262; effects of, 222; electroconvulsive therapy (ECT), 230, 231, 234; origins of, 229–30; in the Philippines, 121
El-Mazri, Khalid, 158
emotions, 4, 87, 276, 280; horror films and, 47; mechanization of, 289
England, Pvt. Lynndie, 109, 124–25, 272; as "bad apple," 273, 277; explanation of torture, 263, 264, 265; in *Ghosts of Abu Ghraib*, 283, 289; sexual photographs of, 110–11; in *Standard Operating Procedure*, 280, 281, 282
Enlightenment, 115
Epstein, Jacob, 29
Europe, historical torture in, 114–16
Every Mother Should Know [*Teda kol em ivriya*] (2008), 202
Execution of Haman, The (Michelangelo), 115
Expendables, The (2010), 3

Facebook, 201–2, 214n25
Falk, Peter, 29–30
Fanning, Dakota, 2, 59
Farewell My Concubine [*Bawang Bieji*] (1993), 82, 84
fascism, 112–13, 229, 251
Fast, Maj. Gen. Barbara, 7
father beyond all laws, 11
FBI (Federal Bureau of Investigation), 11, 26, 31, 58, 112
Fear Up Harsh: An Army Interrogator's Dark Journey Through Iraq (Lagrouranis), 22

Fellini, Federico, 95
femininity/the feminine, 4, 11, 48. *See also* women
feminism, 147, 158, 159
fetishism, 102, 241
Fierro, Adam, 31
film noir, 56
films (cinema): box office revenues of, 55, 73, 129, 131; classification codes, 143, 144, 153; emotions elicited by, 4; film as pluralistic medium, 5; genres, 56; photographic basis of, 5; psychoanalytic discourse and, 102; world articulated by, 4–5. *See also* Hollywood
film theorists/scholars, 4–5, 12
Finnegan, Brig. Gen. Pat, 26
First Blood (1982), 4
First Blood II (1985), 222, 229
Fleming, Ian, 129
FLN (National Liberation Front [Algeria]), 223–25, 259–61, 263, 270n2
Flynn, Michael, 13
Folman, Ari, 191, 203, 204–6, 211, 215n29
food deprivation, 231
foreign films, 3
forgiveness, 40, 113; in Israeli cinema, 14, 192, 195, 207; in South Africa, 14, 168, 170–73, 175, 181–83, 187n26
Forgiveness (2004), 14, 168, 171, 172–76, 181, 187n16
For My Children [*la-Yeladim sheli*] (2002), 194
Foster, Dennis, 198
Foucault, Michel, 42–43, 48–49, 65–66, 148–49, 240, 252; *Discipline*

and Punish, 66, 149, 249; on emergence of "humanitarian" regimes of punishment, 239; on hiddenness of torture, 243; on torture as "limit experience," 261
FOX television, 21, 127
Frederick, Ivan, 273, 282
Frederick II (the Great) of Prussia, 10, 116
freezing, as torture, 231
French Connection, The (1971), 143
Freud, Sigmund, 101, 102
Frist, Sen. Bill, 131
Fromm, Erich, 275, 289, 290
Full Metal Jacket (1987), 195
Fu Manchu novels, 74
"futility" tactic, 124

Gabriel, Ian, 172, 175
Garaje Olimpo (1999), 4, 9
gaze, 96, 99–100; erotic gaze of camera, 100; infantile, 101; of paparazzi culture, 103; in *Peeping Tom*, 97, 98
Gemayel, Bashir, 206
gender, 47–48
Genealogy of Morals, The (Nietzsche), 113
Geneva Conventions, 22, 122, 131, 153, 246, 266; Abu Ghraib prison and, 286; U.S. standards and, 284
Gerstel, Yulie Cohen, 194–95
Gestapo (Nazi secret police), 225–27, 229, 230
Ghosts of Abu Ghraib, The (2008), 3, 15, 230, 276; analysis of, 283–88, 289; female "rotten apples" in, 277
Gibney, Alex, 158, 266

Gibson, Mel, 35–36, 130; anti-Semitism and, 37, 39–40, 41; directorial vision of, 41–42; graphicness of torture as spectacle and, 46–49; moral vision of, 44–45, 48; religious beliefs of, 43, 44–45, 46; as starring actor in *Braveheart*, 36; as tortured hero of filmmaking, 36–42
Gilcrest, Todd, 41
Ginsburg, Allen, 98
Ginsburg, Shai, 207, 209
Goldberg, Elizabeth, 12, 14
Goldfinger (1964), 130
Golub, Leon, 8
Good, the Bad and the Ugly, The (1966), 4
Good Shepherd, The (2006), 3, 9, 129
Gordon, Howard, 27–28
Goren, Amit, 194
Goya, Francisco, 8
Grace, Maggie, 56
Grand Theft Auto: Vice City (video game), 129
Graner, Specialist Charles, 110, 264, 273, 281
Greece, ancient, 8
Greene, Graham, 8
Green Fields [*Sadot yerukim*] (1989), 196, 197
Grossman, David, 215n26
Guantánamo Bay, 122, 132, 133, 254, 266, 275; as anomalous legal site, 241; as behavioral science laboratory, 124; as "death-world," 6; innocent detainees at, 267; interrogation handbook, 118; interrogation techniques copied from television, 21; Rumsfeld-

Hayes memo authorizing torture at, 233; sexualized torture at, 7; source of detainees at, 268; "stolen Soviet techniques" of torture at, 230
guerilla warfare, 54, 223, 257–61
Gugulethu Seven, 182
Gulf War, first, 26
"Gus" (unidentified Iraqi prisoner), 280
Gyllenhaal, Jake, 129

habeas corpus, 266
Haiti, 229
Hamdan v. Rumsfeld, 131
Hamrah, A. H., 3
Harman, Specialist Sabrina, 263, 264, 276, 278–79; as "bad apple," 273, 277; in *Ghosts of Abu Ghraib*, 283, 285, 286–87, 289; in *Standard Operating Procedure*, 279–80
Have You Ever Shot Anyone? [ha-im Yarita Pa'am be-Mishehu?] (1995), 194
Hebb, Donald, 116–17
Hegel, G.W.F., 58
Heiman, Ci, 197
Helms, Richard, 116
heretics, torture of, 114–15, 239
Hero [Ying Xiong] (2002), 88
Herrington, Col. Stuart, 25–27, 28
Hersh, Seymour, 221
Heydrich, Reinhard, 226
Heynemann, Laurent, 270n2
"high cuffing," 233
Hilal, Sandi, 192
Hill Street Blues (television series), 29
History of Sexuality (Foucault), 43
Hitchcock, Alfred, 93–94, 96, 100

Hoffman, Dustin, 1, 257
Hollywood, 25–27, 30, 59, 240; films critical of torture, 129; ticking time-bomb scenarios, 241, 248; torture scenes on film, 126. *See also* films (cinema)
Holmes, Oliver Wendell, 102
Holocaust, 9, 193, 205, 215n32
homophobia, 38, 39, 229
Honduras, 54, 119
Hong Kong, 73, 76, 77, 78
hooding, 124, 231, 268
Horkheimer, Max, 95
horror/slasher films, 3, 4, 47, 96, 101
Horrors of the Black Museum (1960), 94, 95–96
Horton, Scott, 283, 284, 288
hostages, execution of, 252
Hostel (2005), 3, 129
hot boxes, 231
Howl (Ginsburg), 98
Human Resources Training Manual [HRET] (CIA interrogation manual), 54, 119
human rights, 7, 32, 156, 207, 213n6; abrogated in name of security, 158; Abu Ghraib and, 288; abuses in the Philippines, 119; "clean torture" and, 61; Obama administration and, 132–33; in South Africa, 171
Human Rights First, 25, 26
humiliores, in ancient Rome, 8
Hunger (2008), 3
Hunt for Saddam Hussein, The (Maddox), 29
Hussein, Saddam, 29–30, 32, 279, 285

Icon Entertainment, 40

ideology, 4, 77; conservative, 37; of late capitalism, 95; of vigilantism, 63; Zionist, 194, 210, 212
Iganatieff, Michael, 158, 161n28, 164n73
imperialism, 55
Index on Censorship, 152, 161n28
India, 246–49
informants, 3
Inglourious Basterds (2009), 3, 11
In My Country (2004), 168, 181, 182
Innocent IV, Pope, 114
Inquisition, Italian, 114–15
Inside God's Bunker [*be-Tokh ha-bunker shel elohim*] (1994), 214n18
insurgencies, 53, 54
intelligence community, 32, 118
intelligence officers, 7, 8, 25–26, 258, 261, 269
Intelligence Science Board, 22, 29
Internet, 39, 77, 109, 110
interrogation: humane techniques of, 27, 28–29, 32, 33n20; practices influenced by media portrayals, 22–23, 159; of rightfully accused terrorists, 158; training of interrogators, 29, 30, 268
Interrogation: WWII, Vietnam and Iraq (DIA study), 32
In the Mood for Love [*Hua Yang Nian Hua*](2000), 73
"In the Penal Colony" (Kafka), 97
In the Valley of Elah (2007), 3
intifada, first (1987–1994), 191, 195–97
intifada, second (Sept. 2000–2004), 191, 201–3
"Into the Dark Chamber" (Coetzee), 168–69, 176, 184, 185n2

Iran, 54, 118
Iraq, 22–23, 29–30
Iraq War, 32, 33n20; Gibson's criticism of, 46–47; sexualized torture in, 124; torture used in, 55, 242, 246, 257. *See also* Abu Ghraib prison
Islam, 57, 248, 252
isolation, 231, 266, 268
Israel, 14, 197; Ashkenazi elite of, 211; first intifada and, 195–97; loosening grip of Zionist ideology, 212; occupation of Palestinian Territories, 193; public opinion in, 194, 213n6; second intifada and, 201–3; violence in Israeli society, 208; Zionist narrative in, 192, 193–94
I Was a Teenage Frankenstein (1957), 96
I Was a Teenage Werewolf (1957), 96

Jackson, Samuel L., 57
Jagger, Mick, 146
al-Jamadi, General, 282, 287
Jesus Christ, 35, 36, 40, 50n2, 252; Abu Ghraib prisoners likened to, 264; flogging of, 38, 130; Jews and crucifixion of, 40–41; torture and agonies of, 45, 115, 131; as victim of sovereign power, 43
Jews: Gibson's views toward, 37, 39, 40–41; Nazi extermination of, 244–45; as torture victims, 8
Joint Personnel Recovery Agency (JPRA), 122
justice, 65, 83, 149; Truth and Reconciliation Commission and, 167, 170, 171; vigilantism and, 62, 63

Kael, Pauline, 144, 153–54, 225
Kafka, Franz, 97
al-Kahtani, Mohamed, 124
Kangleon, Fr. Edgardo, 120
Kaplan, Mark, 173
Karpinski, Brig. Gen. Janis, 7, 263, 277; in *Ghosts of Abu Ghraib*, 283, 286; in *Standard Operating Procedure*, 279, 282
Kashyap, Anurang, 246, 248
Katz, Evan, 31
Keep America Safe, 133
Keller, Marthe, 1
Kennedy, Sen. Edward, 278, 279
Kennedy, John F., 94
Kennedy, Rory, 276, 278–79, 283, 287, 288
Kesey, Ken, 154
KGB (Soviet secret police), 117
Khalid Sheikh Mohammad, 126, 132
Khulumani Support Group, 171
kidnapping, 2, 59, 60, 65
Kierkegaard, Søren, 253
Killzone 2 (video game), 129
kinship, 42, 44, 48
Klein, Michael, 195
Komer, Robert, 118
Korea, North, 117
Korean War, 230
Krol, Roman, 285, 286
Kubark Counterintelligence Manual (CIA interrogation manual), 54, 117, 118
Kubrick, Stanley, 143, 144, 152, 156; critics of, 155, 157; enfant terrible reputation of, 145–46; on "psychedelic fascism," 155

Lacan, Jacques, 101

L.A. Confidential (1997), 28
Lady Chatterley's Lover (Lawrence), 98
Lagouranis, Tony, 22–23, 29, 284, 285
Laor, Yitzhak, 204, 215n27
Lartéguy, Jean, 227, 228
Last King of Scotland, The (2006), 3
Last Tango in Paris (1973), 71, 76
Latin America, torture in, 61, 118, 119
law, rule of, 6, 133, 152
Lawrence, D. H., 98
Lazreg, Marnia, 14
Lebanon/Lebanese people, 14, 192
Lebanon War, First (June 1982), 196, 203, 204, 206
Lebanon War, Second (July 2006), 191, 202, 215n33
Lee, Ang, 71–72, 73, 75, 88
Lemon Tree, The (2008), 204
Lethal Weapon (1987), 36, 50n1
Lethal Weapon films, 10
Leulliette, Pierre, 259
Leung Chiuwai, Tony, 73, 79
Levin-McCain Report, 273–75, 278, 290
Levy, Gideon, 207
liberalism, limits of, 159
Lie to Me (television series), 29
Lilly, John, 231, 232
lingchi, punishment of, 74–75, 83
Lives of Others, The (2006), 3, 28
lobotomies, 153
Lolita (1962), 145–46
Long Night's Journey into Day (2000), 168, 182, 186n6, 186n15
Lost Command (1966), 228
LOST (television series), 21, 26, 27, 28, 29
Lust, Caution [*Se Jie*] (2007), 13, 70, 71–73; audience reactions in

China, 76–79; German shepherd dog in, 71, 72–73, 72, 75, 76, 79; international failure of, 73–74; sex scenes, 73, 75–76, 78, 84, 89; skeptical attitude toward idealism, 86–88; stereotypes frustrated by, 74–76; torture in, 79–80
"Lust, Caution" (short story), 77
Lyotard, Jean-François, 170

Madaka, Topsy, 175, 177
Maddox, Eric, 29–30, 31
Mad Max (1979), 36
madness, torture victims driven to, 268, 271n17
mad scientist, figure of, 244
Malhotra, Pavan, 247
Malraux, André, 100
Manchurian Candidate, The (1962), 230
Mandela, Nelson, 170
Manet, Édouard, 99, 116
Man on Fire (2004), 2–3, 11, 13, 52, 59–62; ex-CIA agent as protagonist, 55, 59; justice as vengeance of the outsider, 63–64; myth of truthful confessions under torture, 10; racialization of violence, 64
Mao Zedong, 259
Marathon Man (1976), 1–2, 10, 28, 257
Marcos, Ferdinand, 119–20
Martyrdom of St. Bartholomew (Ribera), 115
martyrdom videotapes, 14, 251
Marx, Lesley, 174, 175
masculinity, 7, 45, 228; anxieties about, 228; gender dualism and, 48; hierarchical power relations and, 42, 43; sexualized torture and, 110–11; in spy films, 55; symbolic function of masculine suffering, 35, 36; torturer as real man, 227; war as separation from women, 62. *See also* men
masochism, 48, 112, 129, 131
Massacre of the Huguenots, The (Vasari), 115
Massu, Gen. Jacques, 224, 235n10, 271n5
Maurya, Vijay, 247
Mayer, Jane, 25
McBride, Robert, 186n6
McCoy, Alfred W., 13, 61, 283, 285–86, 288
McDonagh, Martin, 222
McDougal, Stuart, 156
McDowell, Malcolm, 144, 153–54, 159
McGehee, Ralph W., 118
McLuhan, Marshall, 100, 101
Mellor, Alec, 115
men: cliché of men as only victims of torture, 261, 265; sadism and gender dualism, 48; as torture victims in Chinese cinema, 84–85. *See also* masculinity
Mengele, Josef, 244
Meninas, Las (Velázquez), 99
Menon, Kay Kay, 247
Merback, Mitchell B., 115
Merleau-Ponty, Maurice, 9
Merwe, Hugo van der, 171, 187n26
Mesrine: Killer Instinct (2008), 3
Message, The (2009), 89
Mestrovic, Stjepan, 15
Mexico, 59, 62
Michelangelo, 115
Midnight Cowboy (1969), 143

Midnight Express (1978), 4
Mihyi, Farhad, 194
Mikolashek, Lt. Gen. Paul, 23
Milgram, Stanley, 283, 284, 286, 288
Military Commissions Act (2006), 132
military educators, 21–22, 28
Miller, Maj. Gen. Geoffrey, 6, 124, 263, 285
mind-control techniques, 117
mirror phase, in infant development, 101
Missing (1982), 4
Mississippi Burning (1988), 4
Mr. and Mrs. Smith (2005), 3
MKUltra program, 116, 135n18
MNA (National Algerian Movement), 224
Mobutu Sese Seko, 242, 243
Mocking of Christ, The (Manet), 116
modernity, 53, 288
Mograbi, Avi, 207–12
monitoring, international, 229, 230, 242–43
Monroe, Marilyn, 94
Mora, Alberto, 283
Morgan, Ted, 235n9
Morris, Errol, 263, 264, 275, 279, 283; interviews with female Abu Ghraib soldiers, 277–78; mental state of soldiers edited out of documentary, 281
Moss, Carrie-Anne, 58
Motion Picture Association of America, 143
Mthimkulu, Joyce, 173, 187n19
Mthimkulu, Siphiwo, 173–75, 177, 187nn16–18
murder, political, 6, 54

Murdoch, Iris, 159
Murphy, Jeffrie G., 154
music and song, 5, 93, 100, 146; in Chinese cinema, 82; in *A Clockwork Orange*, 144, 146, 147, 150, 151; in Israeli cinema, 211–12; in pornography, 49
Muslims, 57, 115; in India, 246–47, 248; sexualized torture of, 7, 124; as a "torturable class," 8
Mussolini, Benito, 112
My Brother [*ha-Akh sheli*] (2007), 194
My First War [*Hamilchama Harishona Sheli*] (2008), 202
My Land Zion [*Zion admati*] (2004), 194
My Terrorist [*ha-Mehabel Sheli*] (2002), 194

narcissism, 102, 290
National Security Counsel (NSC), 123
Navarro, Joe, 26–27, 28
Nazis, 1, 64, 126, 150, 250; dogs associated with, 215n32; extermination of Jews, 244–45; Gestapo torturers, 225–27; Israeli soldiers and role of, 191; in *Salò*, 112; scale of state violence in Nazi Germany, 245; as source of ticking time-bomb scenario, 228–29
NEC (Non-Enemy Combatant), 269
Neeson, Liam, 56
neoconservatives, 124
neuroscience/neurosurgery, 116, 155
New Left, 153
New Women [*Xin Nüxing*] (1934), 86, 87
Nielsen ratings, 25
Nietzsche, Friedrich, 113

Nieuwoudt, Gideon, 173–74, 177, 187nn16–17
Nineteen Eighty-Four (Orwell), 104–5
1984 (1984), 4
NLEC (No Longer an Enemy Combatant), 269
Noriega, Manuel, 26
NYPD Blue (television series), 126, 228

Obama, Barack, 132–33
Occupied Territories, Palestinian, 196, 197, 198, 199, 202, 208
Olick, Jeffrey, 212
Olivier, Laurence, 1
One Flew Over the Cuckoo's Nest (Kesey), 154
119 Bullets and Three [*119 kadurim ve-shalosh*] (1996), 214n18
One of Us [*Ehad mishelanu*] (1989), 14, 196, 197–201, 210, 214n19
Operation Iron Triangle killings (2006), 273, 284
Orwell, George, 104, 105, 232
Osborn, K. Barton, 118
Oslo Accords, 201
Ourhia the Brown, 225
Our Man in Havana (Greene), 8
Outlook [*Nekudat tatspit*] (1990), 196, 197

Pack, Brent, 280–81, 283, 288
pain, 9, 40, 47, 264; definition of torture and, 160n15; international conventions on torture and, 284; madness or death as result of, 268; "psychological regression" and, 54; purification by, 42–45; scale of pain, 222; symbolic function of, 35; world-destroying, 10–11

Pakistan, 246, 247, 251, 267
Palestine Circus [*Kirkas Palestina*] (1998), 214n18
Palestinians, 14, 191, 197, 210; dispossession of, 194; first intifada of, 191, 195–97; Israeli anger at, 192; in Israeli parliament, 201; killed in Israeli attack on Gaza (2008), 207; murder of, 197, 198–99; Sabra and Shatila massacres of, 203
Panama, 26
Pannwitz, Heinz von, 229
Pan's Labyrinth (2006), 3
paparazzi, 94, 98–99, 101, 103
Pappas, Col. Thomas, 283
Pappe, Ilan, 194
Pasolini, Pier Paolo, 7, 112, 113
Passion of the Christ, The (2004), 3, 13, 34, 36, 130; Abu Ghraib photographs and, 131; audiences/viewers of, 37–38, 47; endurance over revenge as theme, 43; Jesus depiction in, 35, 50n2; Jews portrayed in, 37, 40–41; purification by pain in, 43, 44; violence of, 38, 40
"Passion of the Jew, The" (*South Park* episode), 35–36
patriarchal values, 43, 44
Pavlov, I. P., 230
Payback (1999), 36, 50n1
Payne, Leigh, 192
Pearce, Guy, 28
Pearl, Daniel, 251
Peckinpah, Sam, 143
Peeping Tom (1960), 13–14, 92, 97–101; consumer culture and, 93–94, 95; psychoanalytic theory and, 101, 102, 103

penal theory of atonement, 37
Perkins, V. F., 5
peroneal strike, 233
Perry, Glenn, 232
Petti, Alessandro, 192
pharmacological therapy, 153, 154
Philippines, 54, 118, 119–22
phobias, 281, 286
Phoenix program, 118–19
photography, 94–97, 99; from Abu Ghraib, 6–7, 110, 123, 131, 221; in *Peeping Tom*, 100
Physical Manipulation of the Brain (Delgado), 155
Picasso, Pablo, 8
Pillowman, The (McDonagh play), 222
Pinkner, Jeff, 27, 28, 29
Platoon (1986), 195
PO Box 1142, 32
Poe, Edgar Allen, 105
police procedurals, 56
Politics of Regret, The (Olick), 212
Polonsky, David, 204
Pontecorvo, Gillo, 14, 223, 225, 261
Pontius Pilate, 36
pornography, 3, 4, 112; Abu Ghraib photographs and, 109–10, 134n4; feminist criticism of, 159; gay S-M, 130; Gibson's films compared to, 48, 49; homoerotic, 128
Portman, Natalie, 10
Postmodern Condition, The (Lyotard), 170
postmodernism, 288–89
Powell, Colin, 123
Powell, Michael, 97, 100
power relations: "deployment of alliance," 42–43, 48–49; desire and, 94, 98, 100, 103–5; forced confessions and, 10; sexualized, 112, 113
Pribbenow, Merle, 11
"primal scene," 101, 102
Primetime Torture, 13
prisoners, treatment of, 6, 273
Project Artichoke, 116
propaganda films, 225
Protestantism, 8, 37, 38; Inquisition campaign against, 115; memorization of Scripture, 59; United States as "redeemer" nation, 62
Provance, Sam, 285
Psycho (1960), 13–14, 94, 96, 97, 98; killer as normal person, 101; psychoanalytic theory and, 103
psychoanalysis/psychoanalytic theory, 101–2, 103, 252
psychosurgery, 154
PTSD (Post-Traumatic Stress Syndrome), 274, 278, 281, 282; Abu Ghraib courtroom testimony and, 275; *The Ghosts of Abu Ghraib* and, 285, 287
Public Enemies (2009), 3
public opinion, 126, 194, 213n6, 242, 243
Punisher, The (video game), 129
punishment, 3, 10, 65, 114, 249; cultural values and, 11; dispensed in name of ideal, 7; "humanitarian" regimes of, 239; pharmacological therapy as, 154; shift from body to soul, 66; vigilantism and, 63

al-Qaeda, 21, 33n20, 54, 122, 132; CIA interrogations and, 123, 125–26;

coerced confessions of association with, 267; Geneva Conventions and, 284
Question, La (1977), 270n2
Quinby, Lee, 13
Qur'an, defilement of the, 7

Rabin, Yitzhak, 196
racism, 171, 174, 186n14, 195
Rambo films, 4, 10
rape, 44, 57, 227; in *A Clockwork Orange*, 143, 144, 146; real-life crimes allegedly inspired by film representation, 144; threat of, 7
Rashid, Omar, 285
Raz-Krakotzkin, As Amnon, 201
Real Time [*Zman emet*] (1991), 205
reception studies, 144
Red Detachment of Women [*Hongse Nianzijun*] (1961), 81–82, *81*, 84
Red Faction: Guerrilla (video game), 129
Reflection: A Diary of a Reserve Soldier 1989 [*Hishtakfut: yomanu shel hayal milu,im 1989*] (1991), 214n18
Reid Technique, 286
Rejali, Darius, 14, 64, 242, 243–44, 245; on torturers as victims, 251
"Religious Dimension of the Torture Debate, The" (Pew Foundation study), 37
rendition, extraordinary, 6, 55
Rendition (2007), 3, 129, 158
Republican Party, 37, 38
Reservoir Dogs (1992), 4, 9
Revelation, Book of, 38, 50n2
Ribera, Jusepe di, 115
Rice, Condoleezza, 123

Rich, Frank, 49
Riefenstahl, Leni, 130, 225
Rikli, Eran, 204
Ritter, Karl, 228
Rivera, Israel, 284, 286
Road to Guantánamo, The (2006), 157–58
Robinson, Ken, 28
Rohmer, Sax, 74
Rome, ancient, 8
Rome, Open City (1945), 4
ROTC (Reserve Officers' Training Corps), 28
Roth, Tim, 29
"rotten (bad) apples," 7, 15, 273, 276–77, 283
Rourke, Mickey, 60
Rousseau, Jean-Jacques, 198
Rules of Engagement (ROE), 284
Rumsfeld, Donald, 123–24, 258, 284

Saadi, Yacef, 223
Sabra and Shatila massacres, 203, 205, 206, 207, 215n27
Sacred Landscapes (Benvenisti), 192
sacrifice, 3, 47, 66, 253, 283; ceremonial, 75; of Christ, 40; cosmic order and, 60–61; masculine suffering and, 13, 35; self-sacrifice for Communist cause, 87, 88, 89; symbolic function of, 35, 36, 48
Sade, Marquis de, 112
sadism, 48, 64, 240, 241, 287, 290; control as essence of, 275, 289; physical torture and, 113; postemotional, 289; "rotten apples" portrayed as sadists, 274, 290n4; stress positions and, 286

sadomasochism (S-M), 13, 71, 131;
CIA interrogations and, 126;
cognitive science and, 112; in
gay pornography, 130. *See also*
masochism
Salek, Fabiola, 13
Salò or the 120 Days of Sodom (1975),
7, 112–13
Salt (2010), 3
Sample, Mark, 129
Sanchez, Gen. Ricardo, 6, 124, 286
Sanders, Mark, 182–83, 184
Sands, Philippe, 23
Sarafina (1992), 167
Sartre, Jean-Paul, 174
Saw (2004), 3
Scalia, Antonin, 22
Scarry, Elaine, 175
Schaffer, Kay, 170
Scharff, Hans, 229
Scheider, Roy, 1
science fiction, 146, 244
Scorsese, Martin, 97, 156
Scott, George C., 231
Seigmund, Special Agent James E., 134n4
sensory deprivation (SD), 61, 117, 120, 124, 230–32, 233
sensory overload, 117, 231
September 11, 2001 (9/11) attacks, 6, 10, 58–59, 65, 240; "clean torture" and, 61; television depictions of torture and, 126; torture adopted as formal prerogative of power and, 111, 122; torture as revenge for, 268
SERE (Survival, Evasion, Resistance, Escape), 117, 233
shackling, 268, 286

Shahn, Ben, 8
Shamir, Yitzhak, 196
Sharon, Ariel, 206–7
Shaviro, Steven, 102
Sheen, Michael, 57
Shen Liyun, 78
Shield, The (cable television series), 31
Shlaim, Avi, 194
shock therapy, 153
Shoot 'Em Up (2007), 3
"shooting and crying" syndrome, 197, 204
Siege, The (1988), 4, 28
Si Millial/Ben M'Hidi, 227
Simon, Joshua, 204
Sivits, Jeremy, 273, 282
sleep deprivation, 54, 231
Smith, Sidonie, 170
Society of the Spectacle, The (Debord), 50n12
Soga, La (2009), 3
Solis, Lt. Col. Gary, 25
solitary confinement, 231, 286
Song of Youth [*Qingchun zhi ge*] (1959), 84–85, 86
Sontag, Susan, 74, 97, 109–10, 111
sound, in film, 5
South Africa, 14, 167, 172–81, 183, 186n6
South Park (television show), 35–36, 50n5
sovereign, power of the, 65
Soviet Union, 53, 114, 117, 231, 245
spectacle, 43, 46, 50n12, 96–97, 98; commodity image of, 95; erotic gaze of camera and, 100; of masculine endurance of torture, 35, 38; mass consumer culture and, 93; *Peeping Tom* and, 97

spies, 55
Spinner, Frank, 278, 283
Srivastava, Aditya, 247
Staiger, Janet, 144
Stalin, Joseph, 8
Stalinism, 229, 251
Stallone, Sylvester, 229
Standard Operating Procedure (2008), 14, 15, 258, 262–66, 272, 275; analysis of, 279–83; female "rotten apples" in, 277–78
standing, forced, 54, 117, 124, 231
state, the, 7, 243; agents of, 62; conspiracies against, 10; regulatory function of, 59; science and, 155; state terror, 12, 13, 55; Truth and Reconciliation Commission (South Africa) and, 168–72
Stevenson, Debbie, 277
story (narrative), 5
Strange, Carolyn, 13
strappado, 115
Strawberries [*le-Lakek ta 'tut*] (1992), 214n19
Straw Dogs (1971), 143
Streep, Meryl, 129
stress positions, 117, 231, 267, 286
suicide bombing, 133, 252
Suleiman, Ramadan, 172, 176
Sun Yu, 81
supplice, 75
Sutherland, Kiefer, 27, 127, 228
Syriana (2005), 3, 129
Szasz, Thomas, 153

Taiwan, 76
Taken (2008), 3, 9, 11, 13, 60; ex-CIA agent as protagonist, 55, 56–57; justice as vengeance of the outsider, 63–64; myth of truthful confessions under torture, 10; torture depicted in, 61
Taliban, 267
Tancredo, Tom, 21
Tang Wei, 77
Tatul, Mohamed, 284–85
Taxi to the Dark Side (2007), 3, 14–15, 158, 230, 258; balanced view of torture in, 266–69; science of torture and, 232–34
Tears of Eros, The (Bataille), 74
television, 5, 12, 98, 126, 257
Tenet, George, 123
terrorism/terrorists, 11, 38, 241; interrogation of rightfully accused terrorists, 158; language of martyrdom and, 252; on 24, 24; in *Unthinkable*, 65; U.S. interrogation doctrine and, 112; West's backslide toward torture and, 152
Testimonies [*Eduyut*] (1991), 191
13 Rue Madeleine (1947), 257
Thistlethwaite, Susan Brooks, 37–38
Thompson, J. Lee, 156
3 Kings (1999), 4
ticking time-bomb scenarios, 25, 57, 112, 257; Afghanistan war and, 233; Algerian War and, 224, 227–28; in Hollywood movies, 241, 248; Nazi sources of, 228–29
Time for Cherries [*Onat ha-duvdevanim*] (1991), 205
"Tipton Three," 157
Toren, Dan, 199
torture: in Algerian War, 223–25, 227–29, 235n8, 257, 260; American public opinion about, 131; CIA and, 54–55; civil rights suspended

by, 261–62; "clean torture," 7, 229–30, 242–43; convenient truths and, 221–23; "dark fascination" of, 8; debate on interrogation policy and, 31; dentistry and, 1–2; effectiveness of, 3; historical antecedents, 114–16; iconography of, 5, 14; illegality of, 270; informal, craftlike nature of, 244–45; intelligence officers as critics of, 26; minimized visible evidence of, 73, 83; by Nazi Gestapo, 225–27; photogenic, 94, 103, 105; photography and, 94; physical, 113; pleasure derived from infliction of, 6; pornography and, 109; psychological, 13, 61, 111, 116–19; public support for use of, 37; represented by verbal recounting of past experiences, 4; science of, 103–4, 230–32; self-betrayal as structural component of, 174; in South Africa, 167, 172–81; as spectacle, 46–49; survivors of, 9–10; treaties banning, 6, 7; U.S. penal code definition of, 145, 160n15; visible evidence of, 229–30
torture, politics and, 240–42, 253–54; morality of images, 245–50; self-representations of torturers, 250–53; torture as craft, 242–45
torture, sexualized, 6, 7, 13; at Abu Ghraib, 110–11, 262, 263–64, 286; eroticized decision making of Bush administration, 122–26; in film and television, 126; in the Philippines, 119–22; in *Salò*, 112–13
Torture and Democracy (Rejali), 219, 226, 244

Torture Game 2 (video game), 129
"torture-porn" films, 3
torturers, 9, 222, 232, 263–66; influenced by screen representations, 6; interrogator as father-figure, 117; as messianic figures, 10–11; Nazi, 225–27; pre-September 11 portrayals of, 12; professional, 60; as pure villains in Chinese films, 83; remorse and forgiveness of, 172–76; self-portrayal of, 11, 251, 263–66; U.S. troops in Afghanistan, 267–69; women as, 7, 124, 263, 264–65, 269, 285
torture scenes, 31, 240, 257–58, 269–70; in *The Battle of Algiers*, 258–63; in Chinese cinema, 79–84, *80*, *81*; as convenient dramatic devices, 29; duration of, 2, 29, 30, 38; in foreign films, 3–4; Gibson's confusing depictions, 35–36, 38–39; graphicness of, 4; in Hindi cinema, 247; in *Lust, Caution*, 73; proliferation of, 3; ratings of, 35
Torture Team: Rumsfeld's Memo and the Betrayal of American Values (Sands), 23
Tortyr (Swedish television series), 270n2, 271n16
To See If I'm Smiling [*Lir'ot im ani mehayehet*] (2007), 202–3, 208
totalitarianism, 151, 153, 155
trauma, 9, 65, 180, 286
Triumph of the Will (1935), 130, 225
Truth and Reconciliation Commission (TRC), 14, 167, 177, 178; operations of reckoning placed outside of, 171, 172–81, 184–85; as organ of state apparatus,

171, 181; South African state and, 168–72; *TRC Final Report*, 170, 172; in U.S. and South African films, 168, 171–72, 181

truths, convenient, 219–21, 234; in Algerian War, 224–25; origins of torture methods, 229–30; torture and movies in relation to, 221–23

Tutu, Archbishop Desmond, 170, 182

Twentieth Century Fox, 40

24 (television series), 6, 12–13, 20, 65, 132; actors in, 27; as advertisement for torture, 127–28; appeal and popularity of, 24–25; influence on Army interrogators in Iraq, 23; moral responsibility in, 245; myth of truthful confessions under torture, 10; number of torture scenes in, 21; producers of, 27–28; public figures' references to, 22; ticking time-bomb scenario in, 228; torture scenes on, 23–24; video game version of, 129; writers for, 31. *See also* Bauer, Jack (fictional character)

Two Stage Sisters [*Wutai Jiemei*] (1964), 80–81, *80*, 83, 86

2001: A Space Odyssey (1968), 143

ubuntu (reciprocity), 169, 185n4

Understanding Media (McLuhan), 100

United Nations Convention Against Torture, 145, 284

United States, 6, 7, 111–12, 240, 245; Cold War and, 53; death penalty in, 152; electrotorture used by, 229, 236n26; film classification codes, 143, 144; humane techniques of interrogation used by, 32; *Lust, Caution* released in, 76; as nation in decline, 46–47; reckoning with racist past, 171, 172, 183, 186nn14–15; social imaginary of, 171; torture in counterinsurgency programs, 15; torture in Latin America and, 61; violence in Mexico and, 62

Unthinkable (2010), 3, 11, 13, 57–59; racialization of violence, 64; torture depicted in, 61; torture-truth hermeneutic in, 10

Vasari, Giorgio, 115

Veblen, Thorstein, 275

Velázquez, Diego, 99

Verräter [*Traitors*] (1936), 228–29

video games, 126, 129, 159

Vietnam, South, 54, 118

Vietnam War, 25, 32, 112, 152; American movies about, 195; electrical torture used in, 229–30; French war in Indochina, 229–30, 259; Phoenix program, 118

vigilantes, 62–63

violence, 10, 113, 234; in *24*, 31; conflicts resolved with, 56; "enduring violence" of South Africa's past, 183; good and bad, 60, 66; graphicness of, 11, 143; Israeli narrative concerning, 192, 201; moral, 57–58; in *Passion of the Christ, The*, 38, 40, 47; racialization of, 64; rising rates in industrialized societies, 153; selective, 224; as spectacle, 47; "ultraviolence" of *A Clockwork Orange*, 146; youth violence, 153

V for Vendetta (2006), 3, 10, 11

Voltaire, 10, 58, 116
voyeurism, 96, 100, 102, 113

Walken, Christopher, 2, 59
Wallace, William, 36, 39, 42, 44, 45
Walsh, Richard, 47
Waltz with Bashir [*Valts im Bashir*] (2008), 14, 191, 203–7, 215n27; still from, *190*; *Z32* compared to, 209, 211
Wang Weiqin, 74–75
War on Terror, 6, 111, 145
Washington, Denzel, 2, 28
Wasted [*Mevuzbazim*] (2006), 202
waterboarding, 21, 122, 123, 126, 157, 231; legalization of, 240; as most intense CIA torture, 125
water deprivation, 231
water torture, 54, 57, 121, 231–32
Weegee, 98
Weizman, Eyal, 192
welfare state, 148, 152
Welles, Orson, 96
Weschler, Lawrence, 12
western genre, 56
West Point, U.S. Military Academy at, 25, 28
What's Wrong? [*Ma kara?*] (1988), 191, 196, 197
Whitecross, Matt, 157
Willis, Bruce, 28
Winnicott, D. W., 101
Winterbottom, Michael, 157
Wire, The (HBO series), 29
Witherspoon, Reese, 129
Wolf Creek (2005), 3
women, 7, 62, 261; falling in love with their torturers, 227; guerillas in Algeria, 260; Iraqi detainees, 264; in Israeli military, 201–3, 208; masochism and gender dualism, 48; as torturers, 7, 124, 263, 264–65, 269, 285; as torture victims in Chinese cinema, 80–84, *80*, *81*, *89*. *See also* femininity/the feminine
Wong Kar-wai, 73
Wood, Capt. Carolyn, 7
World of Warcraft (video game), 129
World War I, 233
World War II, 32, 93, 259, 284
Wypijewski, Joanne, 277

Xie Jin, 80, 81, 82
X ratings, 97, 144, 159

Yacef, Saadi, 258, 259, 261
Yoo, John, 123, 133, 283, 284, 286, 288
youth culture, 96
Yueh-yu Yeh, Emilie, 71

Zahalka, Jamal, 201
Zaidi, S. Hussain, 247
Zarqawi, Abu Musab al, 32, 33n20
Zhang Yimou, 88
Zheng Pingru, 77
Zimbardo, Philip, 283, 290n4
Zionism, 192, 194, 200, 201, 210, 212; European culture of early Zionism, 211; mythology of, 204
Z32 (2008), 14, 207–12
Zulu Love Letter (2004), 14, 168; operations of reckoning placed outside TRC, 171, 172, 176–81, 182, 184; still from, *166*

GPSR Authorized Representative: Easy Access System Europe, Mustamäe tee
50, 10621 Tallinn, Estonia, gpsr.requests@easproject.com